AF473933

William Alister Macdonald

Watercolours from Thurso, the Thames and Tahiti

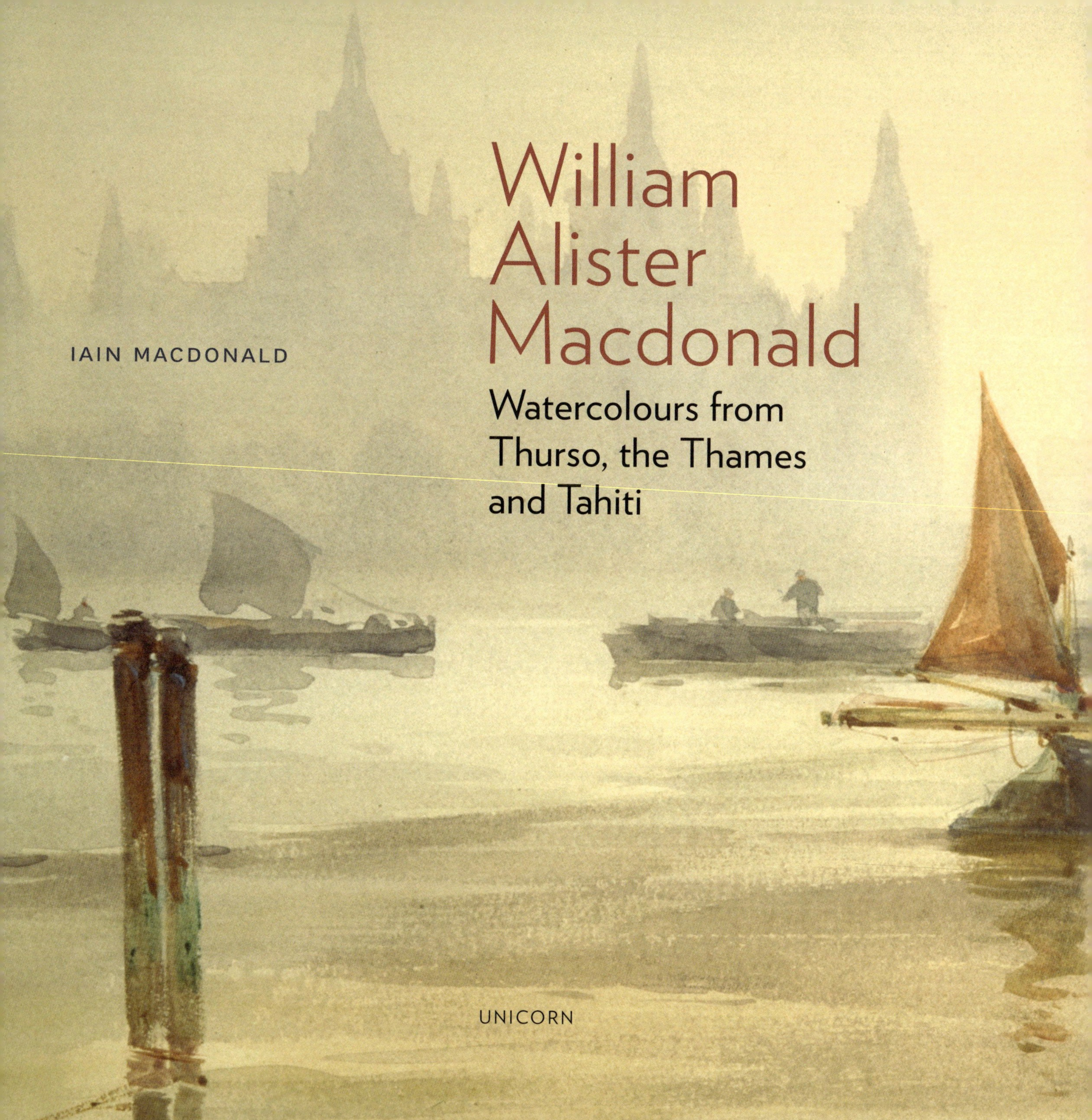
William
Alister
Macdonald
IAIN MACDONALD
Watercolours from
Thurso, the Thames
and Tahiti
UNICORN

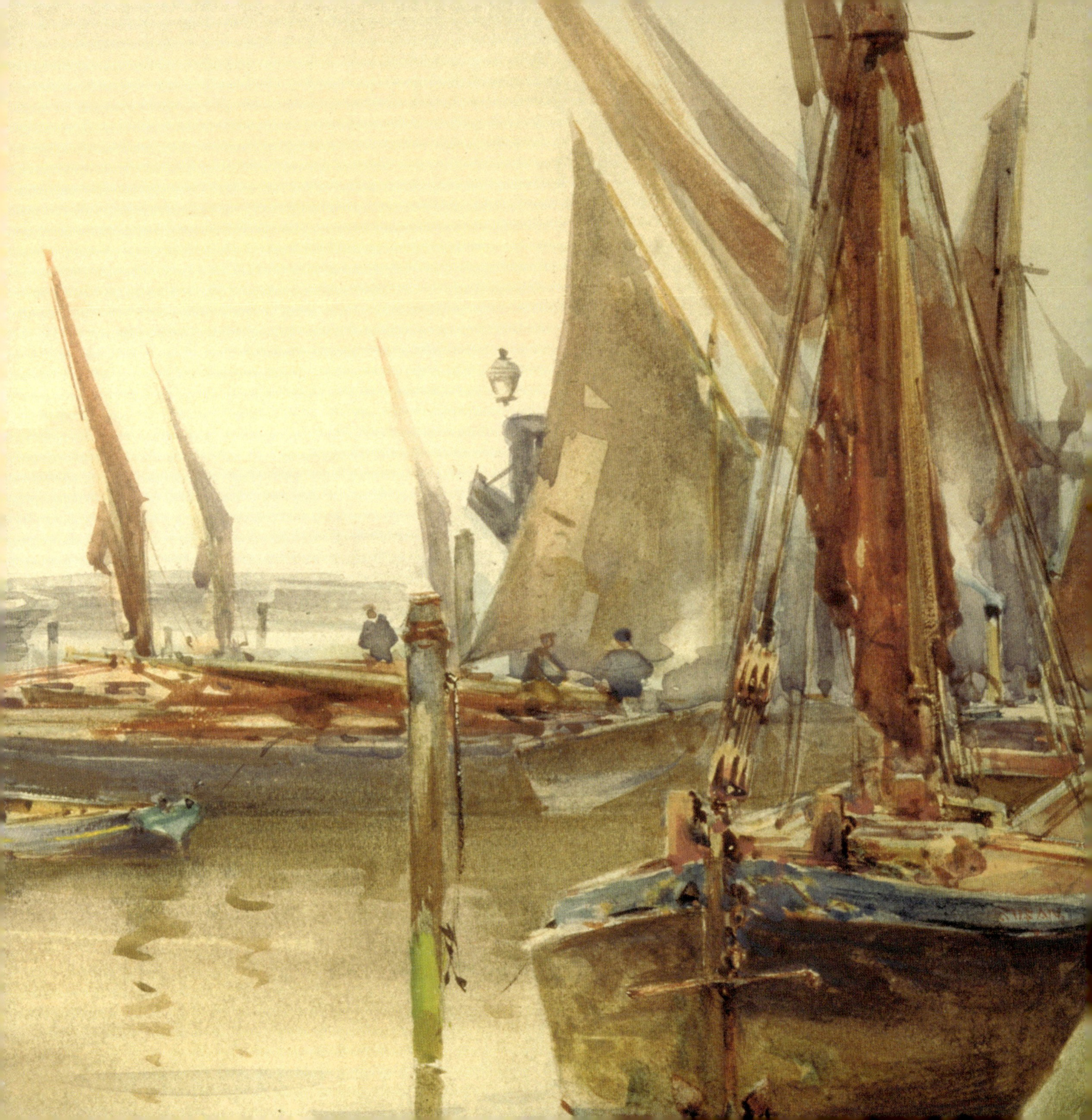

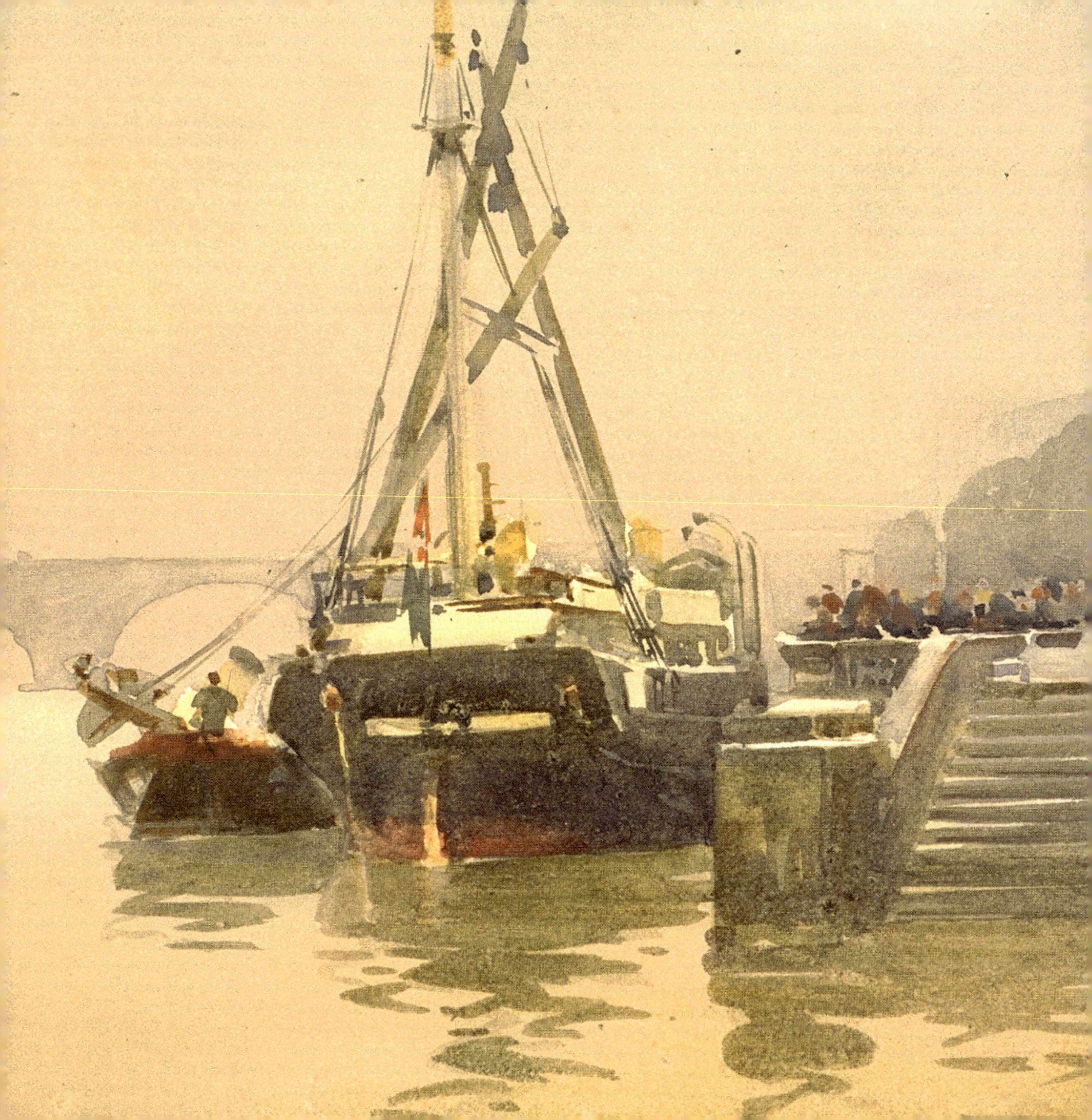

CONTENTS

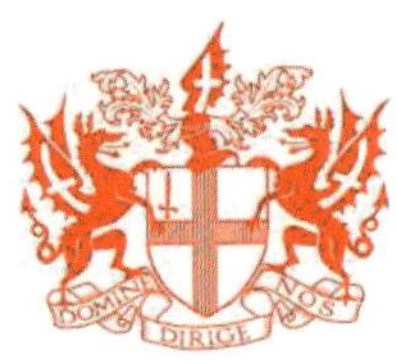

THE RIGHT HONOURABLE THE LORD MAYOR

ALDERMAN PROFESSOR MICHAEL MAINELLI

THE MANSION HOUSE, LONDON EC4N 8BH

TELEPHONE 020-7626 2500

June 2024

It is with great pleasure that I introduce this comprehensive biography of the Scottish watercolourist, William Alister Macdonald, penned by Dr Iain Macdonald. The story of Macdonald's life and his artistic journey offers an extraordinary glimpse into a bygone era, capturing the essence of London's streets and the Thames' vibrant river life at the turn of the last century.

William Alister Macdonald's works, particularly those in the remarkable Wakefield Collection, hold a special place in the Guildhall Art Gallery. Donated by Lord Wakefield in 1935, these watercolours are not only artistically exquisite but also of immense historical significance. They document the atmospheric beauty of London from Kew to Rotherhithe, including iconic views of Westminster, the Temple, and St. Paul's Cathedral. Macdonald's ability to convey the colours and moods of these scenes has ensured his work remains an invaluable asset to our cultural heritage.

In 2001, the Guildhall Art Gallery proudly exhibited Macdonald's watercolours alongside contemporary photographs, highlighting the dramatic transformation of London over the past century. This juxtaposition underscored the lasting impact of Macdonald's artistry and the importance of preserving such works for future generations.

The Lady Mayoress and I recently had the honour of selecting Macdonald's work from the Gallery's collection to grace our invitation cards. We hold a great appreciation for Macdonald's contribution to the arts and his unique ability to capture the spirit of the City of London.

I commend Dr Iain Macdonald for his meticulous research and dedication in bringing this important artist's story to life. May this book inspire a renewed appreciation for William Alister Macdonald's legacy and his contribution to the world of art.

Sincerely,

Michael Mainelli

The Rt Hon The Lord Mayor of London
Alderman Professor Michael Mainelli

ACKNOWLEDGEMENTS

This biography is the first to span William Alister Macdonald's entire life of ninety-five years. Some questions remain, and no doubt some secrets remain undiscovered. It has been a detective story, but newspaper reviews and passenger manifests from British and American archives have revealed many, if not all of his movements between Britain, USA and Tahiti. I am indebted to the National Library of Australia for their excellent archive of *Pacific Islands Monthly* which has provided invaluable exhibition and book reviews. James Giffin at the Guildhall Art Gallery has provided access to the Wakefield Collection and their copies of documents donated by John Macdonald. The London Metropolitan Archive holds a treasure chest of London watercolours, drawings and sketches that revealed much about the artist's methodology and favourite haunts. In Tahiti, the James Norman Hall Museum's curator Vivienne Millet was a conduit to all manner of important people and a portal to the Rutger family, Musée de Tahiti et les Iles, and Allegra Marshall who shared with me the moments of revelation and discovery there.

My quest had been to discover more about Alister's life in French Oceania and experience something of the life there to better understand the artist and his work. Although tourism and commercial exploitation has grown since the opening of the airport in Tahiti in 1962, its rugged mountainous neighbour Moorea retains some remote simplicity and a quieter pace of old. Meeting and getting to know the Tahitian side of my family enabled us to have time and the opportunity to unlock memories and for them come back to life. We shared images from family and museum collections, and carefully sifted through fragile papers, drawings, photographs and letters. Each day revealed more pieces of the jigsaw and illuminated more corridors of doors to be opened.

My sojourn of three weeks in Moorea was made possible with the assistance and generosity of Tipari, Moana, Monique Hepua, Aiden and the friendship of Noha. These men made me feel like 'bond-friends for life', as Robert Louis Stevenson described in 1888 with 'Ori a Ori'. The Scottish and Tahitian brotherhood has a long history. However, a special place in my heart is kept for Alister's two surviving granddaughters Jacqueline Chavez and Andrine Maraea, who read my heart and took me to theirs as aunts. Their lived memories came back to life in front of me, the first Scottish Macdonald to be among them since Alister himself. It is to them that my duty lies: to do my best and honour them as much as the artist himself.

Thanks are also due to John Myhill, Poppy Collinson, and especially the detective work by her father John Collinson who bridged the family histories with John Macdonald; both sadly never got to read or see this book in print. Lastly, none of the Macdonalds would have a handle on the family tree and all its branches were it not for the dedicated research and knowledge of cousin Stroma Riungu.

The author gratefully acknowledges the National University of Ireland for their grant towards the publication of this book.

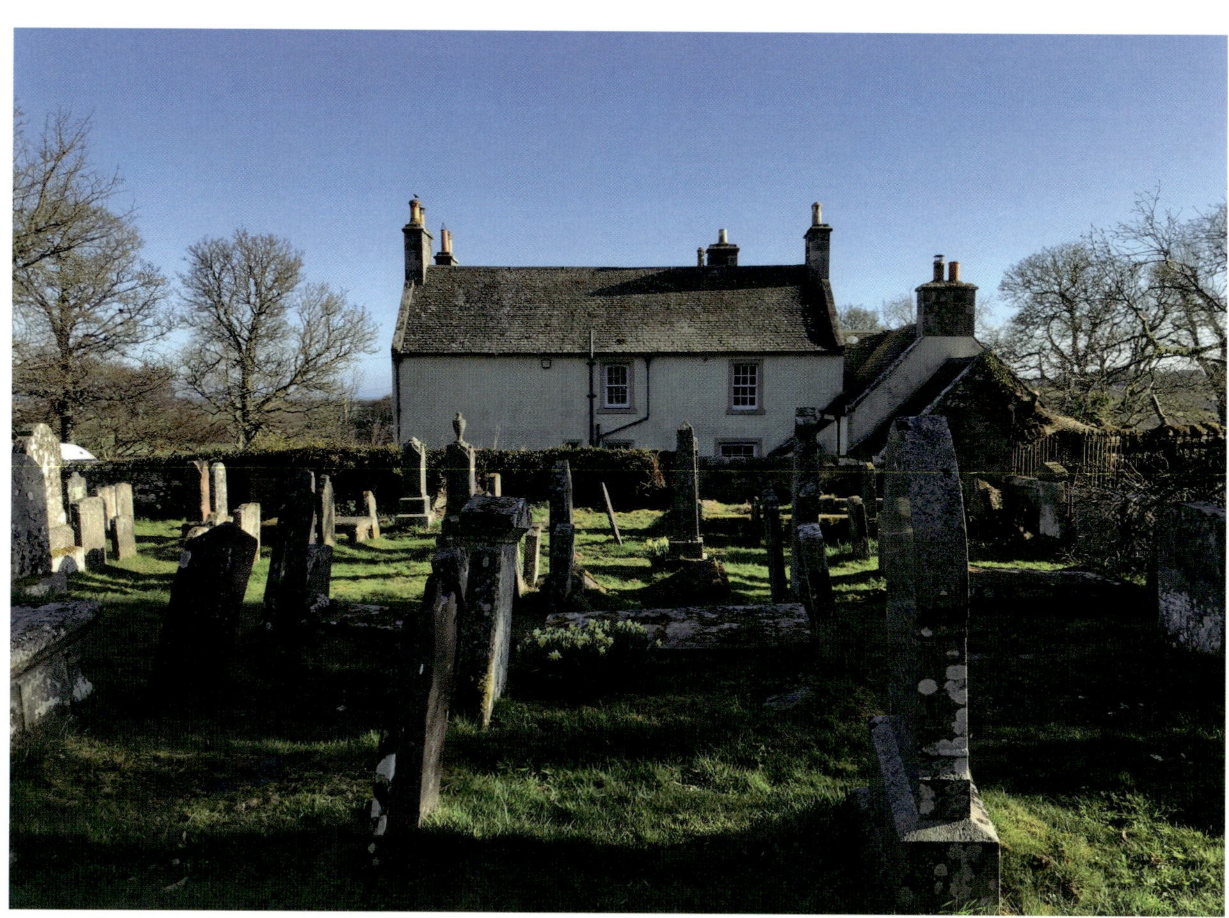

0.1 Clynelish manse, Brora, Sutherland

PREFACE

My life, of nearly a century, I have much wanted to write: as covering a period of complete change. I have the bare facts, up to 1939 or so in manuscript. Now I don't suppose it will ever be written. Mind & hand no longer being what is needed. But the London work will live. Came out here in 1921 at 60! Thinking my life was over. Instead one third of it had to come & another reputation made in Tahiti.[1]

THE QUEEN IS DEAD, long live the King. Breaking news disturbed the still waters as the sun rose over the mountain behind me, casting its warm glow on the lush green mountain ridge opposite. Seventy years earlier my great-great-uncle William Alister Macdonald gazed over the same bay and felt the same moist breeze as he heard 'The King is dead, long live the Queen'. Winds of change for us both, generations apart, united by place, and the enchantment of the Pacific island of Moorea.

This story begins with my uncle Alasdair showing me an old antique book with a hardback red cover by E. Beresford Chancellor and William Alister Macdonald called *London Recalled* (1937). I opened the book to see the delicate watercolours of London scenes, some of which I had walked myself when I lived in Richmond and Barnes, near the Thames. When I discovered he had had a son called Ian, the coincidence propelled me to find out more about the life of the artist, my great-great-uncle.

Family names are important links and identifiers to culture and tradition. In Scotland many names have multiple variants of spelling despite sounding the same. In my case, Iain Macdonald might easily be recorded as Ian McDonald, or my uncle Alasdair as Alister. Ours are near-Gaelic variants, so it is perhaps ironic that the subject of this book, Alister Macdonald, who was brought up in a Gaelic speaking community, had a more anglicised spelling as did his own son, Ian.

Our family roots in the early 1800s can be traced to the far north-east of Scotland. My grandparents' home in Thurso, Caithness has been the sole constant 'home' to me throughout my life. As a child, and still today, I would dream about my return: from the drive up the winding coastal A9, to the front door and hallway of Hillcroft. Sometimes I would stop off at Brora and take a short detour to visit the grave of Rev. John Macdonald and gaze admiringly at the handsome manse that was their home and birthplace of Alister (0.1, 0.2). Hillcroft is special for many reasons, not least that it was designed and built by Grandfather Hugh, an architect of respected calibre and a man of character, much loved and regarded in the region. His father had stayed in Thurso to start and build the family architecture practice, Sinclair Macdonald & Son, while Alister and their other three siblings moved south. Even my grandfather's siblings moved south, as my father and uncle did too. Yet my cousins, brother and I all keep returning with our own children, to keep alive and enjoy, not just the family home, but the freedom of Caithness' barren wilderness, however impractical the journey may appear in our busy lives further south.

It must have been an exotic adventure to reach the South Seas of the Pacific in 1921 by steamship, one that required some bravery or compelling motivation, and not least the financial resources to afford the passage. My journey in 2022 required less commitment and was a lot quicker, but a destination that was similarly inspired by the same books read a century ago.

When Alister returned from Tahiti in 1935 to visit family in Caithness and Sutherland he must have carried a heavy burden. His son, Ian had recently drowned in the Thames, and he had returned to his wife in London, having left behind a 'vahine' (woman) and daughter in Tahiti. If he dared to take his family into his confidence, we can scarcely imagine what reception that news would get in 1930s Scotland, whatever your religion.

Scandal lurked behind the lace curtains, but in Tahiti, then as now, the liberal attitudes of inter-ethnic relationships and children are accepted and commonplace. I noted the polite trepidation in the first contact between relatives in the UK and Tahiti, and other relatives of Alister's liaisons, made by John Macdonald in the 2000s. I am indebted to him for his pioneering research and detective work that established a link to our Tahitian family and the Myhill descendants from Norfolk. He sadly died before a visit to Tahiti could be made, and so I was the first to meet them since Alister himself. My father's cousin, Stroma Riungu, has also done a lot of heavy lifting with the family tree. Timing is everything, and perhaps fortune was on my side rather than on Stroma's daughter when she happened to visit Tahiti in 2000 and we missed an opportunity to engage different branches of the family when Alister's daughter Avril and other granddaughters were still alive.

Finally, as full an account, as possible to this date, of Alister's life can be read and viewed through the accompanying watercolours and drawings. Sometimes described as a 'wandering vagabond', or a 'ruined Lord', he struck a confident pose with his trusty pipe, sometimes in a panama hat with an umbrella under one arm, equipped for whatever life threw at him. It was a long life, a lot longer than his siblings and later generations. He came to Tahiti, thinking his life was drawing to a natural end, but in fact it was only the beginning of an entirely new life that extended for over another thirty years.

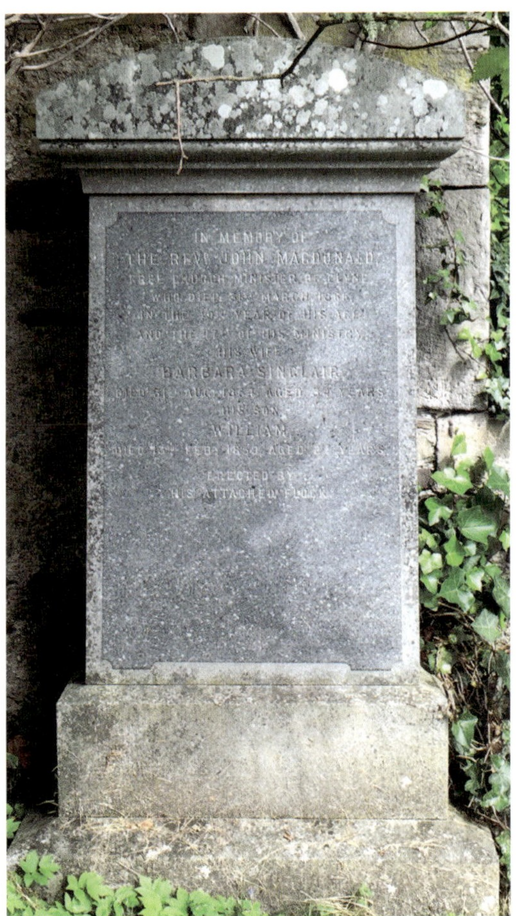

0.2 Rev. John Macdonald gravestone, Clynelish, Sutherland

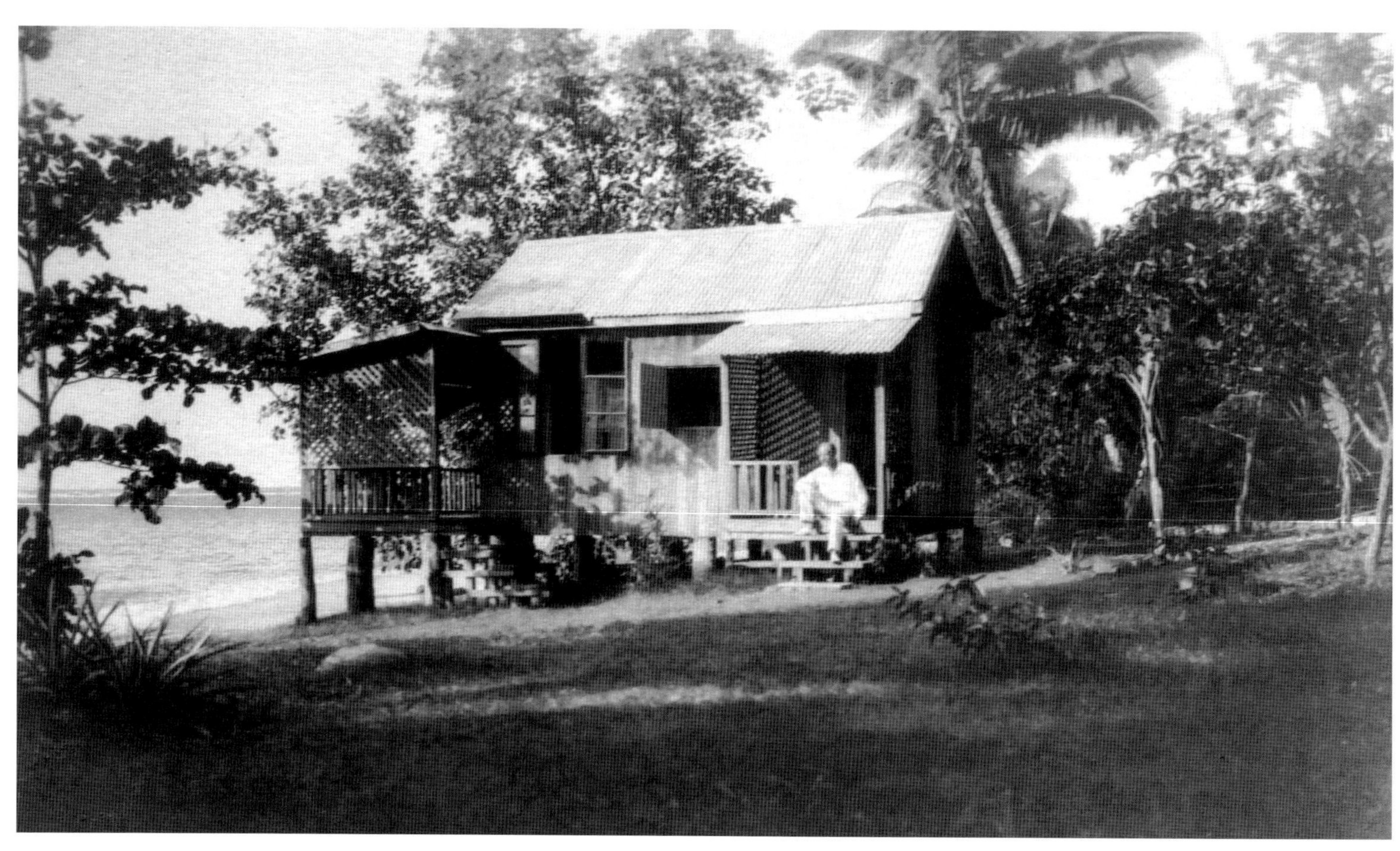

1.1 W. Alister Macdonald by his home,
Paopao, Moorea 1952

Moorea

IN COOK'S BAY on the island of Moorea, at the shore called Paopao, William Alister Macdonald, now in his nineties, lived alone and painted in his bungalow (1.1). It was built by his son-in-law, Ben Teraiharoa, of bamboo and walls of woven palm fronds, a pandanus thatched roof in the traditional manner, on stilts raised above the beach and tidewater. The Tahitian house is designed not to shut out the world, but to allow nature to enter. The bay is only a kilometre wide, the simple houses, known as *fare*, and churches are ringed by the sea at their base and by mountains to the heavens. In the cool morning breeze, as the dawn sky brightened, the bay would come to life with roosters crowing and dogs barking. People here wake early, around five a.m. Taking breakfast of star apple, guava and ramboutan on the verandah, he could hear the lapping water underneath and watch the clouds form over the mountains of Mont Rotui, Muaputa and Tohivea. Looking across the bay to the Catholic mission of St Joseph's he would watch the sun's golden rays track down the dense tropical foliage of the steep mountain opposite. A fisherman might paddle out to the reef in his outrigger, his powerful strokes breaking the glassy surface (1.2). Some mornings there might be a schooner at anchor, with voices from the crew carrying across the bay, providing an opportunity to paint a watercolour and make a sale, a record of their visit to Moorea (1.3).

Breakfast consumed, any debris was distributed over the side to the hungry fish below, darting up to the surface in a flash for titbits.

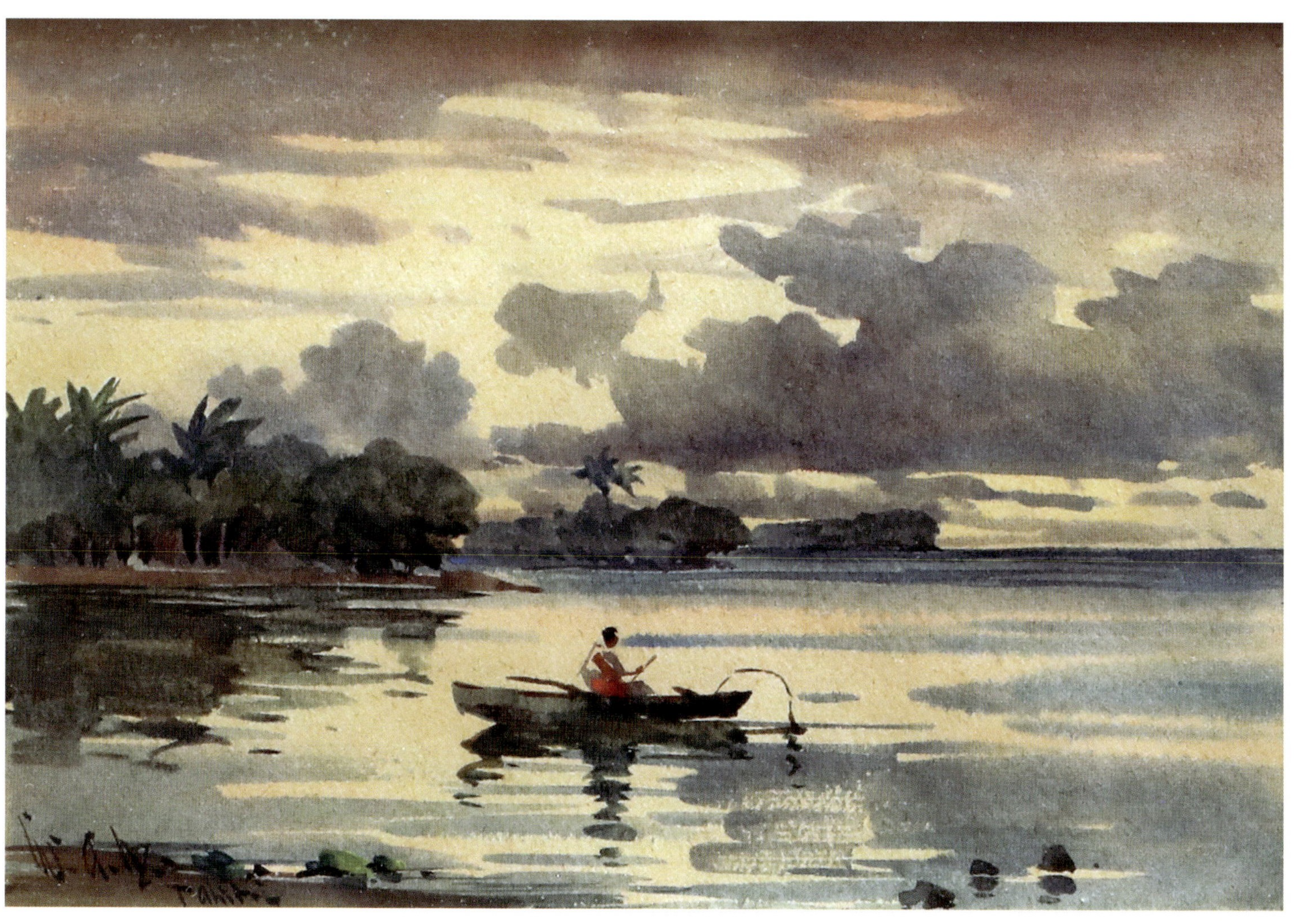

A cold freshwater shower prepared him for another working day, though little he did he know that his 'butt-naked' ablutions would be the source of amusement amongst giggling local girls driving past in their jitney bus!

Dressed in a long-sleeved white cotton or linen shirt, wearing his panama hat, with an umbrella under his right arm, he would walk barefoot along the beach with his letters and any painting orders he had wrapped for the courier, Mr Tiro, whose boat, the *Mitiaro*, was moored at the nearby wharf waiting to depart for Papeete, the main town of Tahiti. On arriving after a two to three hour crossing, depending on the size of the Pacific swell, Tiro also took care of any orders of provisions at the Donald's store on the harbour seafront that would be delivered the following day. A pension of £125 per year from the British government sustained Macdonald's basic needs, and as long as he sold enough to have 'six months expenses in hand' he was satisfied and content to live 'in harmony with nature, totally detached from worldly goods'.[1]

With messages despatched he would take his folding chair, open his umbrella and find a shady spot on the beach from which to paint. A schooner at anchor would provide an ideal opportunity for a painting, and with good fortune, a sale to a flattered owner. Holding the brush in his left hand he would work quickly and precisely, layering colours to capture the atmospheric and translucent light. From the moment he first set foot on Tahiti, he saw this as 'a paradise for watercolour painters'.[2] Then, puffing on his faithful pipe, with a trained and knowledgeable eye for maritime architecture, he would faithfully paint the detail and structure of the boat.

As the day grew hotter he would retire to his studio where he could lower the rattan shutters to shade from the hot afternoon sun. His fair Scottish skin had tanned and grown resilient to the tropical sun under his wispy white beard and receding hair. At four p.m. his daughter, Avril (1.4), would come with tea and a cake, sometimes accompanied by her daughters who might eat or sit with him. Their reward would be a bonbon, known as a sweetie

1.2 Pêcheur en pirogue

in Scotland. This was his daily routine from when Avril had been a small child, and then as now, he would enjoy a little siesta before rising for his favourite part of the day, dusk. Every day had a different sunset that inspired another study of light, clouds and reflections.

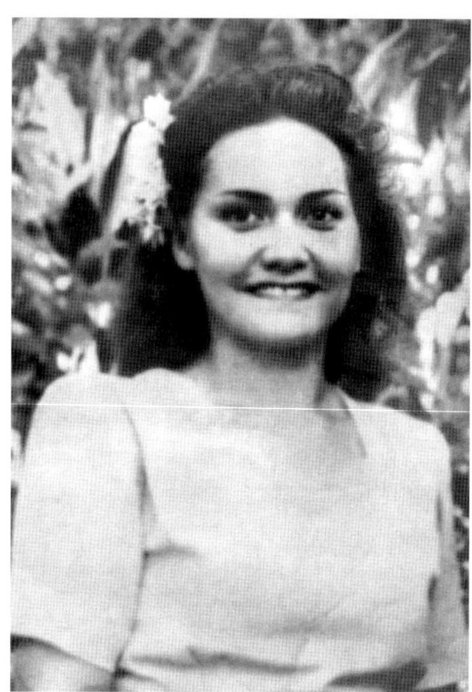

1.4 Avril (Marie) Macdonald c. 1952

As the tide changed direction, large passive coral-pink shark would swim idly by beneath the bungalow (1.5) and ray glide over the sandy bottom like a magic carpet with a tail. A little further out in the deeper water where the coral reef falls away like a cliff edge, the head of a turtle would pop up for air. There is little birdsong, Moorea is an island of peace, silenced after the volcanic explosion one and half million years ago in the Pleistocene era.

Around seven p.m. his evening star, the planet Venus, appeared above the silhouetted mountain opposite and he would retire to write his correspondence by the light of an oil lamp, sustained by his pipe and a dram of whisky. Out from the corners of the room geckos would venture to dine on mosquitoes, chirping to each other as they scampered across the walls. Sometimes he would sit out with Danielle, his eldest granddaughter, and paint the moonlight rippling across the bay and silhouetting the coconut and ironwood trees. As they practised her English, land crabs would emerge around them from their sand burrows and scuttle away to find prey. An occasional dog would bark to make its presence known. Some evenings, the night's tranquillity is enhanced by distant harmonious singing and ukulele. At night it is as if time has stood still.

> I read on till drowsiness overcame me and the pages blurred before my eyes. It was late and the night was very calm; a vagrant night breeze, wandering down from the mountains, rustled gently among the fronds of the old palms around the house. When the rustling ceased – so faint as to be almost inaudible – I could hear the far-off whisper of the sea. The world about me was asleep; I roused myself with an effort, adjusted the mosquito net, and blew out the lamp.[3]

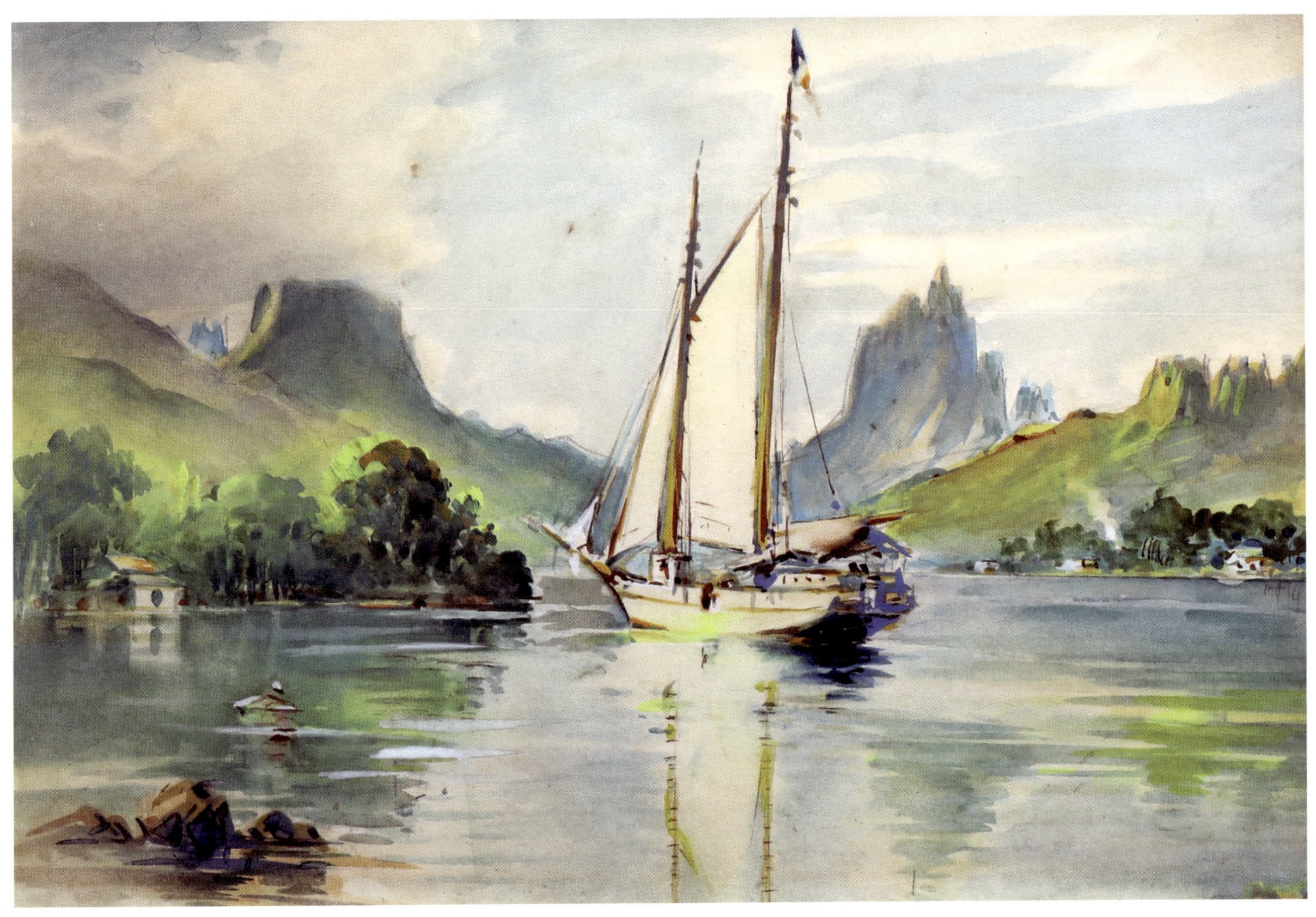

1.3 Voilier dans la Baie d'Opunohu

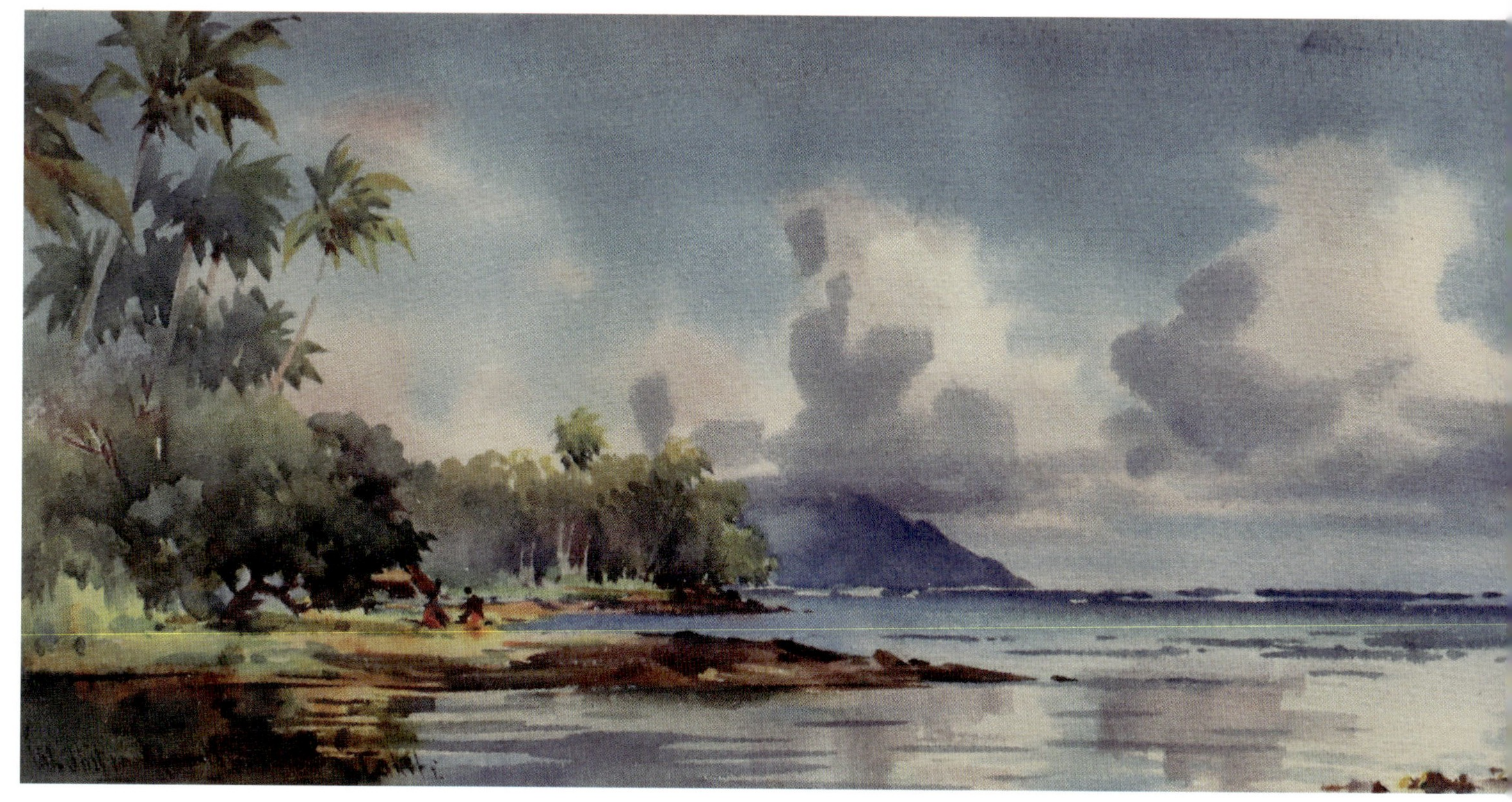

1.5 Vue depuis Tahiti

In the rainy season, between November and April, his painting activity was intermittent, if not completely stalled. Squalls of rain gust across the bay and lash the palm trees bending under the deluge, the noise immense, punctuated with thuds from falling coconuts (1.6). Dampness pervaded everything, an enemy of paper, and the fabric of clothes and buildings. During these days and nights the company of friends and family helped to fill the hours of painting inactivity, now replaced by essential activities to repair damaged or waterlogged homes.

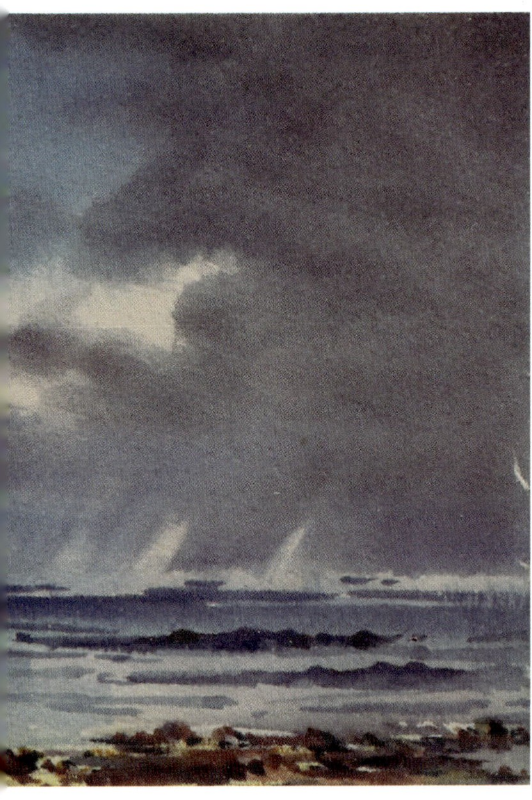

> He reads ordinary print without glasses. He formerly wore glasses, but some years ago he discarded them, and now says that when one has reached a certain age they are not of much assistance to the eyesight. He attributes his longevity to that wise maxim: moderation in all things.[4]

For a man in his nineties, having outlived many of his younger friends and certainly all his siblings who had remained in Scotland, there was time to reminisce and consider at leisure one's life choices. The what ifs, and what might have been. Macdonald was well-read; amongst his friends in Tahiti were the American authors Charles Nordhoff, James Norman Hall, Robert Frisbie and Zane Grey. He was familiar with their attempts to portray the beauty and glamour of the islands in their prose and poetry, but nothing could match the lived experience that is felt, for it is immersive and multisensory.

> The great attraction of the hotel was the view from the upstairs veranda, overlooking the lagoon and the open sea beyond, with the island of Moorea in the background at a distance of twelve miles. I would not venture to say how many hours, and days, and weeks I have spent, all told, merely looking at that glorious panorama of lagoon and sea and sky, with the mountains of Moorea in the distance, so beautiful at any time of day, and particularly so early in the morning, or at evening when the sun had just vanished behind the mountains. Moorea is all that a South Sea island should be, and it surpasses my most splendid dreams of one, as a boy.[5]

After receiving a letter out of the blue from a young American woman, Daryl Broderick, in 1955, he vigorously emphasised that the islands had to be seen and felt (1.7).

> Thank you Miss Broderick for your long letter of the 6th. It is nice to feel that one can give so much pleasure to others & total strangers!. . .

> . . . You are young – thank the Gods for that! Aim high – mediocrity of little use, & specialise!
> You certainly write well. No writing is of much use as regards the Beauty Glamour of the Islands. They must be seen! & felt. You were fortunate.[6]

She had been crewing on the *Nordlys* for a wealthy family from California, Walter and Hathily Johnson, when she visited Moorea in September 1954. She had been hired to look after their three young children, and was looking for a 'once in a lifetime' adventure in the South Seas. Her letter to Macdonald ignited a conversation from afar; she was curious and expressed a love of art and the island, wanting to keep a connection, and not let go of fading memories

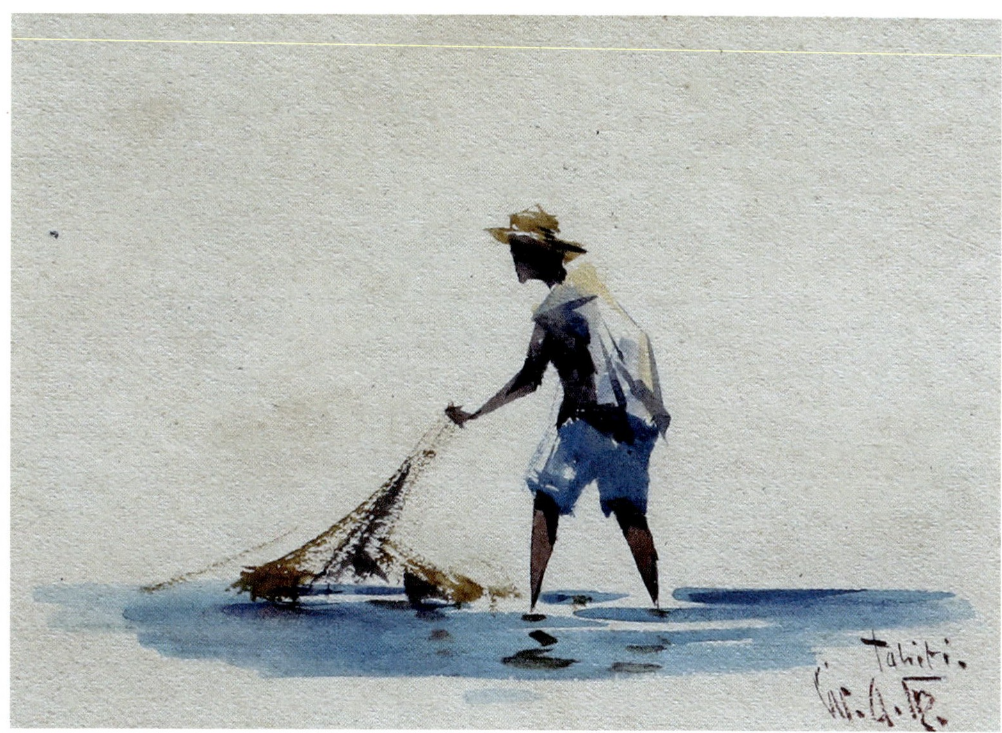

1.6 Native with throw net

of her time in Moorea. He found her enquiry charming and flush with youthful promise. Fortunately, Daryl Broderick kept these letters safe along with some photographs taken at the time. In later life she would reflect that it had been a transformative experience, but one where she had seen the best and worst in people, noting that far away from the 'civilising constraints' of polite society some American men 'revert to becoming lawless and feral'.[7]

Her yacht was moored alongside another called, *Serva la Bari* (or as Daryl quipped 'Serve up the Body'), and onboard was a writer from Chile, Enrique Bunster.

> At sundown – which happens at 7 pm – I had the feeling that it will never be daylight again, after witnessing the night gloom. The only sign of life were the lights on the little houses on the shore, which the indigenous people believe will protect them from the *tupapau* apparitions.
>
> However, one of those houses did not have a light on. Eyzaguirre told me that this was where the English painter William Alister Macdonald lived. These are the wonderful things that happen while travelling. To find in this far-flung corner of the world an artist whose genius was comparable to Turner's and Whistler, and whose watercolours have sold for hundreds of pounds!
>
> Early the following morning we took a boat to get a closer look... We find him on the beach, sitting on a wooden chair, sketching the *Serva la Bari* on a pad he balances on his knees. His appearance is that of a ruined *lord:* thin, hunched-backed, with messy and balding white hair, wiry beard and a thin mouth biting the mouthpiece of his inseparable pipe. He was barefoot and was wearing well-worn clothes. I was amazed by the strength and steadiness of his brushstrokes. I noticed his left ear was eaten away by some sort of cancer. He agreed to be photographed and answered my questions without interrupting his work... He asked me when we were sailing. When

1.7 W. Alister Macdonald, personal correspondence to Daryl Broderick, 27 February 1955

I told him we were leaving the next day, he mentioned he was worried he might not finish his work on time. It was his polite way of asking us to leave him alone.

I walked away feeling a lot richer.

Later I learned he had been the reason behind our docking in Pao-Pao. Giorgio de Giorgio, the shipowner of the *Serva la Bari* had just bought 114 of his paintings. Amongst them were

> some of his golden era: 1928 to 1939. There were Tahitian and Japanese landscapes, boats, fish, the beach of the hotel Rivnac, where I lived... Watercolours so delicate that seemed to have been painted with humidity instead of water.
>
> The pieces had been bought after a two-hour negotiation, as the artist was adamant not to sell. 'I've kept these for 25 years' – said the master painter – 'there isn't enough gold in the world to buy them'... The interested party was very persuasive, sweetening the deal with gifts of whisky and tobacco, which the artist couldn't procure in the island. I don't know which was the agreed price in the end; all I know is that the artist insisted the payment had to be made in dollars.[8]

The captain, young Georges di Giorgio, wrote in his log that day (1.8):

> Since there was patchy wind, we did the 12 miles to the Pao Pao bay (or Cook) using the motors; once we passed the reef, we found ourselves in a 'bowl of milk'. We anchored in the bottom of the bay in 12 leagues deep with sand. In the afternoon we headed off on an excursion to the house of the famous painter Leeteg (dead) and the great English watercolourist Wm Alister MacDonald.[9]

The American painter Edgar Leeteg (1904–1953), once Macdonald's neighbour in Paopao, could not have been a more different painter, christened 'The American Gauguin' by his gallerist Barney Davis in Honolulu, who had spun a story of excessive debauchery and drinking 'worthy of an American TV Soap'.[10] A motorcycle accident cut short his life, but relieved him from an incurable variant of syphilis. Many young men were playboys, looking for women and easy sex, the glamour of the South Seas as portrayed in every book and movie.

Working and living alone it might be considered a lonely life, but Macdonald reassured Broderick this was not the case:

con su señora pero esta no pudo
dejar los niños solos en Tahiti.
Como el viento estaba completamente
empopado hicimos las 12 millas
hasta el paso de la bahía de
Pao-Pao (o de Cook) a motor;
una vez pasado el arrecife
nos encontramos en una taza de
leche. Fondeamos al fondo de
la bahía en 12 brazas, fondo de arena.
En la tarde hicimos una excursión
a la casa de famoso pintor Keeter (muerto)
y al gran acuarelista inglés Wm. Alister
Mac. Donald. A la mañana siguiente
llegaron a Pao-Pao Dolly Higgins
y otros amigos que nos acompañaron
hasta la bahía de Papetoai donde
fuimos recibidos cordialmente por
los esposos Kellum. A Ned y sra.
ya los conocía de mi viaje anterior.
Hicimos una expedición en busca
de limones y camarones con

1.8 Georges di Giorgio Ship's Log,
14 September 1954

> Lonely, O-rarely! As Winston Churchill wrote – 'Happy are the artists for they will not be lonely. Light and Colours, Faith & Hope will keep them company to the end or almost the end of the Journey'.[11]

Young at heart, if not in body, he was much like he was twenty years earlier, 'still imbued with an unbound enthusiasm and activity in the pursuit of his profession'.[12] He still had the wherewithal to give an honest assessment of himself.

> As to WAM he is rather an unusual man I am told, and a 'miracle' as regards his age and health. (Am in my 95th year). But my eyesight is going, nearly gone! & your letter I can only read with difficulty. Glasses no longer help me. But I can still work as my distant sight is good still.[13]

A few months later he reported to Miss Broderick: 'Been ill – a bad tumble. But now all is well & busy! Been disinclined for effort, Lazy in fact.'[14]

In September 1956, *Pacific Islands Monthly*[15] reported W. Alister Macdonald's death in the August, following a fall when he fractured his hip. His daughter Avril put the cause down to bronchitis. While recorded as saying 'he plans to end days in his homeland',[16] maybe by then Tahiti was his true spiritual home where he now rests in the family plot on Moorea, buried with his pipe, folding chair and easel.

A few years previously in 1951, the obituary of his great friend, James Norman Hall, was just as apt for Macdonald, who similarly 'never indulged in excesses', and lived quietly in Tahiti with occasional trips abroad. 'Tahiti he regarded as "a grandstand seat to observe the workings of a mad machine age"'.[17]

As Macdonald gazed up at his evening star, he would have wondered on the remarkable journey that this guiding star had led him, from the chilly and remote coastal highway across the barren north-east of Scotland at the age of four, sitting amongst his recently orphaned brothers and sister embarking on a new life. (1.9)

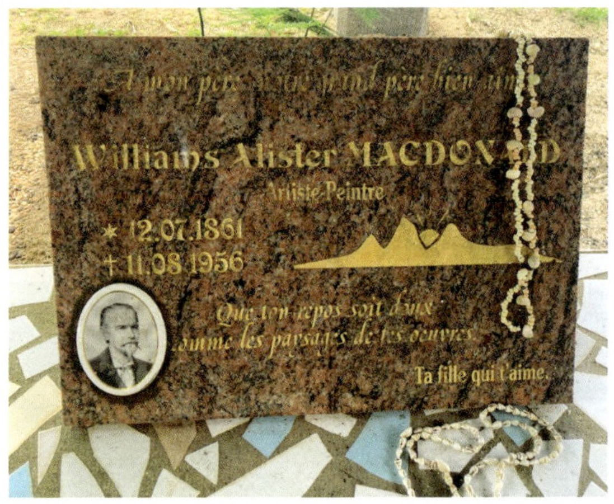

1.9 W. Alister Macdonald gravestone, Paopao

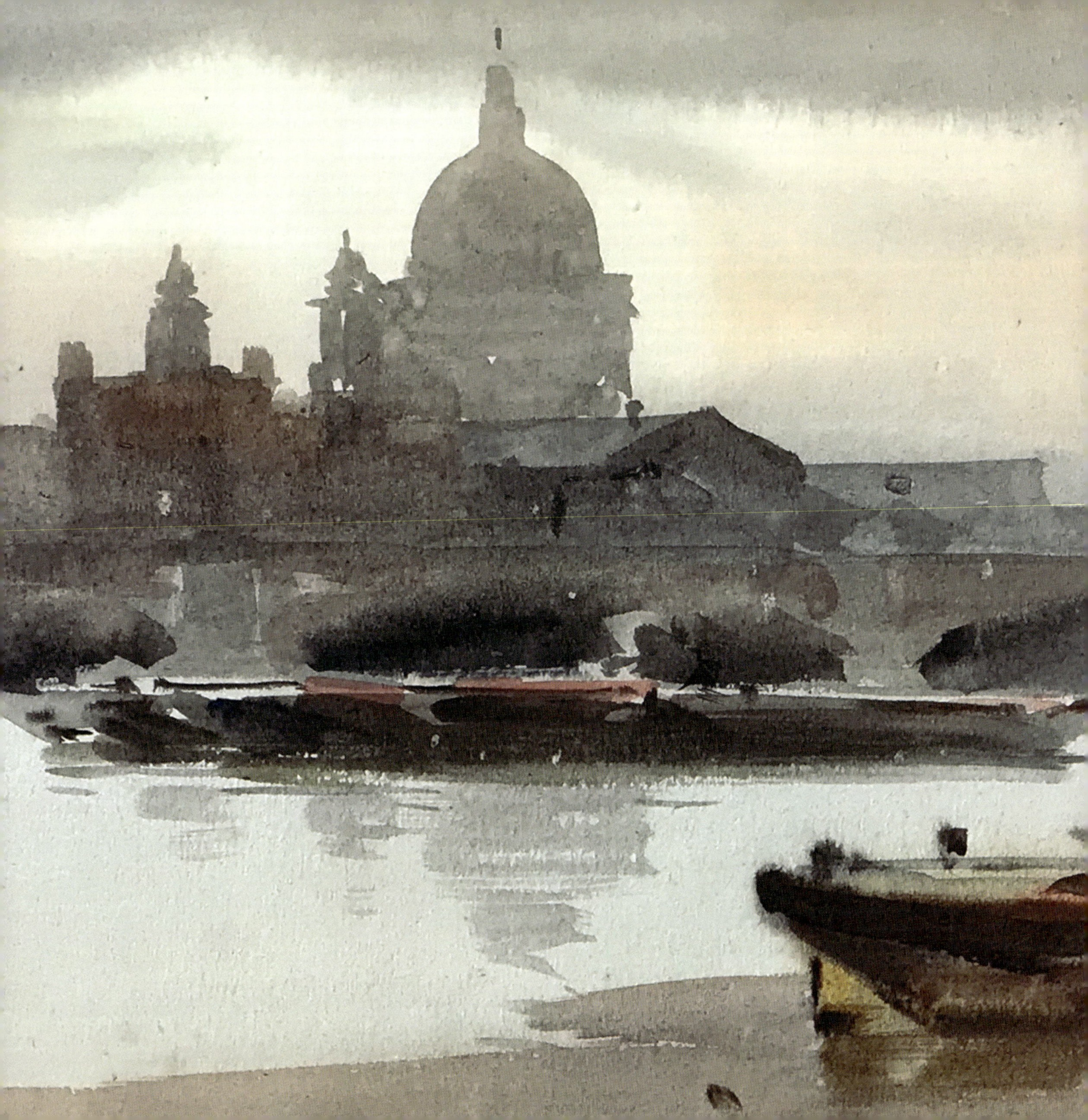

2

Early Life and London

In 1861, W. Alister Macdonald was born on the morning of 12 July in the Free Church Manse of Brora, a parish of Clyne, in Sutherland, of which his father, John, was then Minister of the Parish of Clyne. He was only four years old when both his parents died under tragic circumstances: firstly his mother of puerperal fever after the birth of his brother Sinclair, and then little over a year later his father after a mental collapse brought on by the devastating loss of his wife. This was in a religious community where ill fortune was viewed particularly harshly as God's judgement upon someone for their sins.

> But retribution belonged to God, not man; in one sermon the Rev. John Sinclair, minister of Bruan in Caithness, made the point explicitly: 'It is true that we often see the wicked enjoy much comfort and worldly ease, and the Godly chastened every morning; but this dreadful rest to the former and a blessed chastisement to the latter.'. . . The miseries of this life were not therefore simply to be endured but were in themselves a necessary agony for those who wished to attain eternal salvation in the next.[18]

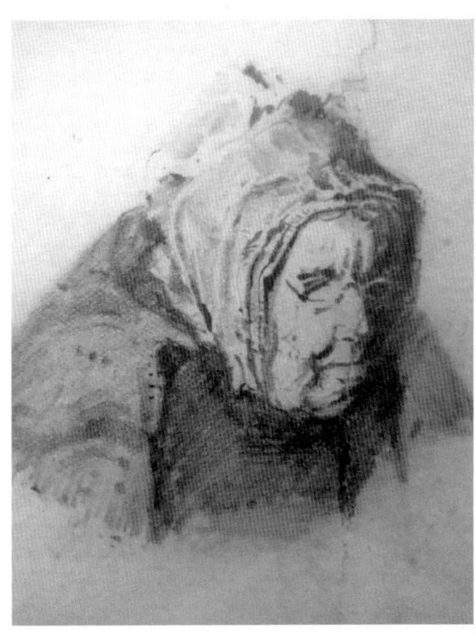

2.1 Grandmother, Mrs Jane Sinclair c. 1885 by W. Alister Macdonald

He and his four siblings were taken into the care of their maternal grandmother, Mrs Jane Sinclair, in the small village of Melvich, under the guardianship of their uncle, David Sinclair, who ran his own drapery business in Thurso. Macdonald later recalled of the road to Melvich, 'characteristically and vividly the moonlight playing over the sea as he journeyed by stage coach (there were no railways then in these remote parts) to the north, as the road wound for miles along the coast'.[19] The Inverness to Thurso stage coach was pulled by a train of four horses that would have strained over the steep braes past the herring fleets harboured in Helmsdale, Dunbeath, Latheronwheel and Wick, before crossing the barren stretch of bog on the Causeymire to arrive at the Royal Hotel with the mail and its many occupants clinging to the roof as well

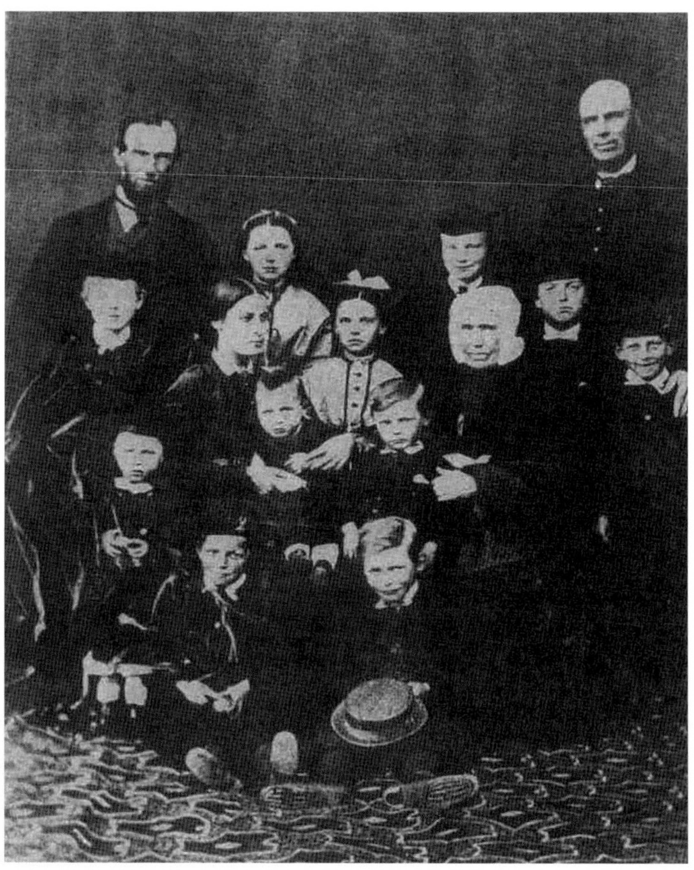

2.2 Macdonald orphans with maternal grandmother, Melvich c. 1870

as seated inside. The Macdonald orphans were not alone as they joined an already established family of three Fraser-Sinclair cousins who had similarly been orphaned in 1862 (2.1 William Alister is sitting bottom right).

For the next six years Macdonald grew up amongst this devout Presbyterian community where Gaelic was often spoken in the home and in sermons, as many who were now living there had been evicted from their villages in the Strathy glen in the brutal Highland Clearances by the Duke of Sutherland's infamous factors to make way for sheep. It was a wild, desolate, treeless landscape washed by the Atlantic and with the high cliffs of the Orkneys glimmering across the sea. Here freedom could be found in solitary wanderings amongst the dunes, and along the salmon river flowing into the bay or watching the herring fleet come into harbour with their catches.

At the local school he was unable to do a sum correctly and 'his chief delight was in caricaturing the masters and pupils and in making sketches – the ruling passion strong in his youth'.[20] Fifty years later on his passage to Tahiti his sketchbook reveals how that skill for observation flourished. But one can assume his competency for numeracy made significant improvements as he progressed to his first job as bank clerk in the Thurso branch!

It was not until later, when he was sent to Rattray's School in Aberdeen, that he had his first lesson painting with watercolours. His drawing master, Mr Kennedy, was impressed and awarded the young student a high commendation. However, his 'rather unscrupulous guardian'[21] was not as impressed with Macdonald's writing and drawing accomplishments, and he was sent at the age of fifteen into a Thurso bank on a salary of £10 a year.

And there he might have remained in a steady job with possible prospects of advancement in the bank in this remote northern-most town. His younger brother, Sinclair (2.2), returned after graduating as a qualified architect in Edinburgh to build a practice that covered all of the Highlands north of Inverness to Orkney, as did his son, Hugh who carried the business successfully on until his death in

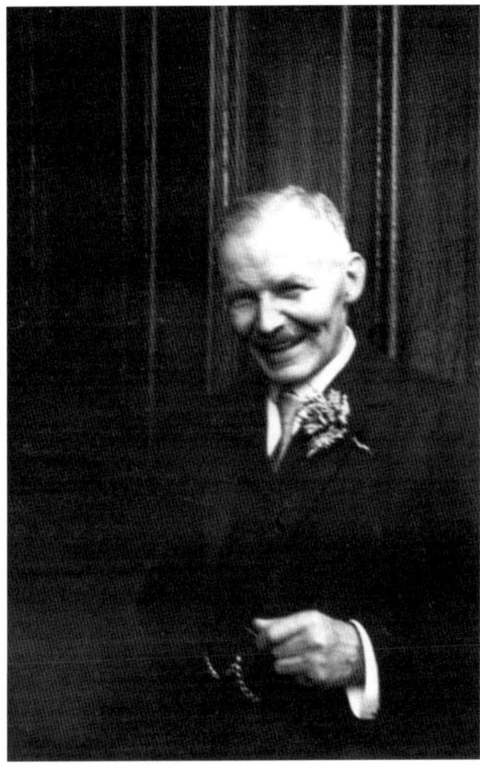

2.3 B. Sinclair Macdonald c. 1920s

1979. Instead, through an intervention from one of his aunts who was married to the then head of the Consul Office in the Bank of England, he obtained a post in the London & Westminster Bank, in Lothbury, right in the heart of the City. In 1880, London was the capital of the British Empire, the largest and richest city in the world; the contrast of Dickensian streets thronging with people, merchants, horses and carriages, could not have been more extreme.

For the nineteen-year-old, while his day was occupied by the bank, he began attending evening classes at St Martin's School of Art, in St Martin's Lane, 'that thoroughfare which for over two centuries had been a sort of Quartier Latin of London'.[22] Perhaps now the budding artist had found his tribe, as under the direction of John Parker RWS, his craft was propelled and led him to the Gilbert Garret Sketch Club. Spending what daylight was available in his leisure hours, most often as the sun was rising or setting, he would draw and paint on the banks of the Thames. What he learned through study and practice over years of dedication and passion for his painting is evident in his complete mastery of the medium of watercolour. In 1885, his early talent was recognised by his peers as he succeeded in taking the second landscape prize in the competition organised by all the London Sketching Clubs and Royal Academy students at the Society of British Artists, as reported in the *Illustrated London News*.[23]

Perhaps that was the nudge Macdonald needed to leave the drudgery, but safe employment of the Bank and take the daring action to make his own way as an artist. With lodgings over-looking the river at Greenwich, almost foretelling his last domain on the shore of Cook's Bay halfway round the world in French Oceania, he paid a modest five shillings a week in rent; 'and records with pride that he lived on another five!'.[24] With a month's salary in his pocket, he cut loose for the unspoilt tranquillity and boating paradise of the Norfolk Broads with two other artists. Here now we see the fascination with water and boats influence the subject of his work that was to last his lifetime.

In London Macdonald was already in good company, as the American artist James Abbott McNeill Whistler (1834–1903) had been painting scenes of the Thames since he arrived in 1861, the year Macdonald was born. In 1882, Walter Sickert (1860–1942) began his artistic career in Whistler's London studio, adopting his tonal approach in oils, painting London street scenes and shop fronts. English maritime artist W.L. Wyllie (1851–1931) exhibited *'Heave Away' Barges upward bound, shooting Rochester Bridge* at the Royal Academy, and further popularity of his paintings of the Thames came through patronage by The Fine Art Society.

In 1886, Macdonald gained his first significant commercial success through the publication of drawings and a story about cod fishing in the North Sea in the *Illustrated London News*. One day from his Greenwich window he observed a cod-fishing smack moored beneath him, which suggested adventure. In his charming manner that would be repeated often thereafter, he approached the captain and owner. The resulting conversation led to the artist boarding the vessel and sailing with the crew to the North Sea. Unperturbed by a south-west gale that forced the captain to lay off the Norfolk coast for three days, he spent the following weeks sketching and fishing on the Dogger Bank, 'and generally enjoying himself'. For this 'first blood' he received 'eleven guineas: ten, he is proud to remember for the drawings and one for the writing'.[25]

Other travels brought him home to Scotland, spending time in Inverness with his nephews Alister and Jack Mactavish (1879–1984), and in Invergordon with his elder brother John, who owned the general store, London House, where he displayed and sold a number of watercolours. In 1892, *Doubtful Weather, Loch Hourn* was his first watercolour to be accepted by the Royal Academy. The coastal landscape of the mountains of Skye, is another image that again almost mirrors the topographic drama of Moorea and his last resting place.

The artist's life was not all plain sailing; there were real hardships and vicissitudes to endure. There was still much to be learned,

2.4 Whitehall 1890

and to improve his drawing technique Macdonald attended the Westminster School of Art. In these hard times the encouragement and attention of a master, in the form of Fred Brown (who later became Professor at the Slade), had all the more impact. Macdonald remembered 'with gratitude, that it was this master who taught him to look for proportion instead of outline, advice which he laid to heart and sedulously followed'.[26] (2.3) This dedicated approach to artistic self-improvement resulted in a watercolour of the Thames from Blackfriars Bridge, which he called *Her Palaces and Towers*, being accepted by the Royal Academy in 1893. 'To his delight it was hung in an excellent place just under the line and won the greatly valued commendation of George Moor, who was at that time art critic on *The Times*'.[27]

No longer able to afford the lodgings in Greenwich he took refuge in a studio in Camden Town to live 'among a colony of artists more or less as impecunious as himself'. To make ends meet he compromised his artistic direction and inclination to paint studio pictures commissioned by dealers looking for work they wanted to sell. This was not sustainable and, tired of the inhibiting contract, he abandoned Camden and took a room in Chelsea, a suburb with a reputation for inspiring the arts and the home of many great artists. More significantly it was on the river, and he set himself to paint and 'to fix its everchanging charms and its elusive attraction',[28] many scenes of which were bought by Lord Wakefield and are now in the Guildhall Art Gallery.

Through the 1890s into the 1900s in pencil and watercolour he recorded the jetties, bridges and wharfs along the Thames. Sometimes drawing from a boat, he recorded mists, fog and dazzling sunsets silhouetting the grand designs of Wren and Pugin. In the winter of 1895 he endured the cold to sketch the ice-locked Thames that brought river traffic to a standstill. He was fascinated by working craft on the river, from wherries to large steamers (2.4, 2.5). In the sketches he was meticulous in writing notes to aid later-finished watercolours: 'Dutch Eel boats' (2.6, 2.7), 'straw barges', 'training ship

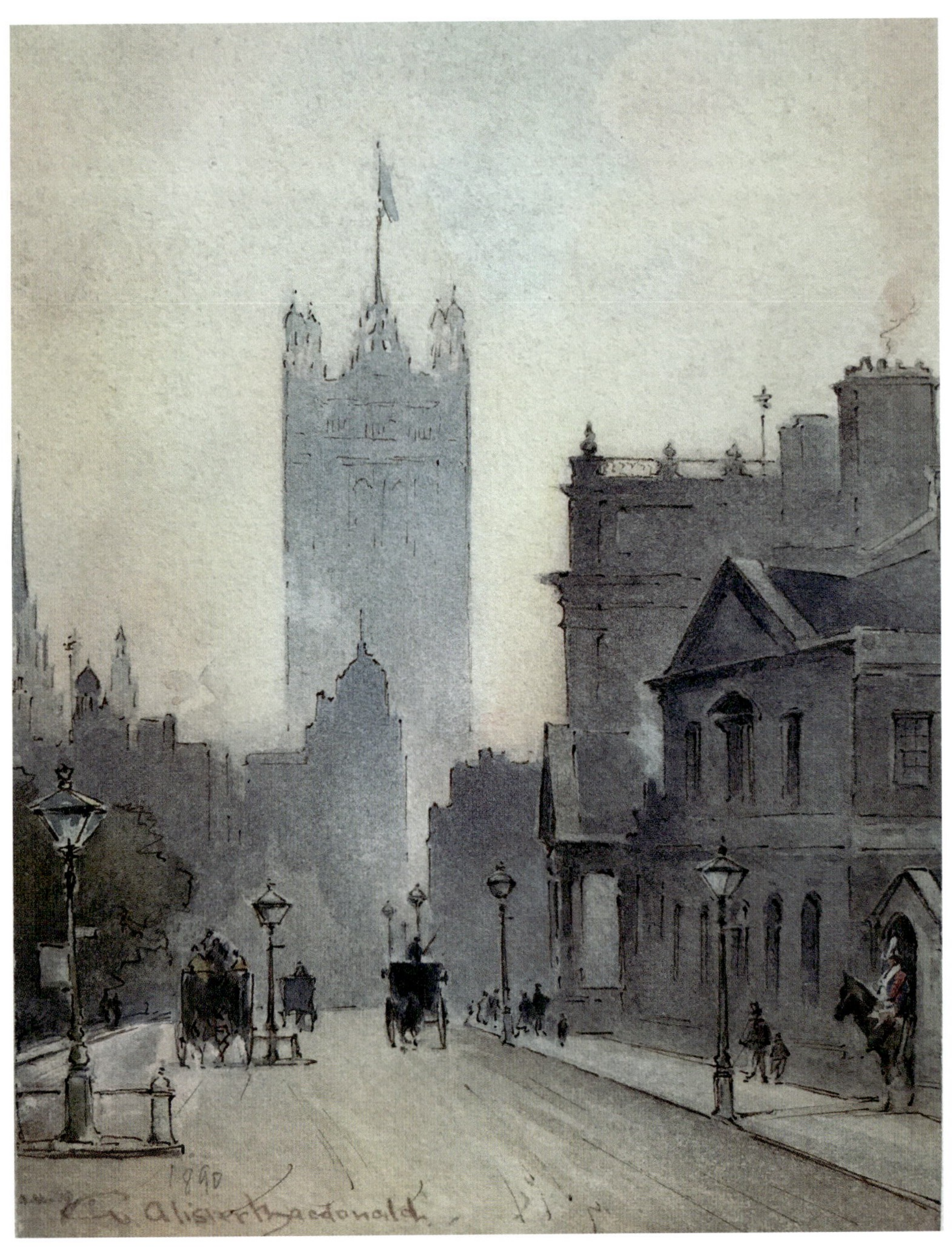

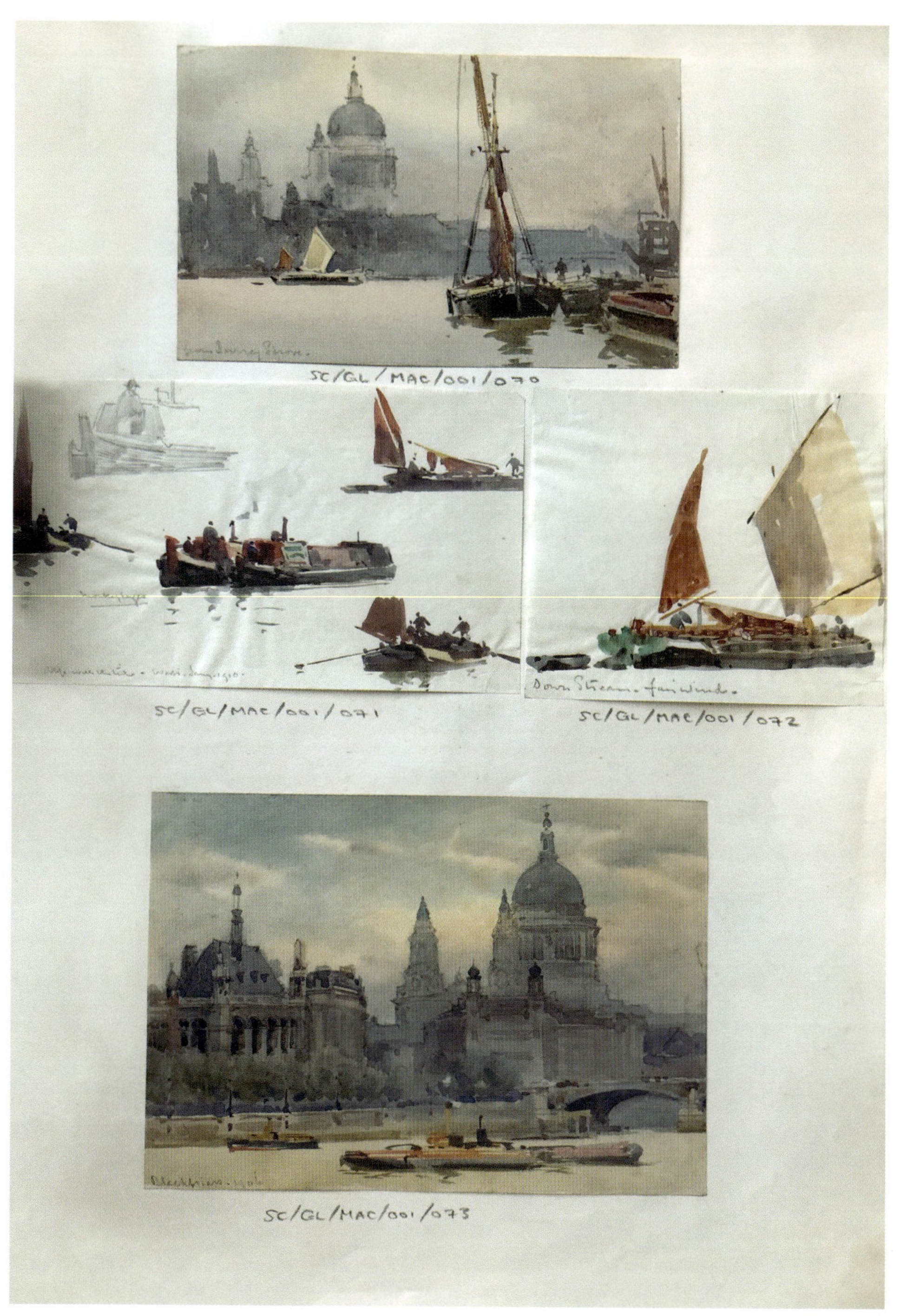
SC/GL/MAC/001/070
SC/GL/MAC/001/071
Down Stream. fair wind.
SC/GL/MAC/001/072
SC/GL/MAC/001/073

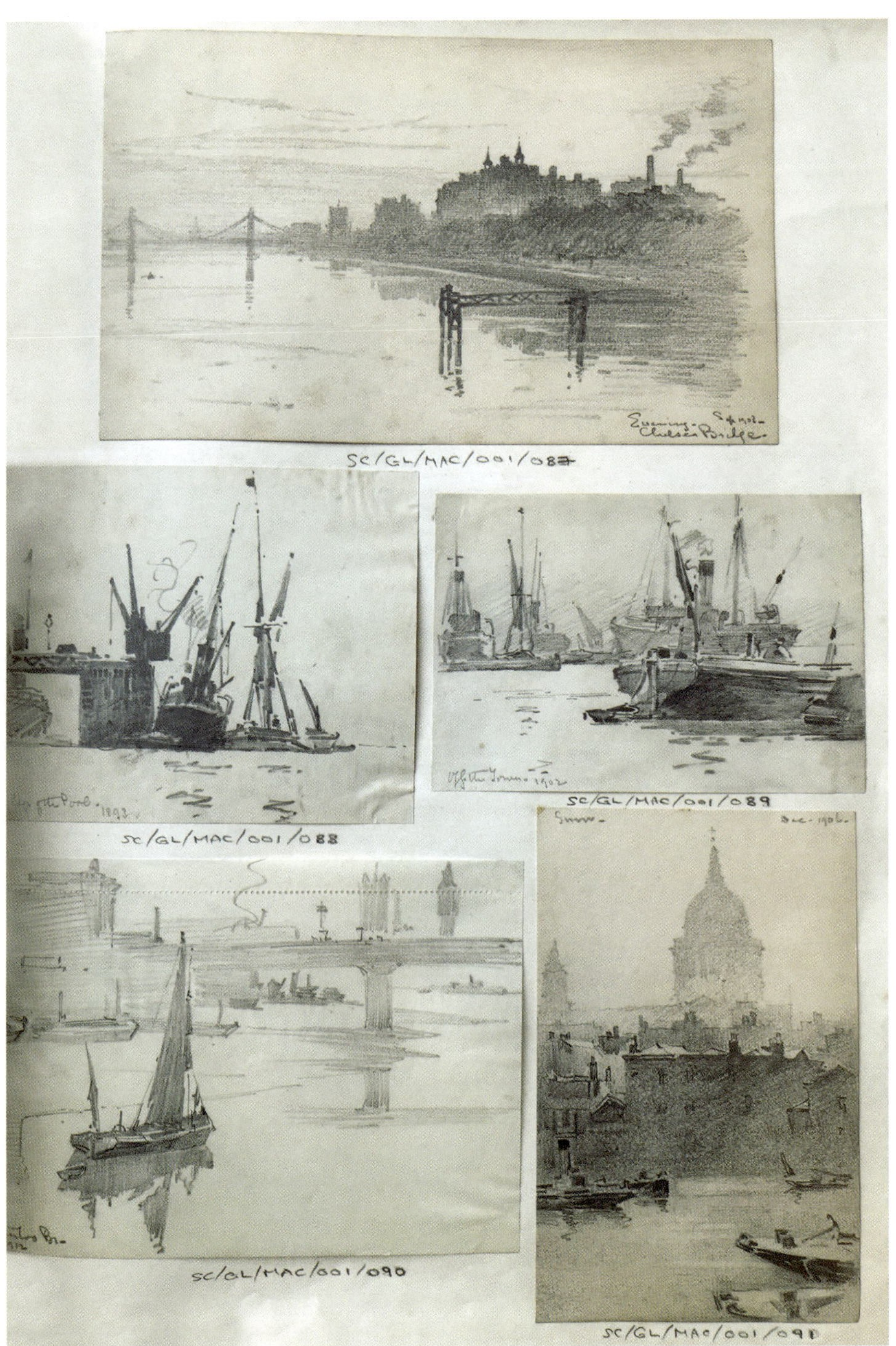

2.6 Sketches of Thames 1893–1912

2.7 Dutch Eel Boats off Billingsgate 1896

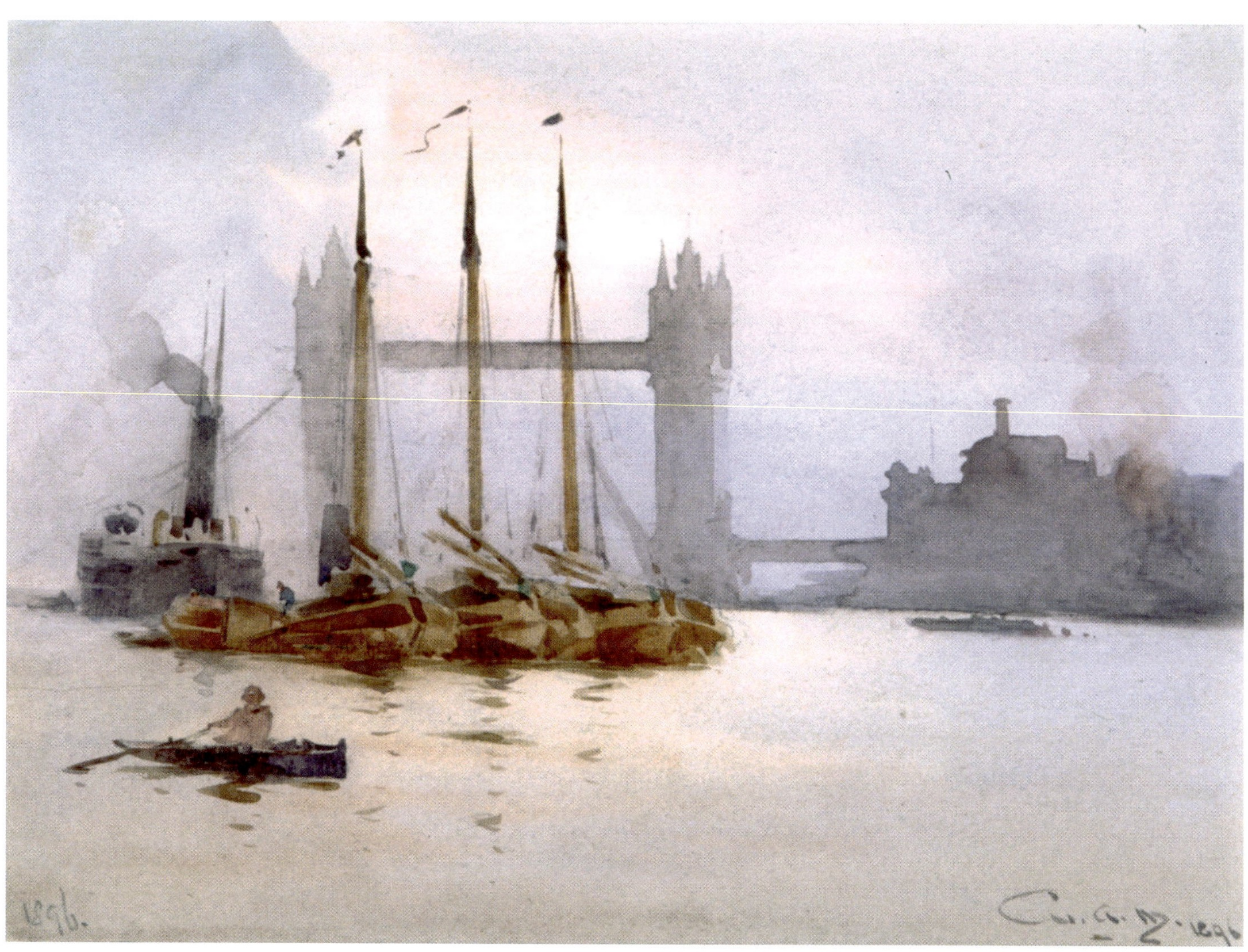

2.8 Sketch of Dutch eel boats and others in colour 1908

2.9 Training Ship Purfleet

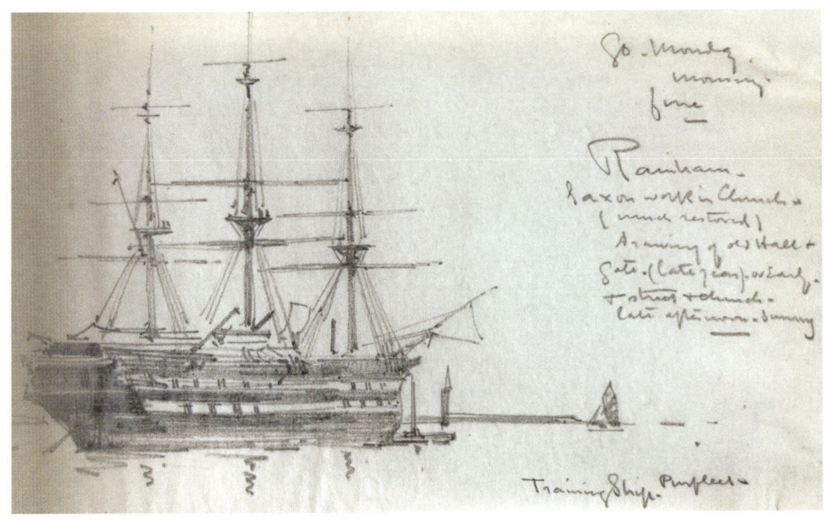

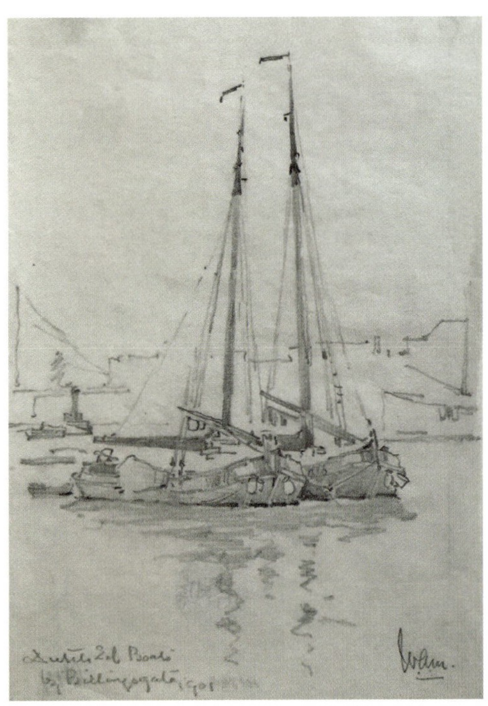

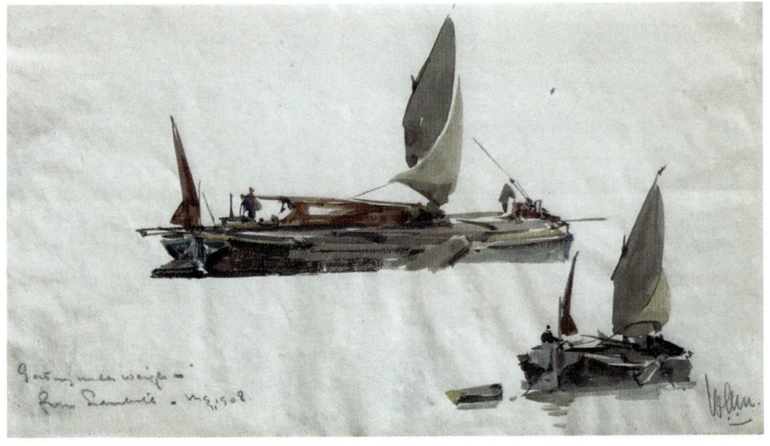

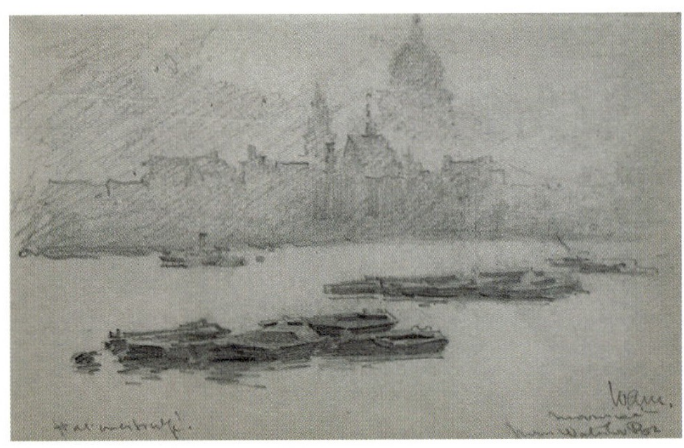

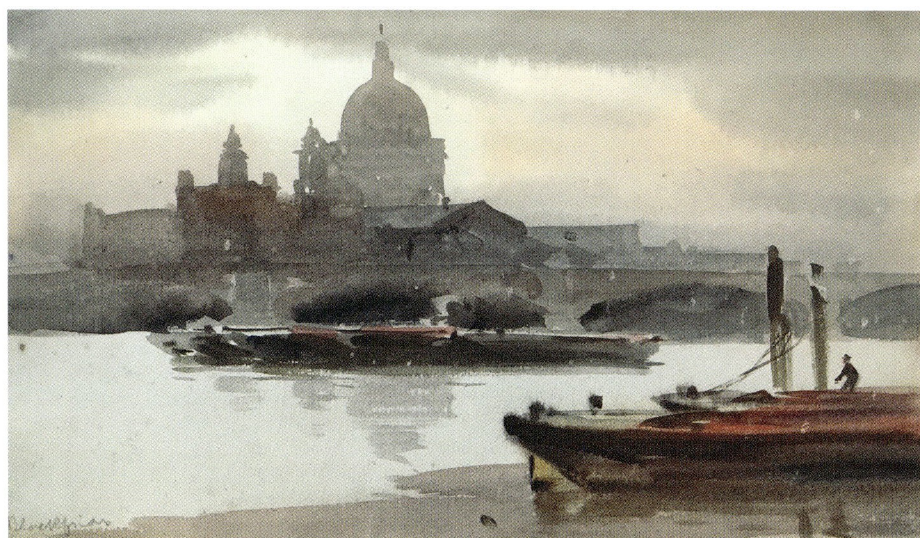

2.10 Impressions of St Paul's

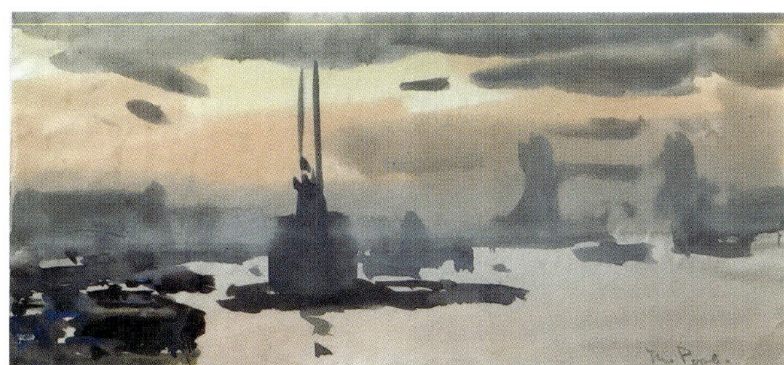

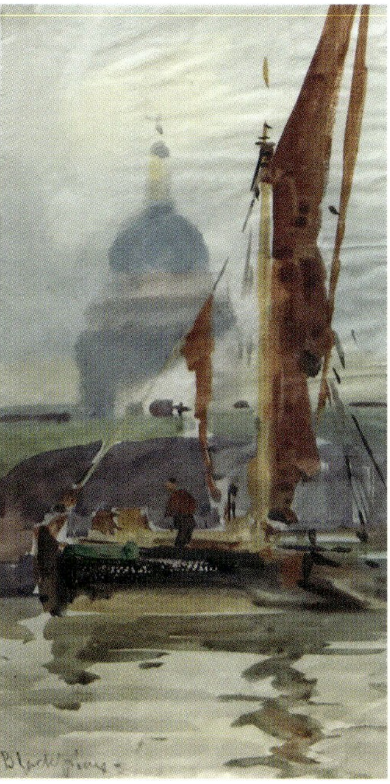

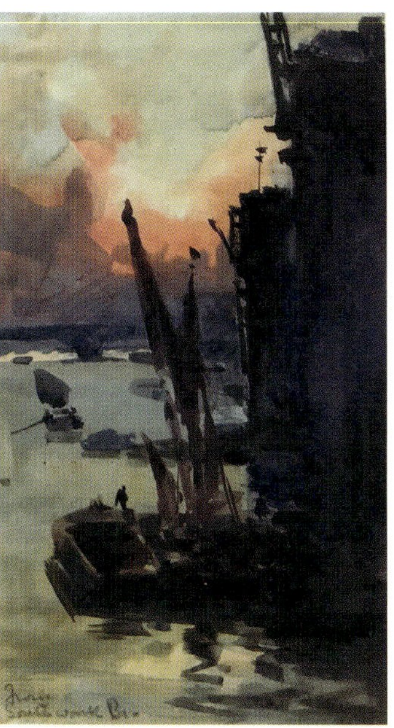

2.11 Impressions of winter evening Westminster and St Paul's

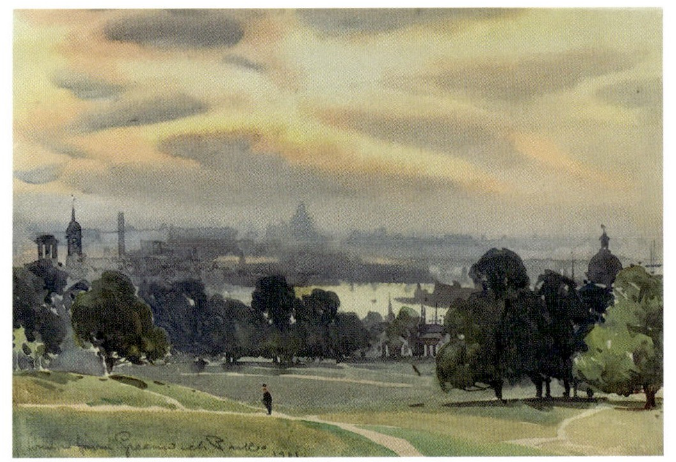

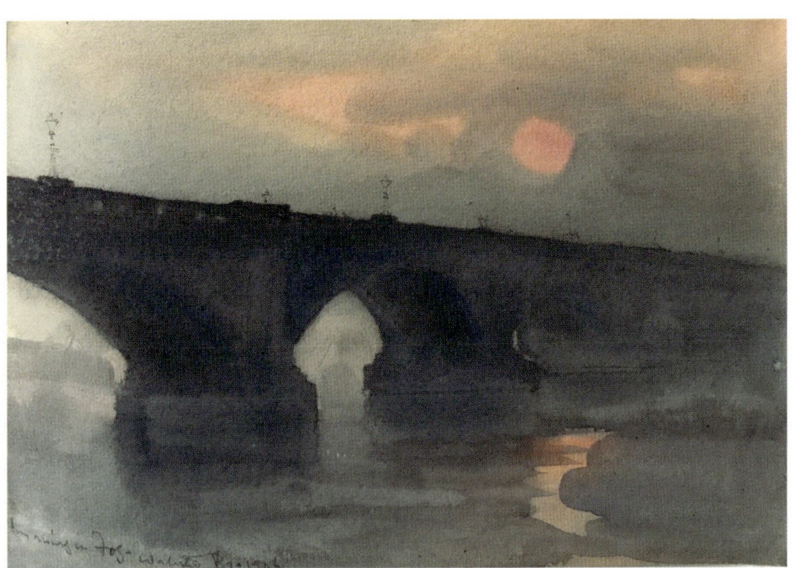

Winter morning. Sun rising in fog. (WAM)

Purfleet, late afternoon & sunny'(2.8), 'downstream fair winds', and architectural notes like 'Rainham – Saxon work in church (much restored)'. In London's less travelled streets around Inns of Court his favourite haunts to paint were 'ramshackle corners such as Cloth Fair or the soon to disappear overhanging houses of Holywell Street. Others show individual old inns and taverns or survivals of early domestic architecture'.[29]

Meanwhile another banker-turned-artist, Frenchman Paul Gauguin (1848–1903), was in Tahiti, and on his return to France caused a sensation with his exhibition of paintings at Durand-Ruel Gallery, Paris in 1894. The men could not be further apart in artistic direction and medium, but perhaps closer in their destiny than might have appeared on the surface, as we shall see in his later life.

Macdonald's London street scenes begin to show more architectural confidence and technical ambition. St Paul's and the Houses of Parliament become regular features in changing atmospheric watercolours(2.9, 2.10, 2.11, 2.12, 2.13). By contrast in Paris, the French photographer Eugene Atget (1857–1927) started recording

2.12 Lambeth Bridge sunset 1909

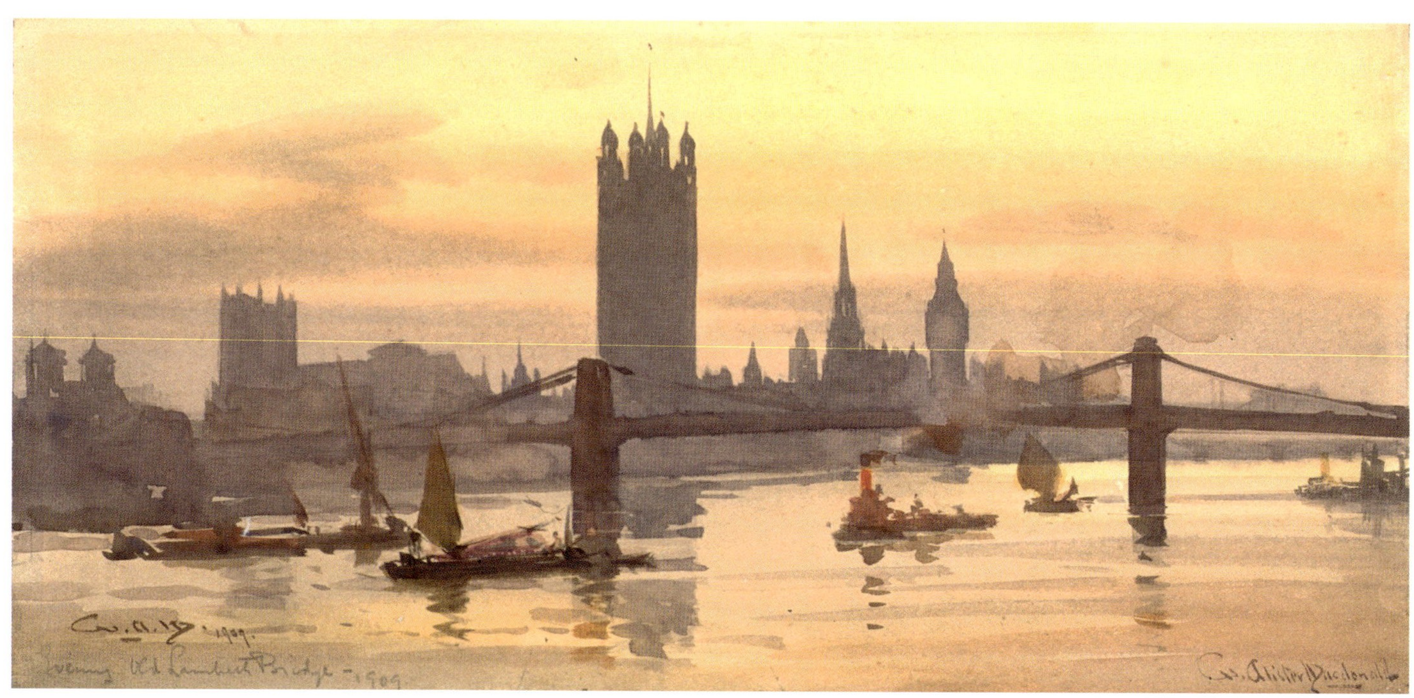

2.13 Impressions of Greenwich 1901 and Waterloo in fog 1906

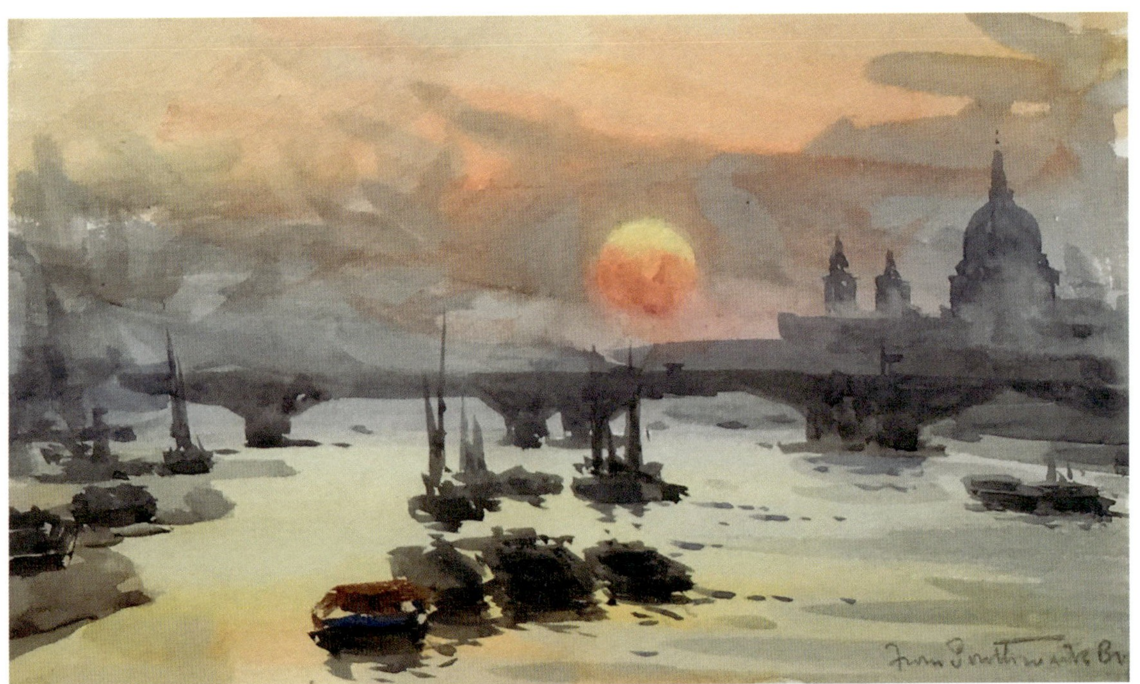

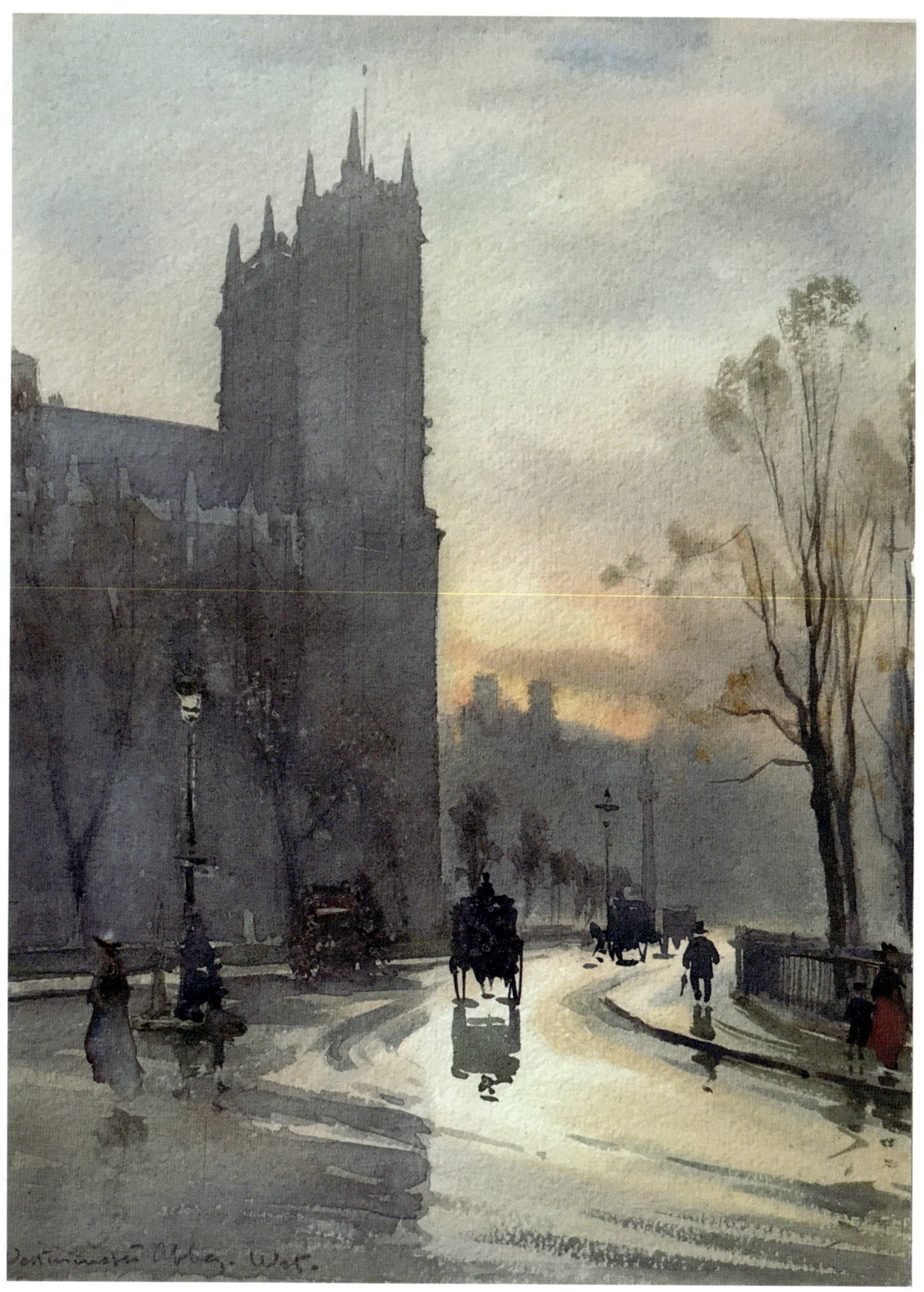

2.14 Impressions of Waterloo in fog 1906

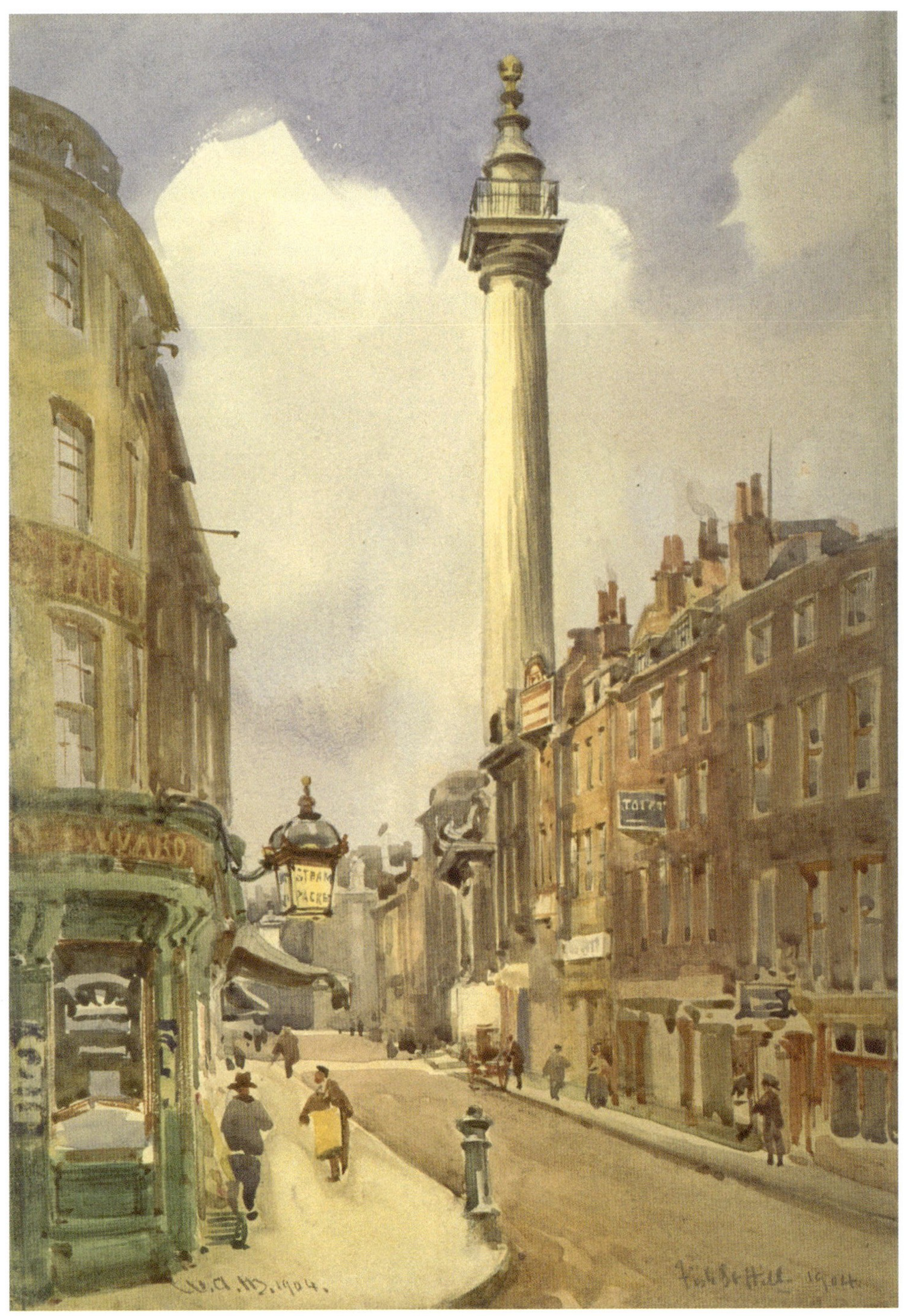

2.14 Fish Street Hill 1904

2.15 Kew Bridge 1897

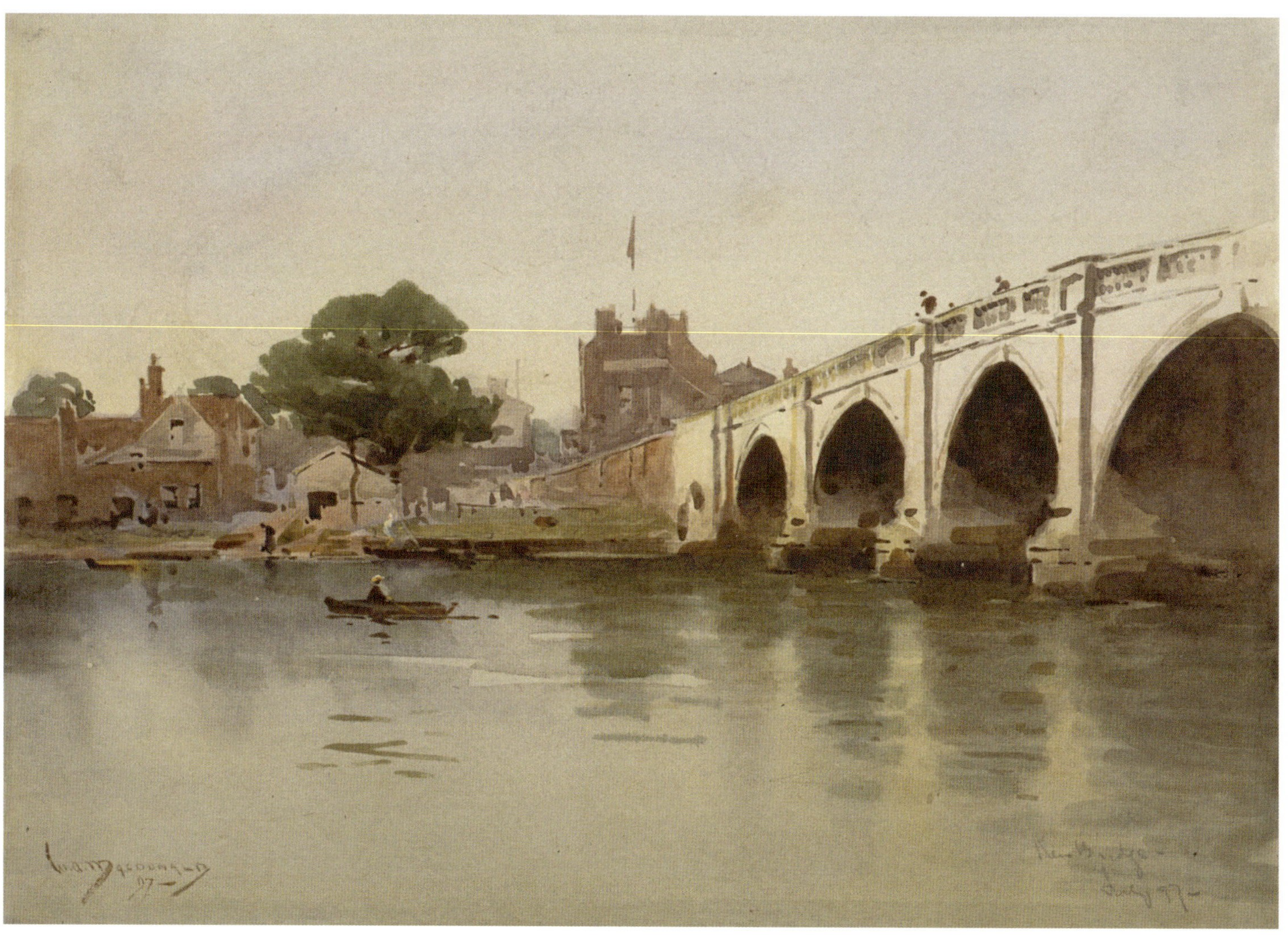

2.16 Old Richmond Bridge 1901

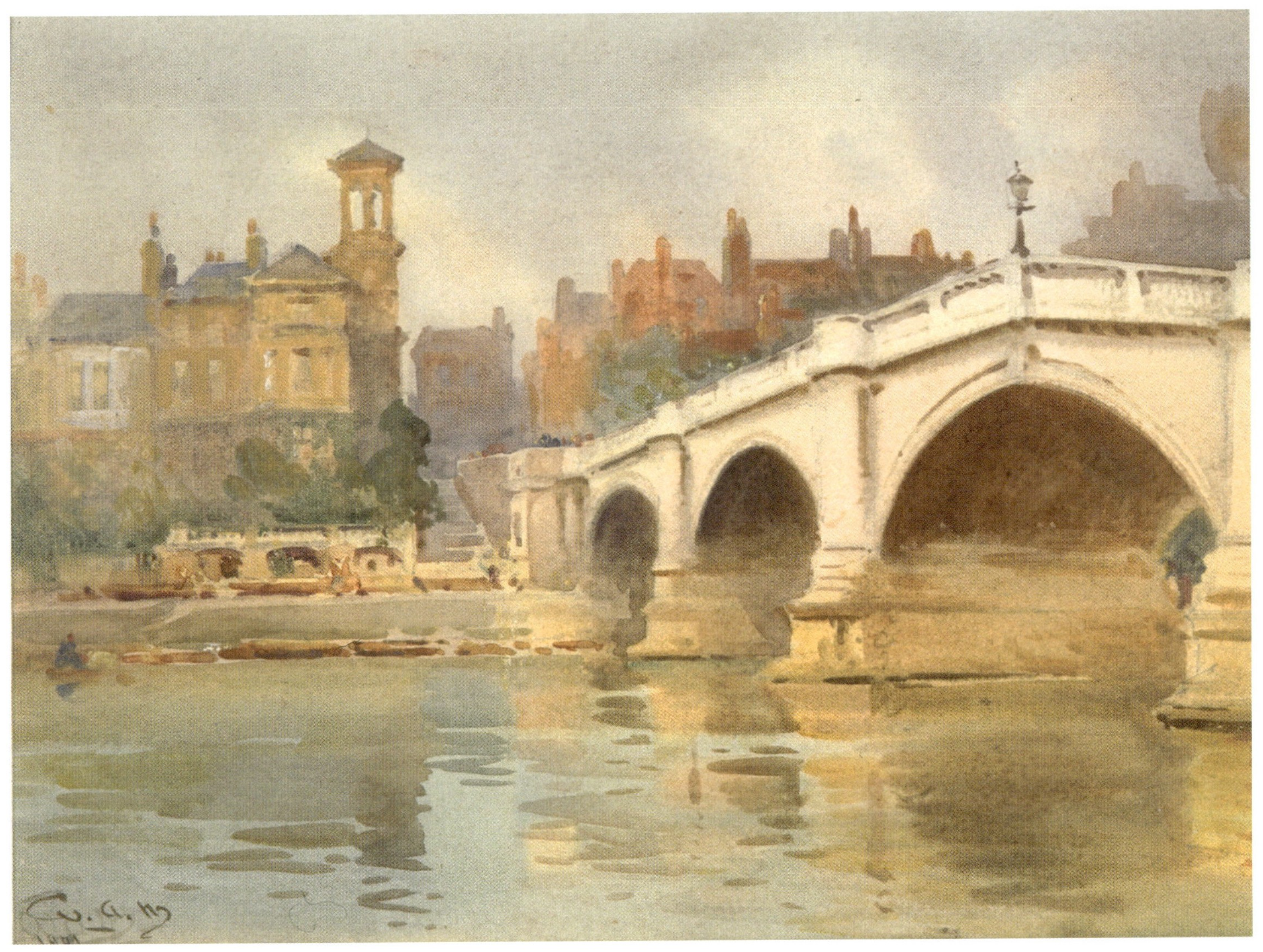

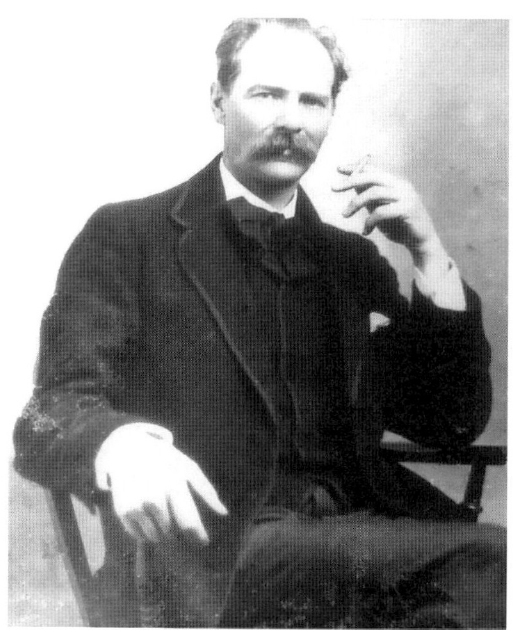

2.17 W. Alister Macdonald photographic portrait c. 1900

2.18 Lucy Macdonald miniature by Mrs W.M.N. Brunton 1914

Parisienne street scenes of its foggy nights, architecture, River Seine and 'humble' urban life. The black and white tonal photographs are crisp, but the empty early morning streets are somewhat haunting by comparison to the watercolourist's warm colour palette.

Macdonald worked on small and highly finished drawings and watercolours which began to find a market through the Kensington Fine Arts Society. He clearly preferred to mix in affluent society circles, perhaps befitting of one born in a church manse and previously employed in a City bank, and so once introduced to the arts patron Lady Freake, he became a welcome guest at her homes in Fulwell Park, Twickenham and Cranley Gardens (2.14, 2.15). His work also caught the eye of Stephen Leitch, a Foreign Office diplomat, who invited him to stay at the British Embassy in Lisbon in 1895. Portugal broadened Macdonald's artistic horizons and gave him his first taste of the sunny south which began a creative fascination with continental Europe.

The wandering artist then met (2.16), and in 1898 married, Lucy Winifred Carey (1872–1951) (2.17), a respected miniaturist painter and gallerist, and daughter of the artist William Carey. Macdonald claimed that this was 'the wisest act of his life', now socially upwardly mobile as she became the Honorary Secretary of the Royal Society of Miniature Painters and widely known in the art world. No longer an 'impecunious artist', 'the happy and well-matched pair' lived in what was an old-world quarter of Danes Inn, in the Strand.[30]

It cannot have escaped their attention that at the turn of the century many of his contemporaries were venturing to Europe to paint. Whistler and Sickert were in Dieppe together, painting street scenes in oils and in a sombre palette. Sickert travelled frequently to Venice to paint repeatedly from favourite spots, exploring shifting light effects at different times of day, taking inspiration from Claude Monet's Rouen Cathedral series. Fellow Scot and one of the finest British watercolourists of the nineteenth century, Arthur Melville (1855–1904), had made his first trip to Venice in 1894, which by then had become saturated with British artists 'that even gondoliers

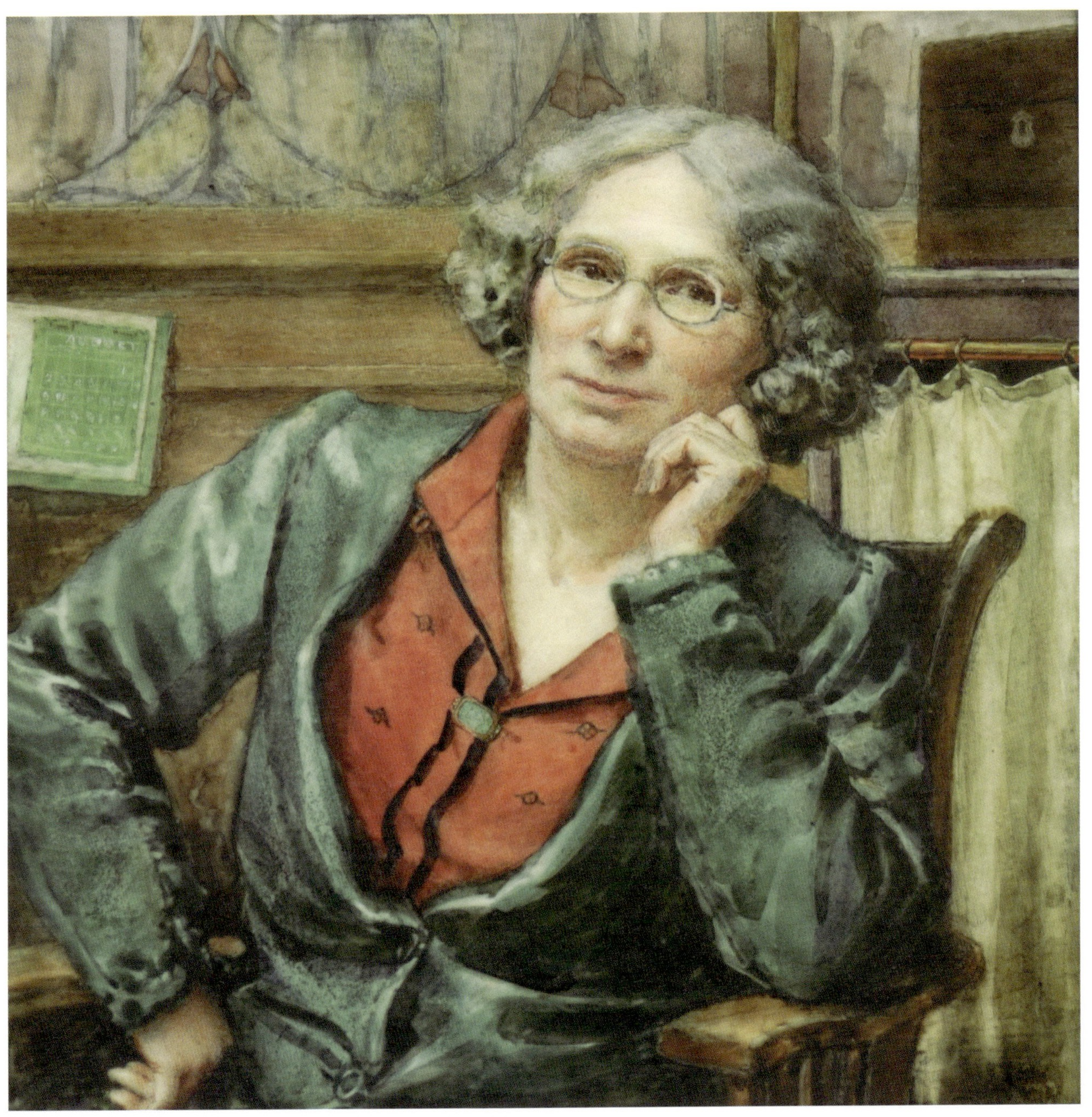

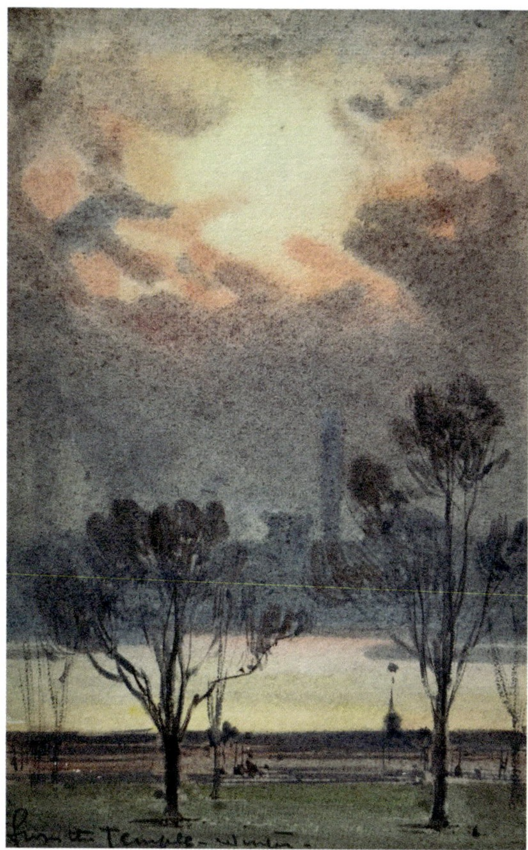

2.19 Sketches from Temple Window

would direct visiting artists to the best places in which to plant their sketching umbrellas'.[31] Seeing a commercial opportunity, rather than inspired to contribute to Melville's advance in 'Impressionism à l'Ecossais', in 1903 Macdonald began annual trips to Italy and other countries in Europe, frequently returning to Florence, the Lakes and Venice. But that year the art world lost two greats with the death of both Whistler and Gauguin.

In 1906 the Macdonalds moved to a prestigious seventeenth century address amongst the Court Chambers of the Temple within sight of the Thames, as seen from a watercolour study from their bedroom window (2.19). It began a fertile period of work and later exhibition catalogues provide evidence of the many locations he frequented, not only around his favourite spots in London and across England, Wales and Scotland during the summer months, but also Europe where he explored in the winter. The age of steam trains and ships facilitated his mobility, in modest steerage. Perhaps this was in part inspired by leading older artists of the English School of watercolours, Rose Barton (1856–1929) and Herbert Menzies Marshall (1841–1913), who were finding new markets and audiences for their work through the publication of illustrated books of their travels, such as *Familiar London* (1904) and *Cathedral Cities of France* (1907) respectively. Macdonald found similar outlets to publish colour plates of London architecture in *Flats, Urban Houses and Cottage Homes* (1906) (2.20), and his travels in *Penrose's Pictorial Annual* (1909) (2.22) and latterly *Hutchinson's Picturesque Europe* (1920) (2.23).

In 1910 Macdonald travelled to Fife, Barra in the Outer Scottish Hebrides, Lincolnshire, Kent, Geneva, Corfu, Naples and Assisi. Consider that itinerary in the same year that their son Ian (8.3) was born, and they opened their own gallery in Westminster (2.21). Lucy now took on new roles of both a mother and business manager of The Little Gallery, while he concentrated on his art with newly acquired liberty to exhibit what he wanted, rather than be frustrated by the taste of dealers in other galleries.

2.20 Flats, Urban Houses & Cottage Homes 1906

2.21 The Little Gallery label

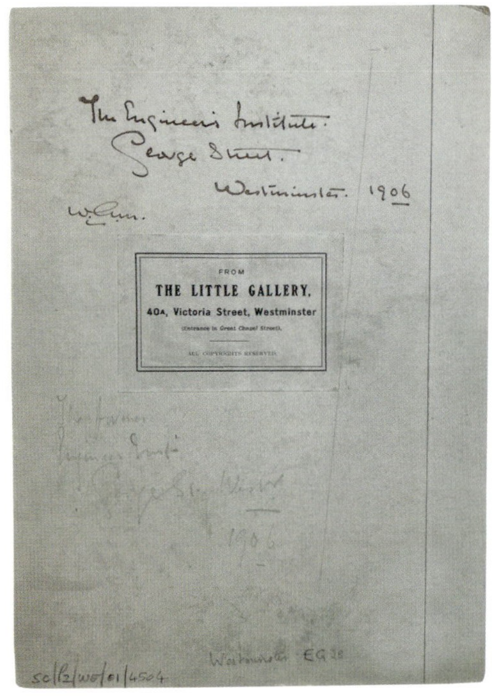

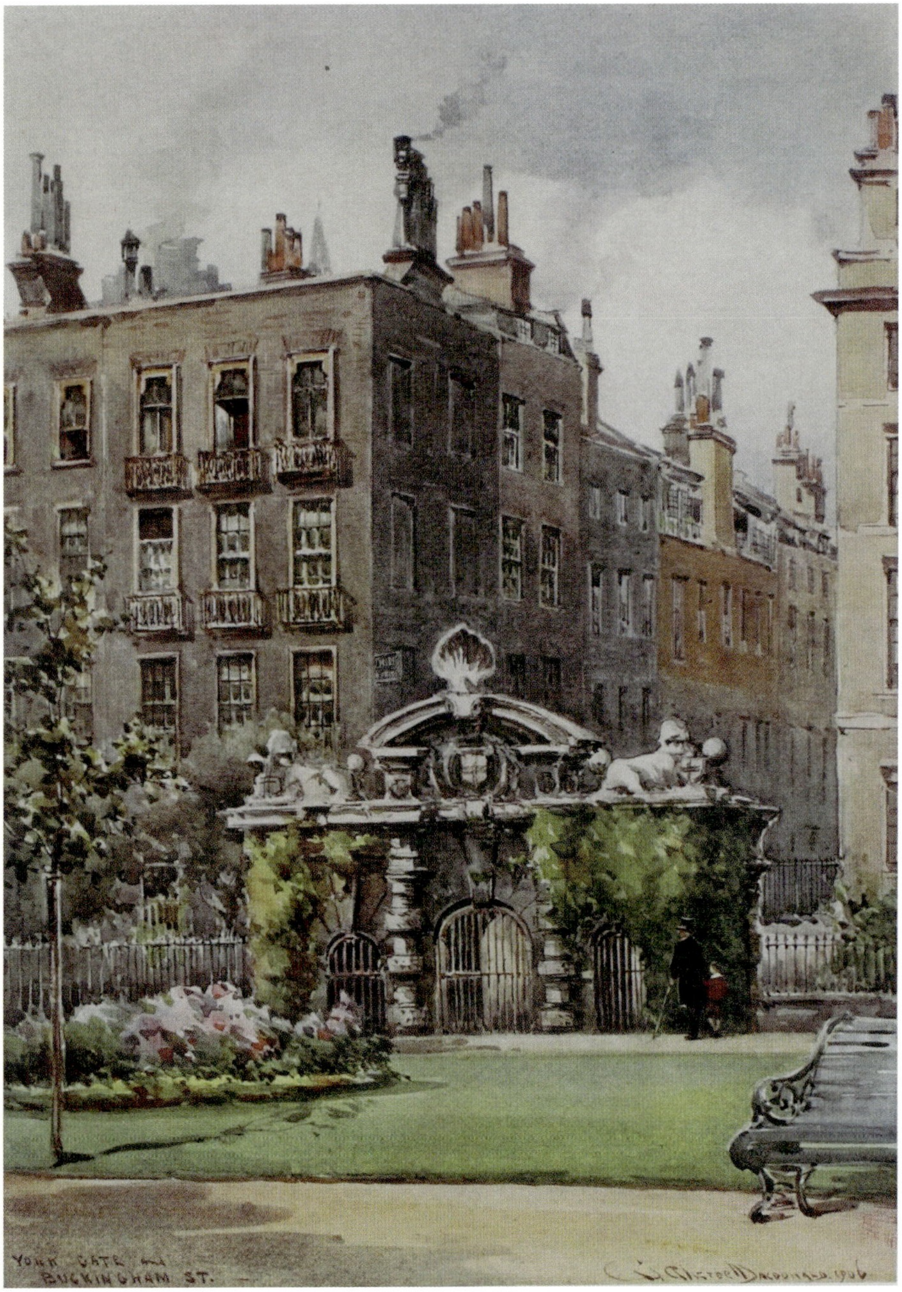

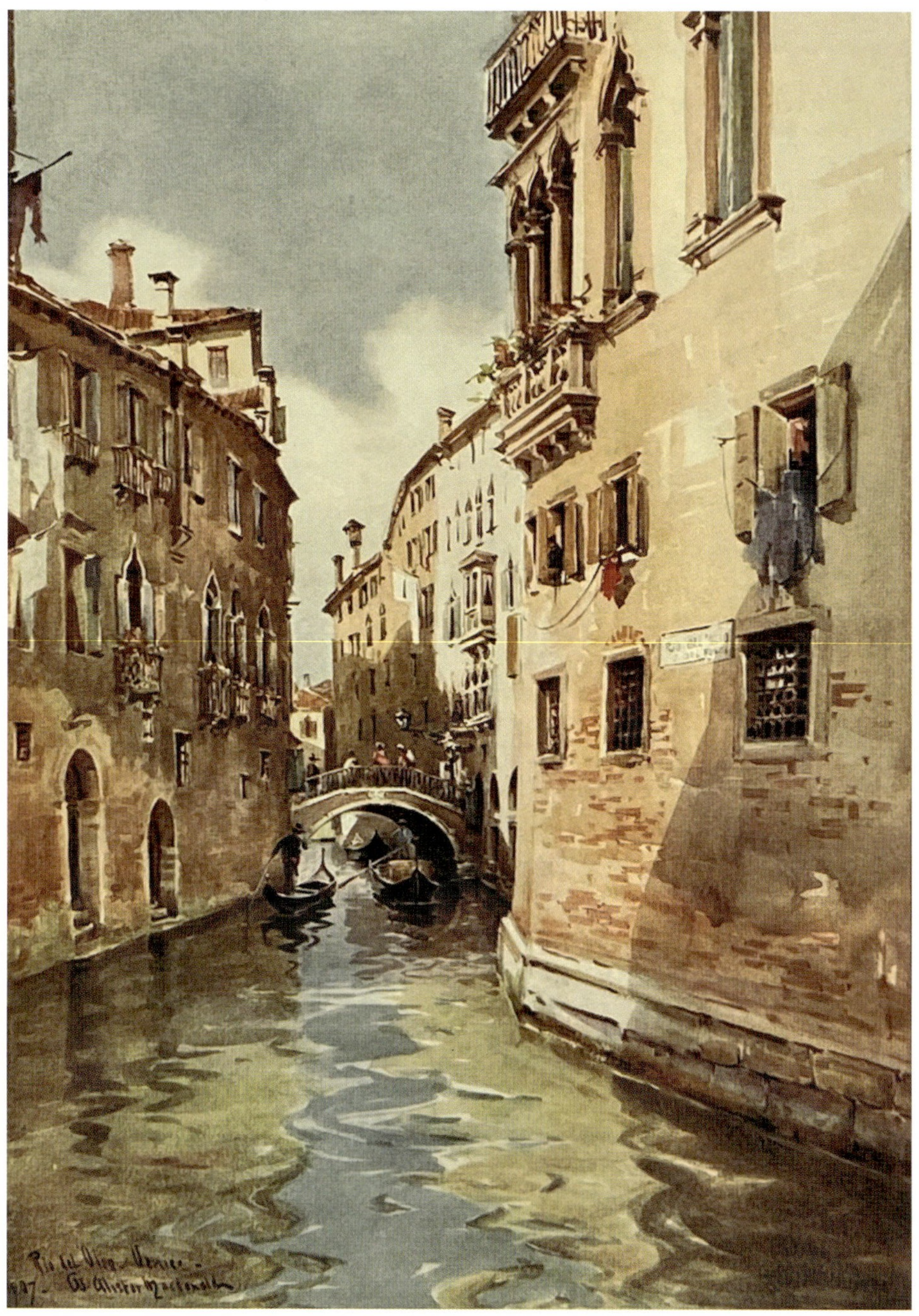

2.22 Rio del Olio, Venice, *Penrose Pictorial Annual* 1909

2.23 Piaza S. Maria Novella Florence, *Hutchinson's Picturesque Europe*

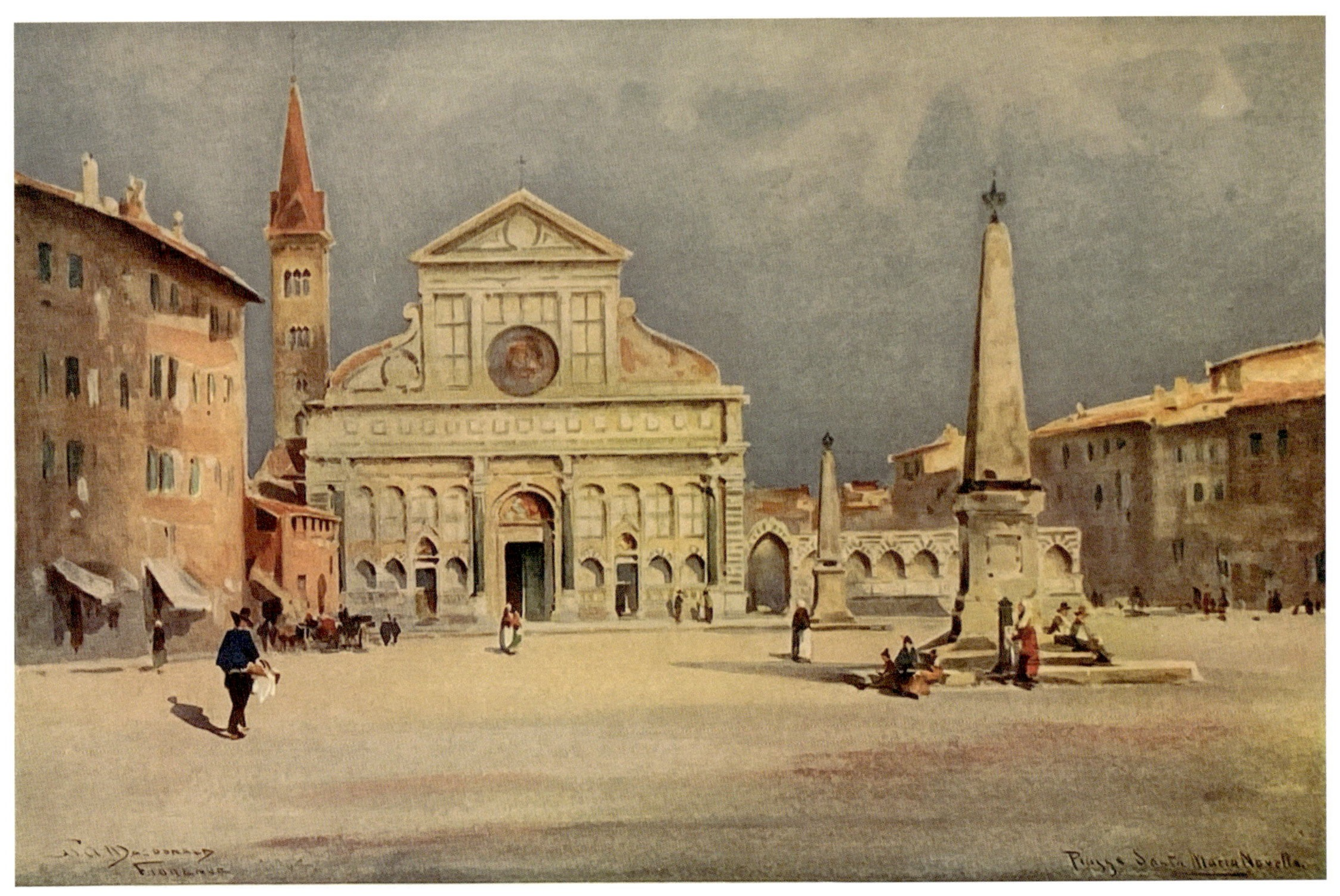

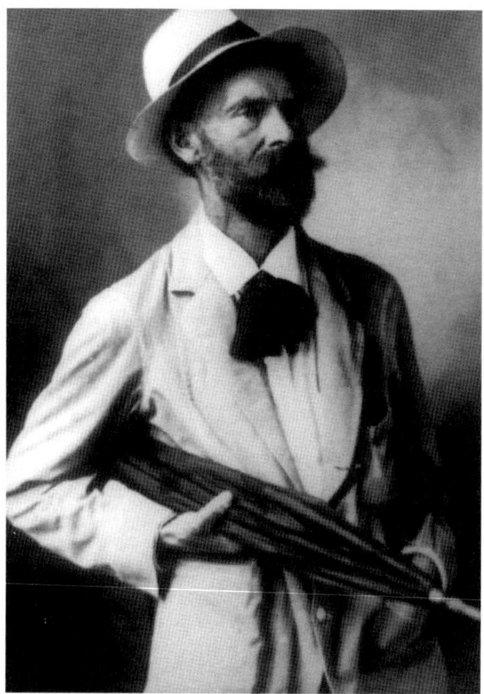

2.24 W. Alister Macdonald photographic portrait c. 1910

The artist's single-minded dedication to his work caught the attention of a London policeman as he was sketching along the banks of the Thames at Billingsgate. 'A burly constable, who had been observing his work, looking over his shoulder, remarked, 'Ah! Some day we shall see these pictures in the Guildhall.' 'How little,' adds the artist, 'did I then imagine that what has turned out to be a prophetic utterance, would be realised.'[32]

In 1912 he took painting trips to the Isle of Wight, in Scotland Loch Maree and the Isle of Skye, and a third visit to Tunisia in North Africa (2.25). Around this time another younger artist from the north of Scotland, James McBey (1883–1959), was immersing himself in Morocco, later made famous for his portrait of T.E. Lawrence, but whose etchings of streets and boats reached an acclaim in Britain beyond Macdonald's. North Africa had been exoticised by the earlier work of Melville, and his masterly watercolours were surely inspirational for Macdonald. The British Museum's collection of Macdonald's work contains studies of boats and people, as well as some landscapes painted on these painting expeditions (2.25, 2.26, 2.27, 2.28, 2.29, 2.30). These sketches in watercolour and pencil often provided reference to enable him to populate streets and complete more finished work later. Punctuated with annotations they capture the costume and characterful faces of that period seen through the eyes of an Edwardian Scottish traveller.

Never once did Macdonald deviate from his focus on the landscape and his meticulous interpretation of it through the medium of watercolour, while artists such as Sickert explored a range of post-impressionist styles in oils, and new Scottish talent led by S.J. Peploe (1871–1935), whose tonal effects were inspired by Whistler, were breaking through to critical acclaim in London and Scotland.

Now an established artist turning fifty years old (2.24), Macdonald began to teach part-time, giving demonstration lessons in his art of drawing and painting. This practical learning by doing was better suited to the nature of a man who had never reconciled to more academic teaching methods. It is perhaps in this role that he was

2.25 Tunis 1912

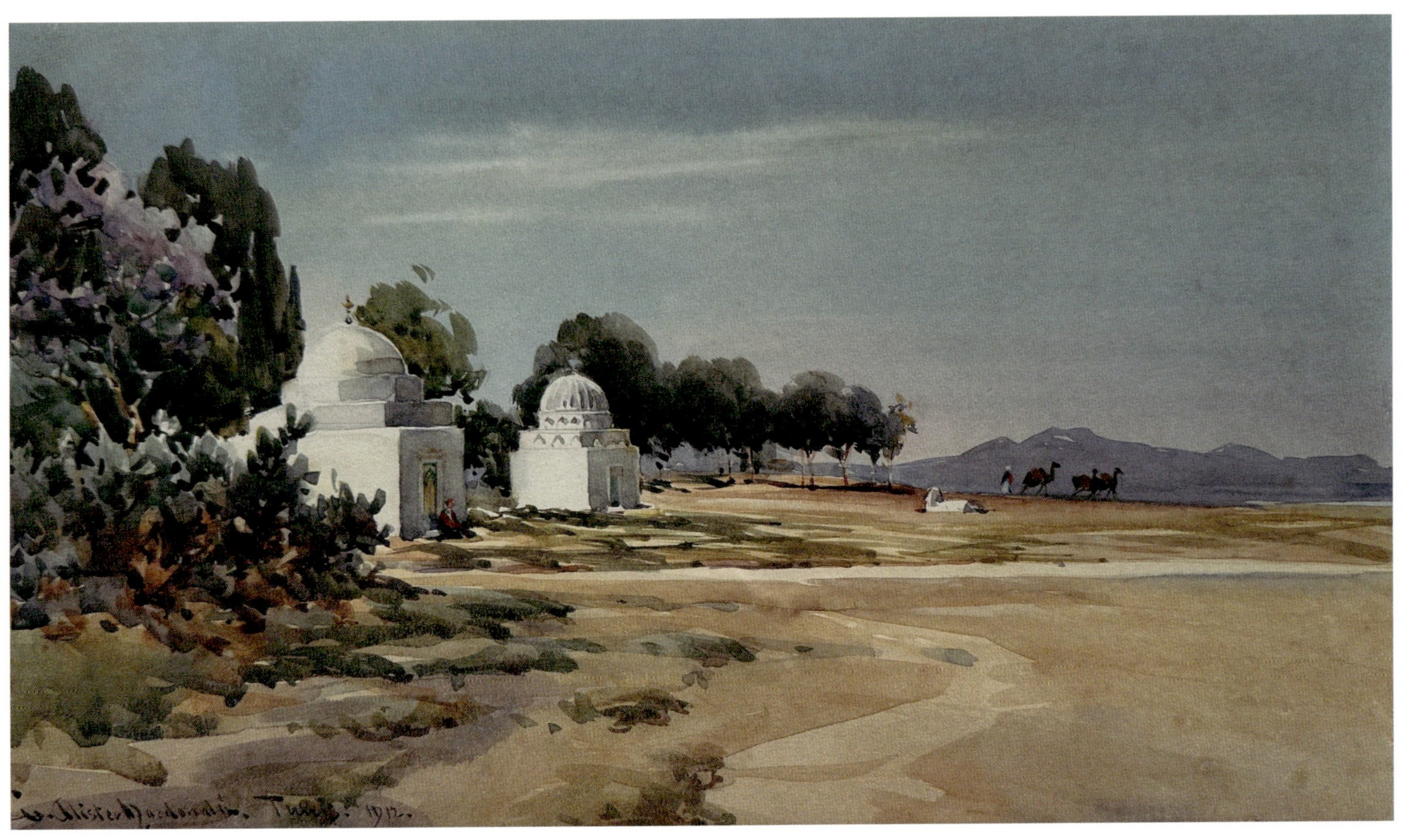

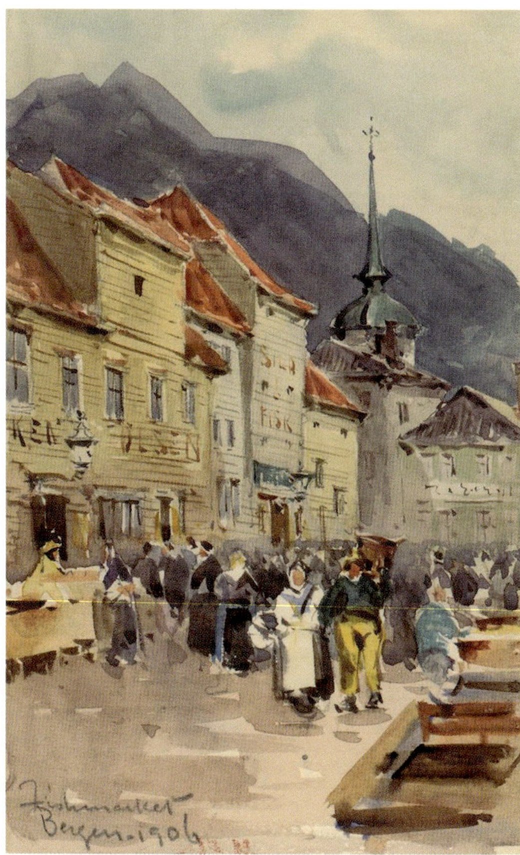

2.26 Bergen; boats moored along quayside, beyond figures and row of buildings 1906

introduced to a young art student Dorothy Myhill, from Norfolk, a county he became familiar with at the start of his artistic career. How they met remains a mystery, but she would later play an important part in his destiny.

With the Great War came the inevitable closure of The Little Gallery, and Macdonald did what he considered to be his patriotic duty and enlisted for military service (2.32). Too old at fifty-three for combat, he was posted to the Army Service Supply Department of the War Office, first under Colonel Morgan in Whitehall, and later under Major Poulton at Reading. In 1918, writing from North Wales to his younger brother, Sinclair, who had remained in Thurso to build a successful architecture practice, Macdonald revealed his political opinions on the leaders and people of the time (2.33):

8, Fig Tree Court
Temple E.C

Written from North Wales
4th May 1918

My dear Sinclair,

Your letter was sent on here by wifie. It certainly is a long time since we saw or heard you and had your news been better, the pleasure would have been greater.

I feel so very sorry for you all. These uncertain 'missings' are hard, very hard when up against it and your boy was sent out there, without leave, on coming back from the East, Willie Macdonald told me. For, of course, they wanted every man they could get then; having run the army short for so long – to suit their own ends. We – as you say – put up with much!

Unfortunately, it is the shirker and job-makers, who are hiring boys. Government Offices are full of them in many parts of the country, apparently. As for Ireland – well there is Politics! – which we so very highly appreciate – and owe so much to!!

2.27 Beguinage in Brugge; river in foreground, flanked by buildings at left, beyond bridge, and in distance church spire 1906

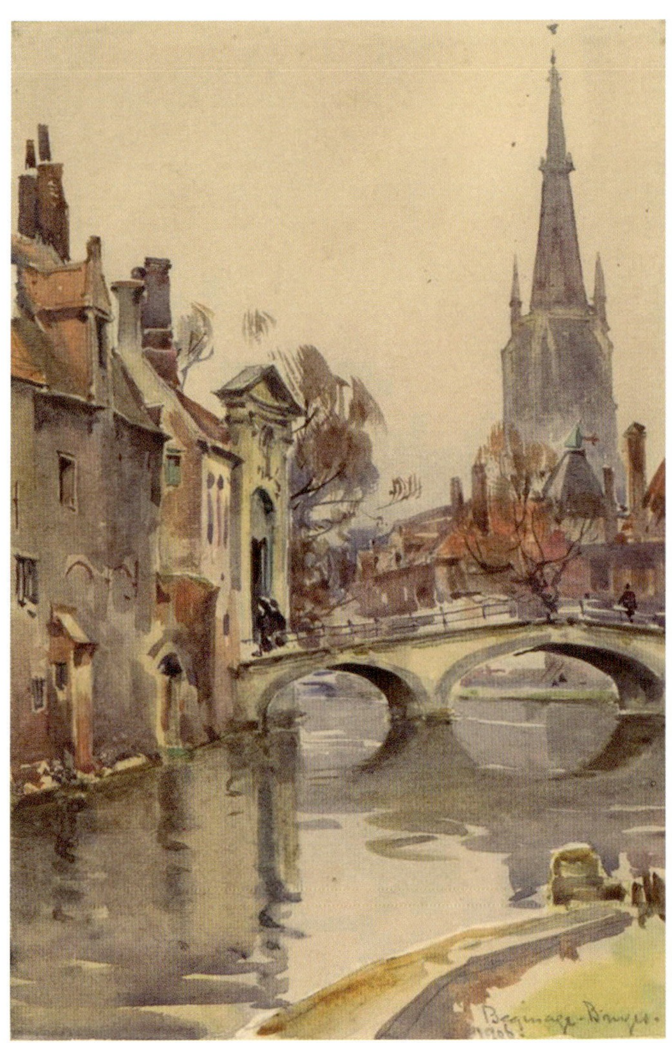

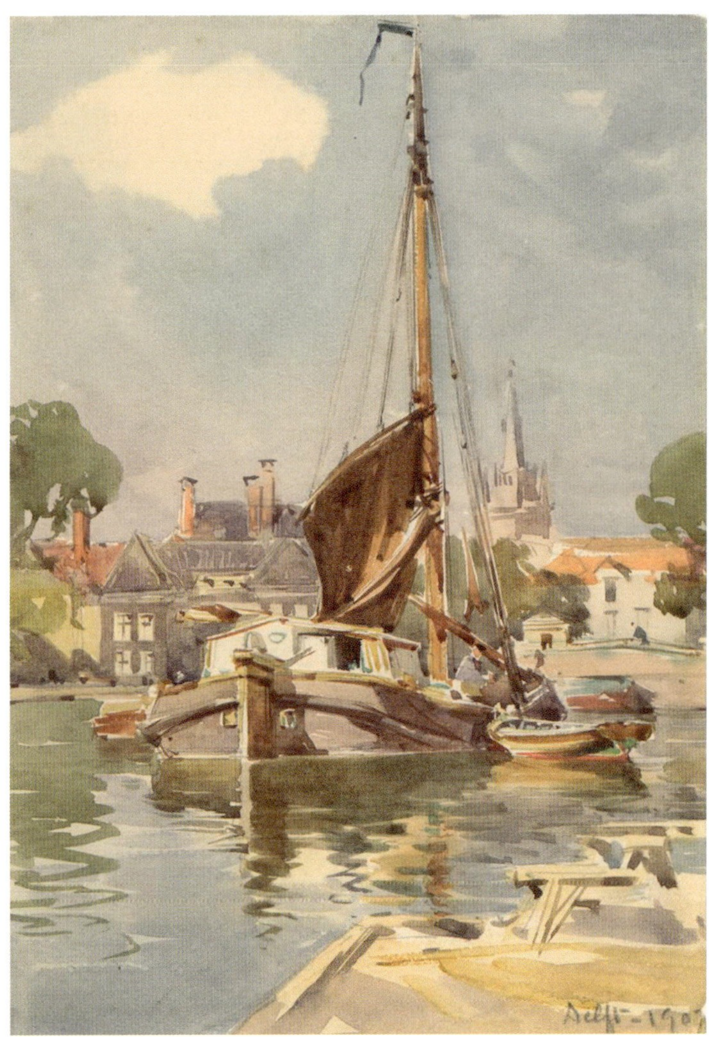

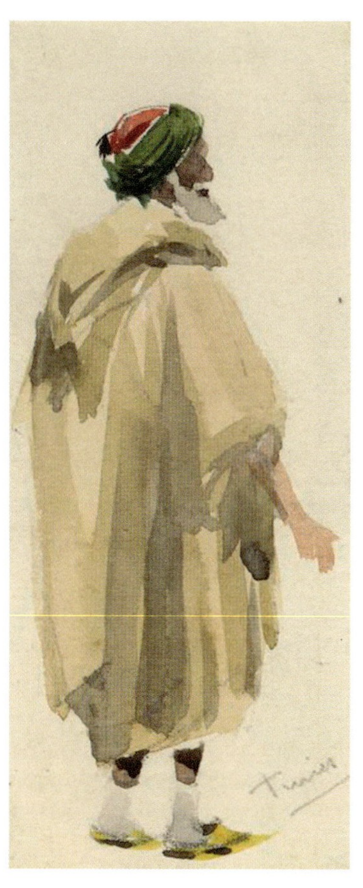
Tunis

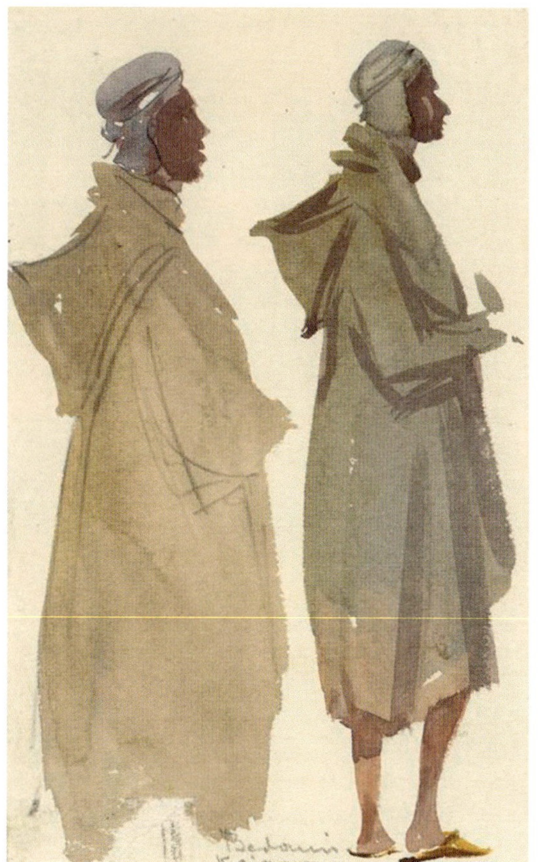
Bedouin
Kairouan.

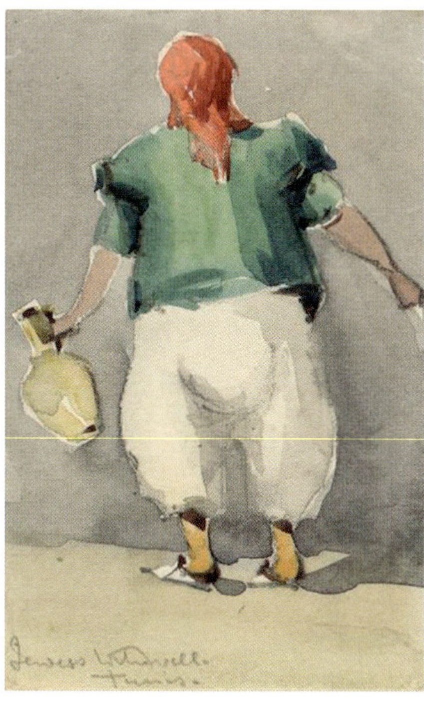
Tunis.

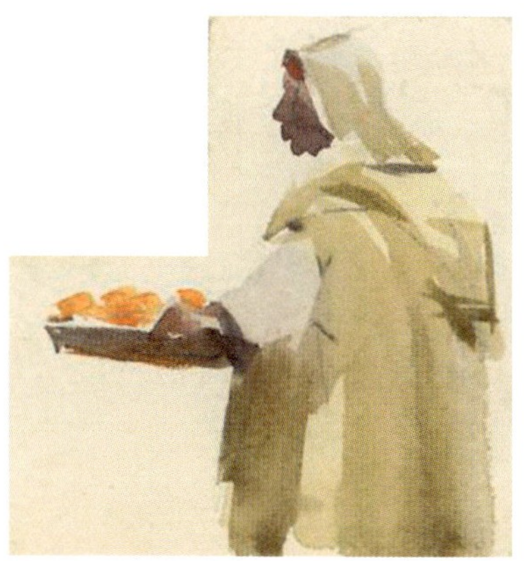

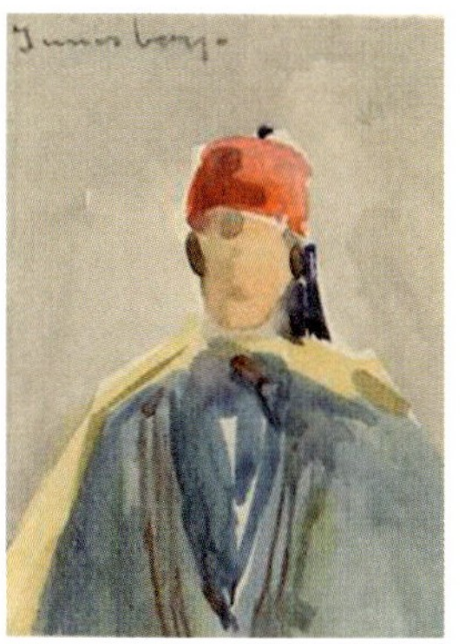
Tunis boy.

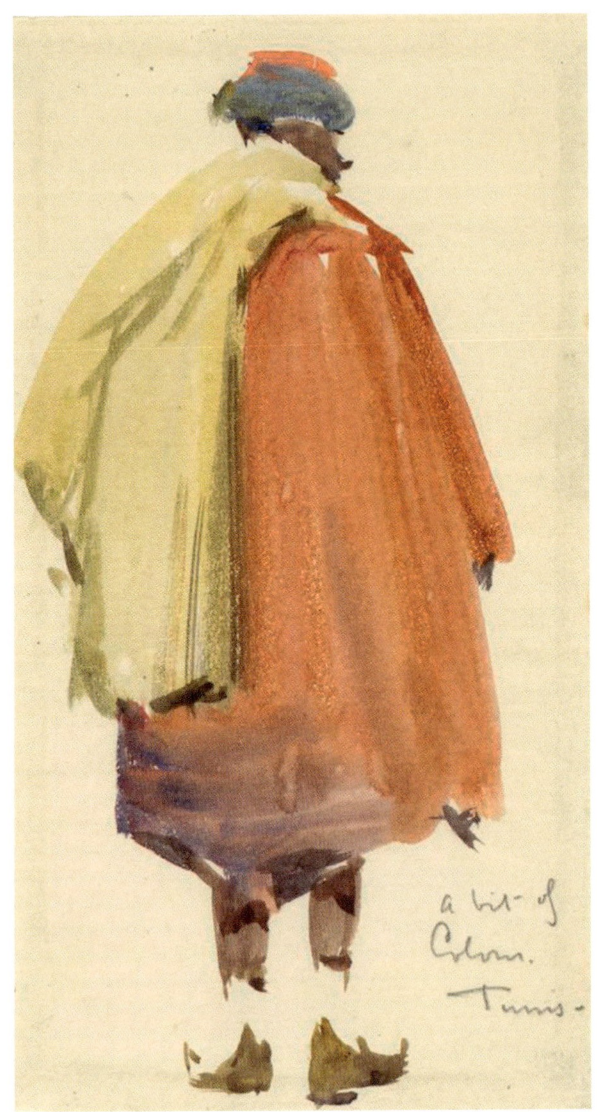

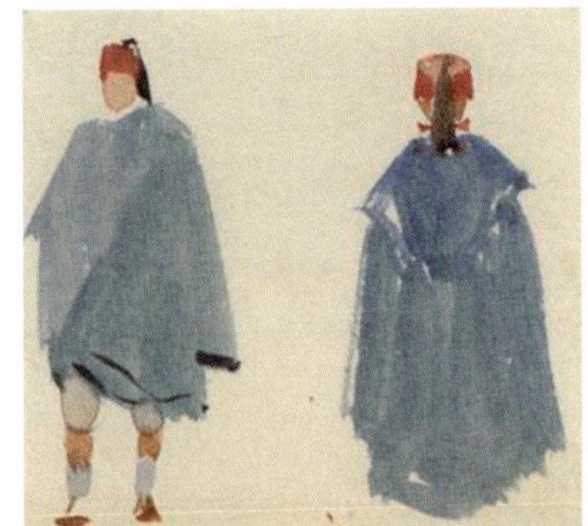

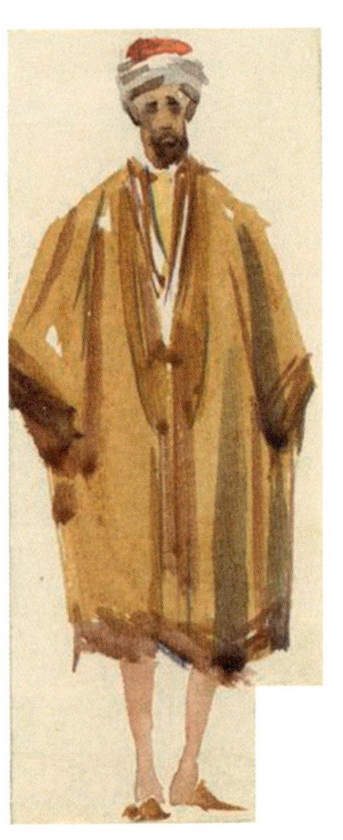

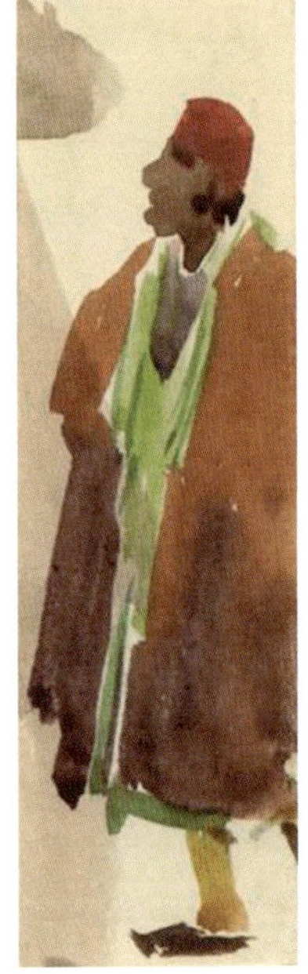

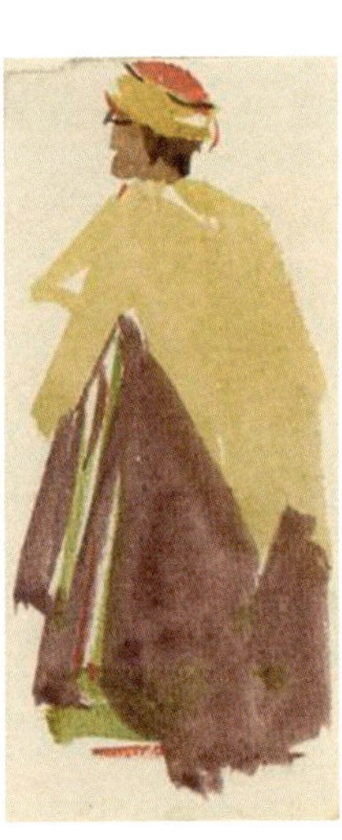

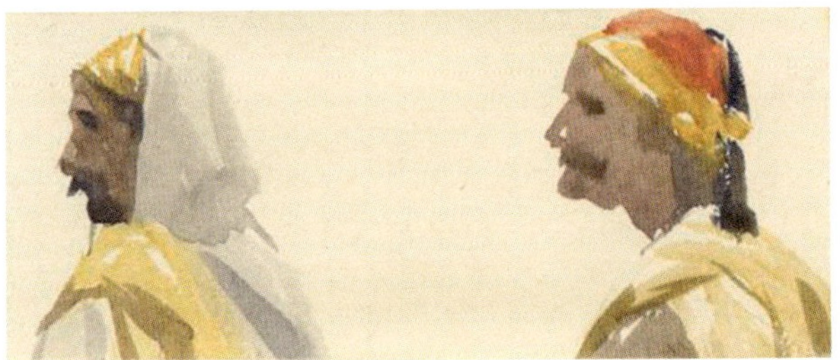

2.28 Study of a Tunisian

2.29 Studies of Tunisians; two figures standing and seen from behind, one whole-length, the other possibly three-quarter length, both wearing a fez

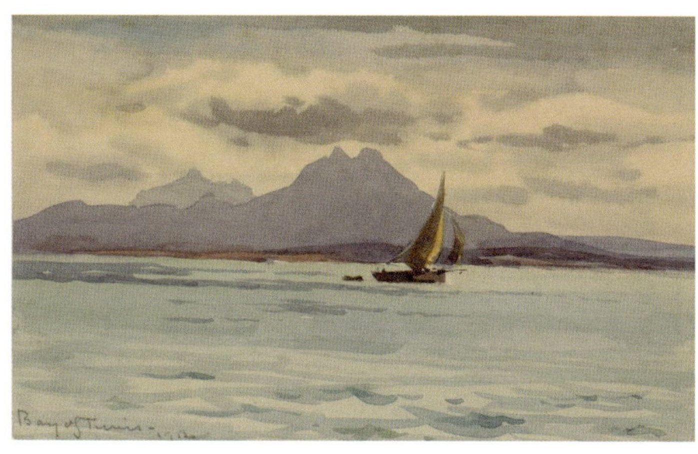
Bay of Tunis -

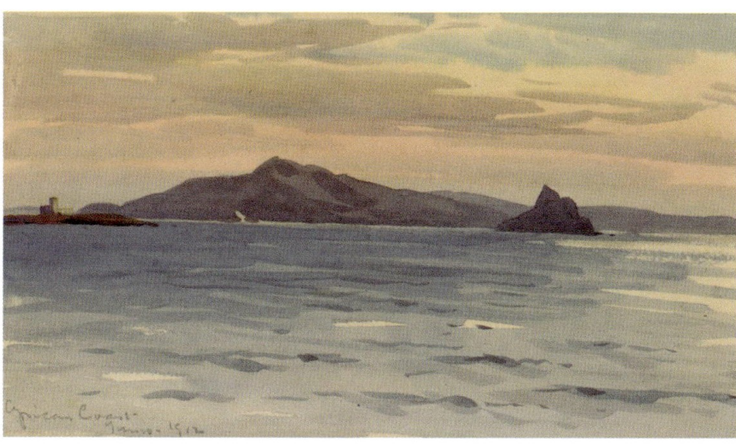
Coast -

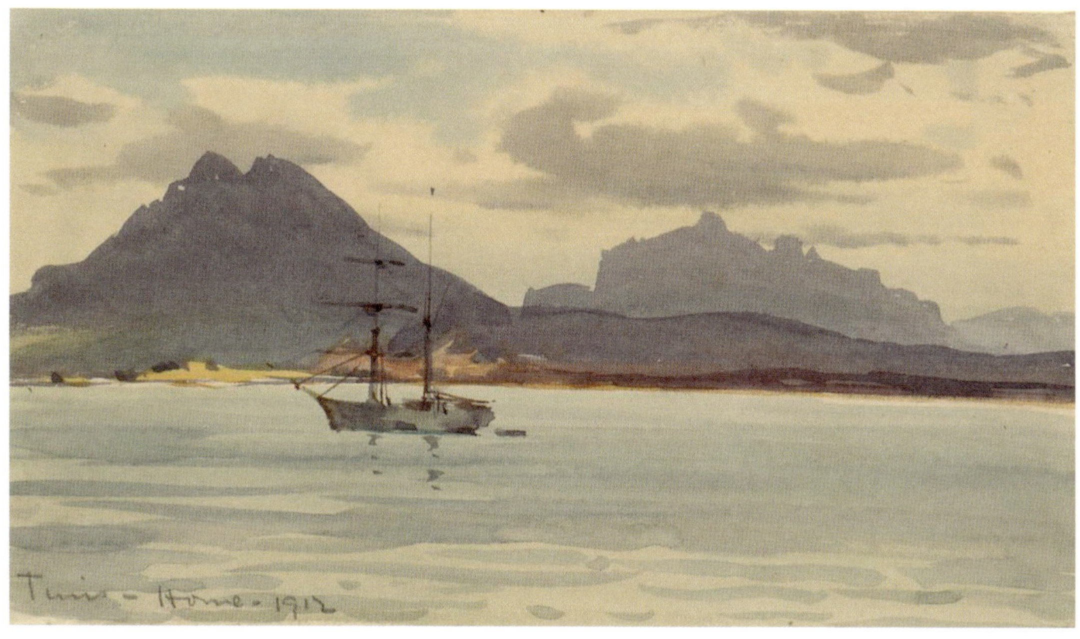
Tunis - Home - 1912

2.30 Tunis; stretch of water across foreground, and ship at left, in distance mountains 1912

2.31 Tunisia, Sidi ben Said, Tunis; buildings, including gate at left 1911

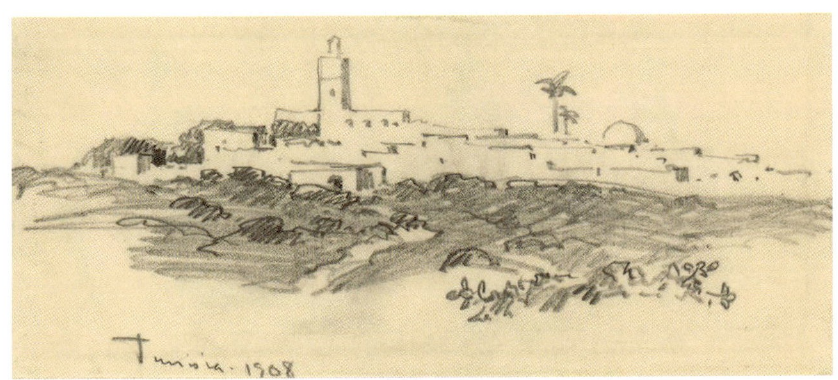

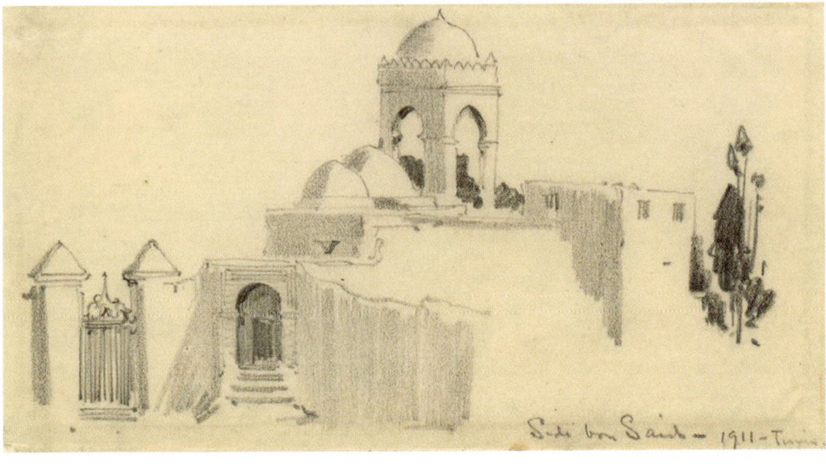

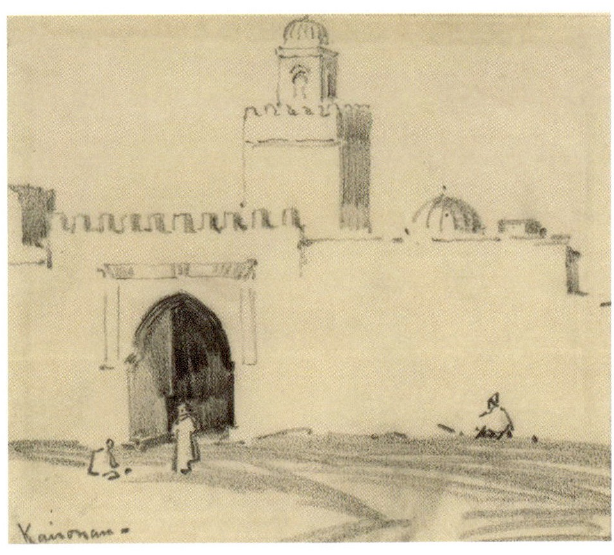

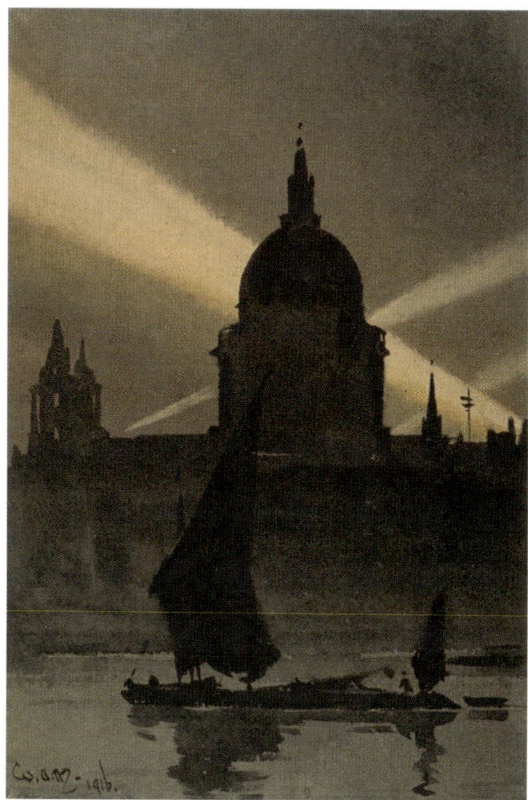

2.32 St Paul's Cathedral with searchlights 1916

Let us hope it will be over before we lose most of our friends and many of our relatives – and while a few years of useful life are still left to us.

I have come down to North Wales. Why? – to get some work done – and move on to Capel Curig on Monday or Tuesday. It is very wonderful country, the hills being of such fine contours. It seems very silly trying to paint these times: but I have had enough of 'useful war work'! – and drawing a good salary for doing nothing of any real use. A year of it was more than enough and left me sadder and wiser. Quite presently we shall get to the stage when but one poor Devil is left to pay taxes – all else are Government Officers!

The Welsh are funny. Some quite nice – others queer. They strike one very much as being a cross between Lloyd George and a weasel. But parts of the country are quite beautiful. However, it will be a joy when one can go abroad again and live among people who are really alive and know how to live.

Saltmarshe, after slicking it in Italy most of these years has now donned a uniform and escorts and pilots the migratory Red Cross nurses and their bundles to and from the camps and the Railway Station in Rome. For an arrant loafer he is quite enjoying himself.

We saw Bessie McPhail a short time ago in London. Very tall and very grave and sedate. She spends her time on Hospital Ships, dodging submarines between Australia and Bristol, having commandeered some odd Water Colours of mine for herself and her mother: I had the great pleasure of hearing from the dear old lady, who seems very well and quite comfortable, near many of her family. She lost one boy in Gallipoli, John.

Oh for a whiff of the sea and the taste of a haddock! Must not go within miles of the Coast with my paint box and have not tried. But they leave me in peace among the Hills.

Now they will probably put a tax on pictures so I had better go back to the War Office and do something to really help the War.

Have had some awful strokes of luck which have enabled us to keep our end up. We got our Russian out of the Temple and it is once more our home. He was of the new Democratic Party. So I wish him luck – but fear damnation.

Ian is now at school and will be 8 in June. He really is quite a nice boy and strong and with apparently a strong dose of individuality: so he may come in at the finish!

I know so little of your folks that I cannot send any really nice messages: but perhaps some day, when wars are over for the time: before we are quite dead.

John seems immersed in Invergordon. Willie is really a nice boy, isn't he? Hope he will come through alright.

So glad to have heard from you and hope you will have better news next time.

Goodbye to you all. Willie

In a letter to his nephew Willie, son of older brother John in Invergordon, he shows his relief that the twenty-one-year-old soldier has survived a gas attack and is safely convalescing in England.

Do you want any books or anything to oil the tedium?

8 Fig Tree Court
Temple E.C.

Tuesday 2 April 1918

My dear Willie

Was so very glad to hear of you from home the other day, as been so anxious about you with the awful struggle in France.

2.33 Snowdonia 1918

I am so very sorry you are gassed rather badly: must be horrible pain & most uncomfortable, but thank the kind fates you are on this side of the Channel & if maimed, mending.

You are lucky: the casualties on both sides are stupendous – but the brutes are held & have failed to break through at Noyon & Arras – so far & the probability now is they cannot. It is hopeful that our expert strategist is at the helm. Divided control is a weakness: & after all the French know much more of the handling of war than we do: & are better trained through practice in the past.

Oh! If it would only be finished before long. How can the Germans hold out much longer against continued failures in the West? Don't you think it rather looks as if this were the last great throw in the gamble?

I do hope you are getting on quite nicely & are comfy & if you have time paler & feel equal to it, you might let me know.

I did write you in France but probably you never got the letter.

You will see I am back at the Temple. Ian is enjoying his Easter holiday.

With all good wishes,

Yours,

W. Alister Macdonald

As the war ended, and after the following Spanish Flu pandemic, many lives were irrevocably changed, if not lost or scarred by bereavement. Being alive could not be taken for granted and the good times of the belle époch were a distant memory. Societal and technological revolutions were consuming countries across Europe, and the art world reflected this change with the advancement of Modernism. Perhaps he found himself a stranger in his own city, unable to adapt and accept such changing times and vogue, his art redundant. More likely the wanderer saw an opportunity for adventure late in life, riding an escapist zeitgeist, to follow his lust for new horizons while he could.

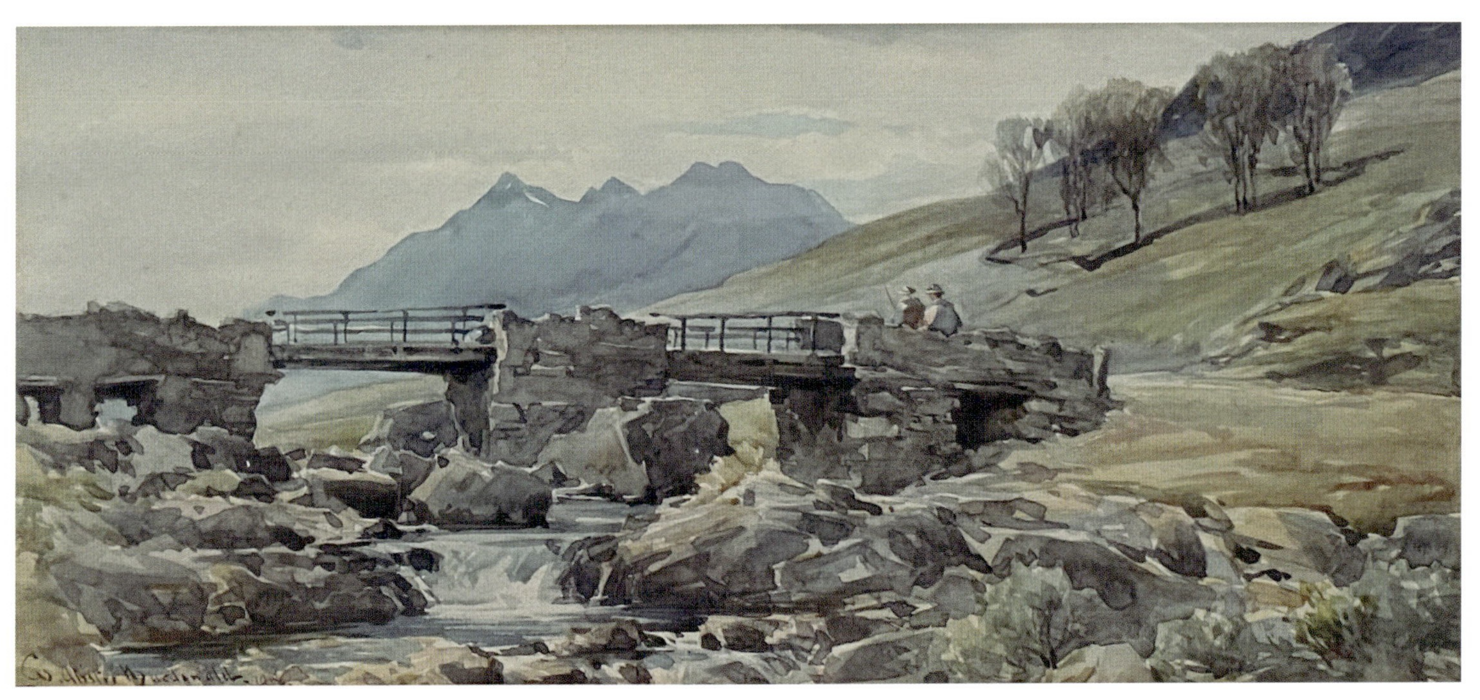

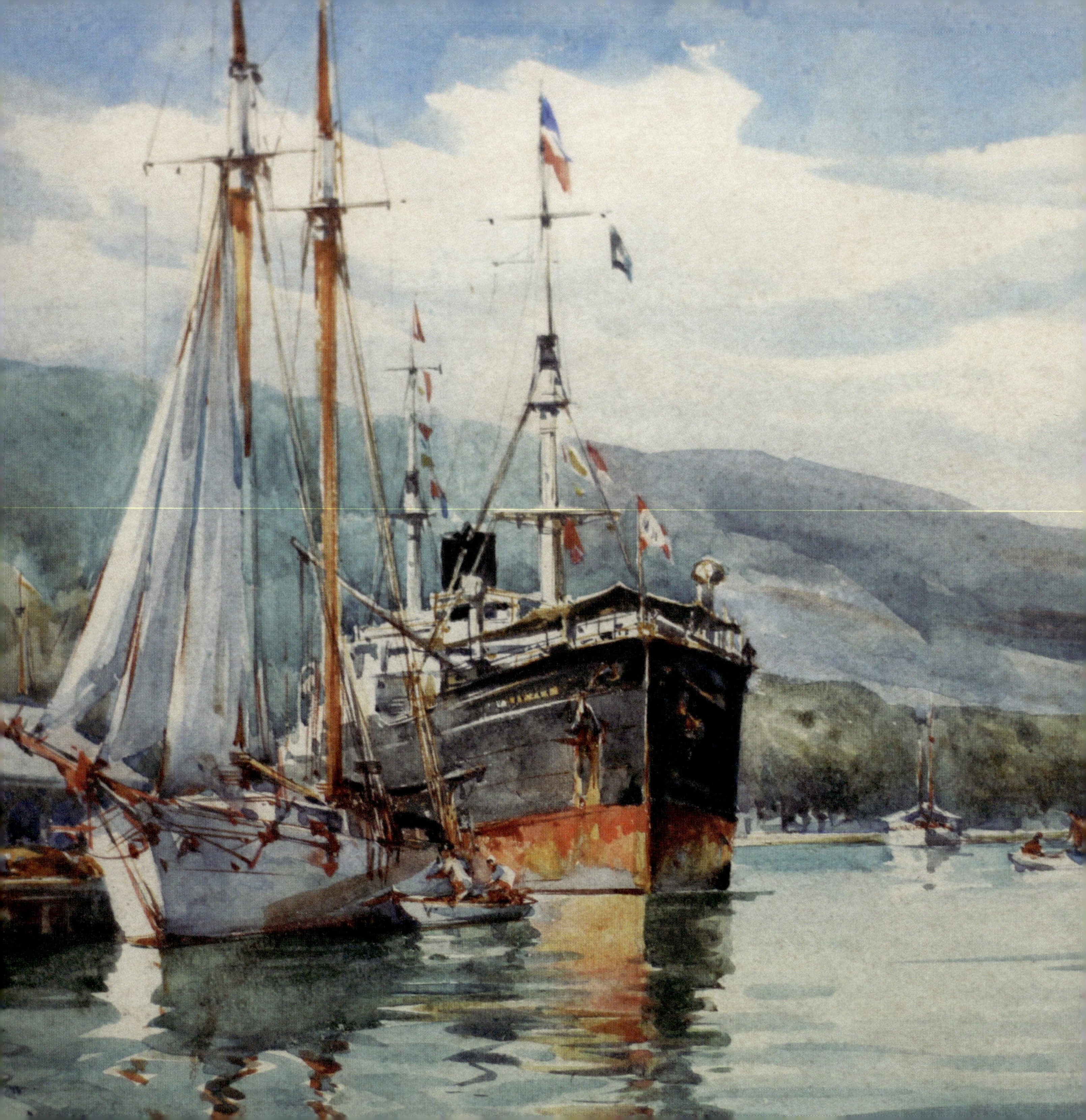

3

Escape to Tahiti 1921

Macdonald was an explorer of sorts, and the titles of his paintings in catalogues now held at the National Art Library in the Victoria and Albert Museum reveal the extent and frequency of his travels, even after his son was born. But we must refrain from applying the norms of the modern age to Edwardian England, for at the same time another gentleman traveller, the arctic explorer Ernest Shackleton (1874–1922) was similarly restless and driven by his work. 'On shore, Shackleton showed little interest in his family, putting all his mind on expeditions, but once away from them, he missed them dearly. Either way, he was never fully content, always chasing something just beyond his reach'.[33] In Macdonald's long life he preferred warmer climes from the comfort of a steamer chair to watch the world go by.

The Allure of the South Seas

Over a century ago, after the devastation and industrial-scale slaughter of the Great War and then the Spanish Flu that followed, there were many in Europe that sought an escape to a far-off paradise. For those that could afford it, and for the large audience of armchair travellers stuck at home who could not, there were many artists and writers who travelled south like migrating seabirds. The American author Zane Grey acknowledged the power of the writings by earlier travellers on his character Donald:

> As long as he could remember, Donald had cherished an unspoken desire to visit the South Seas. In his boyhood he had read Defoe and Stevenson, Melville's *Typee* and the works of Loti, Calderon, Brooks, and Nordoff and Hall.[34]

Nordhoff and Hall, surviving fighter pilots from the poppy fields of France, came to seek a new life but were conscious of the overblown romance of the South Seas that was taking hold in the minds of many in the creative salons and cafes of Europe.

> It became irresistible the more we talked of it, longing as we were for the solitude of the islands. The objection to this choice was that the groups of islands which we meant to visit have been endowed with an atmosphere of pseudoromance displeasing to the fastidious mind.[35]

The French painter Paul Gauguin (1848–1903), who abandoned a wife and family in Paris for Tahiti in 1891, had set the mark at the turn of the century: 'All the joys – animal and human – of a free life are mine. I have escaped everything that is artificial, conventional, customary. I am entering into the truth, into nature.' The manifesto for idealistic island hedonists ever since.[36] Barkham argues that the idea of an island as a pristine paradise was not always the case, like Daniel Defoe's *Robinson Crusoe* (1719); they are seen as wild places to be tamed, or prisons for castaways and condemned men. A widely held concept transformed by the popularisation of Jean-Jacques Rousseau's (1755) romantic idea that islands are the ideal place for finding one's true self.

> . . . an urge to escape to small islands pulses through recent history, usually during times of crisis. When the mainland or mainstream is in crisis, people look to the periphery for escape or inspiration. Many of us are looking there right now. Are small-island values – robust self-sufficiency, for instance, or an integrated, neighbourly community – passé, or are they more pertinent than ever? Small islands may offer a critique

> of our larger island life, but they might also provide salvation for our epoch?[37]

There are certainly parallels in today's uncertain world, and with instant digital communication the world is harder to escape, yet the islands easier to reach. While many were motivated to venture south in search of escape and new start, the simple aesthetic attraction cannot be underestimated. Today the South Seas still maintain a timeless natural beauty that attracts artists.

> Heavy clouds hung over Tahiti and Moorea, clinging about the shoulders of the mountains whose peaks, rising above them, were still faintly visible against the somber glory of the sky. They seemed islands of sheer fancy, looked at from the sea.[38]

Somerset Maugham's novel *The Moon and Sixpence* (1919) was inspired by Gauguin's life, but it wasn't until the writer visited Tahiti in 1914 and experienced it for himself that he was able to create a novel that authentically described the island and spoke with such compelling conviction for the artist through his character Dick Stroeve.

> Why should you think that beauty, which is the most precious thing in the world, lies like a stone on the beach for the careless passer-by to pick up idly? Beauty is something wonderful and strange that the artist fashions out of the chaos of the world in the torment of his soul. And when he has made it, it is not given to all to know it. To recognize it you must repeat the adventure of the artist. It is a melody that he sings to you, and to hear it again in your own heart you want knowledge and sensitiveness and imagination.[39]

The timing of the publication of Maugham's novel and its subject came at a time when Macdonald was living his own melodrama in London and Norfolk. In London he and his wife Lucy ran their Little Gallery together and their son Ian was now at school. The outbreak of war had restricted his painting trips to England and Wales

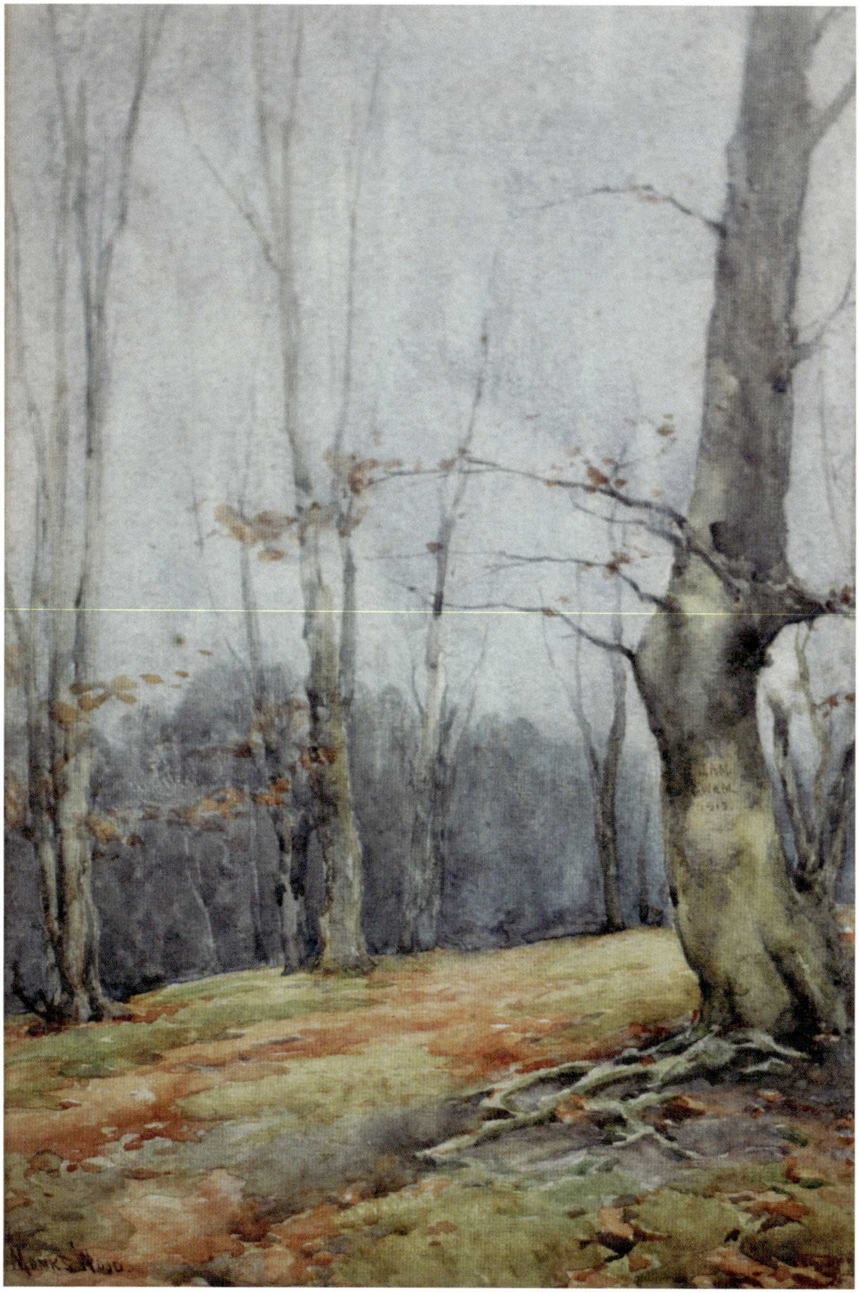

3.1, 3.2 Monk's Wood (detail) 1919

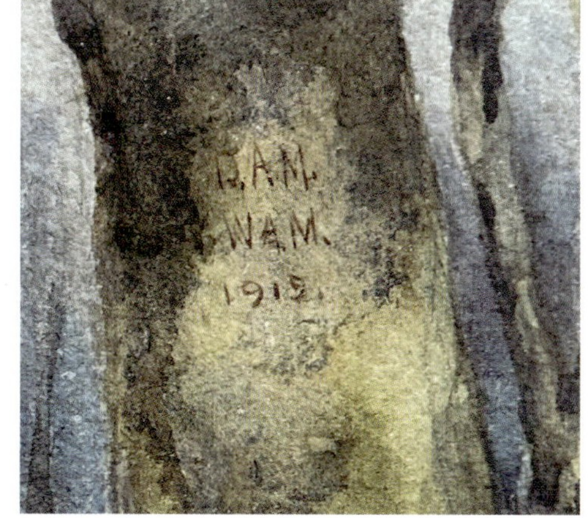

during and immediately after. Norfolk was a place of special significance, as it was where he had launched his artistic career and had published illustrations and his story of a fishing vessel to the North Sea fishing grounds. In 1919, the year *The Moon and Sixpence* was published, he gifted a watercolour of *Monks Wood* to a young civil servant clerk, Dorothy Myhill (1890–1981), from the village of Fundenhall in Norfolk, with their initials inscribed into the trunk of a tree (3.1, 3.2).

According to family folklore, their relationship was actively discouraged by her father, William Myhill (1839–1925). A widower since 1908 who relied on the care of his six daughters, he insisted that Dorothy's relationship with Macdonald be broken off and that he was forbidden to enter the house. The reason being the age difference of twenty-nine years, 'Mac' was old enough to be her father. Perhaps inspired by Maugham's novel they escaped the gossip and scandal of London society and Macdonald boarded the SS *Arawa* for New Zealand on 5 May 1921 (3.3). Maugham understood the sense of shock that he would leave behind in Edwardian England where 'much was made of being seen to be fair and gentlemanly',[40] and Maugham was writing about a man twenty years younger than Macdonald.

> 'Isn't it dreadful? He's run away from his wife?'[41]
>
> 'It can't go on at his age', she said. 'After all, he's forty. I could understand it in a young man, but I think it's horrible in a man of his years, with children who are nearly grown up. His health will never stand it.'[42]

What were their emotions as the ship slipped away from the dock, standing in isolation watching other people lined up waving goodbye to loved ones, the ships horn blasting one last time to drown out the shouts of bon voyage? Later in life Macdonald wrote: 'Came out here in 1921 at 60! Thinking my life was over. Instead one third of it had to come & another reputation made in Tahiti'.[43] Life can take surprising turns.

12

P.M. 21

Name of Ship SS Arawa   *Date of Departure* 5 May 1921

Steamship Line—SHAW SAVILL & ALBION Co., Ltd.   *Where bound* New Zealand

NAMES AND DESCRIPTIONS OF **BRITISH** PASSENGERS EMBARKED AT THE PORT OF Southampton

(1) Contract Ticket Number	(2) NAMES OF PASSENGERS	(3) CLASS (Whether 1st, 2nd or 3rd)	(4) Port at which Passengers have contracted to land	(5) Profession, Occupation, or Calling of Passengers. In the case of First Class Passengers this column need not be filled up.	(6) AGES OF PASSENGERS. Except for First Class Passengers state the age last birthday. Adults of 12 years and upwards: Accompanied by husband or wife — Male	Accompanied — Female	Not Accompanied by husband or wife — Male	Not Accompanied — Female	Children between 1 and 12 — Male	Children — Female	Infants — Male	Infants — Female	(7) Country of last Permanent Residence † England	Wales	Scotland	Ireland	British Possessions	Foreign Countries	(8) Country of Intended Future Permanent Residence †
				Bt forward	2	2	3	25	1	1	-	-							
2388	Mr J Carbines	2nd	Wellington	None			52						1						New Zealand
-	Miss J do	-	-	Scholar				11					1						-
-	Miss Va do	-	-	-				15					1						-
	'Braeside' Ilfracombe																		
2389	Miss M. Eales, 16 S. Andrews Rd Romford	-	-	Shop asst.				25					1						-
2390	Mr O Bubb	-	-	Carman	65X												1		-
2391	Mrs do	-	-	wife		63X											1		-
	S. Littleton Evesham, Worcs.																		
2392	Mr E Preston	-	-	Farming	48								1						-
-	Mrs do	-	-	wife		47							1						-
	15 Kensington Gdns Bayswater W.																		
2393	Mr G Medhurst	-	-	Farming	26								1						-
-	Mrs do	-	-	wife		25							1						-
	24 Crockerton Rd Upper Tooting London S.W.																		
2394	Mrs A Lusk	-	-	Housewife				32X									1		-
-	Miss P do	-	-	Scholar						6x							1		-
-	Miss D do	-	-	-						5x							1		-
	8 Dalkeith Av. Dumbreck Glasgow																		
2396	Mr J Guthrie	-	-	Farming	46										1				-
-	Mrs do	-	-	wife		49									1				-
-	Miss L do	-	-	Child						9					1				-
-	Miss C Rawcenson	-	-	-						14					1				-
	21 Halmyre St Leith																		
2397	Mr W Macdonald, 8 Fig Tree Court Temple EC	-	-	Artist			59X						1						England
2398	Mr E Wakeling, 110 Strand London W.C.	-	-	Clerk			19						1						New Zealand
2399	Mr H Mayes, 71 Carlisle Rd Romford	-	-	Slaughterman			17						1						-
2400	Miss A Millen, Shanlongford Ringsend Garvagh	-	-	Housekeeper				21					1						-
				(21)	6	6	7	30	1	5	-	-	12		4		5		

† By Permanent Residence is to be understood residence for a year or more.

BT27/959

3.3 SS *Arawa* manifest 5 May 1921

Elinor Mordaunt

ELINOR MORDAUNT (1872–1942) was an author, writer, and traveller, brought up in genteel society in the English Cotswolds, she was acclaimed for her short stories that displayed her grim sense of tragedy and humour. In 1923 she set sail from Marseilles for Tahiti on the *El Kantara*, a cargo boat that carried a limited number of passengers on a passage via Martinique and the Panama Canal. In 1919 it had the acclaim of being the first French ship to pass through the Panama Canal.

In her book *The Venture Book* (1926), Mordaunt describes her journey and the company she keeps on the *El Kantara*, a boat 'thick with the grime of ports, her decks foul with the trampling of many feet' (1926: 12), with a cargo in the lower decks 'crowded with livestock' (1926: 11). 'There are some twenty first-class passengers – one Englishman and the remainder French – with a few more in the second class', and a company of French soldiers being carried out to New Caledonia commanded by a single petty officer. In the captain she finds 'a comrade, with a short, bright-brown beard, merry brown eyes, and a bright colour; a man in whom every line and every tint, every movement spoke of a life at sea' (1926: 11). This is not a luxury cruise, but Mordaunt uses the time to complete a series of short stories for her publisher and sketch the people she sees when the ship comes to harbours along the way.

'I like the fact, also, that despite the passengers whom I had not expected and who at first rather appalled me, this is, indeed, a cargo-boat where one need not spend one's time feverishly dragging out boxes from under one's bunk, dressing and undressing, sitting with one's hair in curlers, or clamoring at the hairdresser's door' (1926: 14).

'For the time being, however, there is nothing on earth that I desire so little as human companionship; while the voyage is so uneventful, so quiet, that the days stream out behind me like a long, indefinitely shaded, blue-and-gray scarf' (1926: 20).

The ship and Mordaunt's description of her voyage are significant because Macdonald painted the *El Kantara* in Papeete harbour and gave it to Dorothy Myhill as a gift. This is known because the watercolour remains in her family in the UK. Mordaunt, a seasoned traveller that had already lived in Mauritius and Australia, describes it as the 'steadiest boat I have ever been on'. 'For a ship is like a woman in love: it takes very little to upset her when there is nothing serious at hand' (1926: 13). She describes the loungers, the musicians, the gamblers and a boxing match that saw a tall 'weak-looking and hollow-cheeked' African sailor beat a 'small, strongly built Frenchman . . . with a waxed mustache' (1926: 15). Mordaunt writes in the terms of the period, as a white privileged English woman, that would offend the modern reader.

City Streets, Thames and Boats to Lagoons and Village Huts

For Macdonald, the long passage via the Panama Canal offered adventure across two oceans and an opportunity to exercise his drawing skills along the way. In his sketchbook he captured his fellow passengers and their activities as a pictorial documentary of global travel in 1921. The titles he gives the drawings add an extra dimension to the way he observed and regarded his subjects, such as 'Doyenne – but no saint', and 'Archangel Gabriel "Holy of Holies"'. The attraction of a cruise holiday remains popular to this day, but after a six-week voyage surrounded by the same people bound by the limits of the ship, relations can be strained and boredom can set in. He documented everyday life onboard and drew passengers playing games of chess, draughts, cards and quoits, or simply snoozing and reading (3.4, 3.5, 3.6, 3.7).

After several weeks at sea there are a series of pages that illustrate their passage through the Panama Canal, the monotony of the sea now stimulated by tropical landscapes and other vessels.

At this point of the voyage one must assume that he and his companion, Dorothy Myhill, were still intent on reaching New Zealand. But on landing in Tahiti in 1921 he was captured by its natural beauty and light. 'Artists, thinkers, and philosophers from diverse cultures have commonly identified it as an earthly paradise, a utopian physical environment that nurtures both body and soul'.[44].

It was a paradise for watercolour, where he could apply the same scrupulous care and skill he had developed in England. The translucent qualities of the light in Southern Tropics were best captured in his chosen media of watercolour (3.8). This is what separated his work from his contemporaries in Tahiti who largely worked in oils, and some in gouache.

The goal of New Zealand was abandoned, seduced by one of the most beautiful locations on earth to start a life on the island, perhaps inspired by Gauguin. According to Dorothy, the couple

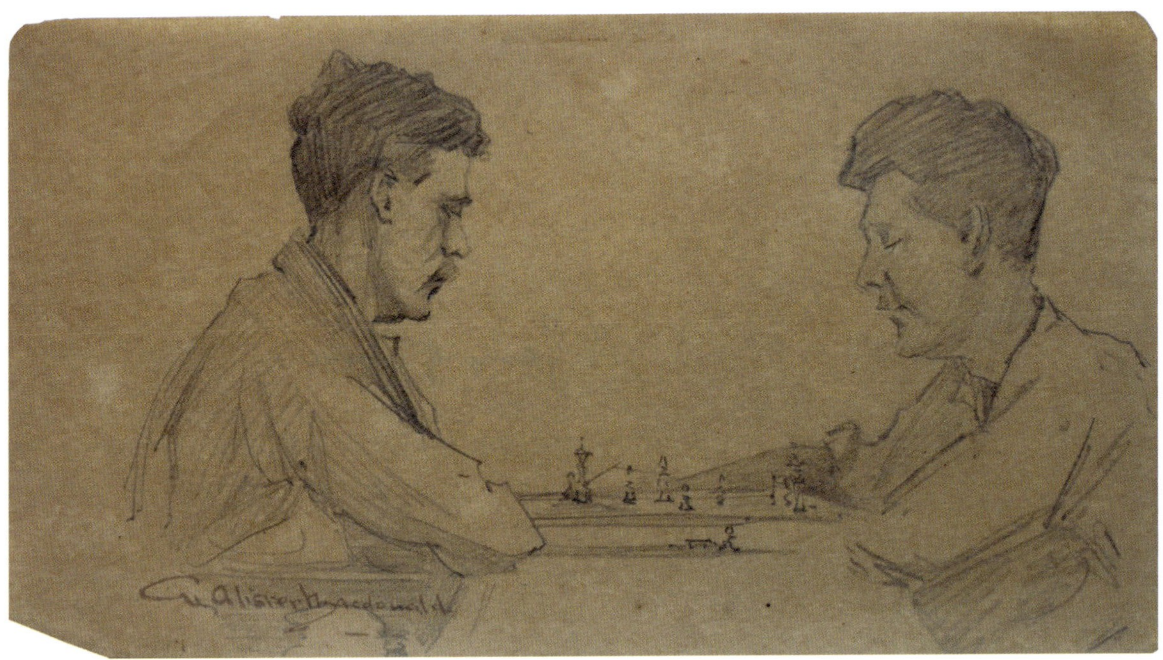

3.6 Game of Chess

lived for a while in the artist's old house. At sixty years of age, some would call the abandonment of his wife of twenty-three years and their eleven-year-old son a late mid-life crisis.

It was also Gauguin that inspired D.H. Lawrence to travel to Tahiti in 1922, though for him reality did not match the promise. In a series of postcards to his friend, fellow author, and lover of islands, Compton Mackenzie, he wrote:

The Cook Islands were 'very lovely'. Tahiti, less so. 'If you are thinking of coming here don't. The people are brown and soft. DHL.' To another friend he wrote: 'These are supposed to be the earthly paradises: these South Sea Isles. You can have 'em.'[45]

The English travel writer Elinor Mordaunt, who was onboard the *El Kantara* in 1923, was more enthusiastic upon arrival in Papeete.

3.5 The Flighty One

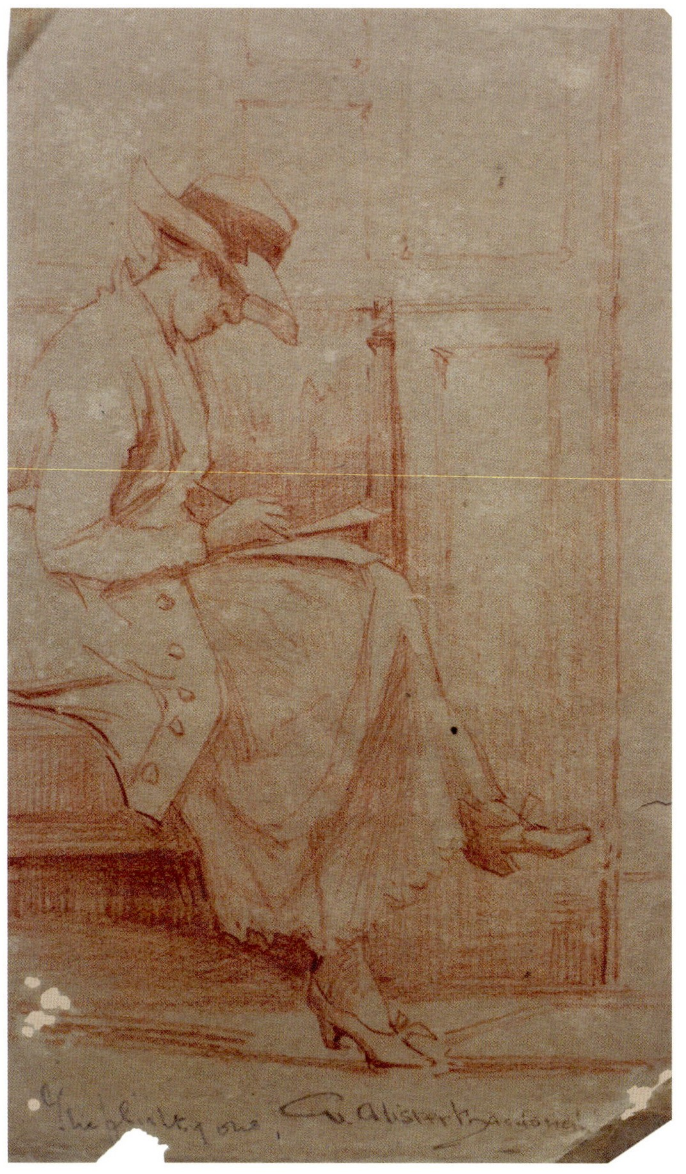

3.4 Doyenne – but no saint

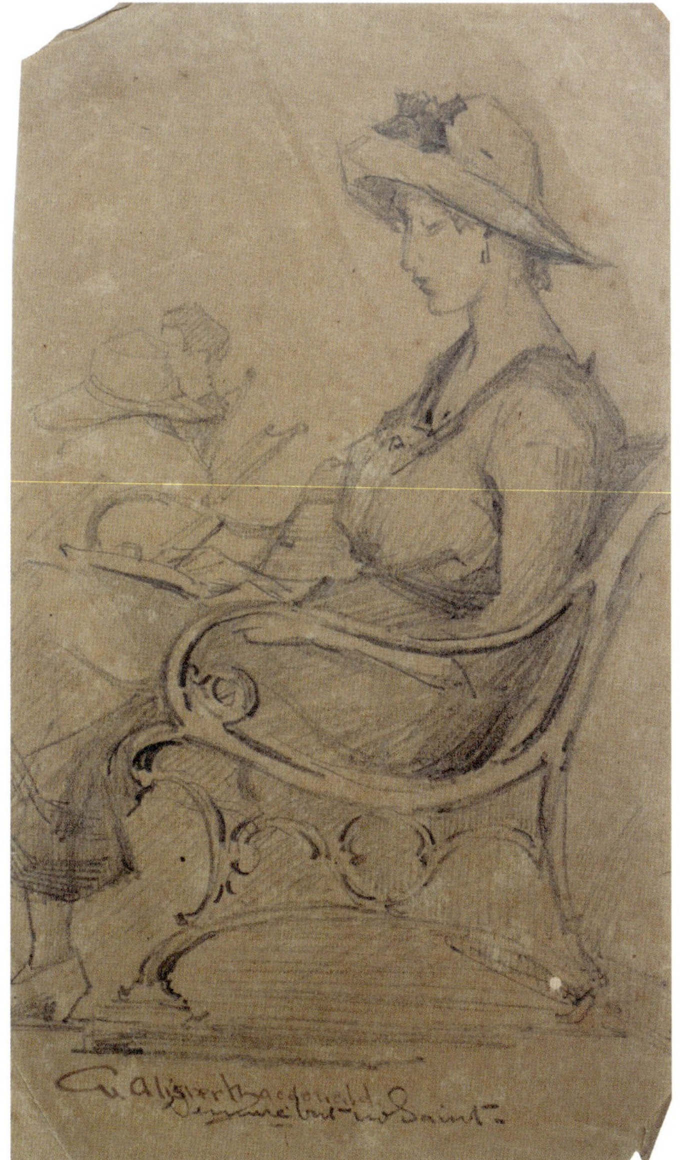

It is late afternoon when we reach Tahiti, and I tremble with excitement at the first sight of it, as something I could never have imagined. I had thought Martinique green, as I once thought Ireland green, but they are drab in comparison with this. It seems, indeed, as though there were no other color in the world which could ever again matter in the slightest degree; as though one not only saw it but was shot through and through with it, permeated with it, so that one's every thought was green, reflecting the glitter of the shining , opaque, enamel-like leaves which cast back the light like mirrors, of the fine transparent leaves, the fern-like foliage. I am old enough now to have schooled myself not to expect much, but I could never have expected anything like this, excelling all expectation, full in the blaze of the late afternoon sun…

…The Diadem, the pride of Tahiti, with her seven piercing peaks of deep indigo, is flung across with no more than the lightest scarf of that mist which lies thick among the innumerable ravines. The foot-hills and lower slopes are of the same vivid and indescribable green, with – and here is an extravagance of beauty – a broken rainbow arched above the town. The white wooden buildings and toy churches are embowered and almost lost in trees deeply green as the velvet of a huntsman's coat, splashed in places with the clear fervent scarlet of the flamboyant, not yet in its full glory.

There is no ugly quay to mar Papeete, the one town and port of the island; no chimneys, cranes, and blackened buildings, the cloven hoof of most seabound towns. The small wooden landing stage, this afternoon, resembles the tulip-beds at Hampton Court, with a breeze-blown parterre of girls in the lightest of muslin and thin silk gowns, – straw-colored and daffodil yellow and white and pink and rose, mauve and fuschia, gray and blue of every shade, – the most of them flounced to the waist. Girls with broad-brimmed hats or with flowing wavy

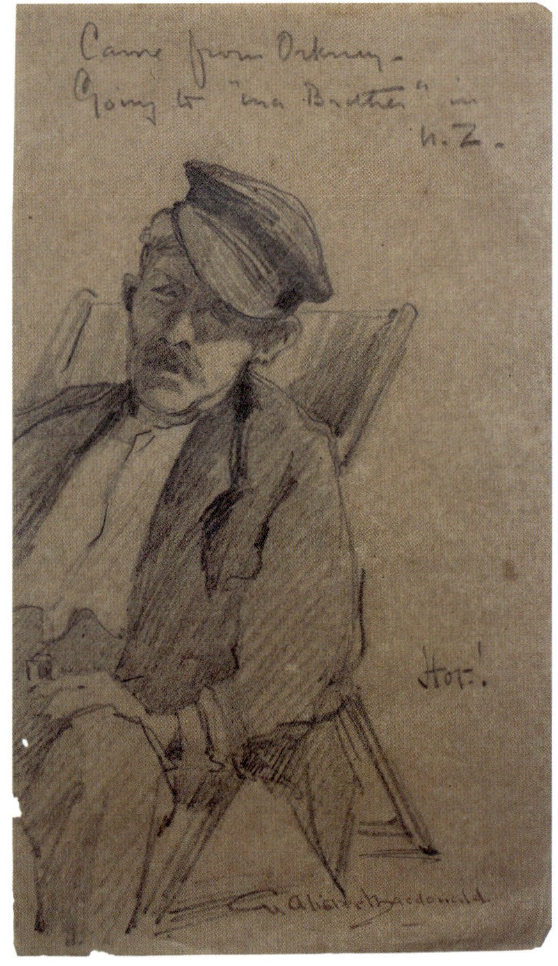

3.7 Orkneyman

3.8 Moorea 1924

> hair falling far below their waists, wreathed with flowers; and mingled with these, young men and old men in white suits or shirts and *paréus*. For the whole of the island takes holiday at the incoming of the French boats.[46]

Thankfully, we have Macdonald's watercolour of *El Kantara* to illustrate Mordaunt's description (3.9). Like Macdonald, she had amused herself by sketching people she found interesting during her voyage, and these illustrate *The Venture Book* (1926). Although educated at home by governesses in the art of landscape painting, fabric and wallpaper design, her eye was overwhelmed by the lush abundance of Tahiti's vegetation.

> More and more I feel that this island is not a place in which to paint. There are too many strong primal colors; it is at once too artless and too passionate. The vegetation is too like the packed hothouse of a millionaire. The background of sky and mountain is purposely set for the life drama of an artless, material, and yet primitive people.[47]

Perhaps it was with this attitude she set herself in conflict with an English artist when staying at Taravao, on the other side of the island from Papeete.

The Artist

The simple bamboo-walled and palm leaf-roofed guest house in Taravao, around fifty kilometres south of Papeete, was owned by Maou-u, and relations between the unnamed male artist and Mordaunt immediately got off to a bad start when they arrived at the same time wanting 'to be put up, greatly embarrassing Maou-u, for he had promised the guest-house to me'.[48] In the end the artists took one of the eight beds in the owner's house where his family of four and two maids slept. The artist was to have his meals with her on her veranda, 'I do not greatly care for the look of him'.[49]

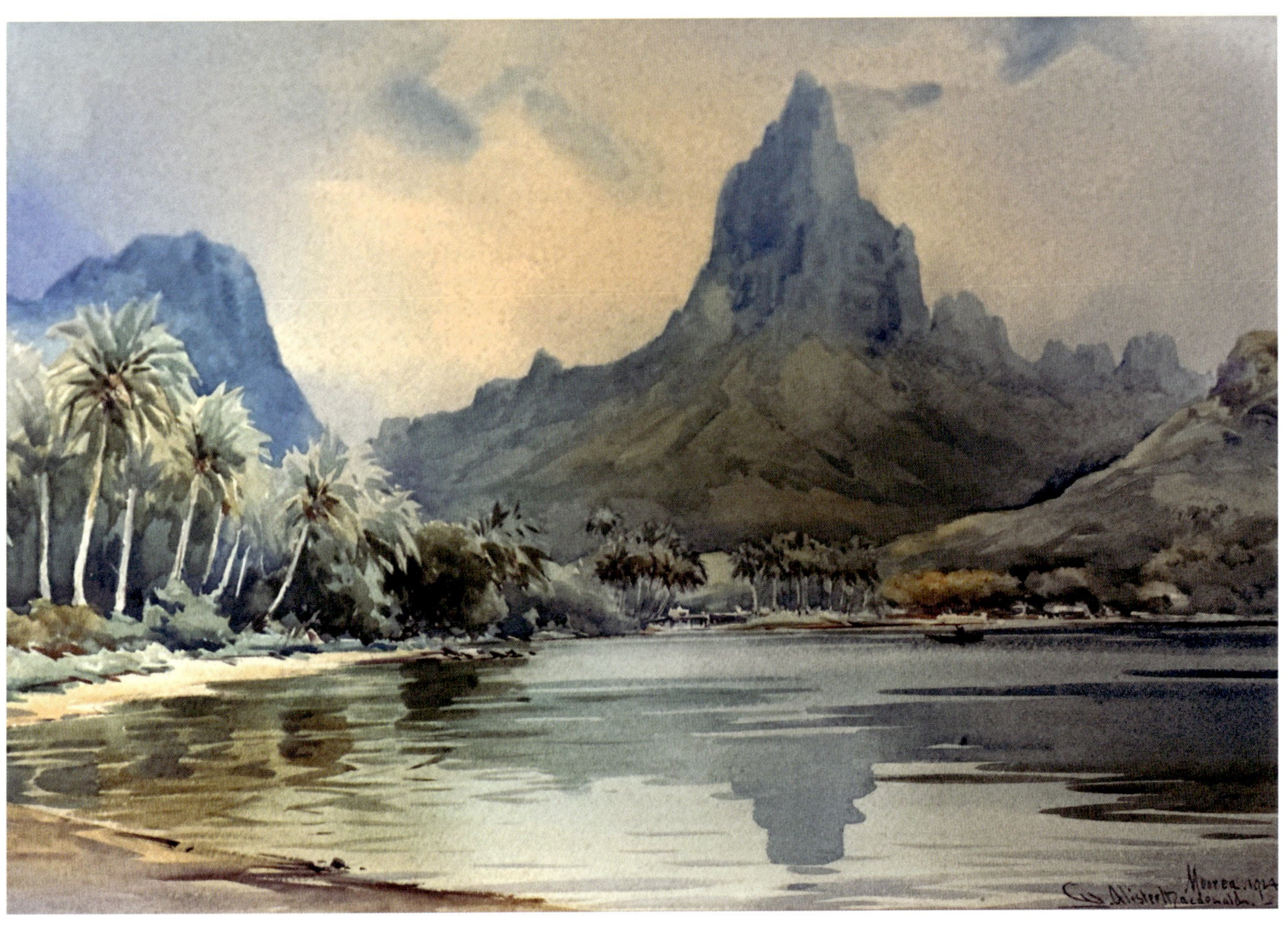
Moorea

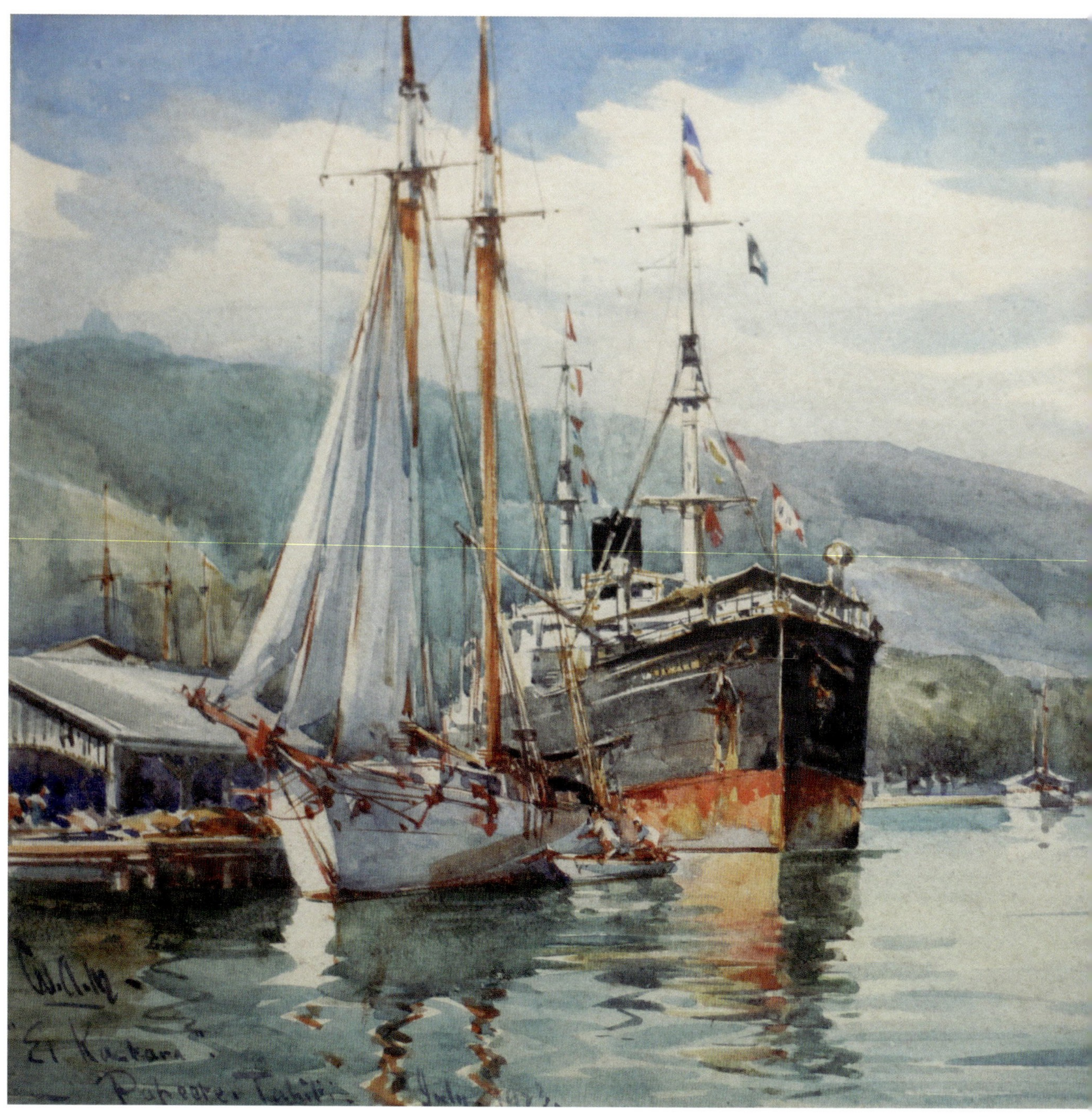

3.9 El Kantara, Papeete, July 1923

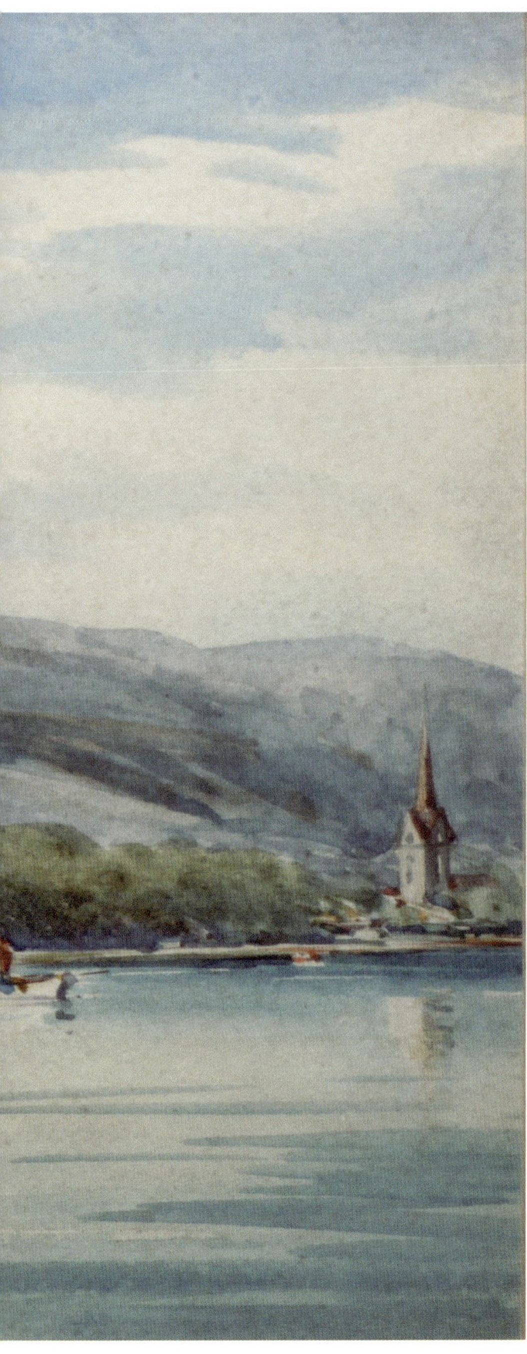

In Mordaunt's account neither do the family.

> All alike, however, detest the artist, whom Marcaline and the other native girls call 'Mam'selle.' . . .when she speaks of the artist she wrinkles up her nose until it is nothing more than a series of creases upon her small thin face, turns down her thumb, and with the greatest disgust ejaculates, 'No good!'
>
> He is, indeed exasperating. This morning he had his 'little breakfast' on my veranda with me, coffee, fresh cocoanut cream, bananas, and oranges still gleaming with dew,-and all the while he grumbled and peeved, declaring that he had lost a silver spoon which he had brought with him; that he had been unable to sleep because of the snoring of his host, the coughing and fidgeting of children; that cocks and hens awoke him at dawn; that he would be sure to get elephantiasis, sleeping among natives. All this in face of Maou-u's wonderful hospitality disgusted me so. . .[50]

Over dinner the artist 'grows to be a more and more unmitigated nuisance' with continuing grumbling and 'when Marcaline says, at the end, in her pretty way: "I hope the dinner was good?" – the dinner, mind you, for which Maou-u would never accept so much as a penny – he snaps out, "The coffee is cold."' That night the artist was moved to the guesthouse veranda.

> There is no other place for his bed save directly against the openwork bamboo wall, on the other side of which stands my washing-stand, and I am rather afraid that he may awake while I am performing my ablutions. Fortunately, however, despite his assertions of insomnia, he sleeps on, even snores; and after all, come to think of it, it doesn't greatly matter one way or another, seeing that he is a landscape and not a figure painter. But –Heavens! – what a setting for a romance! Never, never, or so it seems, were Browning's wonderful words: 'Never the time and the place and the loved one altogether,' more apt.[51]

At breakfast that morning things came to a head and voices were raised.

> ...the artist was in an altogether intolerable humor, and the veranda was a disgusting sight with his unmade bed and all his untidy belongings. I was the offender this time – I under whose mosquito curtain he snored, and snored. I had disturbed him with my fidgeting. My temper broke and turned on him, bidding him, 'For God's sake, shut up!' and informing him that, as I had come there for rest and quiet and not to be bothered by anybody, I should be glad if he would stop complaining.
>
> He turned on me like a cat, hissing and screaming, stuttering with rage. 'You damned civilised women ought n't to be allowed in the place, spoiling everything!' he cried, at which I laughed, for it was really too funny in the face of all his fussing, his silver spoon, his nerves. As to my civilization, what was there to be said for it, considering my costume, a rough-dried dress, my bath-towel over my shoulders, my hair in a plait?
>
> 'That's good! That's very good!' I said. 'Civilised' from a man whom every native girl in the island knows as "Mam'selle." 'An answer which did nothing whatever to turn away his wrath, for he rushed off down the garden and across the road to Maou-u's house, where I heard him shrieking curses, declaring that he would no longer take his meals with "that damned woman."'[52]

Aside from the description of the artist as a male landscape painter with a short temper, Mordaunt gives us no further clues on his appearance or nationality. One could speculate that this artist was British given the very English swearing: 'you damned civilised women'. Perhaps it was Macdonald on one of his forays around the island, travelling alone as he frequently did to paint, leaving Dorothy behind in Papeete. Were relations with his lover strained by conflicting attitudes to the life and culture of Tahiti, and this was just transferred to an outburst at another Englishwoman who happened to be a writer?

Sunrise

It would not be an exaggeration to say that every writer that visits Tahiti will at some point in their story describe a Tahitian sunrise. Mordaunt describes swimming and canoeing with the maid and the children, the exquisite colours and bountiful flora and fauna, without being tempted to use the words 'Eden' and 'paradise', as many male writers have frequently done.

> It is only five in the morning, but I could sleep no longer and am sitting on my veranda, waiting for the sunrise, which begins with a silver-gilt diffusion of light over the entire scene. The fish are once more leaping high in the inner and outer lagoons, as I could hear them doing up to twelve o'clock last night. I see Marcaline's figure out upon the causeway and calls to me, her hands rounded to her mouth, telling me that the sun is about to rise. From the exultation and joy in her voice one might think that such a thing had never happened before. By the time I join her, the outer and inner lagoons are like sheets of gold with crimson roses reflected upon them; the mountains at the back glow with purple and gilt, while in a cleft of the mountains to the right of us the sun comes up, as it seems, with a rush.
>
> Already the children are bathing in the inner lagoon, laughing and shouting, splashing golden drops around them; they bring a small fish to show to me, flat and broad and the color of brilliant blue enamel shot with violet. For a few minutes they play about me, then run back into the water, catching fish in their hands and throwing them up to their two pet frigate-birds, which swoop and swirl above them,

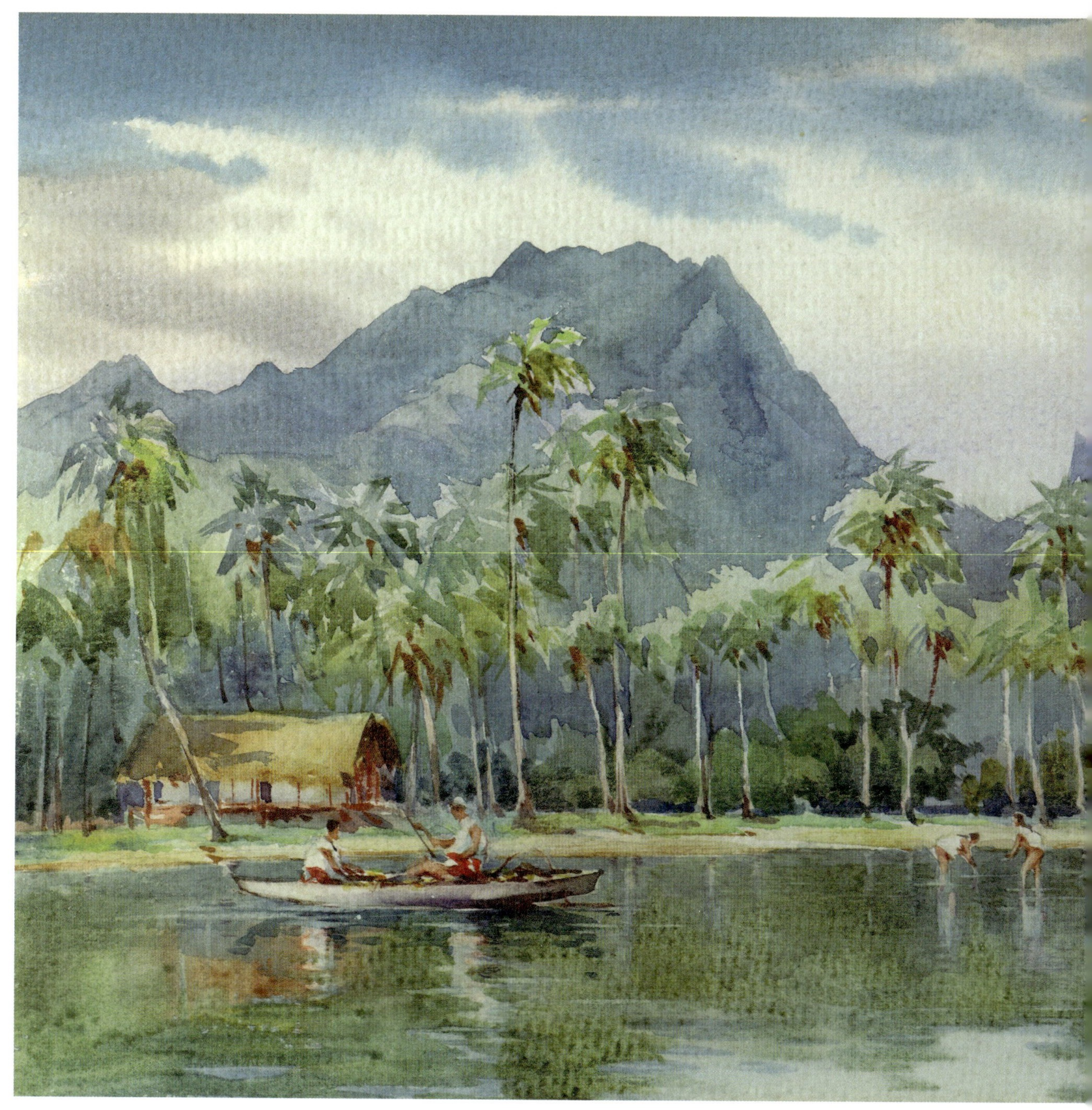

3.10 Tahiti, 1922

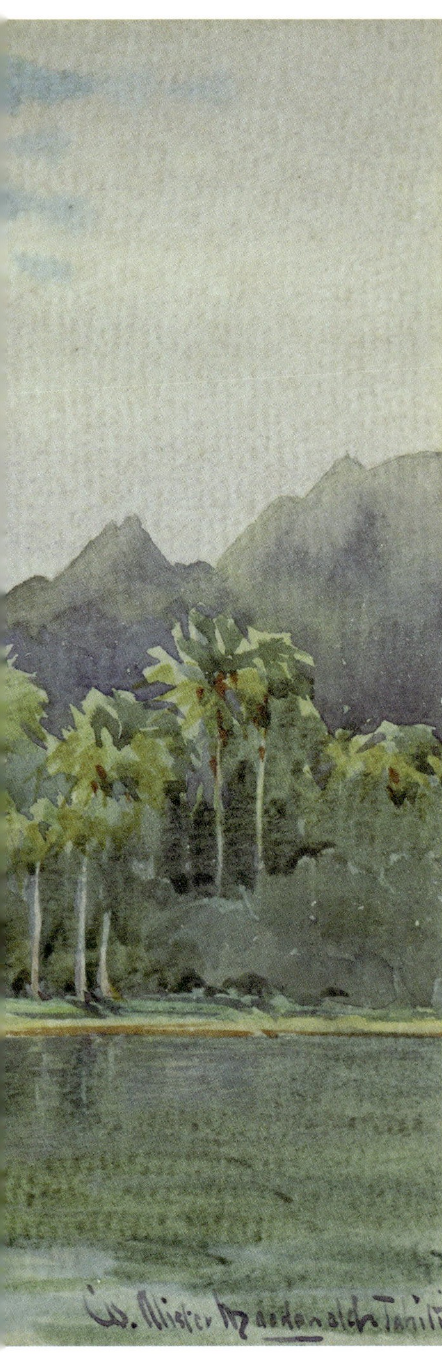

> mount so high that they are lost to sight, then swoop down again.
>
> I am wearing nothing more than my nightgown and the thinnest of kimonos, but I paddle down to the edge of the water and join the children, watching them with delight as they gaze upward, throwing the fish as high as they can, calling out the names of their birds in long-drawn syllables: 'Chacco-o!. . . T-i-t-i!'[53]

While the children appear content and carefree, and 'the girls are always giggling', Mordaunt notices a deep melancholy among the older women and men, an 'air of desperate resignation, far and away beyond despair'.[54]

> I wonder what it is that, without hope, they long for. It may be some sort of subconscious yearning from the land from which their race once came; or it may be that they are forever trying to follow with their eyes those sailing- ships which come and go above the horizon, bearing away, away their loved ones.[55]

An answer to that question may be found in Zane Grey's (1872–1939) last book, *The Reef Girl* (1977), published posthumously, where his protagonist, an American writer travels with his fiancé to Tahiti and is lured away from her by the seductive splendour of the island and by a beautiful Tahitian young woman.

After three years Dorothy parted company with Macdonald, and left with a portfolio of sixteen sketches in a book, one dated 'from Raiatea August 1921', including a painting of Gauguin's house, and another of *El Kantara* in Papeete harbour 1923 (did Macdonald want to purge himself of Mordaunt as well?), that finally returned with her to England. No one can presume to know what really motivated her return, though given the fact that her widower father died the year after her return in 1924, either that was fortunate timing on her part or a return prompted by news from England of her father's declining health.

Macdonald remained in Tahiti and found agreeable company in other Europeans and Americans that were looking for an alternative to the speed and rapid mechanisation of the Modern world. He was also older than many of his contemporaries, and with his reserved nature he found steadfast friends amongst other like-minded creatives that were forging new lives as frontier men of the arts.

A year or so after Dorothy left, he met a Tahitian widow, Tipari Tuera (1885–1950) from the island of Rapa in the Austral Islands. Despite being in his sixties and still legally married to Lucy back in London, they had a daughter in 1926 called Avril Tuera, that he called 'Marie Macdonald'.

Neighbours

Tipari and Macdonald established a new family home together in Pirea, just outside Papeete (3.10). One of their neighbours was a young Australian writer, George Farwell (1911–1976) and his friend Pat O'Brien. Later in his autobiography, Farwell gives an amusing account of a neighbourly quarrel his Irish housemate O'Brien had with Macdonald. Farwell and O'Brien's housekeeper Titine was often to be seen exchanging gossip with Macdonald's 'now middle-aged mistress, Tipari. . . unintentionally adding to his feud with Pat'.[56]

> I found their Scots-Irish antipathies embarrassing for this white-bearded painter was a kindly, sensitive character. We had long discussions together amid his easels and water-colours and he lent me books of philosophy, art and fiction from his excellent library. His great joy was their seven-year-old daughter, a slender, happy elf of a child who often followed me into the lagoon, dived from my shoulders or clung to my back as I swam out to an anchored raft. The old man would often come down to the shore to watch us. If Pat appeared, he turned abruptly and went in.[57]

The root of the feud was said to be Macdonald's chickens that trespassed into O'Brien's seeded garden, so frequently that he devised a trap to remove any offending fowl without a squawk and into his pot.

> He did it once too often. The bearded old man threw open our rickety gate, demanding that O'Brien show his bog Irish face.
> 'I'm having you charged with theft,' he shouted. 'Just keep your dirty fists off my fowls.'
> Pat appeared at the door, innocent and without fowl. 'Sure, mister,' he yelled back, 'and I'll be asking any MacDonalds [*sic*] to stay out, or I'll have proceedings agin you for trespassing.'[58]

Having retired in his mid-thirties as a successful Hollywood film editor for Warner Brothers, O'Brien would be fluent with a blade cutting celluloid, and now as crafty with fowls and traps.

Paradise is never quite what it seems, as each man's fantasy borders another. However, more agreeable company was not far away, a short walk along the beach towards the port a merry band of frontier men could be found drinking at the end of the day in the Cercle Bougainville.

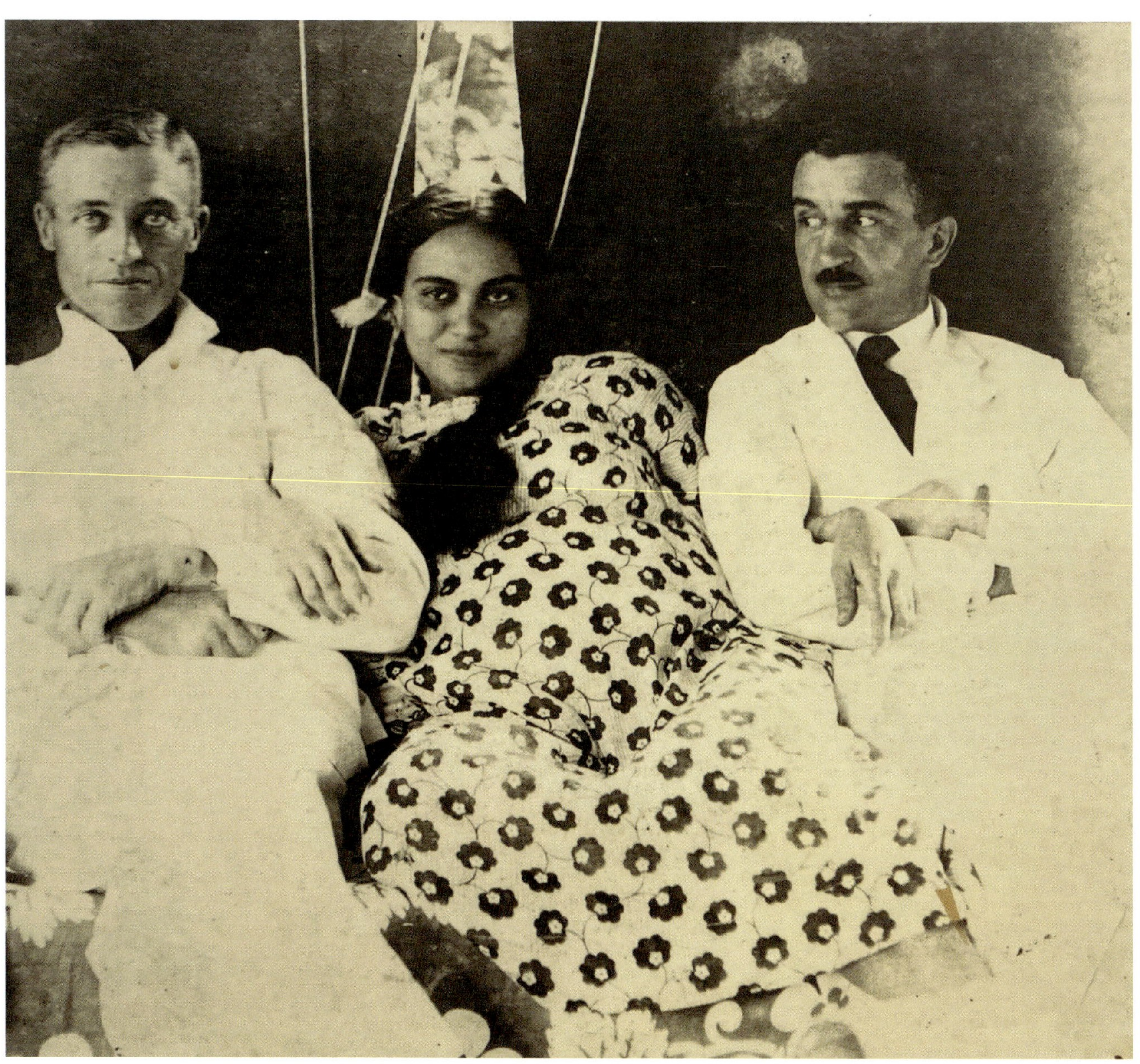

4.1 Charles Nordhoff, his wife Vahine, and James Norman Hall 1926

4

Frontier Men Drink, Sail and Fish Together

Tahiti, and the hospitality of the Cercle Bougainville, was also the new home to the young writers Charles Nordhoff (1887–1947) and James Norman Hall (1887–1951) (4.1), both thirty- three years old, when they set sail from San Francisco in January 1920, both seeking solace and peace from their wartime experiences as fighter pilots over the battlefields of France where 'eight million people were pointlessly slaughtered in
five years' (Hall 1934: 10).[59] Hall describes their motivation in response to the lost opportunity for humanity to take a new turning at the Peace Conference in Versailles, 'Our best course,' said my friend (Nordhoff), 'is to retire as far as possible from the mess and muddle to come. . . . A discreet withdrawal before we should be sucked into the bog seemed a sensible proceeding, and what better refuge could we find than upon some remote island in the South Sea?'[60]

At the start Nordhoff and Hall lived on a monthly allowance of fifteen dollars,[61] accommodation was affordable and they assimilated with the islanders' harmonious ways with the natural resources around them. The soils were fertile, bananas were readily available and the fishing was good. Once acclimatised the writers went on their separate ways to accumulate stories and adventures as lived material for their planned books and newspaper articles. Waiting on their return to Papeete was a colonial social life around the Cercle

Bougainville bar verandah that provided convivial conversation and an exchange of ideas and experiences. Friendships grew with fellow Americans, such as Harrison Smith, a naturalist, English writer Robert Keable, Norwegian Vigo Rasmussen, a schooner captain, and Macdonald, whose paintings hung on the walls. In Nordhoff's letters to his parents back in California he describes his friends and in one shows a learned appreciation of European art: 'it is hard to do fine and masterful work when one has Gauguin, Whistler, Degas, or Manet in mind!'[62] That Christmas in 1924 he commissioned Macdonald, 'the best of friends', to paint a watercolour:

> By the way, I am sending you for Xmas, a watercolor of my little place. I asked the artist, an Englishman named MacDonald – the best of friends – to make it more of a representation than a work of art. I hope he will have combined the two to some extent at least. But in any case it will give you an accurate idea of the place and the cottage.[63]

As they began to carve out their artistic careers in Tahiti one can imagine Macdonald living as frugally as his younger American friends. A photograph of Macdonald's studio in Patutoa from the late 1920s shows the arrangement of window blinds, thatched roof and bamboo matted construction on stilts (4.2). He then moved to Pirae and Farwell, who lived across the lane from him, describes Macdonald's home in 1933:

> a modest little cottage: walls of woven palm fronds, a pandanus thatched roof, one large room with built-in day beds, walls that propped open to reveal the lagoon only metres away, a small kitchen, cold shower and at least a hectare of garden under tall, leaning palms. . .It was the perfect place to live; in a perfect setting. The light of the Tahitian houses, wrote Gauguin in *Noa Noa*, is the way they were designed not to shut out the world, but allow nature to enter.[64]

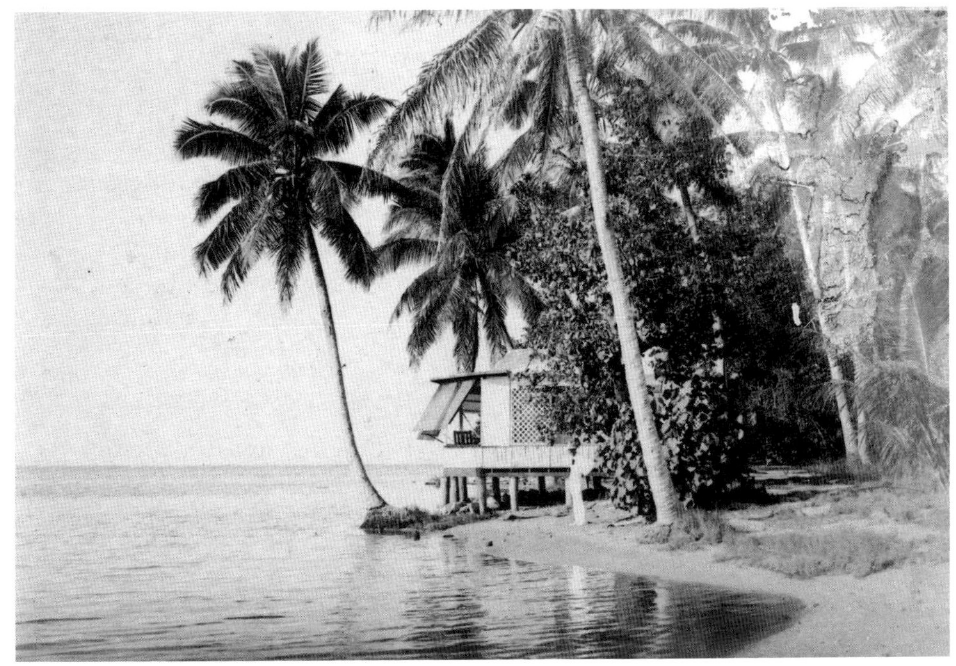

4.2 W. Alister Macdonald's home studio, Patutoa 1926

4.3 W. Alister Macdonald and Mrs Hall, Pirea 1927

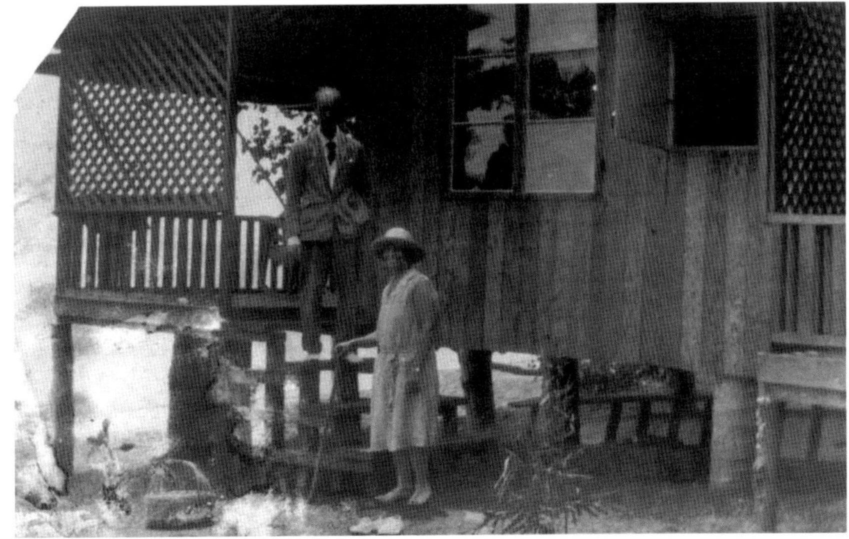

4.4 Arue, Hall family home 1931

In Papeete larger buildings such as the hotels and town hall were French colonial style brick and wood construction.

It did not take long before the white settlers took a Tahitian wife and had families to root them deeper into the island. Hall married Sarah (Lala) Winchester, who was part-Polynesian and had two children, Conrad and Nancy. Nordhoff married a Tahitian woman, Christianne Vahine Tua Tearae Smidt and had four daughters and two sons. Macdonald followed suit, despite being twenty-six years their senior, and still legally married to Lucy back in London, he took Tipari as his 'mistress',[65] and in 1926 they too had a daughter, Avril. Years later she recalled how she went to school in Pirae and 'from time to time, in the afternoon, when my father went to visit (the Hall family in Arue), I went with him. We would walk along the beach. Their daughter was my friend.'[66] (4.3, 4.4)

The Australian George Farwell in his autobiography, *Rejoice in Freedom* (1976) describes Tahiti in 1932 as 'the last truly pagan society on earth, based on the pleasure principle, not supernatural fears or a cult of death'.[67]

> Like some tropical infection, Tahiti worked its way into the bloodstream, dooming a man forever. Many others had no intention of quitting. They belonged. The world began and ended at that beautiful, encircling outer reef. What happened beyond was no longer their concern unless it came under discussion at the Bougainville. To join to this leisurely, unpretentious club on the *quai*, you needed only five francs and a jacket.[68]
>
> ...local beauties greatly enhanced the evening sunset view from the verandahs of the Yacht Club, Cercle Bougainville, and other popular male lounging-places, as they passed between sun and viewer in their promenade along the Broom Road.[69]

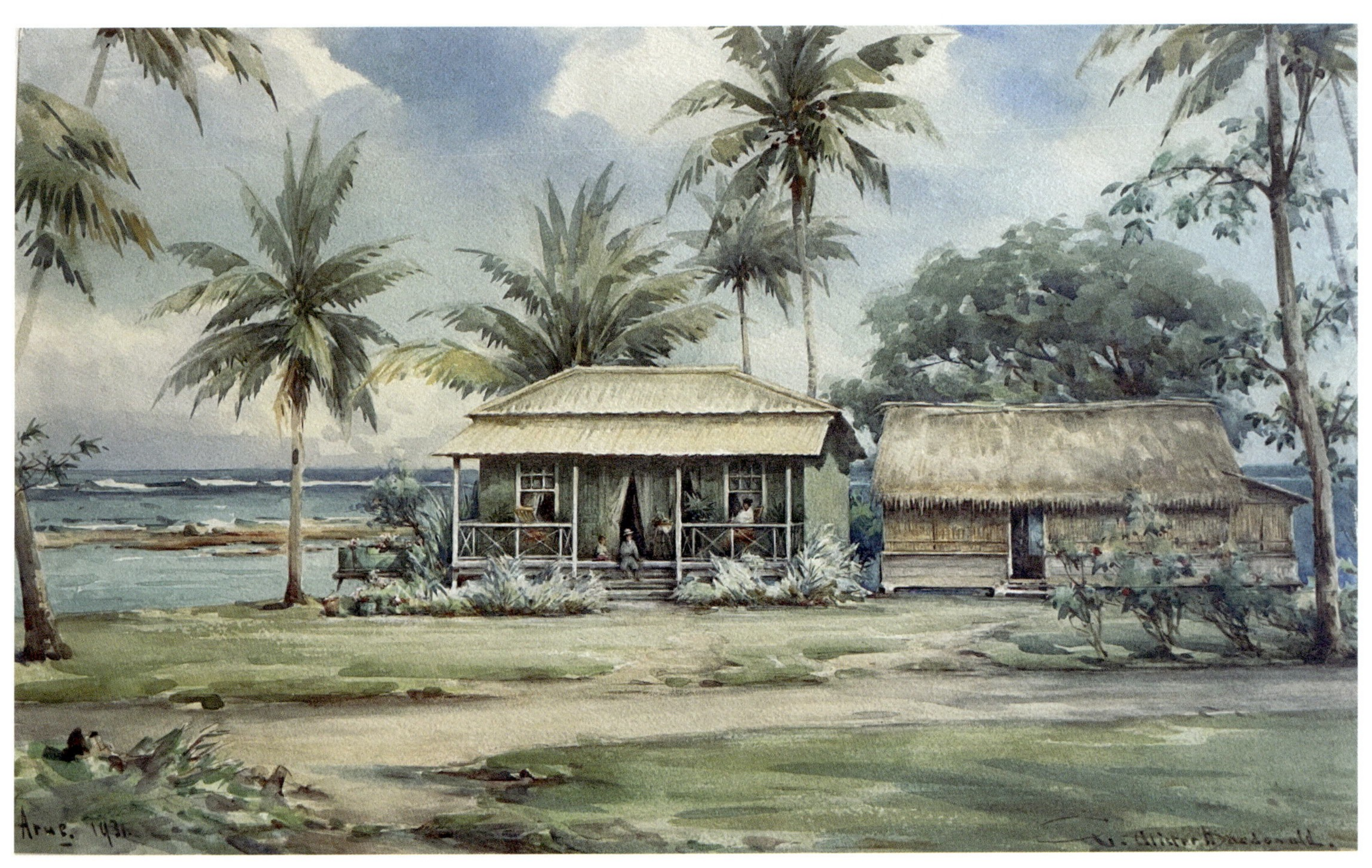
Arue. 1931.

On the verandah with a rainbow cocktail in hand, sitting under the rattan sunblinds with a view of the moored schooners at the quay below, merchants, writers, artists and adventurers could socialise. These American, Norwegian, Russian, Polish, Czech, Greek, French and British men 'were of a kind the South Seas will never again know'.[70] Amongst them he records 'the quiet, white-haired terrier of a Scotsman, Alister MacDonald [*sic*], painter of exquisite watercolours'.[71] There they would sometimes be joined by Hall and Nordhoff after a day's collaborative work in their town office, now on the crest of fame with the success of their novel *Mutiny on the Bounty* (1932). These men were also voracious readers and each generously shared and exchanged their books, with the proviso they would be returned.[72] Without the distraction of radio the art of conversation kept them intellectually stimulated and entertained. Later in his autobiography, Farwell writes:

> ...this white-bearded painter was a kindly, sensitive character. We had long discussions together amid his easels and water-colours and he lent me books of philosophy, art and fiction from his excellent library.[73]

As for the ambiance of the Cercle Bougainville:

> Behind those bat-winged doors, M. Bohler had brightened his whitewashed walls with French posters, advertisements for Dubonnet and grenadine and out-of-date calendars reproducing Alister MacDonald's evocative paintings of schooners and outer island lagoons.[74]

It might be an easy speculation that it was on this verandah that Macdonald's reputation as a watercolourist was enhanced and that commissions were made, but evidence suggests he had a more direct approach from the beach.

Book Commissions

In the period between 1930 and 1934, Macdonald was commissioned to illustrate several books by American writers that sought to capture the exquisite and unique life of Tahiti and French Polynesia. In each case the writer was aware of the temporal nature of the island life they lived amongst and all too aware of the tsunami of mechanisation and commericalisation that they felt would catch them up on these remotest of islands in the Pacific Ocean. As a watercolourist Macdonald's technique and media were regarded to be the most immediate and responsive to the light conditions and atmospherics of Tahiti, rather than oils, which the artist considered a 'loud medium'[75] that would render the island scenes in a more gaudy palette.

In 1927 a millionaire's three-mast schooner called *The Fisherman*, moored off a beach in Tahiti.[76] Macdonald had a particular eye for boats, a fascination from his childhood in Melvich, Sutherland, looking out to the cargo vessels sailing between the North Sea and Atlantic, and the herring fleet from nearby Scrabster off the north coast of Scotland. Boats were the subject of many paintings, honed from his early work published in the *Illustrated London News* of a cod-fishing trip off Norfolk in 1884, and followed by many scenes of the Thames until his departure for the South Seas in 1921. How better to earn a living than by flattering a millionaire with a painting of their schooner in Tahitian waters. Zane Grey (1872–1939), the most successful author ever at that time[77] of *Riders of the Purple Sage* (1912), *The Lone Star Ranger* (1914) and other Western novels and movies, was undoubtedly his wealthiest client. Zane Grey's *Tales of Tahitian Waters* was published in 1931 and Macdonald provided the cover colour illustration (4.5) and two other black and white illustrations in the book. These accompanied many black and white photographs of Grey's fishing trophies, records of his world breaking catches of marlin and sailfish, his boats and landscapes of Tahiti. Grey describes his meeting with Macdonald, 'an English artist' whose home was near where *Fisherman* was anchored.

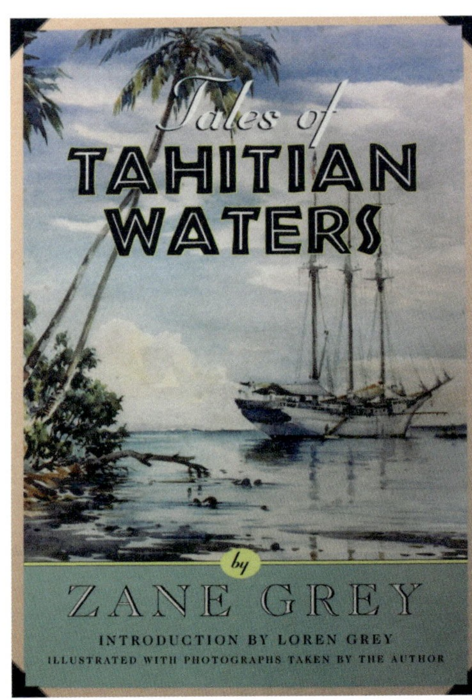

4.5 *Tales of Tahitian Waters*
Zane Grey book cover 1931

> He showed us his fine water-colours, rich in the gold shades and white shadows that make Tahiti so exotic. He had made a very beautiful painting of my ship. Mr. Macdonald was something of a fisherman himself, with trout tackle, and he interested us much by telling about the *nato*, a beautiful little fish inhabiting the Tahitian streams. He caught them with the lightest of fly tackle and claimed they were very gamey.[78]

And he clearly admires the extra dimension that his watercolours capture of the exotic light of the islands to include them amongst his own landscape photography, even when printed in monotone.

> Four miles out and somewhat to the eastward of our anchorage I had my first view of the most beautiful part of beautiful Tahiti. Nordhoff and McDonald [*sic*] had not exaggerated the magnificence of the scenery. The eastern end of Tahiti was cut into sharp peaks and deep gorges, all mantled in exquisite soft green. . . Some of the clouds were letting down misty veils of gray rain; some of the canyons were full of golden light, others dark in purple shadow. I gazed until my eyes ached, and forgot I was fishing.[79]

Like a modern-day correspondent, Macdonald was embedded into the fishing entourage camped at Vairao, south-west Tahiti, sketching and accompanying their big game fishing expeditions. Something of Macdonald's character is exposed by Grey:

> We had Alistair [*sic*] Macdonald, the English artist, visiting us at camp, and he went out with us occasionally. Once he complained to Captain Mitchell in this wise: 'My God! Man, if you don't stop eternally watching that bait, I'll go mad.'
>
> That is a clever way to illustrate one of the features of this class of fishing. Not one man in a million would want to do it, and less than that could stand it. . . I have a peculiar habit of watching my bait, then shutting my eyes for a second, and so on, over and over again, endlessly.[80]

The book had a wide readership, not least among the big game fishing community, where the account of one particular expedition is believed to have been the inspiration for Ernest Hemmingway's *The Old Man and the Sea* (1951).[81] The two writers were fiercely competitive over their record catches. As such Macdonald's work would have been given a wider audience and appreciation than previously encountered.

In December 1932 the *Pacific Islands Monthly* reported that:

> Mr Alister MacDONALD [*sic*], our celebrated local artist, returned recently from a tour of the Marquesas Islands and the Tuamotos, on the schooner 'Moana'. Many exquisite examples of MacDonald's water colours are to be seen in Tahiti residences, but as the present trip was undertaken expressly for 'L'Illustration' (Paris), we shall have to wait events before any comments may be made on his latest work.
>
> Mr. James Norman Hall, the novelist, was also a passenger on the 'Moana', having spent several weeks in the Marquesas in search of new impressions.
>
> Mr. Hall and his collaborator, Mr. Charles Nordhoff, are to be congratulated upon the outstanding success attending the publication of their latest book, 'Mutiny on the Bounty', which has been chosen by the American 'Book of the Month Club', this alone ensuring a large circulation.[82]

The trip to the Marquesas also resulted in a series of large illustrations to represent the Phosphate Mining Company for the French Exposition Coloniale's Oceana Pavilion in Paris. This exhibition of French colonial wealth and industry, and cultural diversity included twenty-six different countries and aimed to advance the notion that France was associating with colonised societies, not assimilating them.

After the success of *Mutiny on the Bounty* (1932), Hall had some unfinished business and in 1934 he published *The Tale of a Shipwreck* of his voyage to retrace *The Bounty*'s last voyage to Pitcairn with

4.6 *Tale of a Shipwreck* illustration

ten black and white illustrations by Macdonald. These works are of delicate detail and atmospheric, at once showing the drama of the Pacific skies and surf, but also the drama of sailors rowing launches through the reef, and later salvaging what they can from the surf (4.6). He described them in a letter: 'the drawings for *The Tale of a Shipwreck*' were in monochrome only and simply done for illustration'.[83]

Macdonald had returned to England before MGM Studios began production for the movie of *Mutiny on the Bounty* in June 1935. Two and a half thousand native Tahitians were employed as extras in the film with one hundred outrigger canoes, but the stars Clarke Gable, Charles Laughton, and Franchot Tone remained in Hollywood where their Tahitian scenes were filmed using rear-screen projection. The film was the highest grossing film in 1935 and won the Academy Award for Best Picture. It seemed the whole

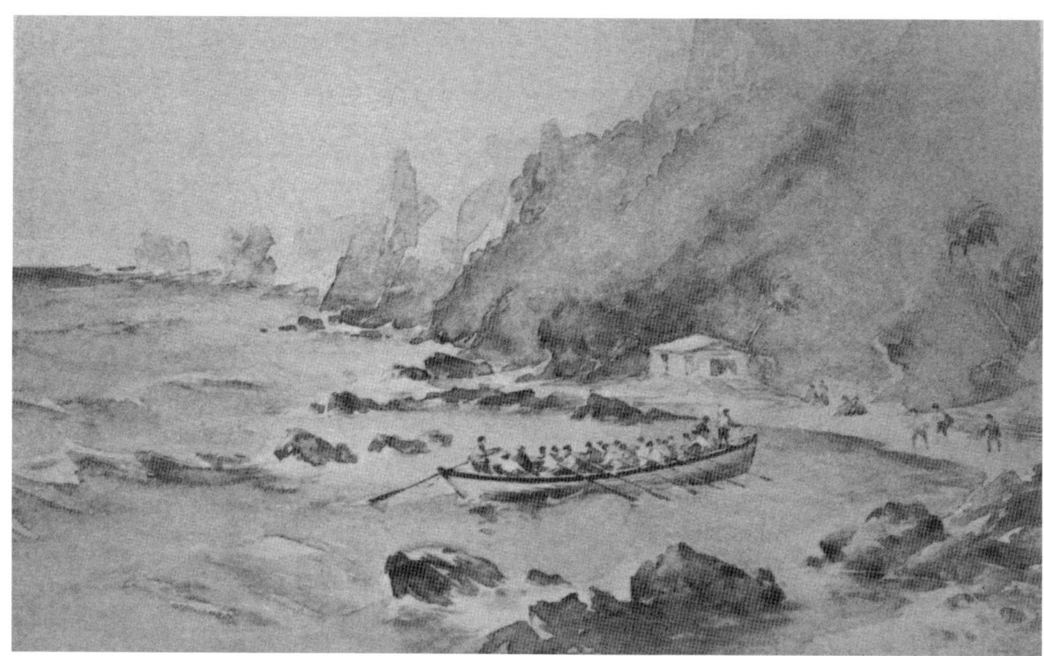

world looked to escape the aftermath of the Great Depression and flee to paradise.

Later in 1937, Robert Dean Frisbie (1896–1948) published *My Tahiti* with a colour dust jacket (4.7) and eleven black and white illustrations by Macdonald. One of these is dated 1931, confirming they were painted before his return to England in 1934. The book, Frisbie's second publication, describes his first arrival to Tahiti in spring 1920 as an adventurous twenty-four-year old, clearly influenced by Robert Louis Stevenson and following in the footsteps of other famous nineteenth-century South Seas writers.

> Fed up with the complications of a routine world, and imbued with a strong desire for solitude, Mr. Frisbie fled to Tahiti in 1920. Here is his account of his first five years there. Lightly written, full of the charm and grace of the island, the naivete and sincerity of the natives, it shows how those very qualities eventually brought an end to the Golden Age in Tahiti.[84]

Largely forgotten sixty years after his death, his books are rarely in print. He was a tall, humorous, skinny American who, in the words of James Michener, was 'the most graceful, poetic and sensitive writer ever to have reported on the islands'.[85] In the late 1920s Frisbie lived on the Cook Islands and on returning to Tahiti in 1930 with his young wife and family he began to write *My Tahiti*. Macdonald would make an ideal choice having arrived in Tahiti at the same time a decade before and being amongst their social circle.

Some of the illustrations are of a very different quality and style to his previous book illustrations; they show island people more close up, there is detail of their clothes as a man labours under a bending pole carrying five large bunches of bananas, in the background the design and structure of the village houses clearly drawn. In another, six young local men fish from an 'outrigger' in sail, surrounded by a flock of diving seabirds.

Frisbie's account shows that the 1920s brought considerable change to Tahiti, so that by the time Macdonald left in 1934, at the

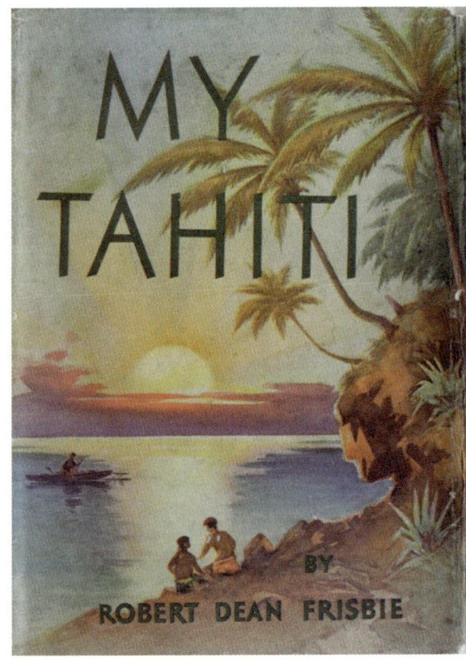

4.7 *My Tahiti* Robert Dean Frisbie book cover 1937

end of his first of three periods of residency, it was a different place to where they had all escaped to in the aftermath of the Great War. Perhaps Frisbie found his paradise too intense to endure, as Farwell recalls a rum-fuelled shouting match in the Cercle Bougainville?

> 'Puka Puka's where everything is still real. I've gotten a whole beach to myself, all the fish and fruit on God's earth, a new girl when I want her.'
>
> In a few days he was gone again... He had found his utopia. Yet years later he was reported to have died out there, the cause given an excess of morphine.[86]

In a letter to his young American pen pal, Daryl Broderick, Macdonald explains his version of Frisbie's demise:

> Frisbie I think, I know him as well as anyone – until I left Tahiti in 1939 for some fifteen years! His life is in his book 'Puka Puka'... Self centred yes, but not arrogant. His own worst enemy; too fond of Orange Beer, which he was always concocting. Sociable, distinctly. I liked him & think he had really more of the 'Divine Fire' than either Hall or Nordhoff. And Puka Puka will live because of its unusual setting & experience... Drink & elephantiasis at the end, was too much for him & he died in the Hos. In Samoa (USA) partly disappointed man I am told.[87]

In James Norman Hall's view Frisbie 'was by no means an alcoholic, but he was so highly strung that two rum punches could make him drunk: a physiological rather than a moral defect, as it seemed to me'.[88] Hall kept a long correspondence with Frisbie, and these were published in his book *The Forgotten One* (1952).

> He borrowed many volumes from my library, and I remember what a find Logan Pearsall Smith's *Trivia* seemed to be for him, at first. There, he thought, was another explorer of Self: a

> man who could look within and write with complete detachment of what he discovered...But, later, he revised his opinion of *Trivia*. It was what the name implied...[89]

Hall empathised with the struggle Frisbie had as a writer and did his best to support his friend through their letters. There was a moral struggle within, as a civilised American contending with the social norms of the island peoples that he wanted to embrace and protect. 'What Frisbie particularly admired in the natives was their lack of hypocrisy in their personal and social relations. He considered the loss of it and the necessity for losing it a heavy price to pay for being "civilized"'.[90] Hall admired his knowledge and understanding of the people he lived with on Puka-Puka, and the value of his writing to those living in the multi-ethnic islands of the South Seas.

> If all the white men who have 'jumped ship' in the South Pacific during the past two hundred years – whether exploring ship, whaler, sealer, Botany Bay transport, man-of-war, cargo steamer or private yacht – could have had Frisbie's understanding of native character and his perception of their attitude toward white men, and if they could have profited by it, what a difference it would have made in the relationships between whites and Pacific Islanders, whether Polynesians, Micronesians or Melanesians.[91]

Anthony Weller provides a modern re-evaluation of Frisbie in his Biographical Afterword to the reissue of *The Book of Puka-Puka* (2019).

> As the observed experience of a man living in a close relationship with nature while questioning the tenets of his own civilization, thankfully left far behind, they compare favourably with Thoreau. And Frisbie's writing is always sublime. In *The Book of Puka-Puka* he writes, 'Without a thought for the white man's code of ethics, I have been happy, enjoying a felicity unknown in right-thinking' realms.'

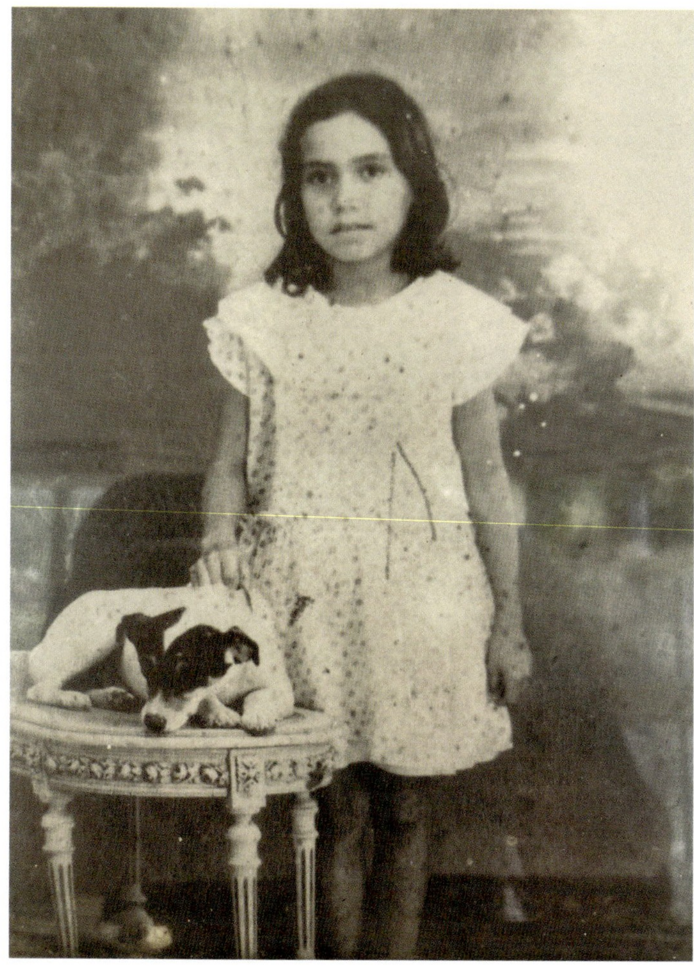

4.8 Avril, aged nine

> ...Time after time, in both books, he caught exactly the sense of island life: 'Of a sudden I understood: all this land and sea, dormant by day, had awakened at dusk, refreshed, hungry...'[92]

Macdonald was as immersed in island life, now living with his *vahine* Tipari and daughter Avril outside Papeete. Living with them freely without prejudice, and able to provide for them as an artist, to travel with them or not as he pleased, he was far removed from his past life in London. Could these lives ever be reconciled?

In 1934, tragic news of the death of his son compelled Macdonald to return to England. As he prepared to leave for England, he packed a portfolio of his Polynesian paintings and said his goodbyes to Tipari and Avril, now nine years old (4.8). He made preparations with an agent to keep them in funds and would write frequently. Before departing he had one 'final exhibition' in Papeete which was reviewed in the *Pacific Island Monthly*. The reviewer held a view that was no doubt shared by others: 'he will be greatly missed in Tahiti, but we hope that it may yet be possible to persuade him to remain with us'.[93] They could not, but he would be back sooner than anyone could have expected.

Would he have returned to England had it not been for the tragedy of his son's death? What kind of reception would be waiting for him? There is no correspondence from this period to rely on. Would he have to keep his daughter's existence secret for fear of scandal and risk jeopardising his wife's gallery business that so depended on society patronage? Never mind the possibility of moral outrage amongst his Scottish family that he had fathered a child with a Tahitian. A mixed-ethnic child would have been taboo in the Scottish Highlands at that time.

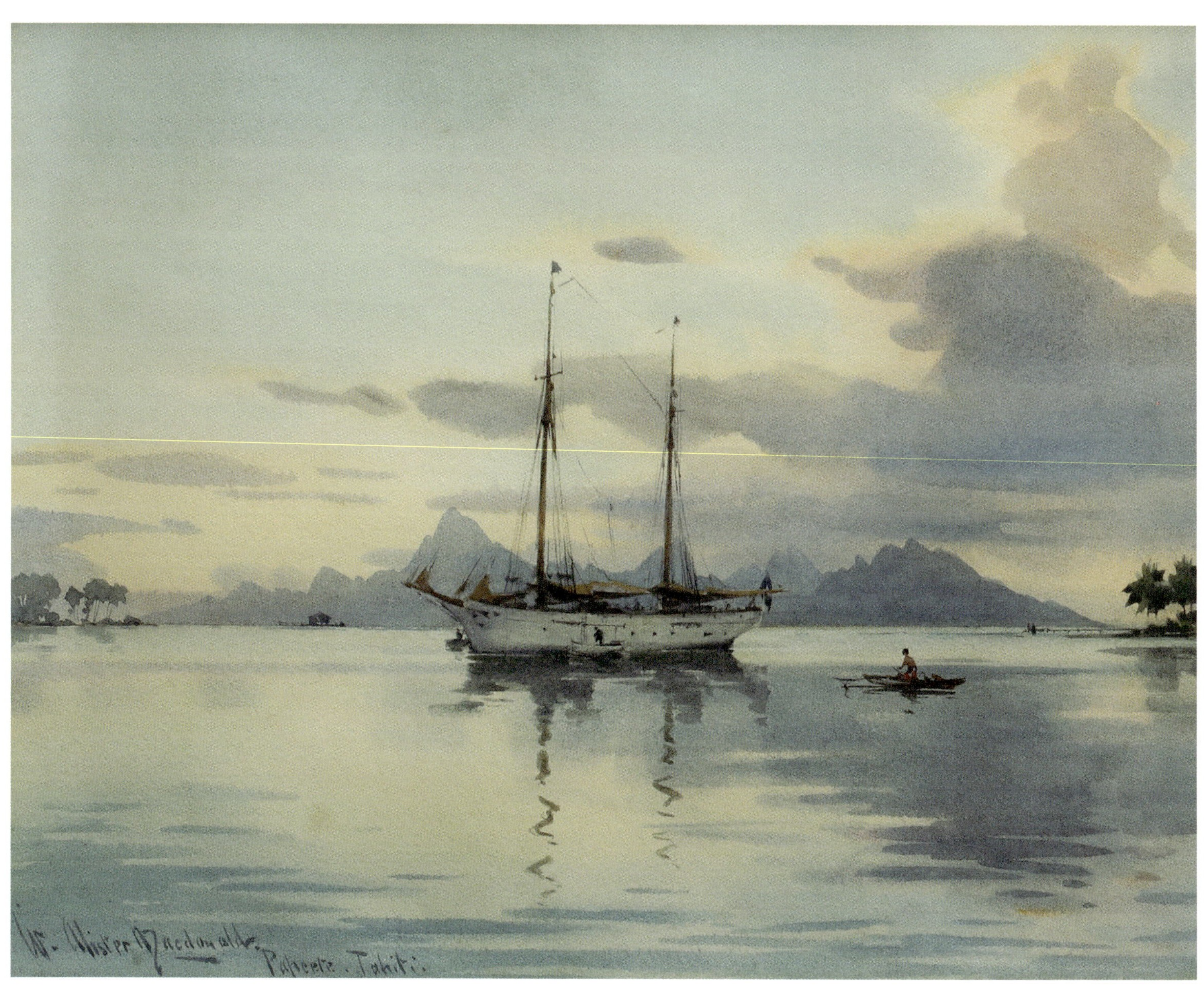

5.1 Voilier à Tahiti, Moorea en fond

5

1930s, Return to UK and Back

In July 1935 Macdonald returned to Britain, via Sydney, and the Suez Canal on SS *Barrabool*. A year earlier he had received tragic news of the death of his son, Ian, drowned in a sailing accident on the Thames at Greenhithe. He left at a time when, like other painters in Polynesia such as Mordvinoff, Machecourt, Gres and Leeteg, were 'unaware that an era was coming to an end'.[94]

Pacific Islands Monthly made several reports of Macdonald's work and exhibitions over his time in Tahiti. The January 1935 edition reported:

> Mr. Alister Macdonald, the celebrated water-colour artist, whose exquisite reproductions of Island scenery and colour are so well known to Tahiti visitors, is now holding a final exhibition of his works in Papeete, preparatory to leaving this colony, where he has been a resident for many years. Some of his finest examples – the result a mature experience – are contained in the present collection...
>
> ...He has been a life-long devotee of the brush, and is a realistic artist of the old school, who believes in fidelity to nature-something which is rarely found these days.[95] (5.1)

On returning to London and after a reconciliation with his wife, Lucy Macdonald (2.17), she organised an exhibition of his 119 Tahitian paintings at her Arlington Gallery in Old Bond Street in October. *Among the Islands of the South Seas* was a critical success.

This may have been in part motivated by the exhibition earlier in the season in June around the corner at the New Burlington Galleries of paintings by Serge Gres (1899–1970) following a three-year stay in Tahiti. The artists' styles and choices of media could not have been more different with Gres focusing on figure studies as well as seascapes 'with an uncommon skill, using an unusual technique in which gouache, oil paint, and shading with pencils of many grades are cunningly mingled'.[96] *The Times* art critic was no less impressed:

> THE SOUTH SEAS Though they do not present any new artistic discoveries, the 119 water-colours 'Among the Islands of the South Seas,' by Mr. W. Alister Macdonald at the Arlington Gallery have the attractions of their subject-matter and they are extremely accomplished in execution: crisp, clean, and direct. The frequent changes in form of picture, with the long horizontal pre-dominating show that the artist is alert in matters of composition, and he seldom fails to put the right thing in the right place. 'Polynesian Hut,' 'Deck of an Island Schooner,' 'Fish and Coral,' and 'Loading Copra, Off the Marquisas,' are specially good drawings. A note on the Islands in the catalogue adds to the interest of the exhibition.[97]

Perhaps by some miracle of oversight, one day following his return, Macdonald and Lucy discovered a cache of forgotten paintings in a cabinet. It was a find of great significance because these were watercolours he had painted of London before the war, and before automobiles had replaced horses and carriages in its streets. They worked quickly to frame 101 watercolours and in December the show opened at their Arlington Gallery. They came at a time ripe for nostalgia, but after the rapid expansion and redevelopment of London's buildings and streets, also a realisation that these were unique records of an old London that had gone or was vanishing before their eyes. The entire collection was bought by Lord Wakefield for the Guildhall in London, for a record price of £750 (5.2).[98]

At the age of seventy-five this would have been a welcome pension for the Macdonalds to live on through their old age.

Following the earlier favourable review *The Times* art critic wrote another appreciation of Macdonald's work:

> On their own lines the 101 water-colours of Old London by Mr. W. Alister Macdonald now on view at the Arlington Gallery, 22, Old Bond Street, could hardly be bettered. Mostly small, they are accurate in drawing but still broad in treatment, with an articulate touch which is a pleasure in itself, and a disposition of light and shade which seldom fails to enhance the architectural character of the subjects. Since the subjects are now mostly demolished the collection has historical interest, but the watercolours can hold their own as attractive little pictures of a kind not often produced nowadays.[99]

A month later, in a letter to *The Times*, the Director of the Guildhall Art Gallery wrote:

> TO THE EDITOR OF THE TIMES Sir, – You will remember that in the issue of The Times for December 18 last there was an appreciation of the water-colour drawings by Alister Macdonald now on view at the Arlington Gallery, Old Bond Street. I have the pleasure to announce that this collection has been purchased in its entirety by Viscount Wakefield, who, I understand, proposes to offer it to the Art Gallery of the Corporation of London. I am, Sir, your obedient servant. J. L. DOUTHWAITE, Director. Guildhall Art Gallery, Jan. 16.[100]

A few weeks later *The Times* reported:

> At yesterday's meeting of the Common Council of the City of London, at which the Lord Mayor presided. the Library Committee reported the presentation by Lord Wakefield of a collection of water- colour drawings of London. The Committee recommended that the special thanks of the Court should be

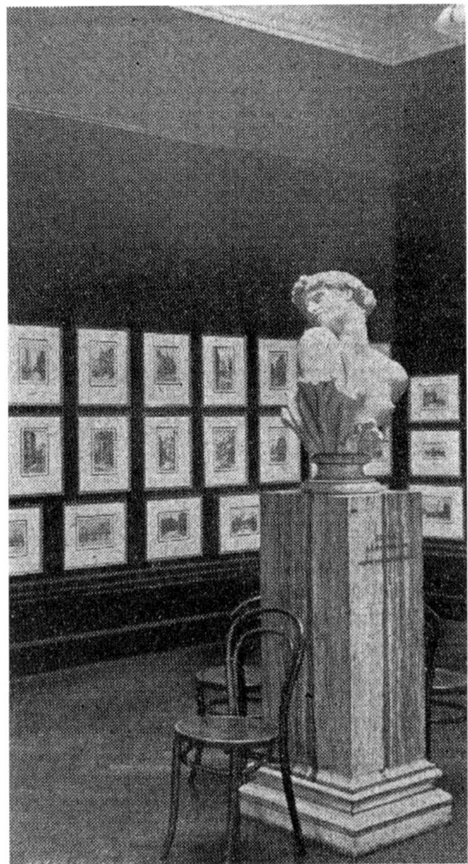

5.2 Guildhall Art Gallery Exhibition of Old London 1936

given to Lord Wakefield for his gift. Mr. ALFRED ROBERTSON (chairman of the Library Committee) said that the late chairman, Mr. E. H. Anning, received the following letter from Lord Wakefield, dated January 17:- 'Dear Mr. Anning, – You will notice in to-day's Times that I have purchased the collection of water-colour drawings by Mr. Alister Macdonald now on view at the Arlington Gallery, Bond Street. I shall be greatly obliged if when the Library Committee next meet you will convey to the members an expression of my hope that I may be allowed to present this series of drawings of London to the City's Art Gallery. Yours sincerely, WAKEFIELD.' The views, Mr. Robertson said, were in the main sketched by the artist during his residence in England more than 30 years ago, and as a representative collection of drawings portraying picturesque parts of London that had almost disappeared were of, considerable historical interest. The Committee felt that no more appropriate home could be found for the drawings than the City of London Art Gallery. LORD WAKEFIELD had made many generous donations to the City and to the Guildhall in particular. It would be within the recollection of the Court that he gave the manuscript entitled the Great Chronicle of London now in course of printing. It was a matter for additional gratification that he had now offered not only the pictures but also the entire cost of mounting and framing them. He moved that the special thanks of the Court should be given to Lord Wakefield for his interesting and valuable gift, and for the deep interest he continued to show in the Corporation and its institutions. Mr. FREDERICK ROWLAND, – the Chief Commoner, seconded the motion, which was carried unanimously, with applause. An appreciation of the drawings appeared in The Times of December 18, and three of them were reproduced in The Times of January 17.

WATERCOLOURS OF OLD LONDON LORD WAKEFIELD'S GIFT TO THE CITY[101]

Clearly Macdonald's work as an artist was now admired and celebrated in newspaper reviews across the United Kingdom, and 'well known on both sides of the Atlantic',[102] described as 'exquisite' by Farwell, and 'fine water-colours' by Zane Grey. The millionaire Grey, not known as a serious art collector, did nevertheless articulate an informed appreciation of Macdonald's ability to capture the specific qualities of Tahitian atmospherics.

This late appreciation of Macdonald's meticulous watercolours of street scenes and views of the Thames set him apart from his European contemporaries who had worked in oils, and who he had outlived. But it is in his rapid watercolour studies of sunsets over the Thames (5.3) that he demonstrated an impressionistic and fluid response to the scene in front of him, in order to capture the rapidly changing atmospheric light. More in the vein of Turner and Whistler's sketches who had preceded him than the darker tones of Sickert. While living in a flat at the Temple before the 1914–18 war, he even had a viewpoint of the Thames from his bedroom window.

Whether it was a humble barge in front of St Paul's cathedral, or a ship moored beside the Tower of London, Macdonald displayed an understanding of the construction of major architectural landmarks as well as the variety of vessels working on the Thames. His pencil sketches and quick watercolour studies would inform more finished watercolours that articulated greater detail. During the period he was painting these river scenes he never found the same success as W.L. Wyllie (1851–1931), another painter in the English tradition, who had found popularity through the patronage of The Fine Art Society and the Royal Institute of Painters in Water Colours.[103] It is unknown whether Wyllie's manual *Maritime Painting in Watercolour* (1901) could have aided Macdonald's early development, yet his studies of architectural building details: masonry and ironwork, in boat fitting and rigging, show a rigour and scientific enquiry into the form as well as an understanding of the engineering of buildings and ships (5.4, 5.5, 5.6). A fascination he no doubt shared with his younger brother and architect, Sinclair Macdonald, while growing up on

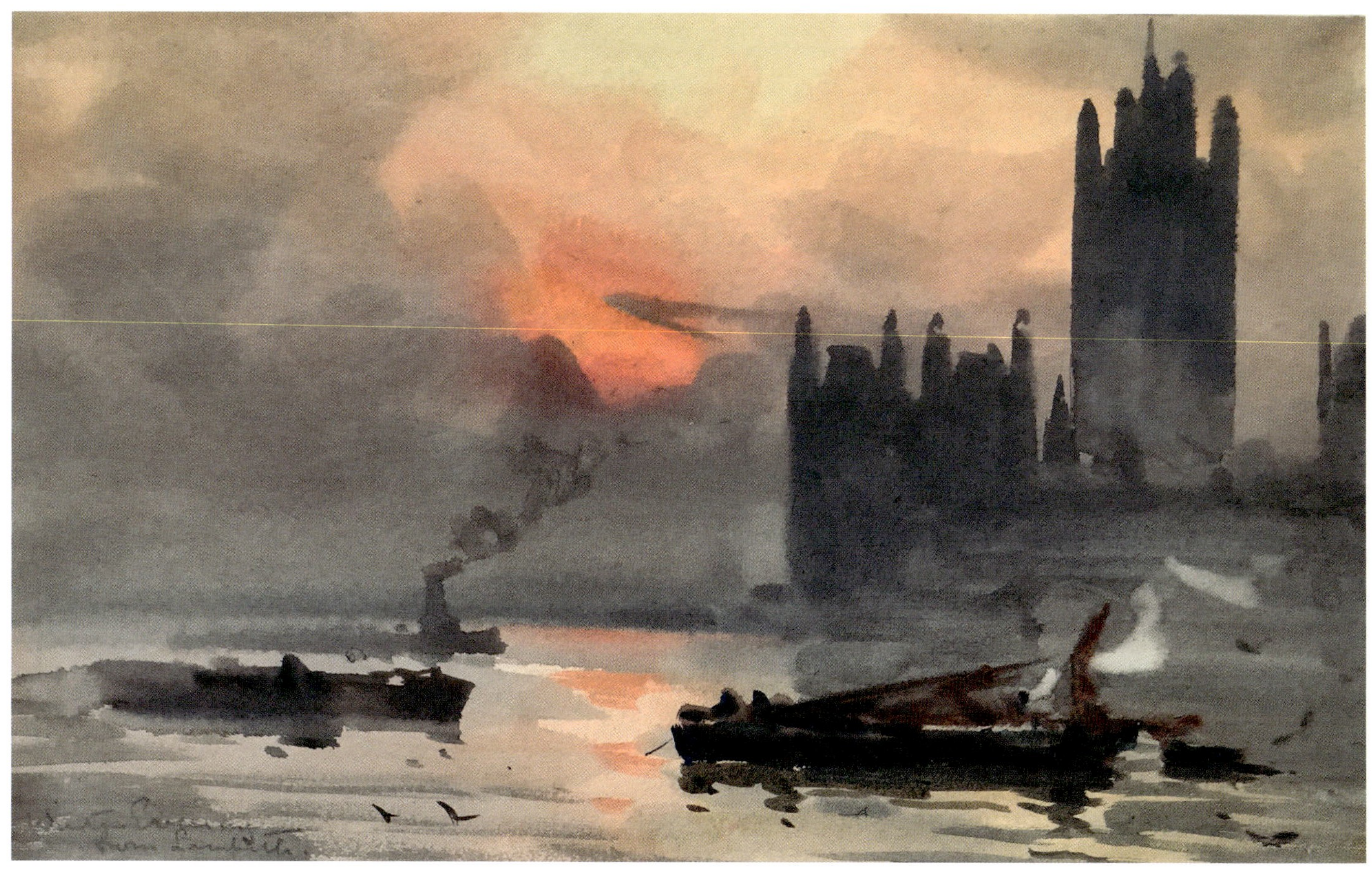

Sundown. Winter. (WAM)

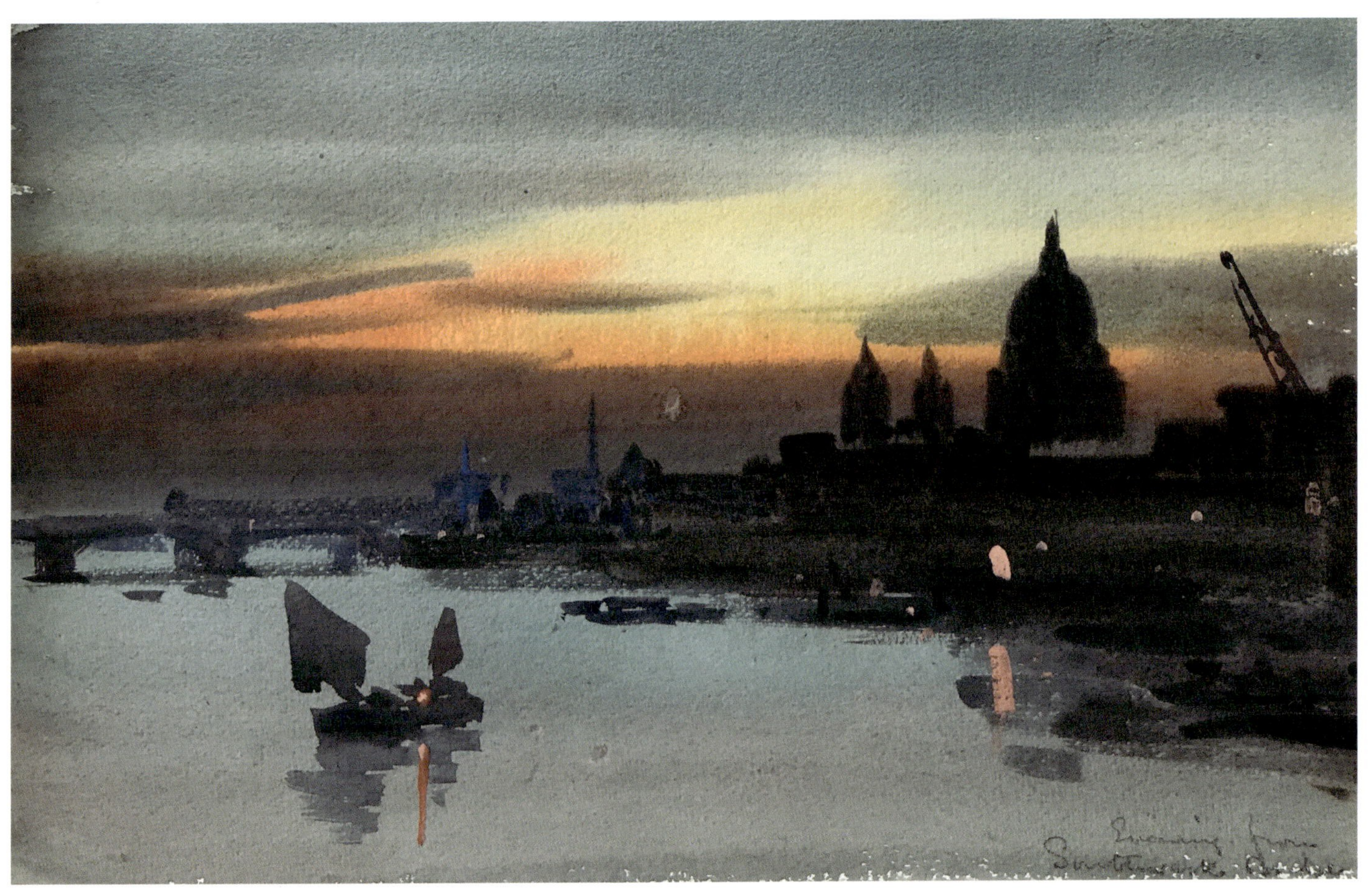

Evening from Southwark Bridge. (WAM)

Scotland's north coast. On the horizon they could see the cliffs of the islands of Orkney, and around them the simple fishermen's cottages of Melvich, along the coast to the town of Thurso there would be the occasional castle then on to the opulence of the Duke and Duchess of Sutherland's French-style chateau at Dunrobin Castle, designed by Sir Charles Barry.

A lasting recognition of Macdonald's life and London work came in the publication of a book written with E. Beresford Chancellor, *London Recalled* (1937). It gave an authorised biography of his life but omitted to explain his motives to venture and stay for so long in Tahiti. In fact the book makes clear the gratitude owed to his wife, Lucy Macdonald, for keeping safe the London paintings and for standing firm and faithfully through the long fourteen years of separation.

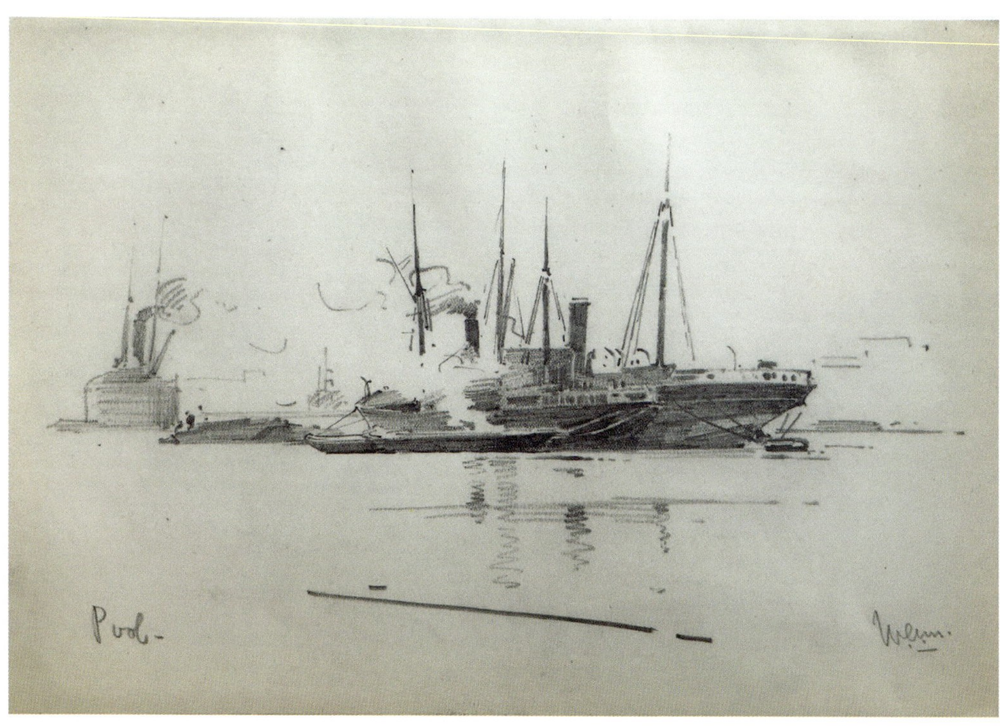

5.6 Sketch of steamer in London Pool

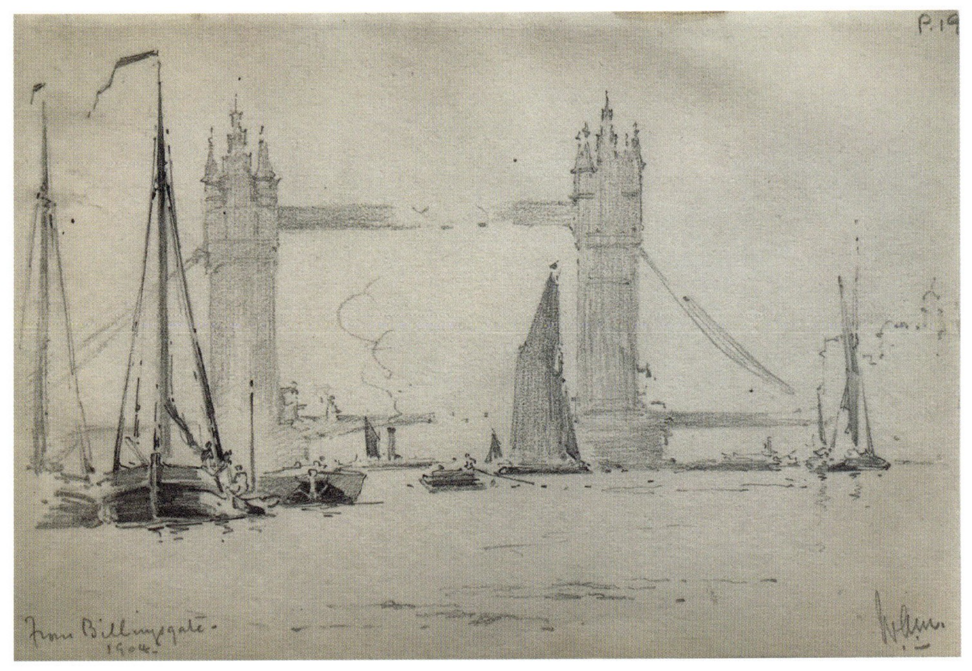

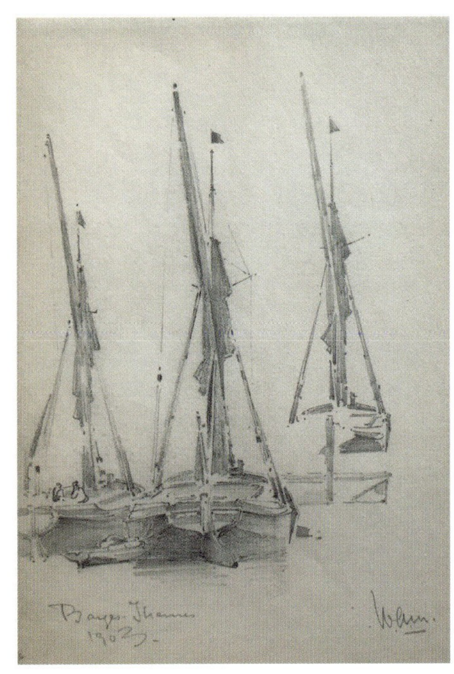

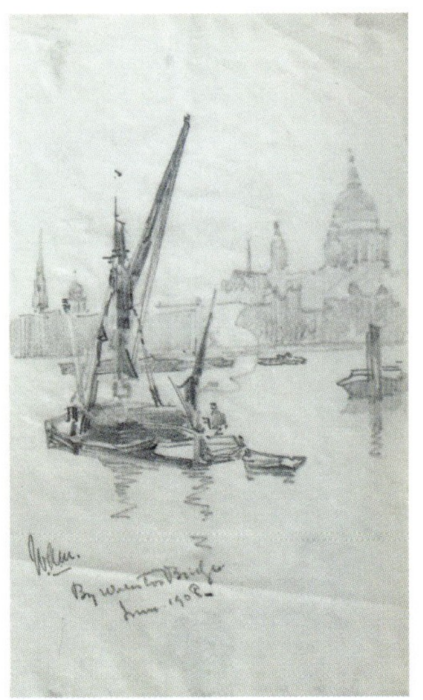

5.4 Barges and boats sketches 1903 and 1908

5.5 Tower Bridge from Billingsgate 1904

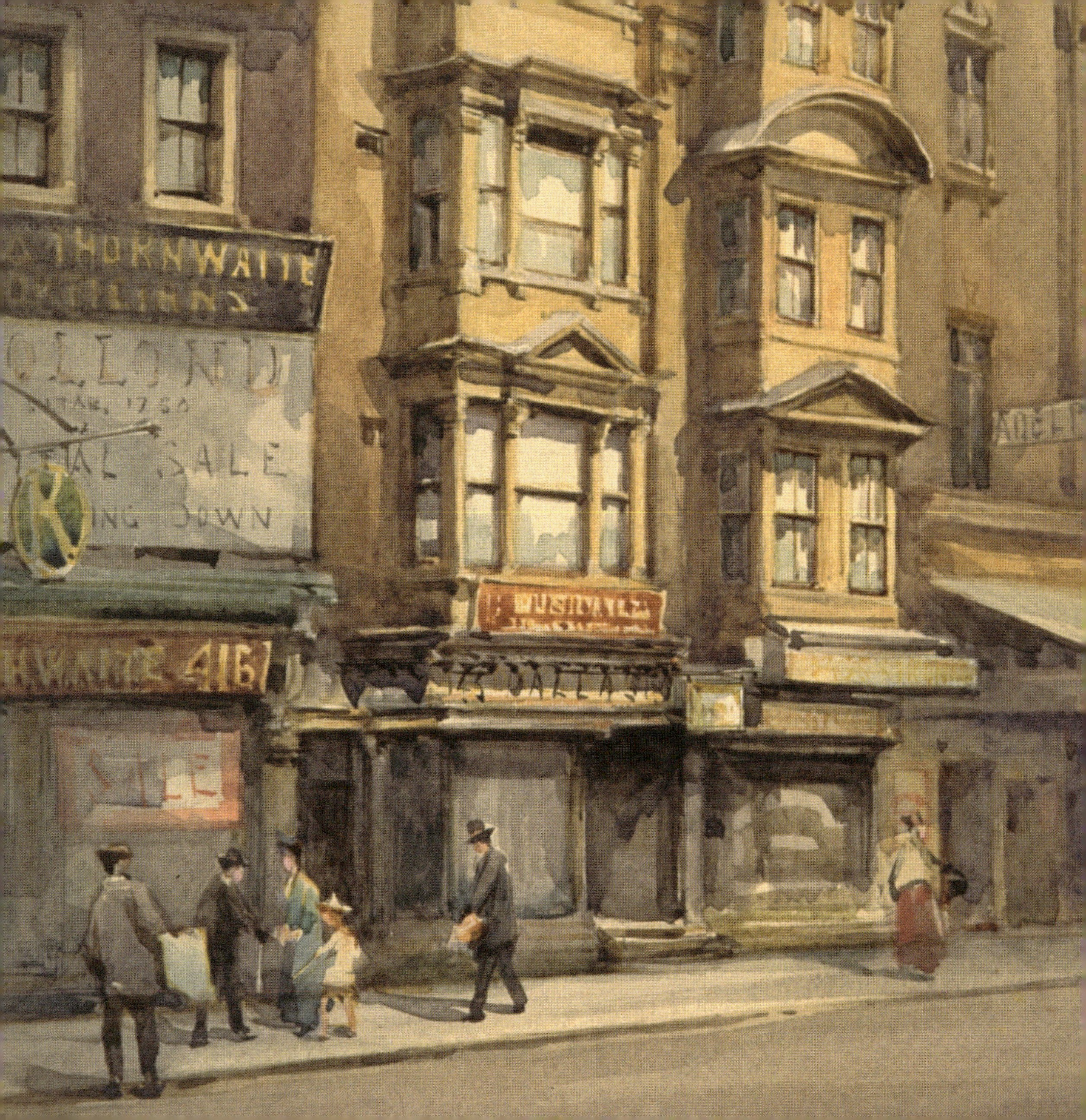
A THORNWAITE
ESTAB. 1760
AL SALE
ING DOWN
HWAITE 416
SALE

6

The Guildhall Watercolours

Chancellor's book, *London Recalled* (1937) provides a valuable historical account of the architecture and London landmarks in the Wakefield Collection of Macdonald's watercolours in the Guildhall Art Gallery. In one of the last exhibitions of Macdonald's work at the Guildhall in 2001 the watercolours were exhibited alongside contemporary black and white photographs of the same street view. The City of London then and now in the twenty-first century would be largely unrecognisable to the artist. Even in 1937, Chancellor wrote with a degree of sentimentality for the lost buildings and streets of historic London (6.1). As such the value of Macdonald's watercolours has even greater academic value for anyone interested or studying London's architectural history.

> Those who examine the reproductions here made by Mr Macdonald's achievement, and add to their knowledge by studying the rest of his work in the Guildhall Art Gallery, will realise, not only that he is a curiously observant portrayer of the structures he has selected for delineation, but also that he has caught in a remarkable way those atmospheric effects which may be regarded as the poetic setting of his subjects. It is in this that he differs from many artists who have restricted themselves (if I may so phrase it) to the prose of their architectural models. The 'correctness' of these leaves nothing to be desired. Mr Macdonald has added to this essential point

6.2 Unloading a Straw Barge, Bankside (No date)

> his feeling of the poetry of London's atmosphere, which adds so much to the beauty and attraction of his work. How many objects would be dull and commonplace were it not for that illusive something which, like the half-lights of early morning, or the coming on of night, invests them with ethereal charm? Whistler, in works not to be forgotten, has shown us how, veiled in the mists of London's atmosphere, the verist commonplace seems clothed in an aura of beauty, and how even the least interesting edifices may appear as veritable palaces, domes, and turrets of a fairy city.[104] (6.2)

The oldest landmark is *St Bartholomew and old Cloth Fair* (1908) (6.3) in Smithfield, 'only a fragment of the once huge monastic establishment founded by Rahere in the reign of Henry I. . . There are four paintings that have the ancient church and its precincts for their subjects'.[105] Chancellor (1868–1937) provides a series of historic vignettes over eight hundred years that occurred in and around these scenes, as if conjuring up actors in front of them in our imagination, such as medieval murders, the burning of martyrs, or the rowdiness of Cloth Fair. 'Happily, as we look at Mr Macdonald's representations of the old church, so fascinating to him and to us, we can forget such tragic happenings and feast our eyes on what time's ravages have left for us'.[106] His knowledge of history and architecture would rival that of the later art historian, and more well known, Nikolaus Pevsner (1902–1983).

A nostalgia for the pre-mechanised age is evident, not just for buildings that have disappeared between the turn of the twentieth century and the 1930s, as the words of the poet Henry Wadsworth Longfellow (1807-1882) illustrate : 'Another is the old Smithies' Yard, near the church, where, in the days before the motor drove nearly every horse-drawn vehicle from the streets, one 'could catch the burning sparks that fly like chaff from a threshing floor'.[107] Macdonald's watercolours provide the only pictorial record of many ancient landmarks that had disappeared by then: Old Dick

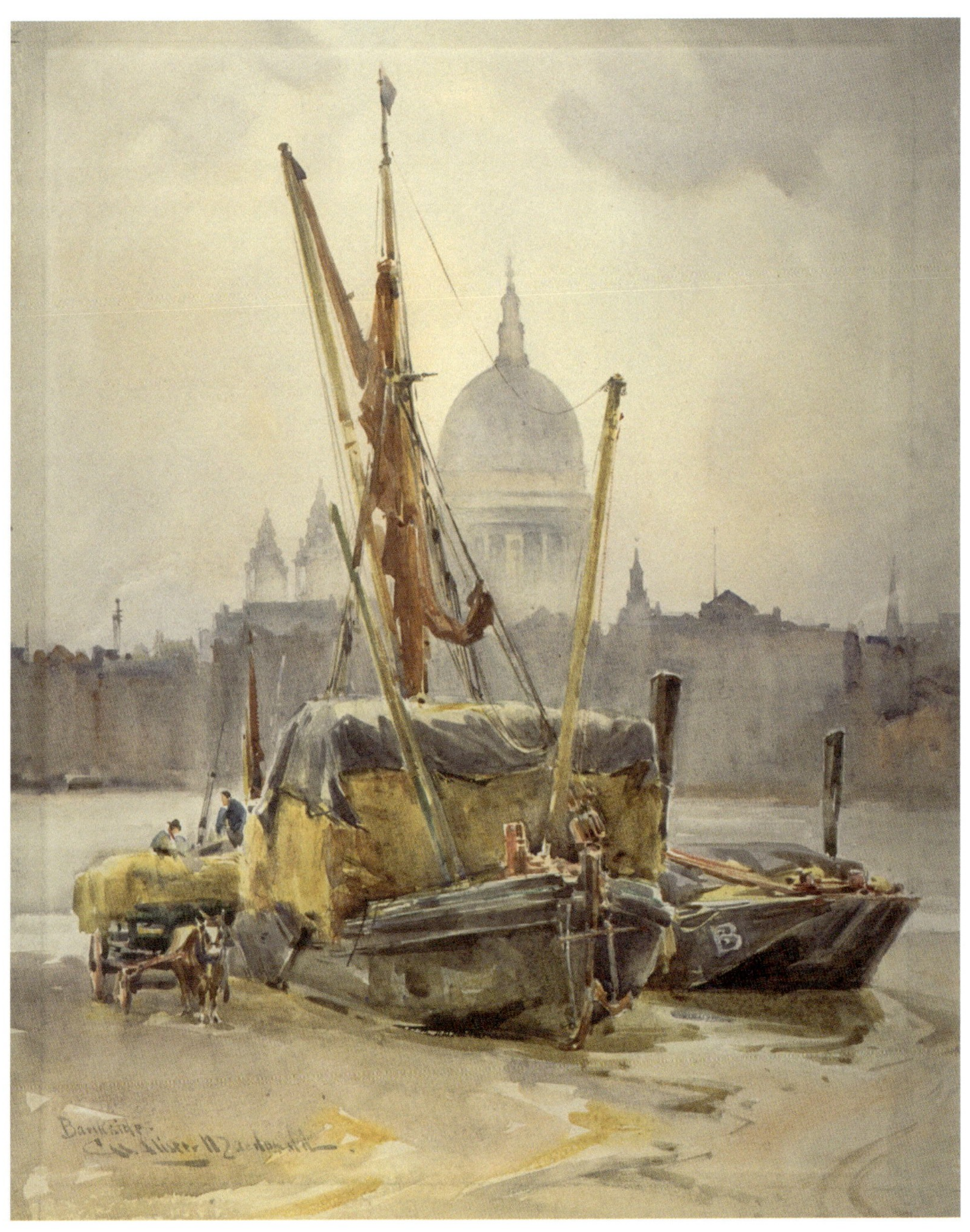
Bankside.

Whittington tavern, established in the 1400s, and *The Little Wonder Eating House, Smithfield* (1907) (6.4), *Saracen's Head Yard, Bishopsgate* (1912) (6.5). But unlike his predecessor, also an artist who lived by the Thames two centuries before him, William Hogarth (1697–1764), the 'Father of English Painting',[108] he never revelled in capturing the drama and character of the patrons of these social meeting places.

Macdonald painted many of the large City thoroughfares, with St Pauls and the spires of other masterpieces by architect Sir Christopher Wren (1632–1723). But what clearly captured the delight of Chancellor were the many paintings of the lost hidden alleys linking these landmarks, such as *Watling Street* (1910) (6.6). It 'was always a narrow and even dangerous one, as indeed it is to-day. But this very fact adds to its picturesqueness...forming a dramatic antithesis to the larger and more impressive thoroughfares that run close by it'.[109] The references to Wren's building and restoration work after the Great Fire in 1666 are a reminder of London's previous upheavals and destruction, and the importance of preserving its historic architecture.

Another important topographical record of a lost landmark is Macdonald's watercolour of *Catherine Court, Trinity Square, looking East* (1912) (6.7), a little tributary of *Seething Lane* (1912) (6.8), once the home and haunt of diarist Samuel Pepys (1633–1703). The painting preserves 'the quiet distinction of the domestic architecture... with their matured red brick-work and their decorative over-doorways, and that repose which seems to-day as much as they a thing of the past'.[110]

In contrast to this, Macdonald and his wife Lucy lived in the Temple, not far from *Lincoln's Inn Fields* (1912) (6.9), an area occupied by lawyers since the Stuart reign in the seventeenth century, but also of many distinguished residents including Dukes, Duchesses, Earls and Lords. The artist returned frequently over the years, attracted by the classical grandeur of buildings by Inigo Jones (1573–1652) and other 'splendid houses, many of them still full of the delicate carving and decorative audacities of an earlier time'.[111] In an earlier sketch of *Lincoln's Inn* (1899) (6.10) the artist uses tantalisingly sparse mark-making and blocks of wash to block and plot out the proportions and perspective of the street.

Around the Temple, Chancellor commends the artist for 'exercising wise discretion in limiting himself to certain outstanding features' (1937–60), such as *Middle Temple Lane* (1901) (6.11), *Fountain Court* (1910) (6.12) and *Brick Court* (1908) (6.13). These stairways and lanes were once occupied by notable writers such as Oliver Goldsmith (1728–1774), Samuel Johnson (1709–1784), Edmund Burke (1729–1797) and later William Thackeray (1811–1863). Chancellor also notes the medieval history dating from the Knights Templars, and the white and red roses, emblems of Lancaster and York in the Fountain Court gardens depicted by Shakespeare.[112] Other corners frequented by lawyers are *Field Court, Gray's Inn* (1904) (6.14), *Staple Inn Courtyard* (1906) (6.15), *Old Houses in Fetter Lane* (1907) (6.16), *Clifford's Inn, Fleet Street* (1906) (6.17), all gone by the time they were exhibited in 1936.

The first matrimonial home of the Macdonalds was off the Strand, where he painted frequently. Before it was built up during the Elizabethan period, it was a resting place for Canterbury Pilgrims at the Holy Well leading to the Roman Baths. *Old Houses, Strand* (1913) (6.18) presents a view that was soon lost, to be replaced by New Zealand's government offices, no doubt to cope with that country's growing economic development and population. It was there that Macdonald himself set off for in 1921, before alighting in Tahiti en route.

In Westminster, Macdonald found a constant source of inspiration and fascination, buildings ranging from the ancient ecclesiastic to many eras of government reflecting national history. *Abingdon Street* (1907) (6.19) records the last remains of domestic architecture of previous centuries capturing the sweep of the street and contrast to the Abbey and Whitehall in middle and distant background, while in *Doorway in Great College Street, Westminster* (1907) (6.20) he deftly records the decorative ironmongery and masonry detail that surround a domestic doorway. The Houses of Parliament are a frequent subject in his paintings, sometimes in the atmospheric background as in *Storey's Gate, Westminster* (1910) (6.21), or the main attraction, reflected in the Thames in *Westminster Abbey and Houses of Parliament from Lambeth* (1910) (6.22) (2.12) where stately grandeur is offset by the humble river boats in the foreground.

Recalling Victorian poet Matthew Arnold, and others long forgotten, who described Westminster, Chancellor regards Macdonald as the more effective visualiser of London's masterpieces.

> 'What shadows we are, and what shadows we pursue,' once wrote Matthew Arnold; and these men are among those who thus fitfully emerge, ghost-like, reluctant, as it were, from their long sleep, to illustrate the memories of this quarter of London which Mr Macdonald has illustrated in a much more effective way.[113]

From the Pool of London in the East to the upper reaches of the tidal Thames in Richmond, Macdonald spent many years painting from the bankside and sometimes from boats. One of the earliest in the Wakefield Collection is *Hay's Wharf, Tooley Street* (1896) (6.23) where ships' masts and cranes play counterpoint with ghostly Tower Bridge in the background. *Waterloo Bridge and the River* (1898) (6.24) is more of an impressionistic study of cloud and water movement, what Chancellor describes as a 'Turneresque treatment of the river',[114] compared to the attention to nautical rigging detail in *River Thames at Westminster* (1905) (6.26) and architectural perspective in *By Westminster Bridge* (1908) (6.25). Both these attributes are combined in *Off the Tower* (1895) (6.26):

> It will be observed that although that landmark forms his background the artist has concentrated on that riverside atmosphere which is now such a feature of its liquid foreground. This beautiful picture was made in 1895, and in view

> of the destructive work going on in London then and since, Mr Macdonald may have thought that even the Tower might not always be safe from depredation and that like Temple Bar and Crosby Hall, to say nothing of a whole series of splendid palaces, it might one day be removed stone by stone in favour of a block of flats![115]

In *Clearing the Site for the new County Hall, Westminster* (1910) (6.27) we see a scene of demolition amongst working London that would have been commonplace along the Embankment and the South Bank of the Thames. Chancellor notes that even here the artist finds something of aesthetic value worthy of his attention.

> It might be supposed that with the overflowing of London on the south of the Thames and the development that took place there at the beginning of the nineteenth century, together with the forming of the Embankment and the gradual destruction of old landmarks, few, if any remains could exist sufficiently alluring to win the attention of the artist. That this is happily not been entirely the case is proved by what Mr Macdonald has left us of views taken over so wide a range as that extending from the Port of London to Millbank.[116]

But aside from the changing landmarks it is the ability to capture the sunshine through the fogs and mists, that magically transform 'the rotten, often entirely disused, wharves and warehouses, dreary when the tide is up, and unutterably depressing when it is low'.[117]

> In all the river views of the Thames, of which there are a number among the Macdonald pictures, one cannot fail to realize how the very spirit of that mighty stream has entered into the artist's conception. Whether he be picturing it in daylight, or as it appears when clad with the mists of evening, or irradiated by the dying sun, he reveals something of its mystery and of the intrinsic beauty which is made doubly effective when reflected in its waters.[118]

6.1 St Martin le Grand 1913

Wren's masterpiece, St Paul's Cathedral, is another fascination for Macdonald. Some paintings are made at water-level in *St Paul's from Bankside* (1904) (6.28), others from the street in *Ludgate Hill, Bank Holiday Morning* (1908) (6.29), but one of his smallest watercolours, almost a miniature, and most haunting prediction of the Blitz, is of it illuminated by searchlight.

In other paintings he follows the path of Whistler, *The Harbour Master's House, Limehouse* (1907) (6.30). In another *The Nimrod* (1910) (6.31), he pays tribute to another wanderer, Ernest Shackleton, whose ship took him on his first expedition to the Antarctic.

London's bridges are also a fascination, and from 1898 *Old Vauxhall Bridge* (6.32) to 1914 he captured London, Southwark, Blackfriars, Waterloo, Westminster, Vauxhall , Lambeth, many of which were rebuilt or replaced by 1936. Lambeth Bridge is the subject of five watercolours in the collection taken from various points of view (2.12, 6.22).

> In some it is outstanding, in others a subsidiary, object of his drawings, certain of which are obviously intended rather to convey atmospheric effect than to be a special study of a particular object, for several of the works have been executed when the setting sun was glowing over the river and the evening mists clothing even a suspension bridge with a sort of incommunicable charm. In many of them it will be seen that the else-commercialised and desolate south bank of the Thames wears that air of mystery which is able to endow commonplace things with an unexpected beauty.[119]

These meticulous paintings, and sketches that led to many of his works, remain important topographic records of old pre-mechanised London, that have rarely been seen and have largely been overlooked by historians and art critics. It is hardly surprising as art historians have largely focused on the many Modernist movements of the twentieth century and photographic and digital media have overwhelmed us with images of London.

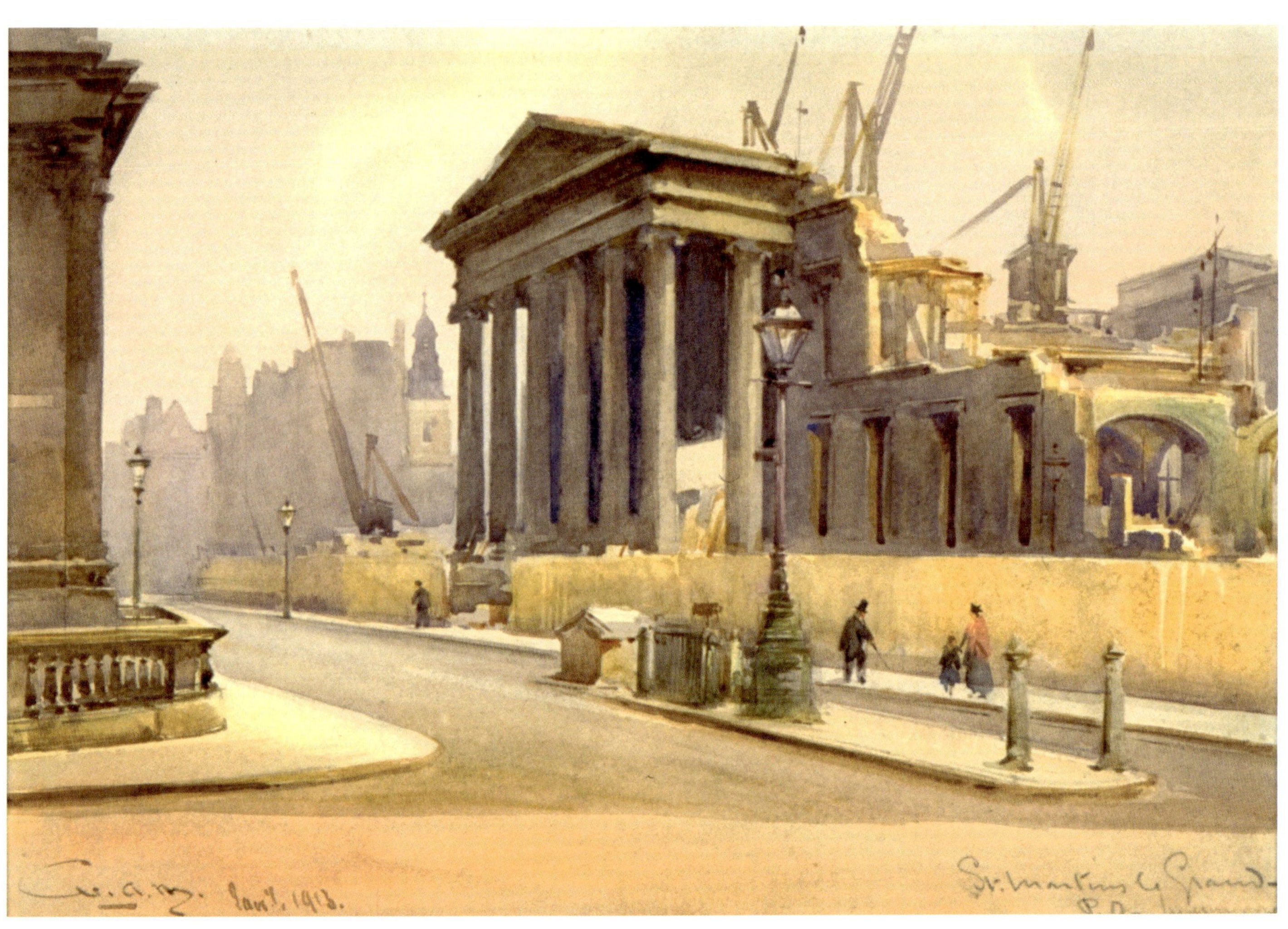
St. Martins le Grand

6.7 Catherine Court, Trinity Square, looking East 1912

6.8 Seething Lane 1912

6.6 Watling Street 1910

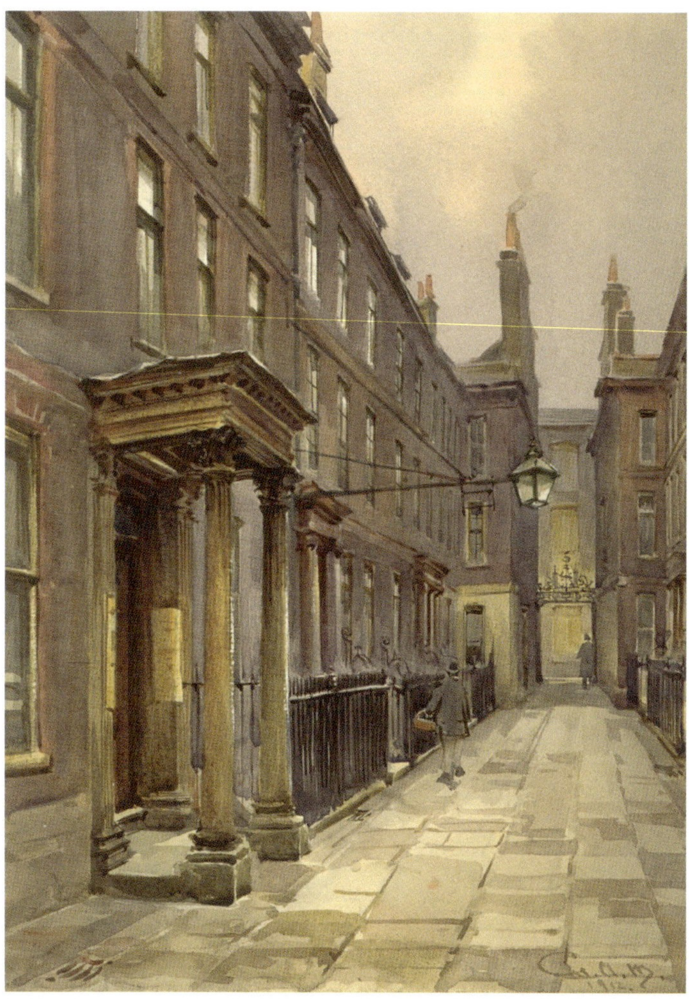

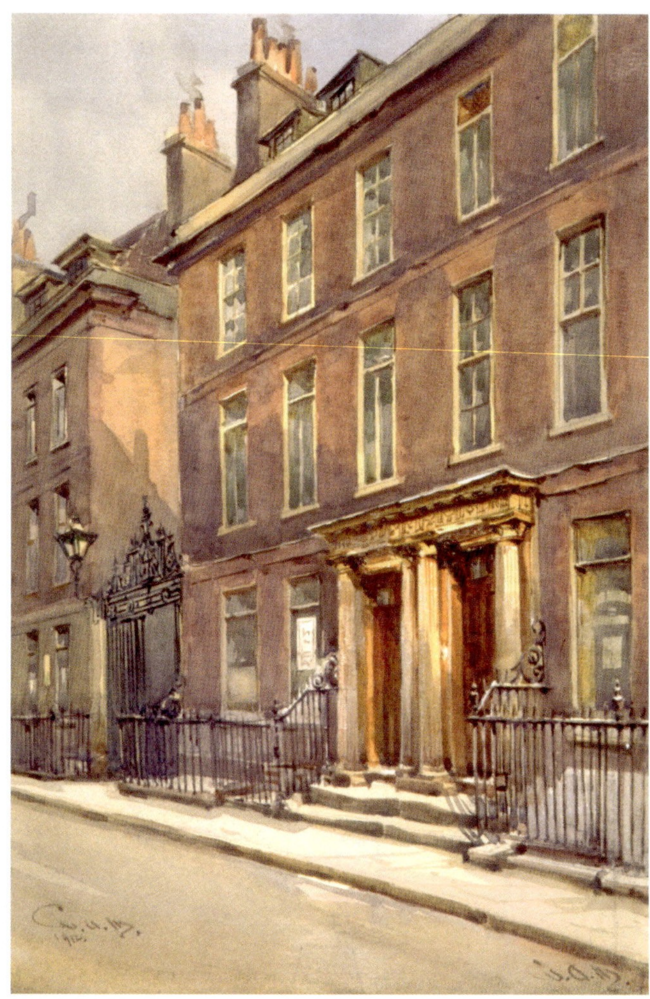

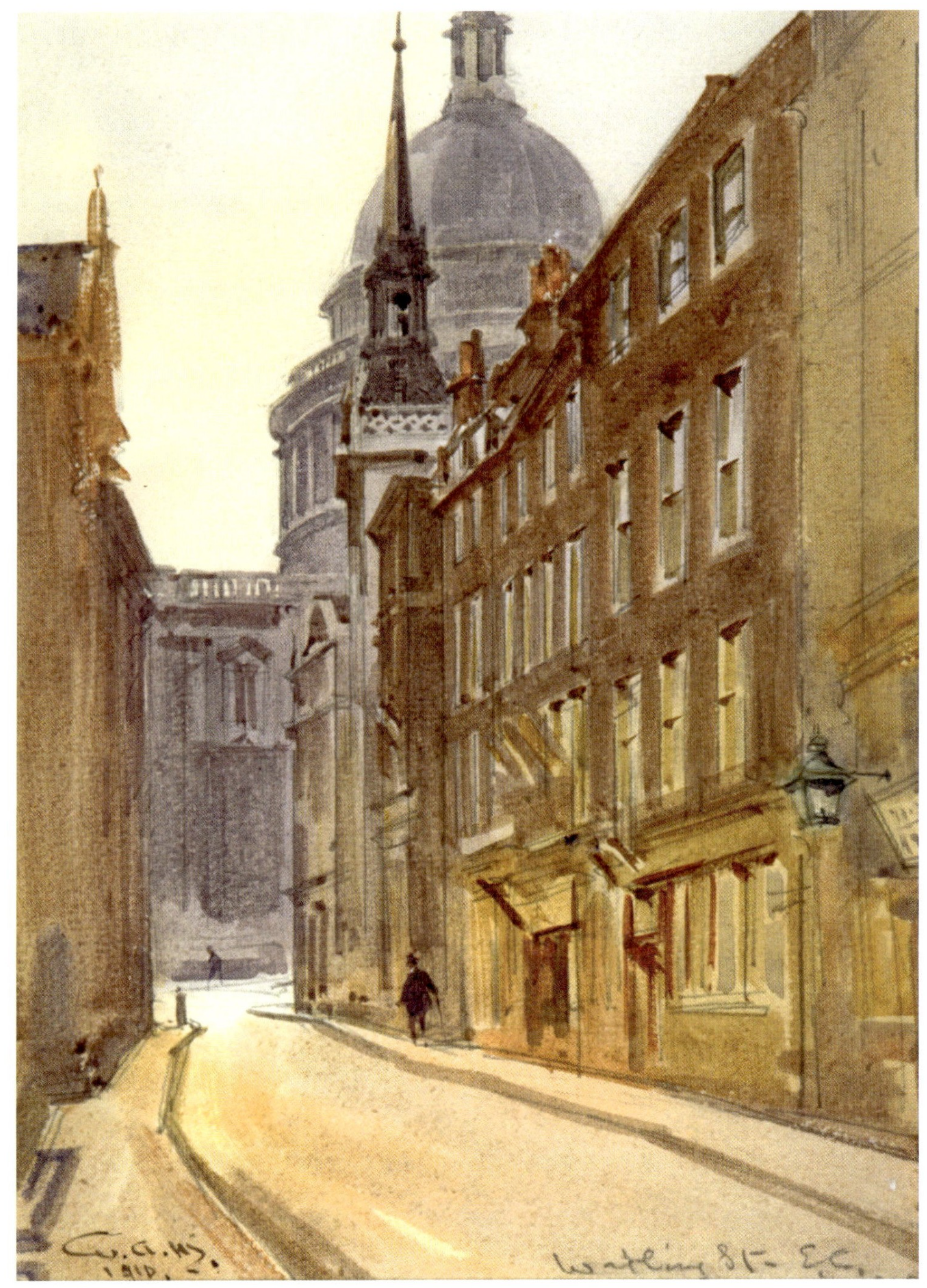
Watling St – E.C.

6.4 The Little Wonder Eating House, Smithfield 1907

6.5 Saracen's Head Yard, Aldgate 1913

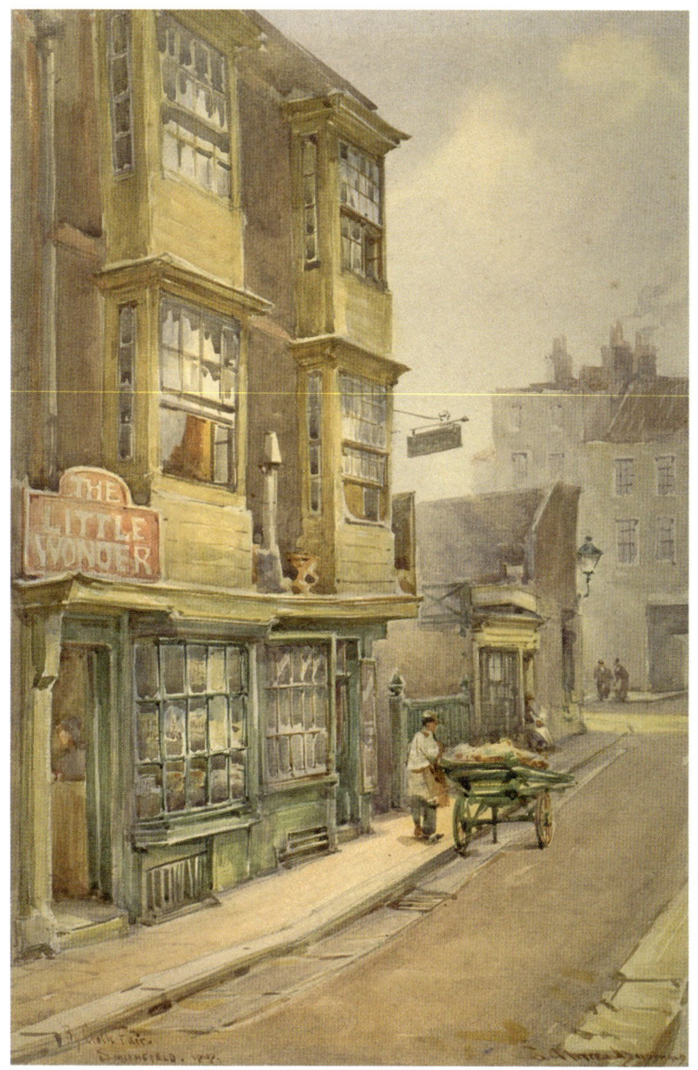

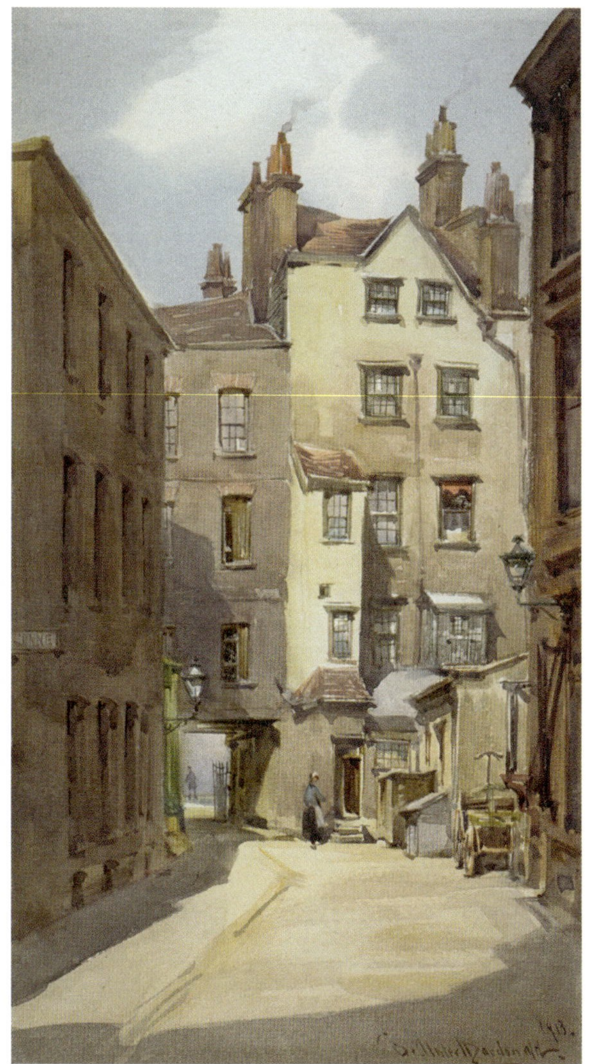

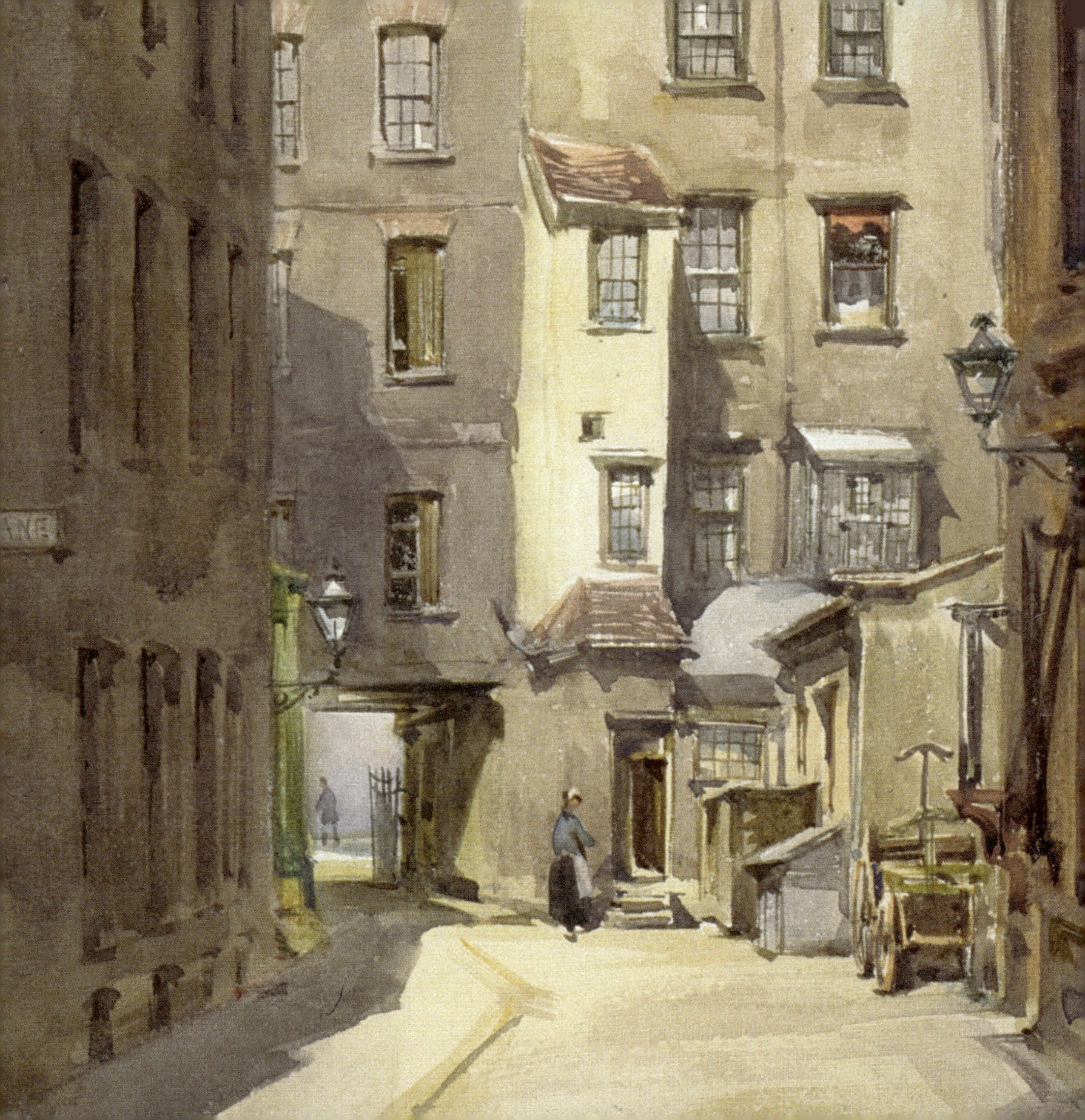

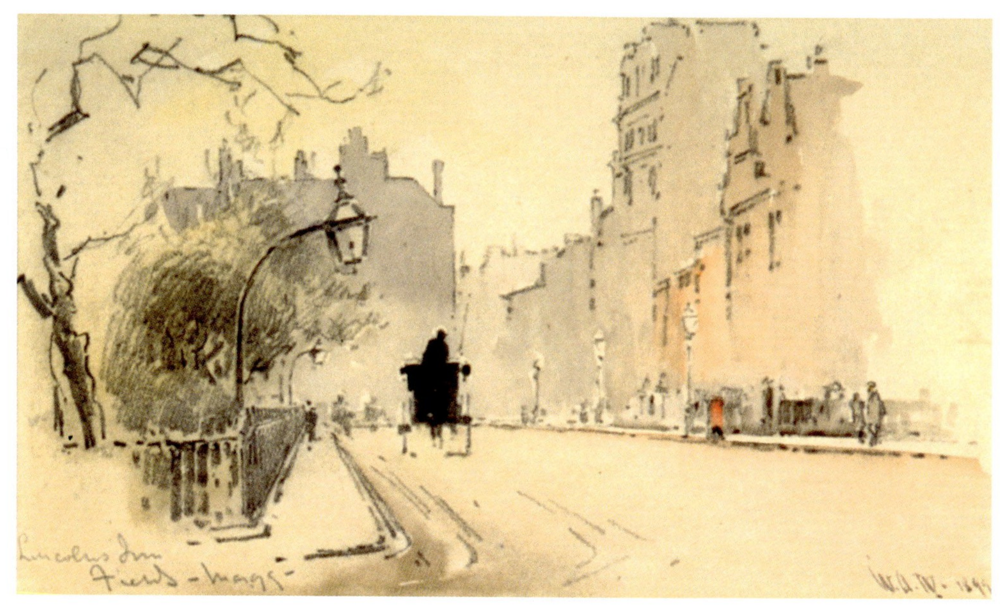

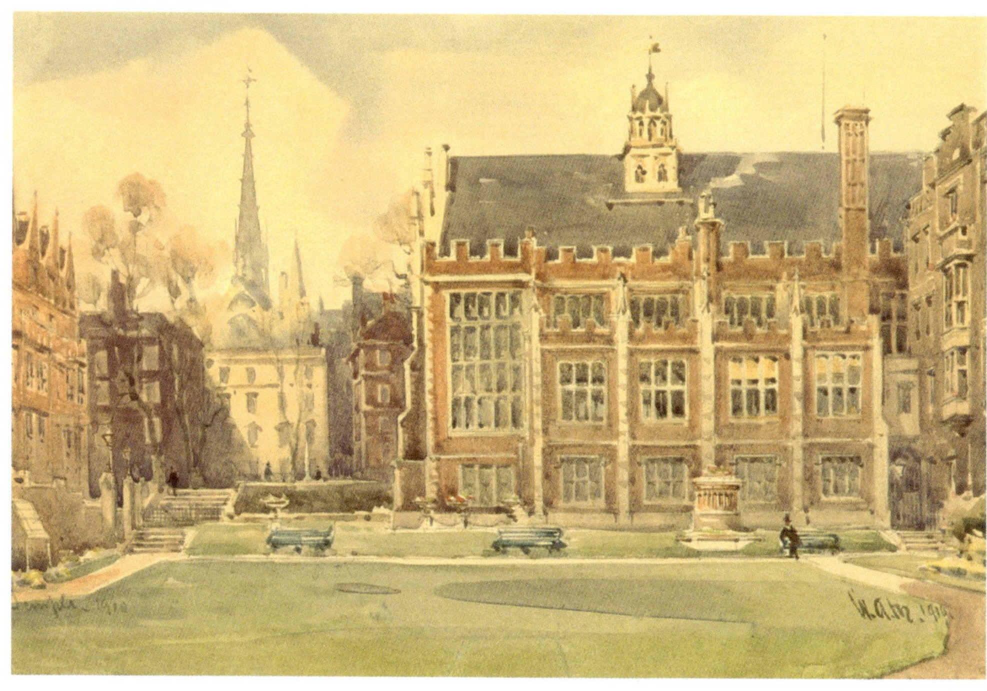

6.10 Lincoln's Inn Fields 1899

6.12 Fountain Court and Middle Temple Gardens 1910

6.9 Lincoln's Inn Fields 1910

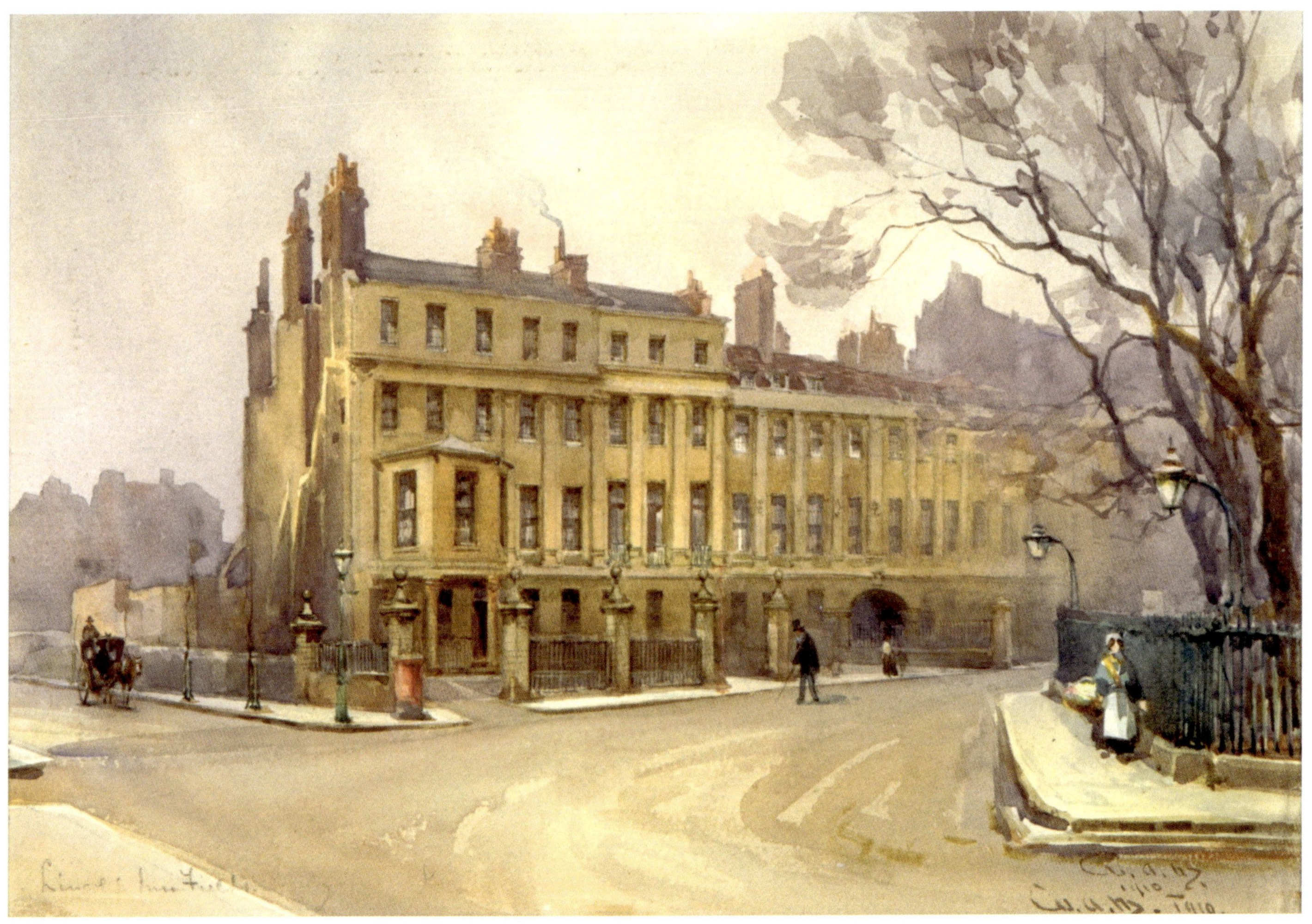

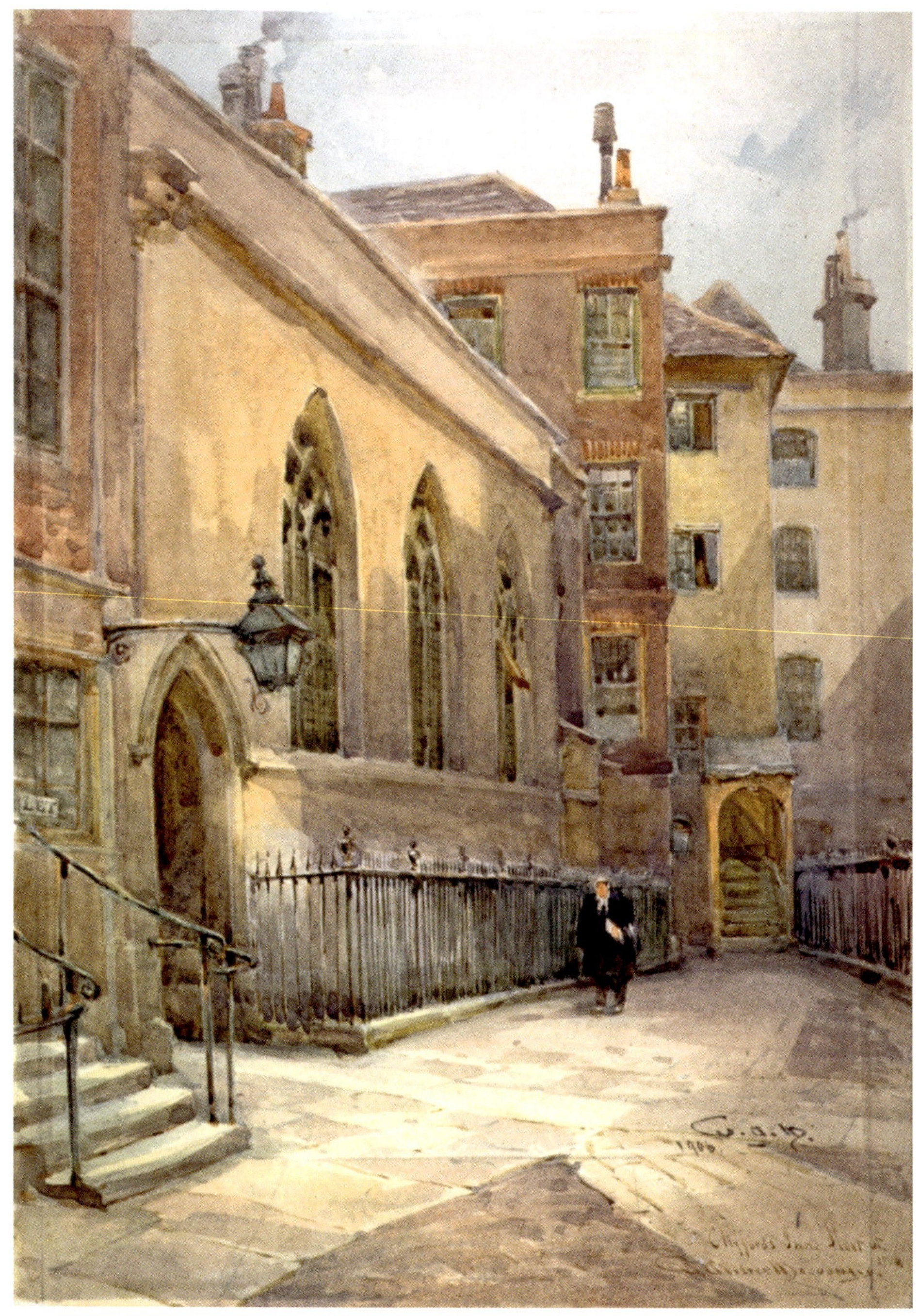

6.17 Clifford's Inn, Fleet Street 1906

6.20 Doorway in Great College Street, Westminster 1907

6.14 Field Court, Gray's Inn 1904

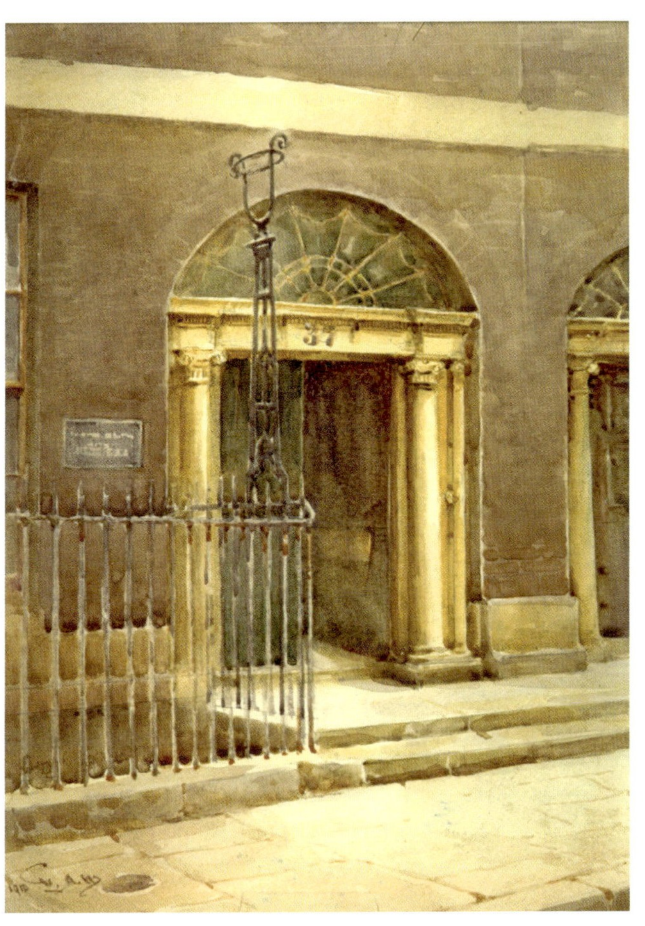

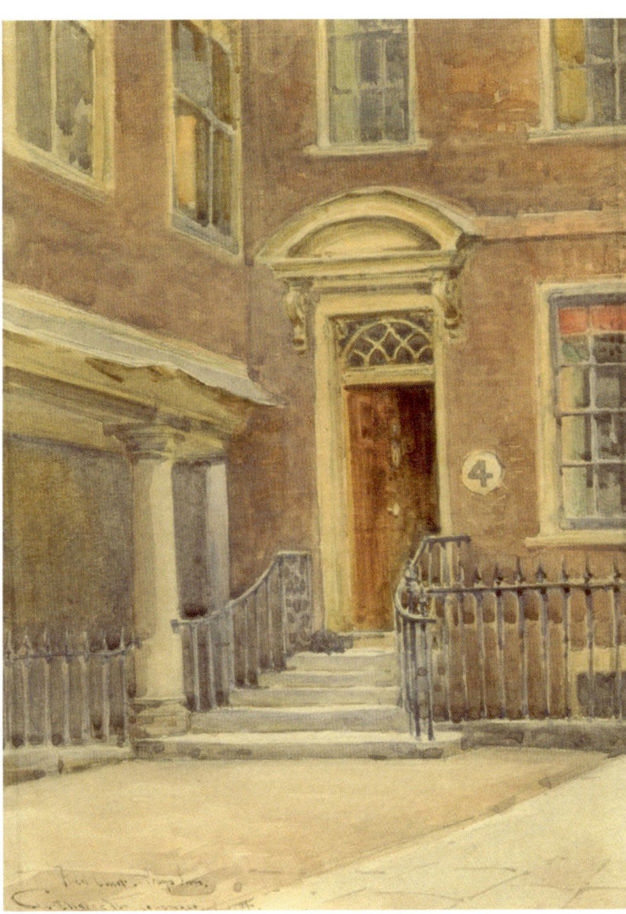

6.11 Middle Temple Lane 1901

6.13 Brick Court 1908

6.15 Staple Inn Courtyard 1906

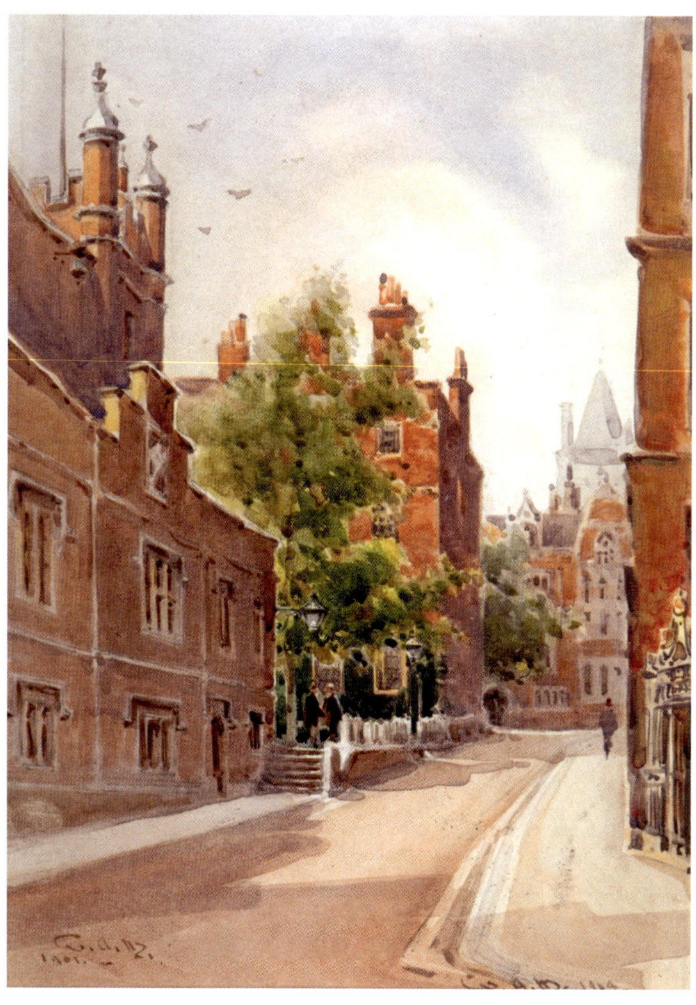

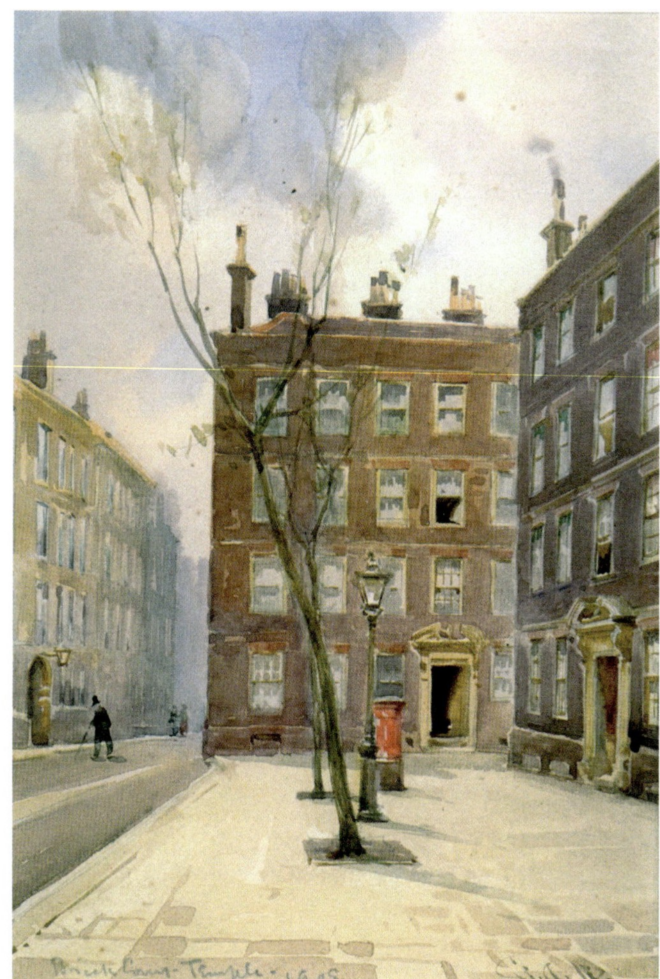

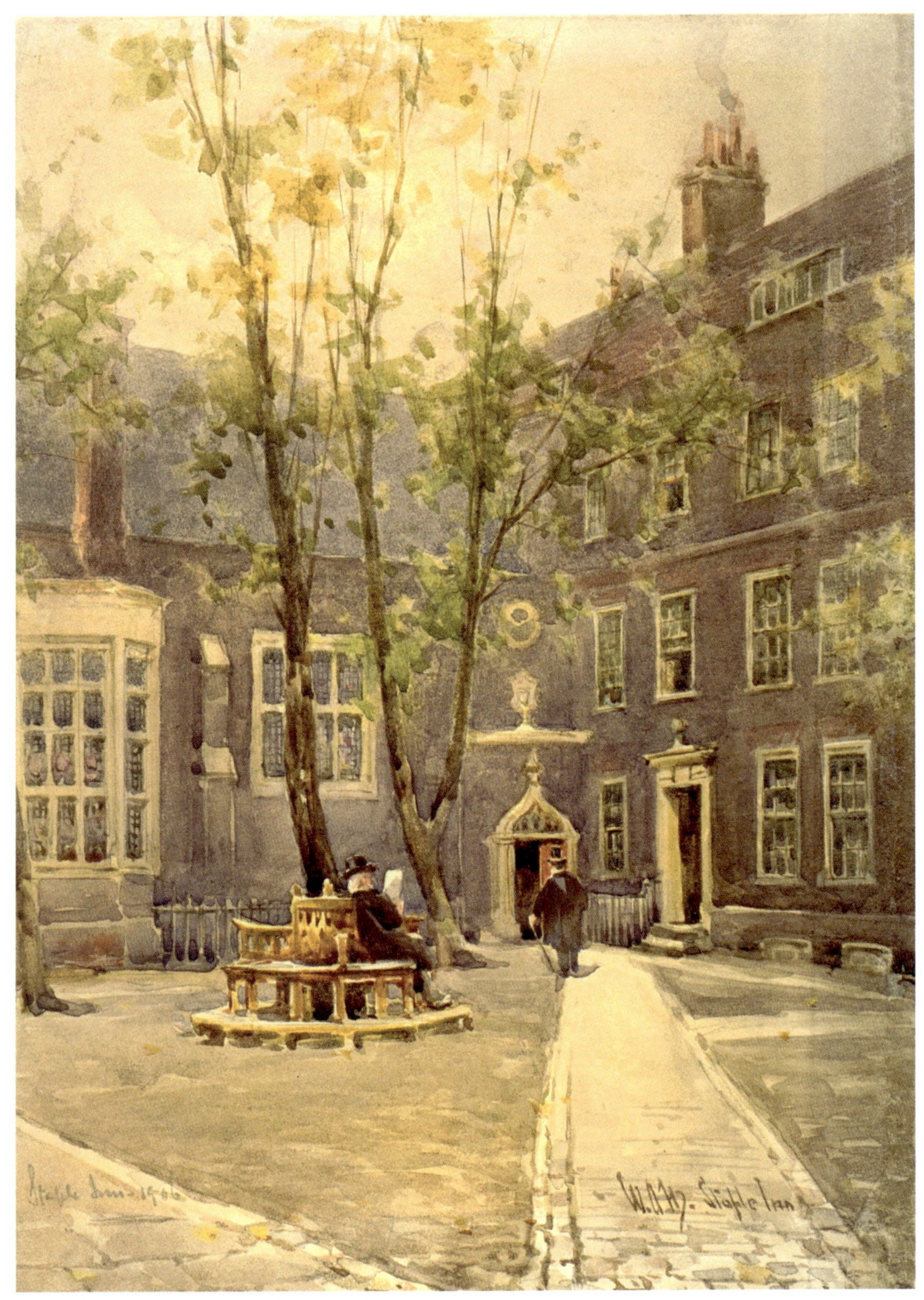

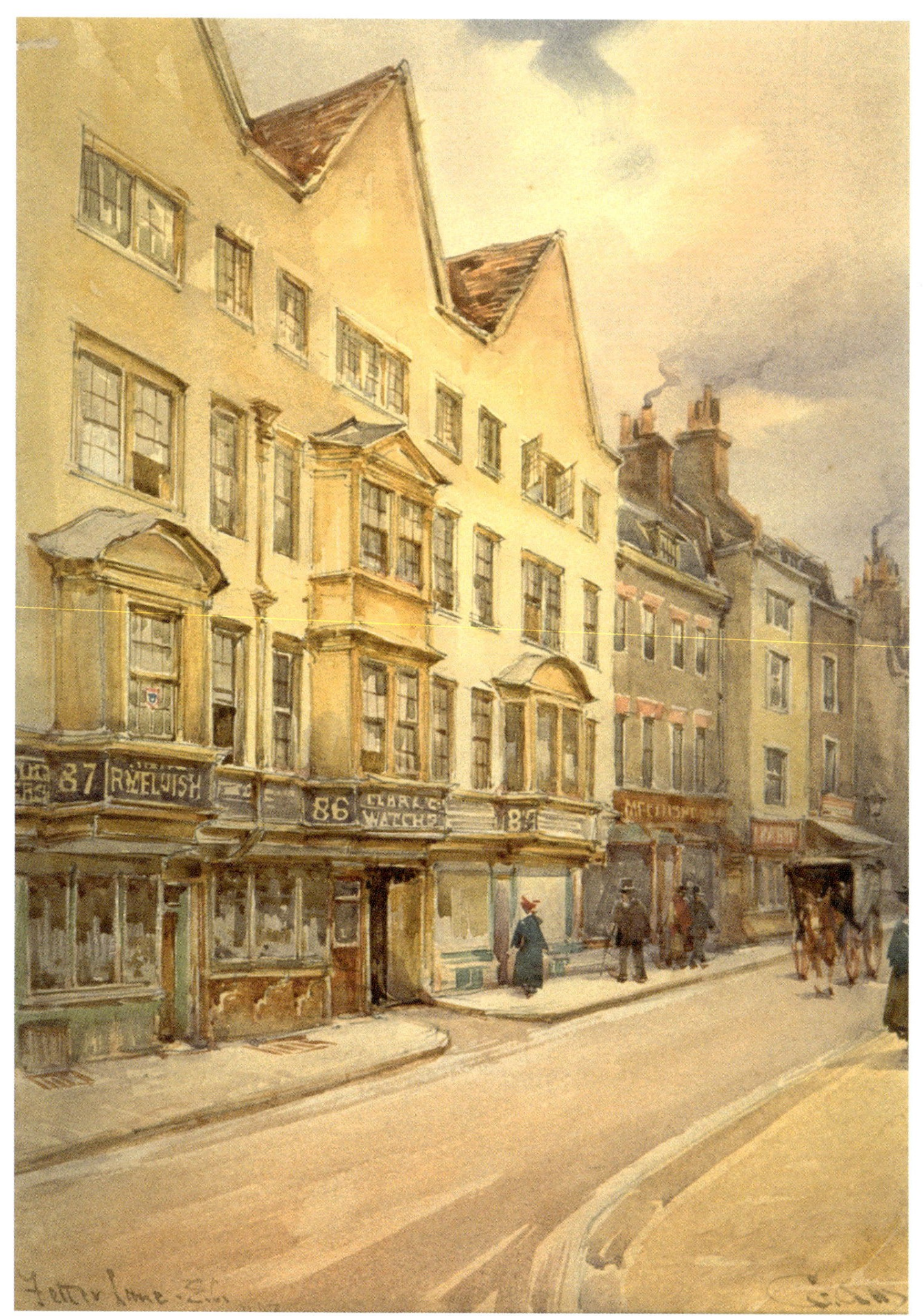

6.16 Old Houses in Fetter Lane 1907

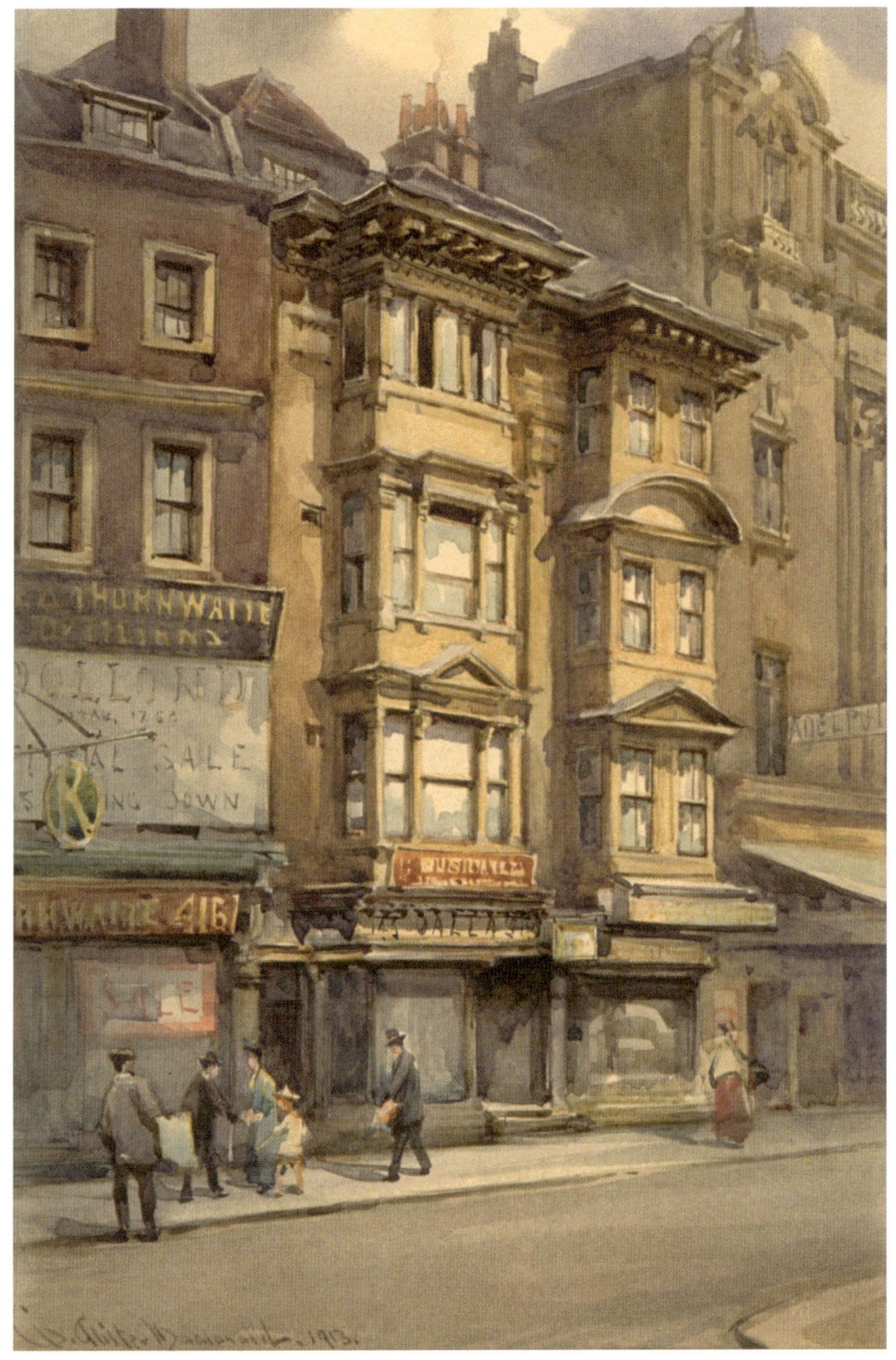

6.18 Old Houses, Strand 1913

6.19 Abingdon Street 1907

6.21 Storey's Gate, Westminster (detail) 1910

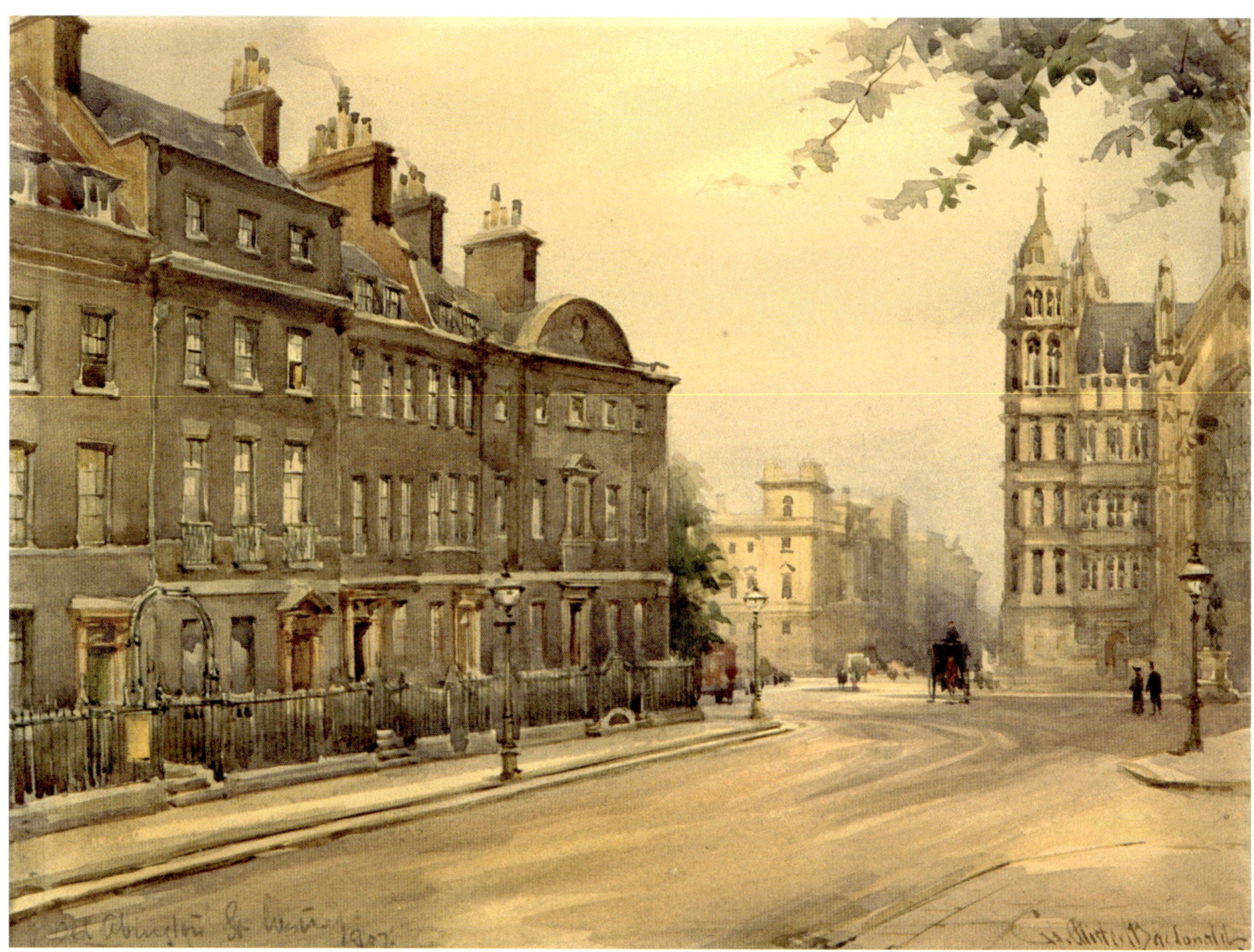

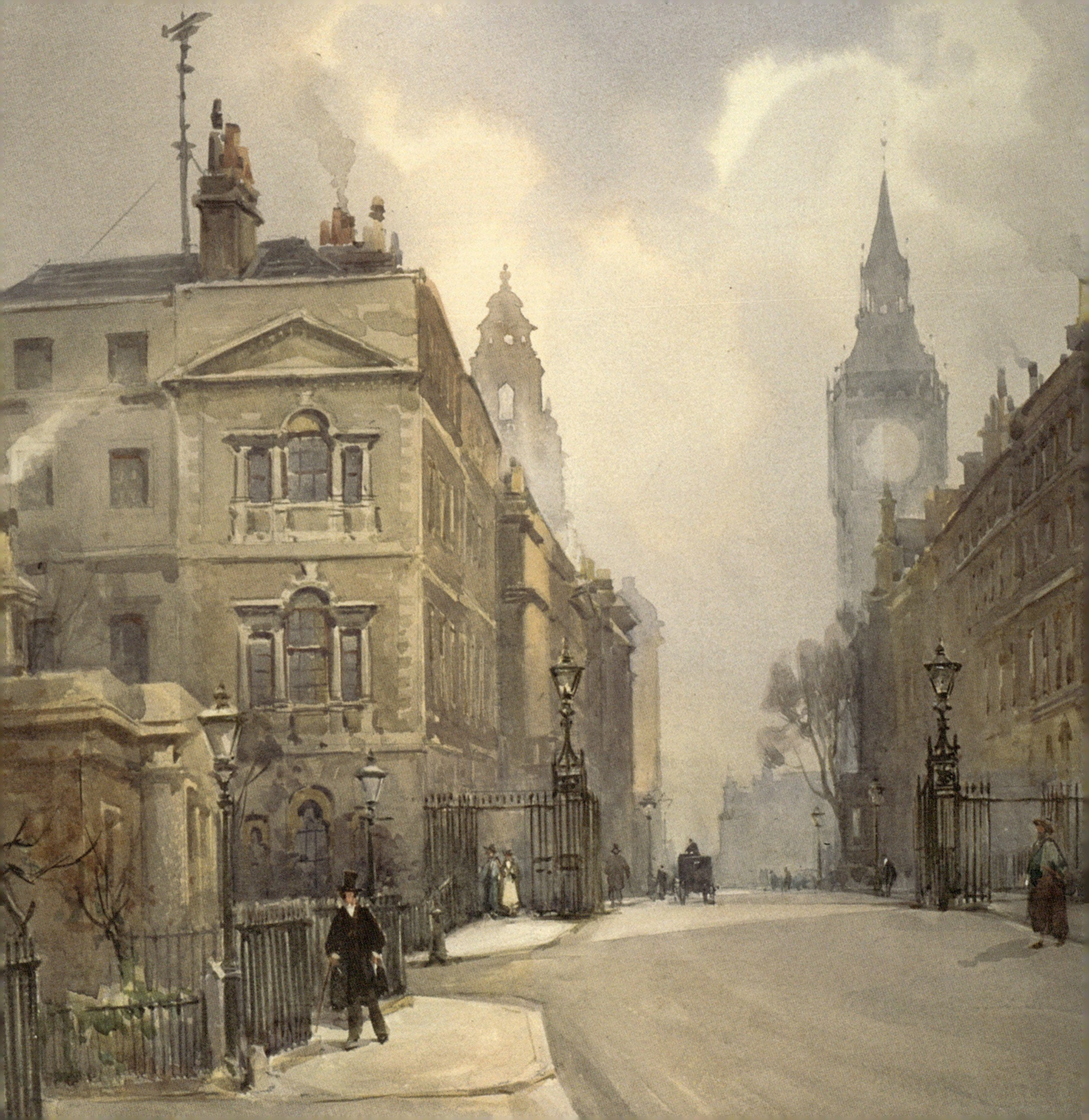

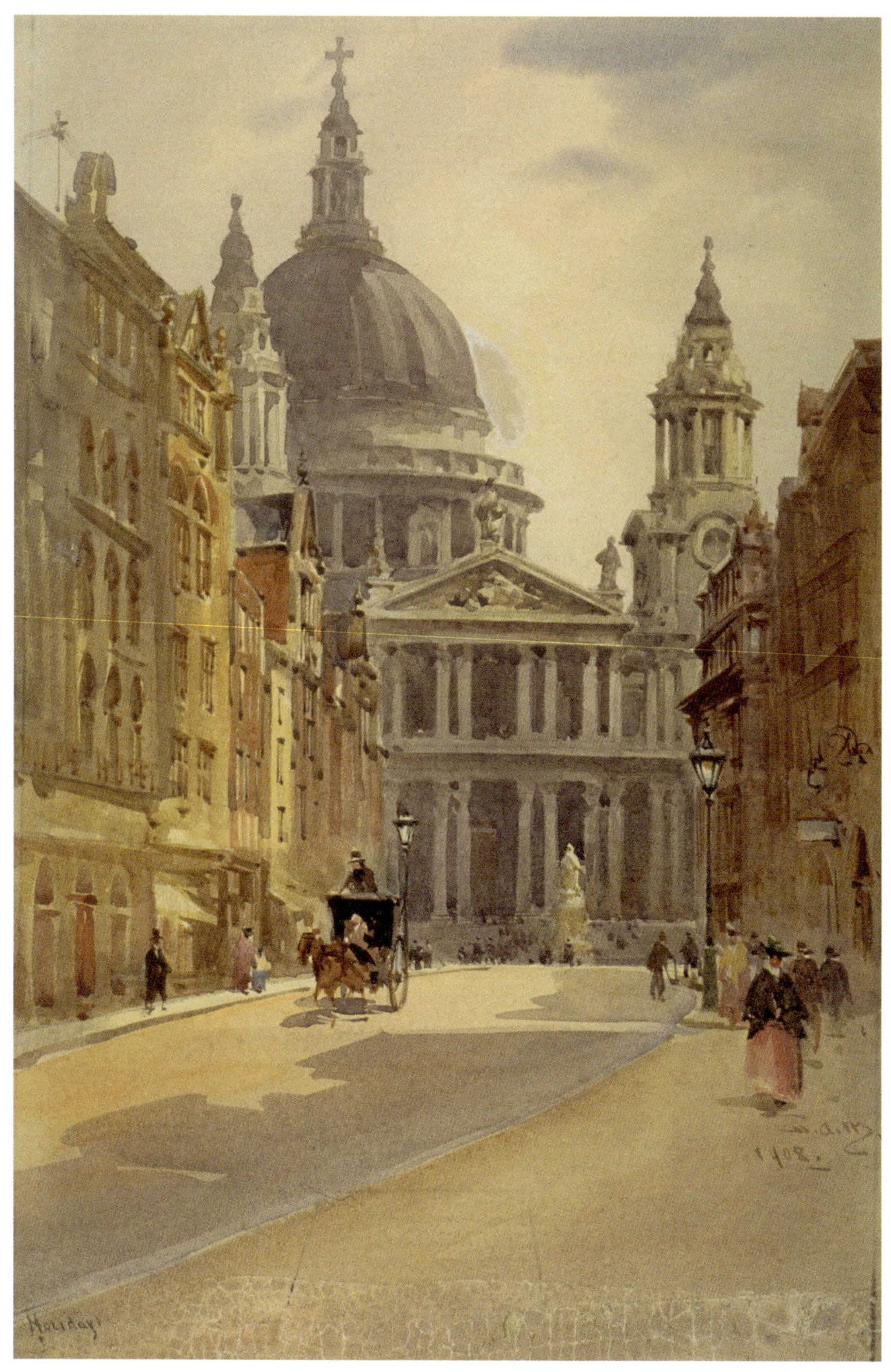

6.29 Ludgate Hill, Bank Holiday Morning 1908

6.23 Hay's Wharf, Tooley Street 1896

6.28 St Paul's from Bankside 1904

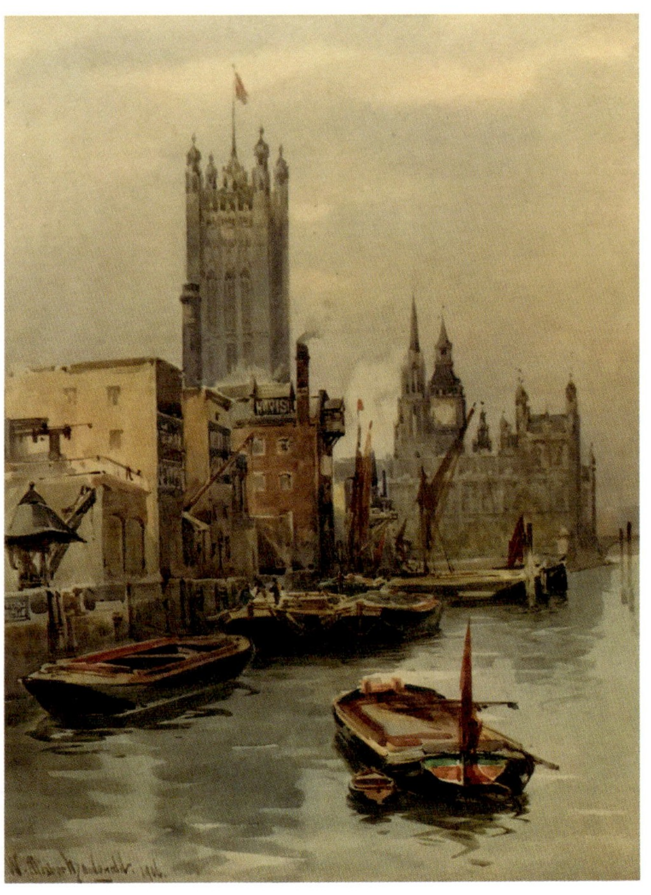

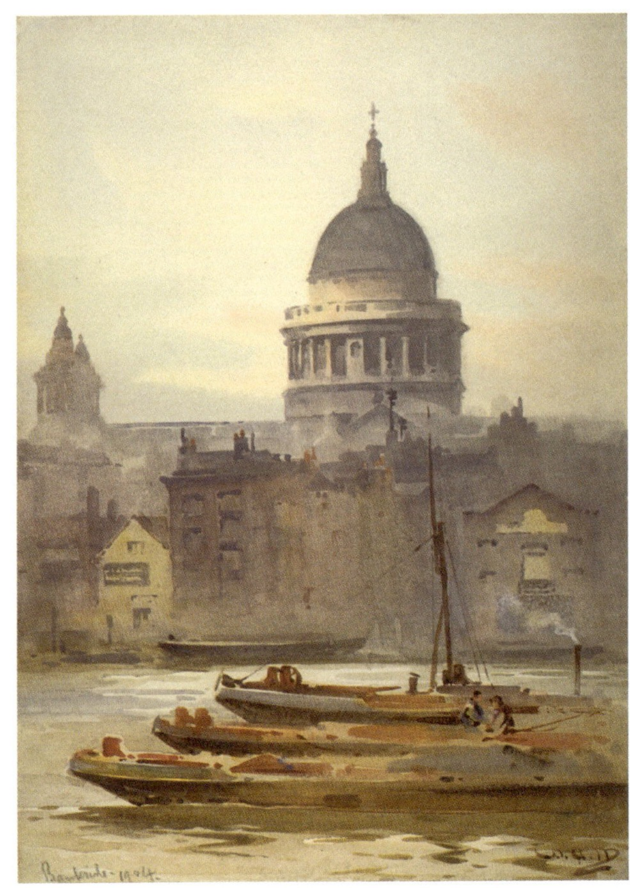

6.23 Hay's Wharf, Tooley Street 1896

6.30 The Harbour Master's House, Limehouse 1907

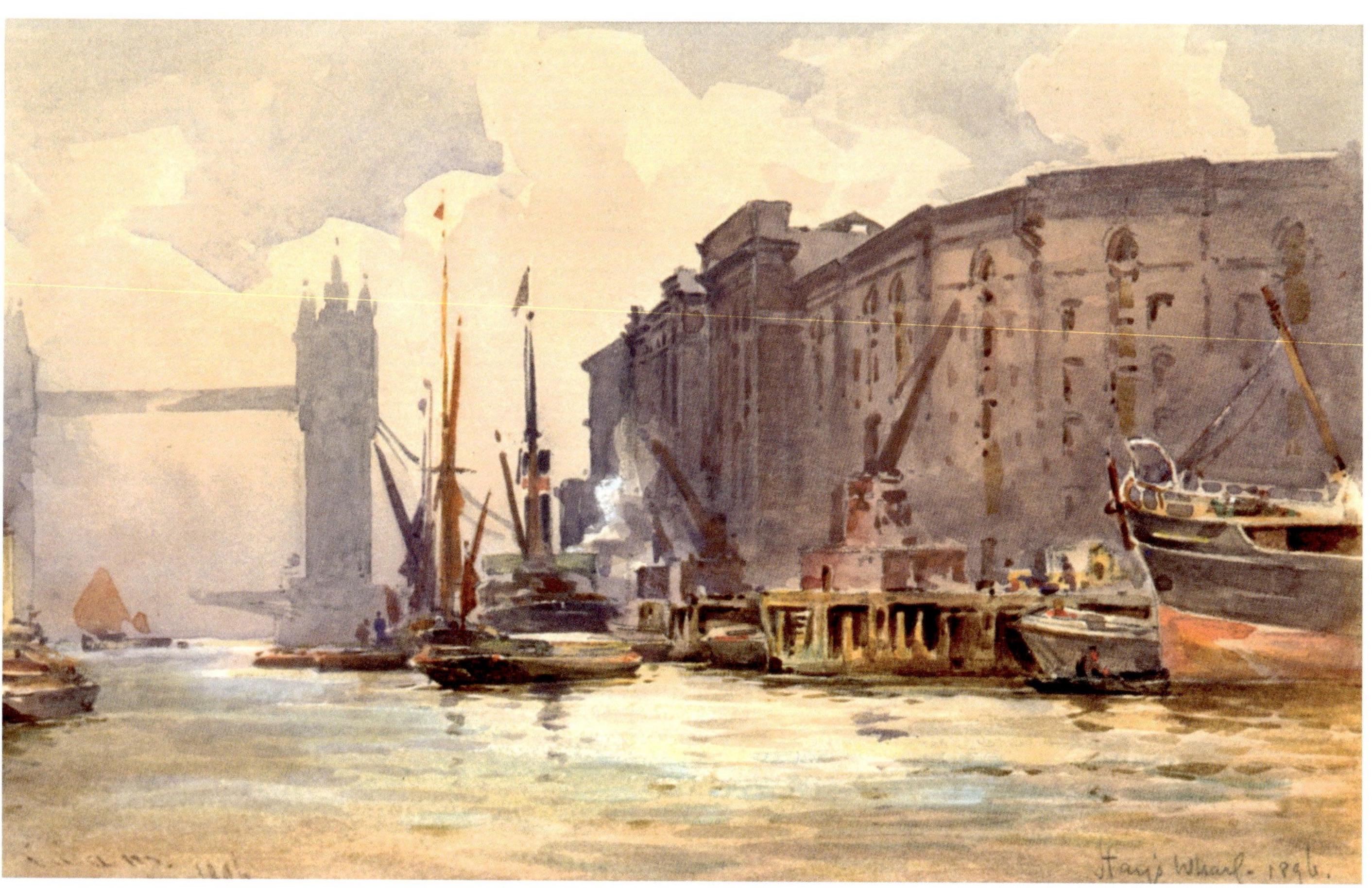

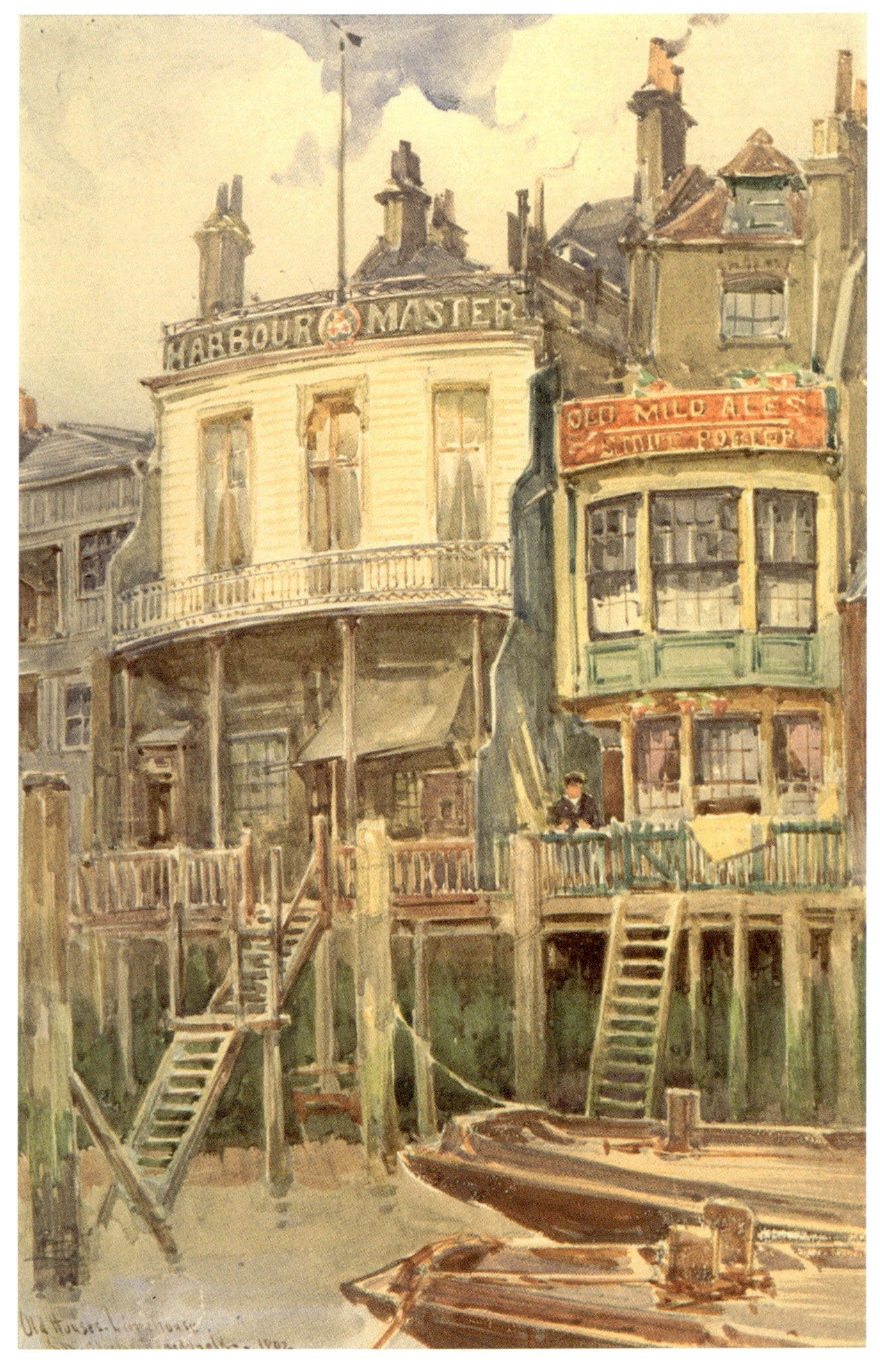
HARBOUR MASTER
OLD MILD ALES

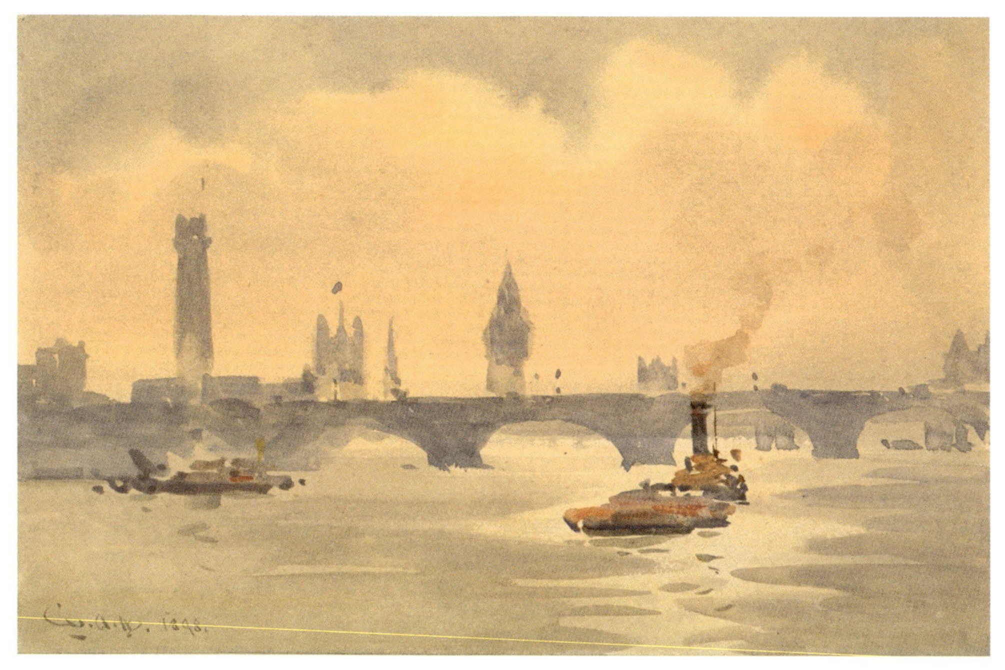

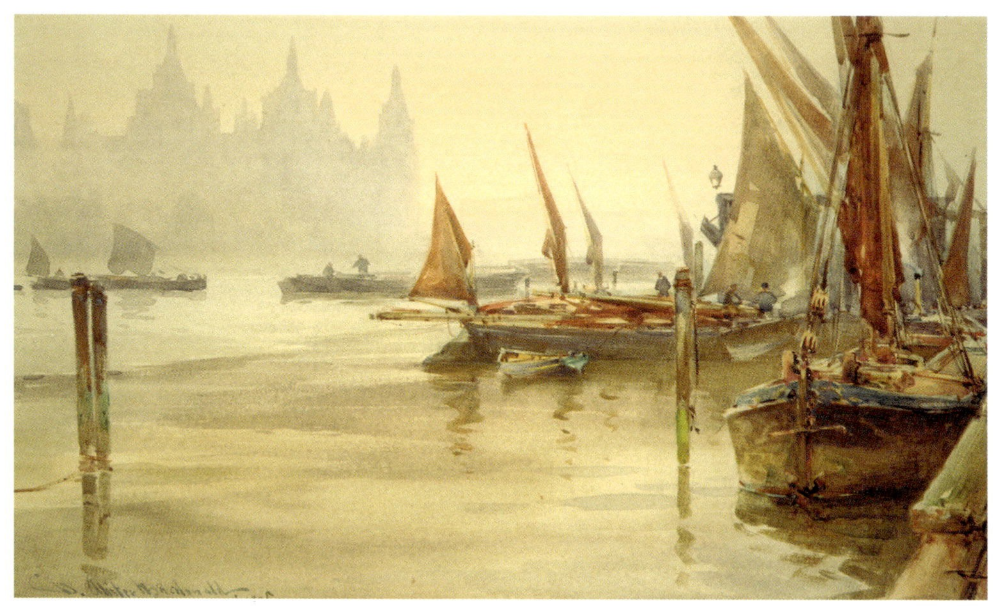

6.24 Waterloo Bridge & the River 1898

6.25 River Thames at Westminster 1905

6.26 Off the Tower 1895

6.22 Westminster Abbey and Houses of Parliament from Lambeth 1910 (OVERLEAF)

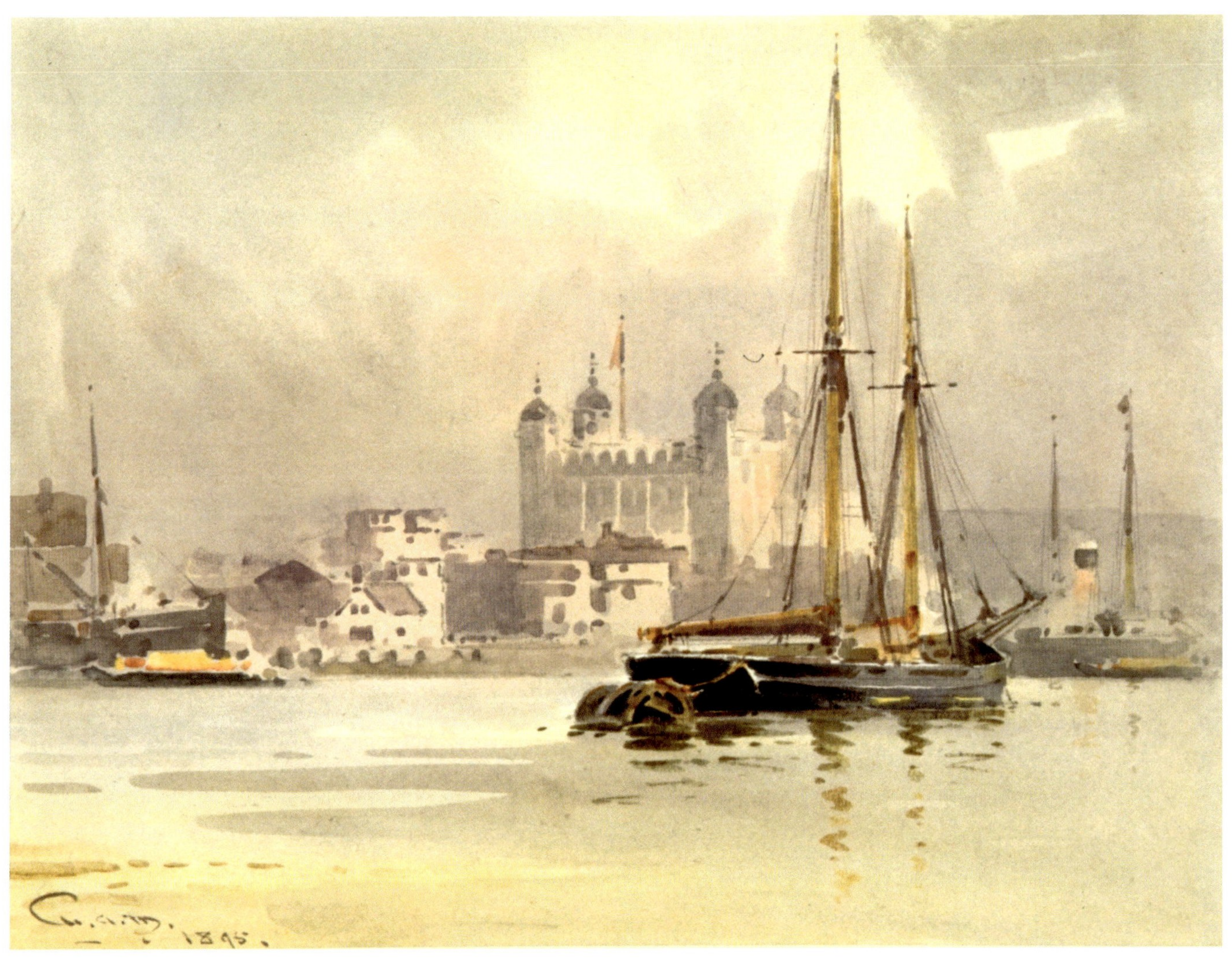

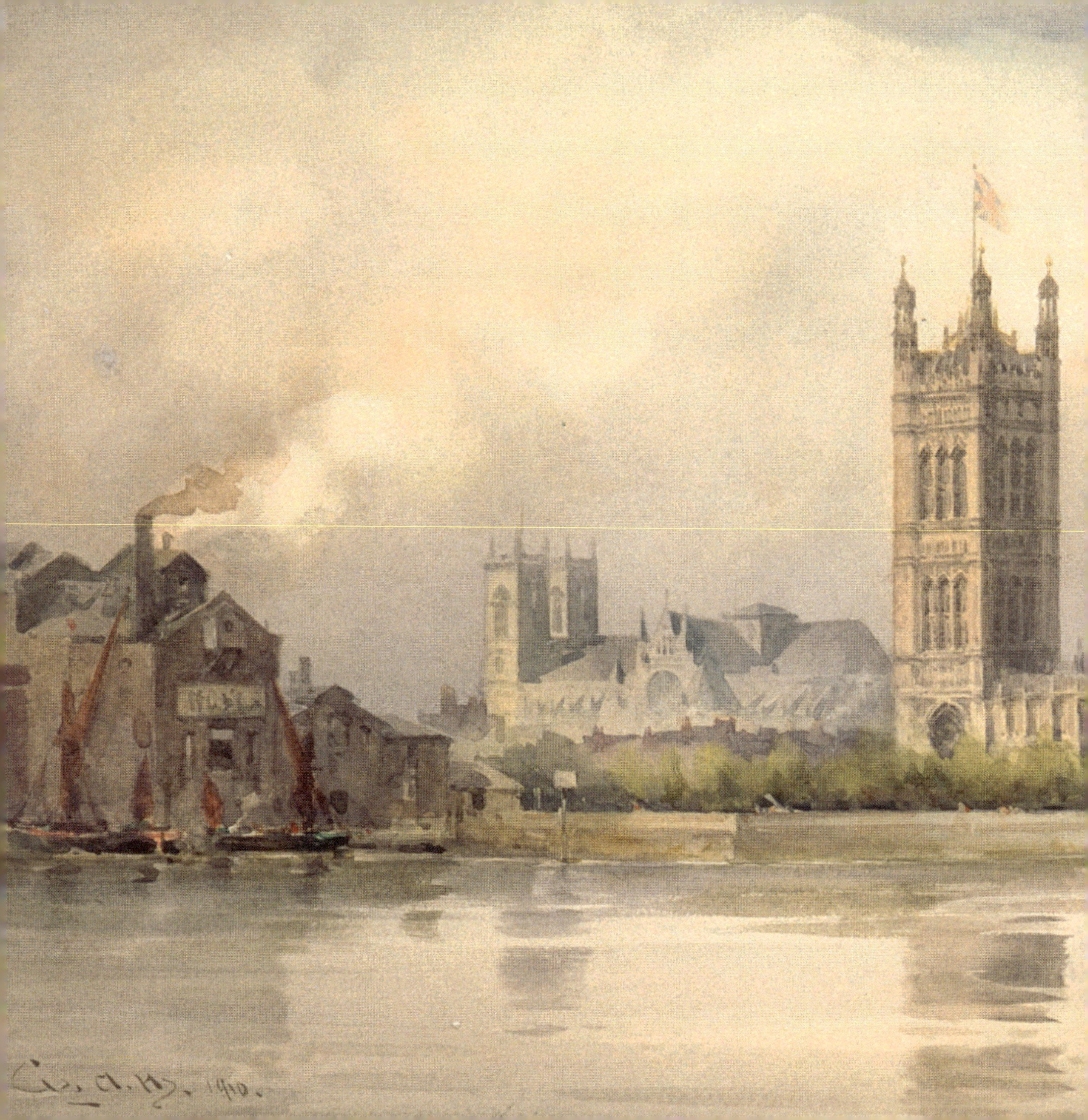

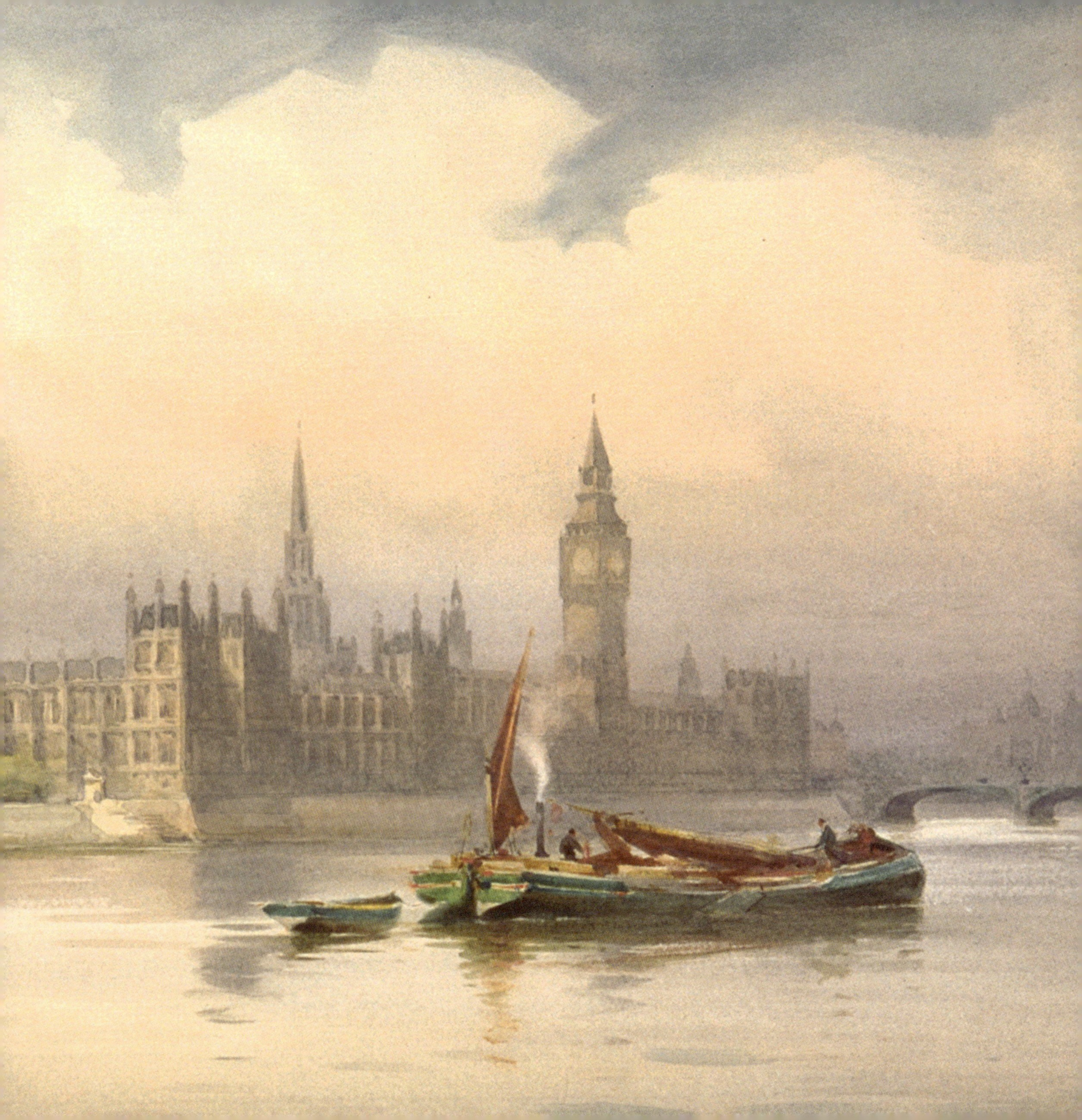

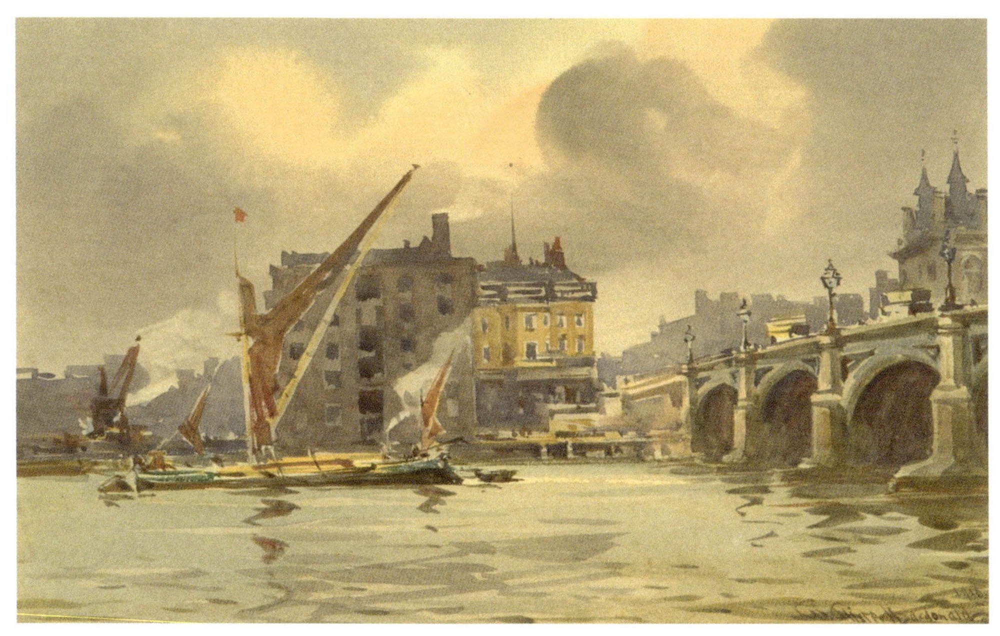

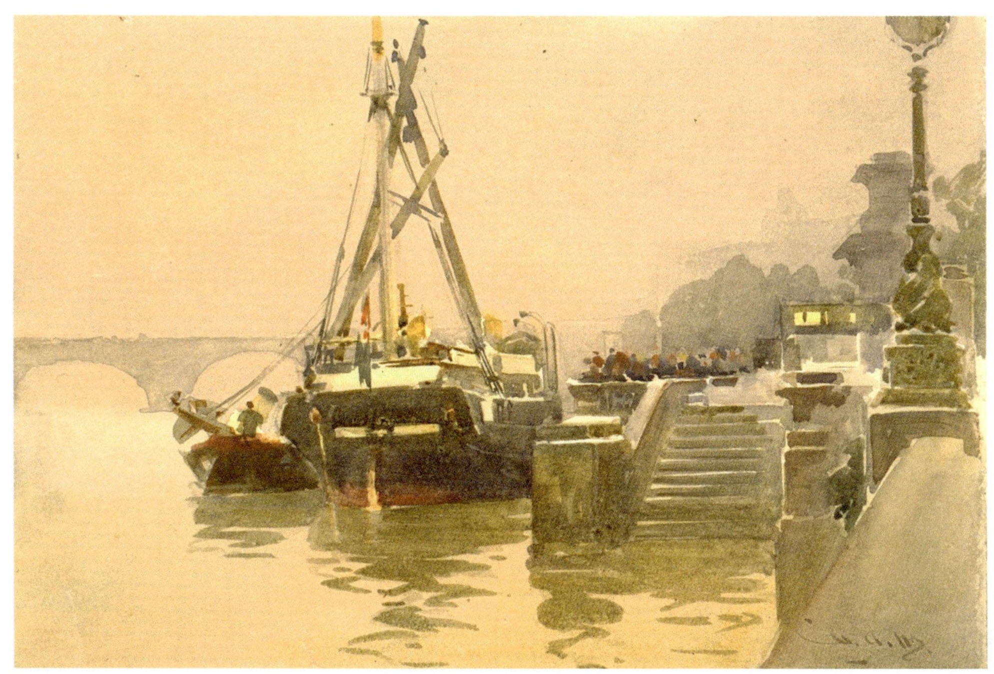

6.27 Clearing the Site for the new County Hall, Westminster 1910

6.31 The Nimrod 1910

6.32 Old Vauxhall Bridge 1898

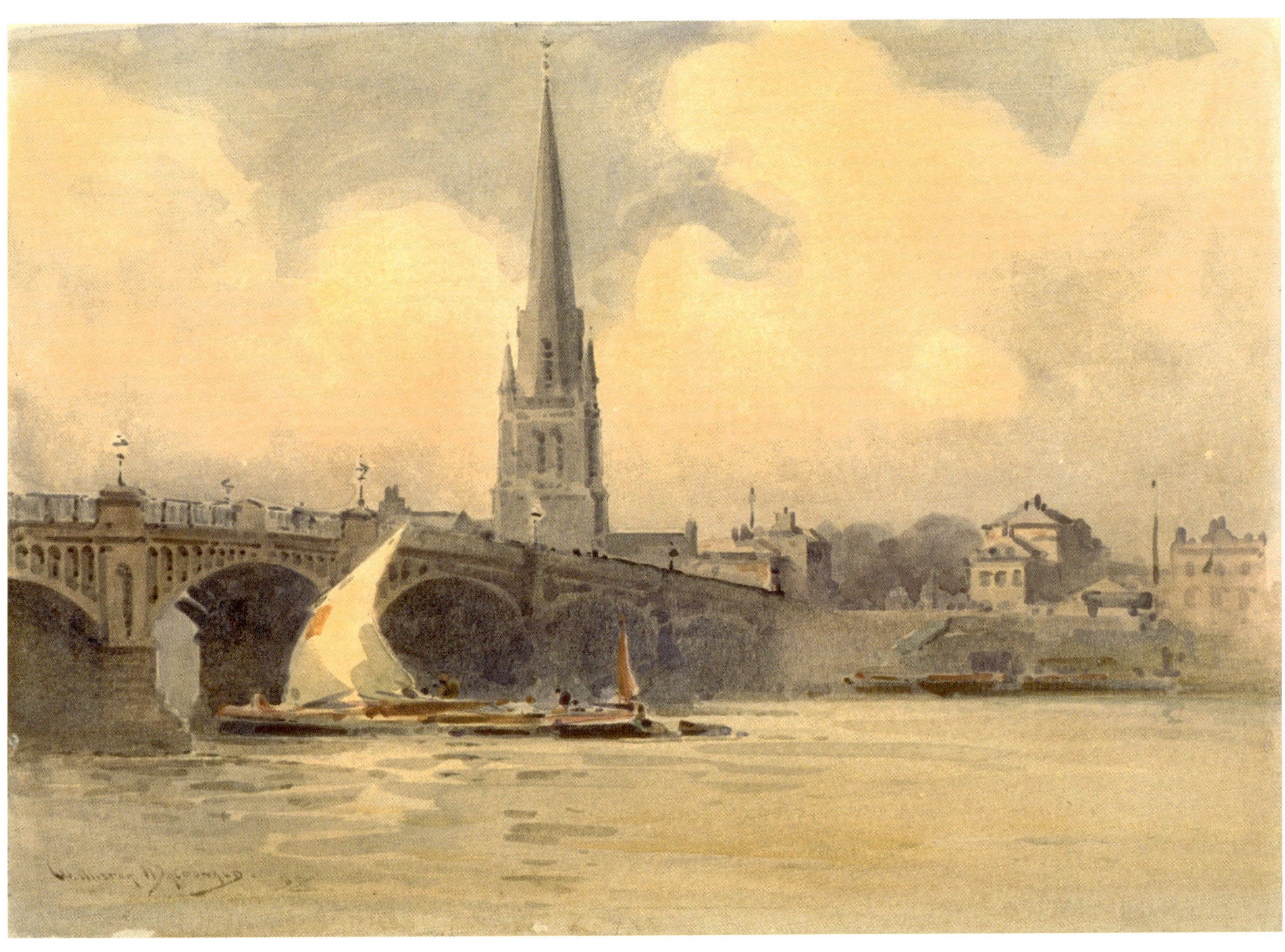

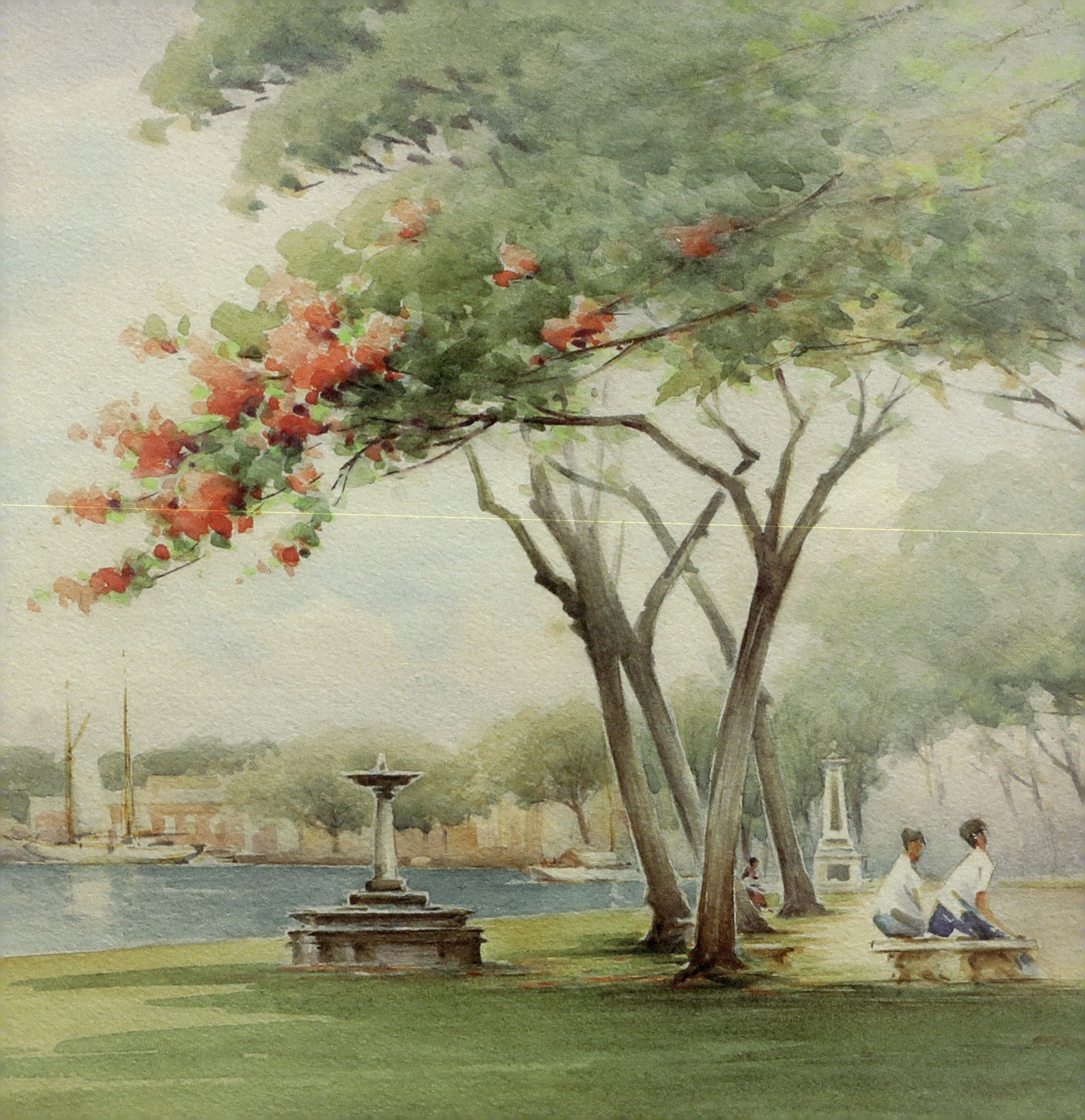

7

Back to Tahiti via America 1936

While Macdonald's return to the London art scene with three consecutive exhibitions at their Arlington Gallery were well reported and received glowing notices in *The Times*, aside from Lord Wakefield's entire purchase, the rest did not sell in large numbers. In Chancellor's book that celebrated the Wakefield Collection at the Guildhall, he (and by extension Macdonald himself) gratefully acknowledges that the paintings were 'carefully kept by Mrs Macdonald during the many and difficult years that followed after they were made ...Mrs Lucy W. Macdonald must share in our gratitude as its foreseeing preserver'.[120]

Macdonald, forever the wanderer, was soon back on the move, eager to capitalise on his work's newly acquired public recognition, and with some money in the bank. Using their contacts in the London art scene and following the wide press coverage of his exhibitions he assembled a portfolio of unsold watercolours of his pre-war wanderings in Britain, Europe, North Africa and French Polynesia, and took them to America. He departed Liverpool on 27 November 1936 on the SS *Scythia* for Boston, Massachusetts. He was likely banking on catching the popular wave of excitement and interest in Tahiti following the cinematic release of *Mutiny on the Bounty* which had become the highest grossing movie in 1935 and had won the Academy Award for Best Picture.

His exhibition of watercolours at the Robert C. Vose Gallery opened on 7 December until 9 January 1937. It featured sixty- three paintings, ranging from the pre-war period including *Old Market Cross* (1901), *Salisbury*, *Dordrecht* (1904), *Tunisian Doorway* (1912), *Snowden from Capil Curig* (1914) to his time in Tahiti with the unashamedly commercially titled *Mutiny on the Bounty Bay* (ND). This was the first and only time a collection of his British, European and North African travels had been exhibited with his Polynesian work. In December 1936 the *Boston Globe* art critic A.J. Philpott reported:

> As an example of the technical perfection of the English school of water color painting, the exhibition of W. Alister Macdonald's work...is complete.
>
> Here it is – smooth, clean, precise; one color blending into another as softly as the colors on the breast of a tropical bird; and all in a clear transparent wash. That sort of thing requires brush skill of a high order...And there are few English painters in watercolors who can equal him in the perfection of his brush work.[121] (7.1)

Philpott recognised Macdonald's love for the countryside and capturing its beauty like 'Turner, Cote and Birket Foster, charged with that spirit. There is an atmosphere in them, rather removed from "the madding crowd".' In Tahiti, he noted that this was a place that held Macdonald, where 'he found surcease from the restlessness of civilisation'.[122]

> And he liked Tahiti, as much as he had liked England, and painted it in much the same way. No two artists have ever painted the Tahitian scene the same way. It would seem as if each artist had gone there with some sort of a dreamlike ideal in his mind of what it would – or should – be. And they nearly always made the scene fit that ideal.[123]

The reviewer leaves Paul Gauguin out of his argument, but instead proposes, 'if Corot had gone to Tahiti he would have hunted around until he found something that reminded him of the banks of the Seine'.[124] He excuses Macdonald and favourably compares him to

7.1 *The Boston Globe*
Tuesday, 22 December 1936

THE BOSTON GLOBE—TUESDAY, DECEMBER 22, 1936

W. ALISTER MACDONALD SHOWING WATERCOLORS OF ENGLISH TYPE

Technical Perfection Seen in Paintings Made in Europe, North Africa and Tahiti

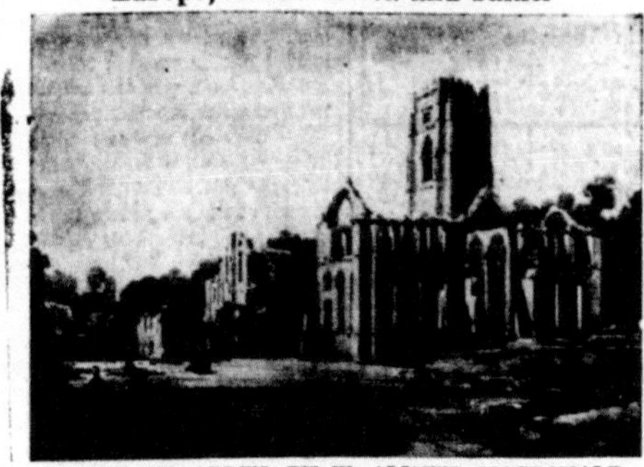

FOUNTAIN'S ABBEY, BY W. ALISTER MACDONALD

As an example of the technical perfection of the English school of water color painting, the exhibition of W. Alister Macdonald's work in the Robert C. Vose galleries in Copley sq, is complete.

Here it is—smooth, clean, precise; one color blending into another as softly as the colors on the breast of a tropical bird; and all in clear, transparent wash. That sort of thing requires brush skill of a high order. W. Alister Macdonald put in 12 years in London studying and acquiring this technique.

He is a Scotsman and first studied in Scotland. The English method fascinated him and he determined to acquire it. And there are few English painters in watercolors who can equal him in the perfection of his brush work.

He Fell in Love with English Moors

Incidentally, he fell in love with those scenes the English watercolor painters loved to portray; the Moors; the low long stretches of meadow land through which the rivers curve and placidly flow, with the town and the Gothic church tower in the distance—all against a softly-clouded sky. Turner and Cote and Birket Foster loved Irish scenes. It is a landscape domesticated by 1000 or more years of husbandry. There is nothing quite like it in the world. It has a beauty of its own.

And evidently Mr Macdonald loved it, for his English pictures are charged with that spirit. There is an atmosphere of meditative contentment in them, rather removed from "the madding crowd." He liked the old abbeys also.

Got Away From Crowds

And it was probably to get even farther away from "the madding crowd" that W. Alister Macdonald pulled up stakes and visited Holland, the Riviera, Italy, Sicily and North Africa and finally sailed away to the Southern Pacific and landed at Tahiti, where he remained about 10 years. He has interesting water colors made in the various places he visited, but Tahiti held him. There he found surcease from the restlessness of civilization.

And he liked Tahiti, mich as he had like England, and painted it in much the same way. No two artists have ever painted the Tahitian scene in anything like the same way. It would seem as if each artist had gone there with some sort of a dreamlike ideal in his mind of what it would—or should—be. And they nearly always made the scene fit that ideal.

Of course there are certain definite characteristics in the Tahitian scene that cannot very well be changed; such as the shape of the mountains, the tropical character of the vegetation and the natives. These are fundamentals.

But these fundamentals are usually incorporated into that prepossession of the artist. If Corot had gone to Tahiti he would have hunted around until he found something that reminded him of the banks of the Seine.

Beautiful Little Tahiti Scenes

In a way, of course, this is all perfectly natural and it is not surprising to find that Mr Macdonald found little bits of scenery there which reminded him a little of those English scenes he had been painting—a little more intense and tropical in color, however.

And they are certainly beautiful little scenes which he found in Tahiti, but he never lost his Scottish reserve. He never "ran wild" in his color—nor in his compositions. And it is fair to assume that one gets a fairer idea of Tahiti in there water colors than he gets even in Lafaige's work. For Mr Macdonald is at heart a realist.

And there Tahitian scenes are painted with the same scrupulous care as the English scenes—with the same fine technical skill. The exhibition is open free to the public.

A. J. Philpott.

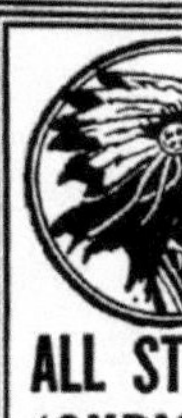

7.2 W. Alister Macdonald, personal correspondence to W.C. Thompson, 25 January 1938

the American painter John La Farge (1835–1910) who had travelled to Polynesia with Henry Adams in 1890:

> In a way, of course, this is all perfectly natural and it is not surprising to find that Mr Macdonald found little bits of scenery there which reminded him a little of those English scenes he had been painting – a little more intense and tropical in color, however.
>
> And they are certainly beautiful little scenes which he found in Tahiti, but he never lost his Scottish reserve. He never 'ran wild' in his color – nor his compositions. And it is fair to assume that one gets a fairer idea of Tahiti in there [*sic*] water colors than he gets even in Lafarge's work. For Mr Macdonald is at heart a realist.
>
> And there Tahitian scenes are painted with the same scrupulous care as the English scenes – with the same fine technical skill.[125]

Similar to Macdonald, La Farge 'was no avant-garde hero' and had a similar personal style of 'urbanity and sense of decorum',[126] but the American artist only spent a matter of months in Tahiti, whereas Macdonald had lived there for a period of fourteen years at that time. La Farge only accomplished thirty-six paintings while in Tahiti, and his vividly hued and somewhat clichéd work was successfully directed at collectors in New York, Boston and even Paris, whereas Macdonald sold locally in Tahiti before returning to London.

Priced between $40 and $125 the Vose Gallery ledger records only four sales, one gifted and three returned. The Vose archive also holds later correspondence between Macdonald and the gallery manager Mr W.C. Thompson in January and February 1938 following his return to Tahiti (7.2). Thompson writes: 'You were most kind to present the Eton College to Billy and I assure you he will be more than pleased with it.'[127] It was a generous gift as its list price was $75. Macdonald is also evidently active as an art dealer in works by other artists, as he has a 'Rowlandson' that he is seeking an

Box. 202.
P.O. Papeete-Tahiti.
French Oceanie.

25. Jan. 38.

Dear Mr Thompson

Your letter of 1. Nov. can only be answered now. Our mails are very irregular!

Have written Mr Croie that you will send on the rest of the Drawings as soon as possible. I am sorry he did not have them all at once! But that cannot now be helped.

Please let me know what I owe you for expenses.

Will you please accept of the Eton Drawing for your boy. Shall be so pleased.

And perhaps you will send me back the Raolandoon. As it does not meet with the approval of U.S.A. Dealers. I can repair the damage in a few minutes. Tis caused by a little insect we have here, having a partiality for Colour!!

I hope things are moving upwards with you &

American buyer for. This is likely to be a lithograph by the English caricaturist Thomas Rowlandson (1756–1827) celebrated for his political and social satire. Unfortunately, no one will offer more than £2, perhaps because it is slightly damaged and so it is returned to Macdonald, who replies: 'I can repair the damage in a few minutes. Tis caused by a little insect we have here, having a partiality for colours!!'[128]

A year later, five days after the outbreak of war in Europe, he writes to Mr Thompson and offers a Manet that he has acquired from a small auction house in London. The letter, similar to correspondence to his younger brother Sinclair in 1918, shows he has not lost his appetite to openly display his opinions on world affairs (and other artists), which in hindsight seem naïvely optimistic:

> 8 Sept '39
>
> Dear Mr Thompson,
> The 'Rowlandson' arrived all safely, and thank you so very much. I was very pleased to see it again, as it has associations for me.
>
> Your Mr Vose wrote me from Liverpool + was to have sailed on the 3rd. I hope he gets through all safely. But one can't trust those diabolical Huns. He wrote me a very charming letter which I am acknowledging.
>
> I think we had better call off the possible Ex(hibition) Things are now far too much in the air + we wait patiently for developments.
>
> It wont last very long. Deserted by Japan. Spain + Italy on the fence. Hitler has his job cut out for him: T Monsieur Gamelin (Commander in Chief of French Armed Forces) will give him fits on the Western Front. Germany wont like being invaded, nor will she enjoy short commissions and ere long she will tire of the present regime - + kick!
>
> And we, the French, are really doing things well this time. Experience has been gained. And if we can but smash the submarine horror, things will move.

Thank you very much for your most kind letter + all your courteous interest. And I hope business will improve with you.

I don't think your Gov. will keep up its non supply of armaments re. for long.

All quiet down here in the depths of the country. London has been badly scared, but is recovering as the defence seems good.

Best of good wishes + very many thanks

Very sincerely yours

W. Alister Macdonald

I got a lovely Manet oil. A woman in Spanish dress, with a fan when in London: prowling around auction rooms – But not in Christies!!

Tis a great joy to me. Its marvellous directions of touch + technique, + depth of colour! As for this rage for Cezanne I don't understand it! He could not paint, nor draw.

But the critics are wonderful!

WAM[129]

Vancouver to Tahiti

The front page of Vancouver newspaper the *Daily Province* on 4 February 1937 informs us that 'One of Famous "Bounty" Writing Team is in City', James Norman Hall, on his way back to Tahiti accompanied by his wife Sarah and daughter Nancy Hall, Mrs W.W. Atwater and 'W. Alister Macdonald, an artist who illustrated Mr. Hall's book, *The Tale of a Shipwreck*.' (7.3) It locates a photograph now on display in the James Hall Museum in Tahiti, as Macdonald, Mrs Hall and daughter Nancy are dressed for winter in front of a Vancouver department store. (7.4)

> Then there is Nancy, a daughter who announces proudly that she is six and half and, in the same breath, demands to be taken out to play in the snow. Snow is a novelty to Nancy and

One of Famous 'Bounty' Writing Team Is In City

J. N. Hall Sailing for Papeete to Get Back To Work—Tells How He and Partner Work on Book—Plans Botany Bay Story.

By TORCHY ANDERSON.

THERE'S an often-repeated legend to the effect that the South Seas leave a white man with more ambition to lie on his back sipping long drinks than to work.

It's very much a legend so far as James Norman Hall, Iowa-born author, who has collaborated with Charles Nordhoff to write a series of modern best-sellers that ride the literary seas in the wake of the good ship "Bounty."

Mr. Hall is in Vancouver, impatient to sail back to Papeete and work. For eight months he has been on this continent. He can't settle down to work here.

Legendary lassitude of the tropics?

Mr. Hall never felt it and his partner, Nordhoff, takes time off from writing to climb the most difficult peaks of Tahiti.

FAMOUS LITERARY TEAM.

How does this Hall-Nordhoff combination, one of the most famous teams of modern literature, work?

"Well," answers Mr. Hall, "you see, we have both much the same outlook on life, seem to see things in about the same light.

"We do a lot of talking first—hit on the subject, discuss the plot. When we have the story well in mind we go to work. It develops and we do about 50-50 on the work on a book. Nordhoff does most of the sea stuff—he knows it.

"I can't remember without looking at a copy just how we divided up 'Pitcairn Island' but it worked out that we did alternate bits. The big fight? Well, we both had a hand in parts of that. That bit where they chased the crazy sailor across the island? That was mine."

DOES NOT LOOK HIS AGE.

Slender, brown-eyed, wearing a close-clipped mustache, Mr. Hall does not look the 50 years he owns to—that despite a touch of grey in his black hair. Incidentally, his writing partner is the same age.

With him awaiting sailing is his wife, a charming brunette whose conversation carries a telltale French accent.

Then there is Nancy a daughter who announces proudly that she is six and a half and, in the same breath, demands to be taken out to play in the snow. Snow is a novelty to Nancy and her mother. This trip is the first time either of them has seen it. Nancy will tell you that she left her brother, 10, at school in California.

WAIT TILL SHIP SAILS.

"Don't write about my dad until after the ship sails, then he won't have a lot of people looking for him," she gravely instructed The Daily Province.

With the Halls also Tahiti-

(Continued on Page 2.)
See BOUNTY.

Flood Relief Gains $400 as Ginger Sells Kiss

HOLLYWOOD, Feb. 4.—(UP)—A kiss for Ginger Rogers brought $400 on the open market here last night.

Ginger auctioned off her kisses to the highest bidder, and Harold Lloyd bought the privilege after outbidding Cary Grant. It was all for the benefit of the mid-western flood sufferers.

The benefit, staged by screen celebrities, netted $12,000 in all.

Snow Clearanc[e] Record Total

Work of Removal H[...] Days of Em[...]

Winter is costing the City of Vancouver more than it has ever done before and if streets are clogged by new falls of snow the inclement season may make a serious dent in the civic budget.

More than $30,000 has so far been spent in keeping clear the roads, gutters and catch basins and in sanding icy streets.

This sum, all of which has been expended since the second week in January, when "extras" were first employed on city gangs, is six times more than the snow appropriation in the average winter.

The record snow cost set by recent falls may be still further heightened if feathery flakes continue to besiege the city.

HELPS UNEMPLOYED.

There is a brighter side to the snow picture, however, an aspect that is better appreciated among the unemployed.

Since snow first fell on the city more than 3000 days' labor have been offered to workless by the city engineering department. The "extras," who supplement regular engineering department gangs, earn

7.3 *The Daily Province*, 4 February 1937

> her mother. This trip is the first time either of them has seen it. Nancy will tell you that she left her brother, 10, at school in California.[130]

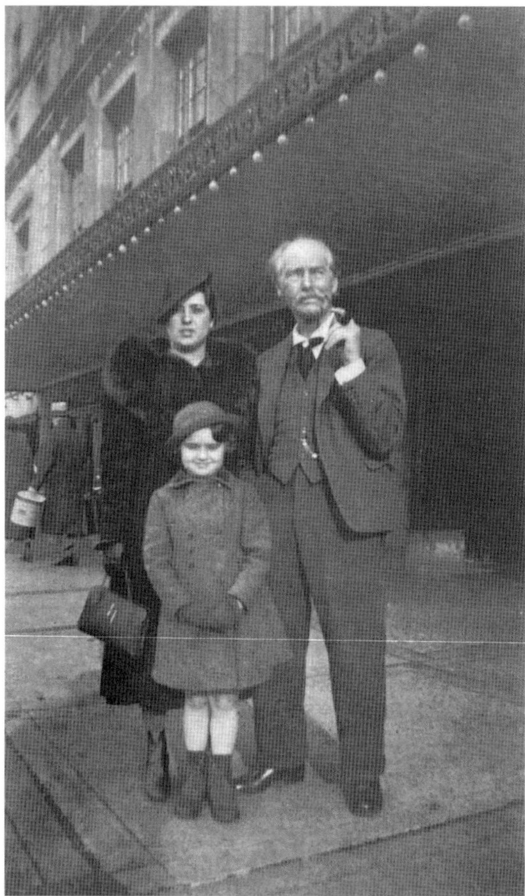

7.4 Mrs Hall, Nancy Hall and W.A. Macdonald, Vancouver 1936

In 1937 the 'most sought after mode of transport'[131] to make the transcontinental journey of 2,886 miles across Canada from Montreal to Vancouver was by Canadian Pacific Railway, which took over five days. Unfortunately, unlike Macdonald's first voyage to Tahiti in 1921, there are no surviving sketches or proof of this journey, but it would have been a spectacular view from the newly air-conditioned observation car of the Rockie Mountains and prairie fields. It is easy to imagine the forthright and social artist engaging in conversation with the international company to be found in the dining car, when sharing a meal or afternoon tea, or in one of the adjoining solarium-lounge cars named after rivers, such as the River Clyde and Thames, to enjoy his favourite pastime of smoking his pipe.

Return to Tahiti

There is no doubt that Macdonald returned to Tahiti with the Hall family in February 1937, but there is some conflict of memory and evidence regarding who was with him. In a written account his daughter Avril recalls a meeting in this period, and discussion she had with her father and a woman pertaining to be the 'mother of his deceased son':

> My father returns 5 years later with a lady who claimed to be the mother of his deceased son. They live in Paea where I go to see him from time to time. He wants me back and offers me to go back to England with him to continue my studies. I don't want to because I prefer to stay with my mother. He continues to paint, travels a lot in the islands of Polynesia, then ends up leaving. He returned to Scotland or England and stayed for many years. He writes to me from time to time to give news and to hear from me.[132]

There is no record of Lucy Macdonald on any ship manifests at that time and she is not mentioned in the *Daily Province* newspaper report previously mentioned. Their Bond Street gallery never closed and remained in business. Arlington Gallery catalogues held in the National Art Library at the Victoria and Albert Museum show a busy schedule of exhibitions: ten in 1937, eleven in 1938, and nine in 1939. The range of artists, many female such as Mrs W.M.N. Brunton RMS, watercolourists, portraits and oils remains consistent. Either she left very strict instructions after planning a long programme of exhibitions, or she did not leave London and was once again left to hold the fort alone. That does not explain Avril's recollection, and so perhaps another English woman stepped in to support Macdonald in his plea to adopt Avril? Had Avril returned to England with her father they would likely have come face to face with prejudice at best, or in some quarters racism and bigotry amongst British society with a morality code at odds with Tahiti's values and social customs.
For his grandchildren and their families still living in Tahiti and Moorea there is no doubt that Avril's decision to remain with her mother was the right one.

> The story is an old one, repeated over and over again in every group: the white cross; the half-white children at the parting of the ways; their turning aside from the stony path of their father's race to the pleasant ways of the mother. And so the end of the strain of white, further diluted with each succeeding generation, shows itself in nothing more than a name... seldom used and oftentimes forgotten. It is Nature at work, and she is not always cruel.[133]

A few years later Nordhoff and Hall wrote *The Dark River* (1938), a story that may have been inspired by Macdonald's circumstances discussed with his friend Hall on their voyage back to Tahiti from Vancouver. The book, like many of its predecessors, highlights the innate racism and bigotry of many Europeans at the time. The story centres around the tragedy and romance of two young lovers,

7.5 Vue de Papeete 1938

one English and the other brought up as a native Tahitian. The drama revolves around the dynamics of mixed marriages, how they are perceived differently in Tahiti and in Britain's polite society, and the wrench of leaving and returning home, be it Tahiti or Britain. 'The mere thought of his son's marrying a girl with native blood in her veins would be horrible to him.'[134]

Written around the time Macdonald returned to Tahiti to seek the adoption of his Tahitian daughter, there are some parallels that can be drawn from the book. Without straining the coincidence of the timing, and the friendship that Macdonald shared with the writers, it is possible that the 'MacLeod' story may have had some inspiration from Macdonald's own life. A father returns from England to seek the return of his English son, and to abandon his Tahitian baby with the native family, but unlike the bigot 'General MacLeod', Macdonald was not in the least racist and saw no social impediment to bringing his Tahitian daughter back to England to complete her secondary education. What stopped him was his daughter's insistence and will to remain in Tahiti with her mother and family, and live the life she knew and loved. It was perhaps this debate of the virtues of remaining in Tahiti as a European, and how it is the upbringing within the culture, rather than the bloodline, makes a person a native of Tahiti, versus the challenge of returning to industrialised and scientifically advanced society in Europe after a simpler life in harmony with nature on the flip side of the world. It perhaps also gives us a glimpse into the conversations, both internalised and shared over evening cocktails on the Cercle Bougainville verandah (7.5).

Return to England 1939

Sensing the impending storm of another war Macdonald returned to England, no doubt concerned for their gallery in Bond Street and home in Earls Court, as well as their extended family and a sense of obligation to do his bit for his country. As when the American painter John La Farge returned home after his period away in the

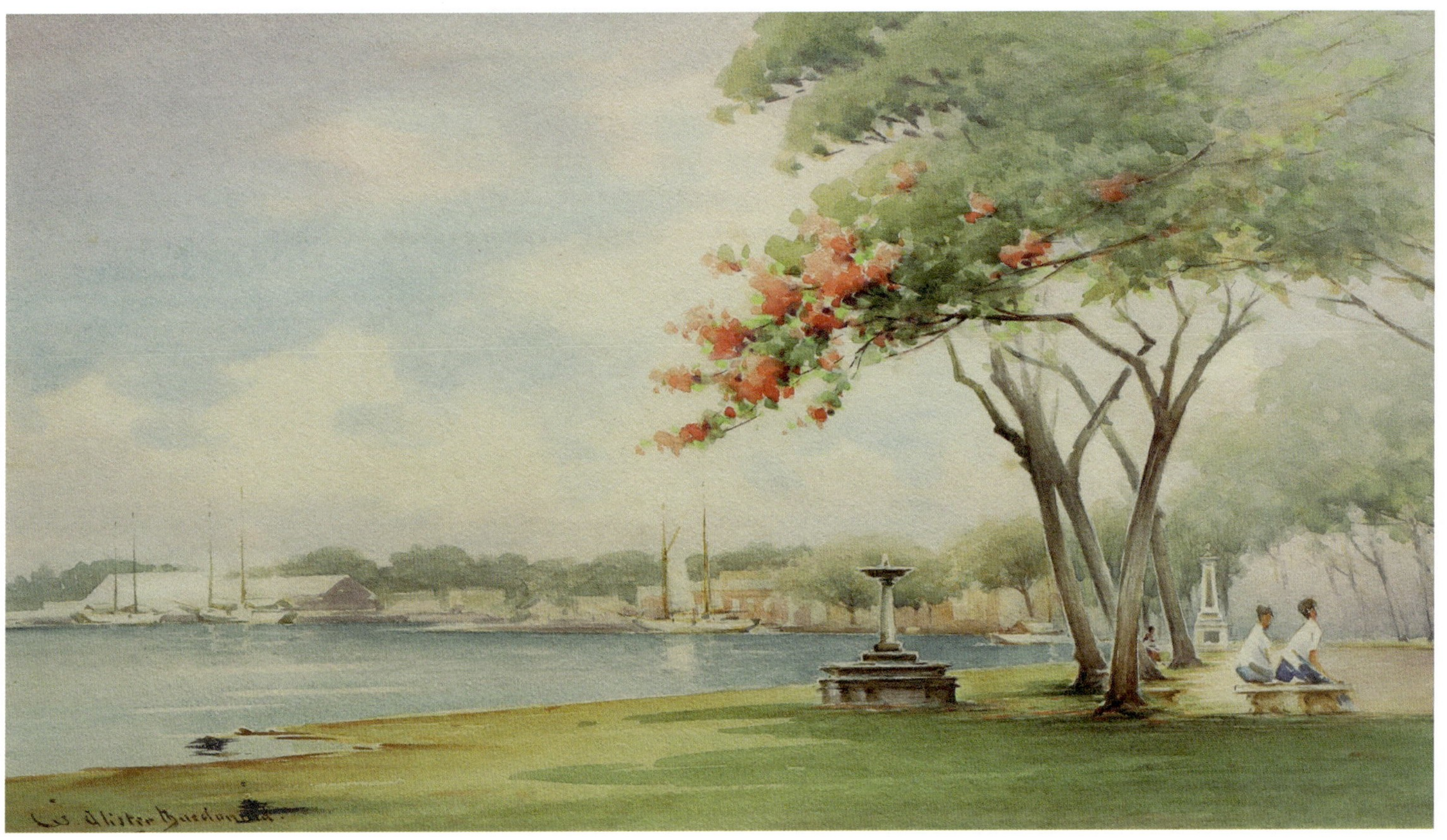

South Seas decades earlier to reconcile with his wife and family obligations, Macdonald must have wondered if his days of travel were now at an end. There is a complexity to the Scot's drive for adventure in contrast to some Victorian values of duty, for him perhaps in part due to a strict Presbyterian upbringing by his maternal 'Grandma' Jane Sinclair, anecdotally 'a force of nature'.

Living now in Wiltshire, and nearing his eightieth birthday, he openly aired his concern for the lack of contact with his family in Scotland in a letter to his niece Jeannie Macdonald (1890–1969), elder sister of war-wounded Willie and daughter of his older brother John in Invergordon.

15th May 1941

My dear Jeannie
Can you give me any news of the folks up north?

Have written Mary Mactavish with P.O. Melvich: & to Jack Mactavish (nephew) at his old habitat at Queensgate Hotel, Inverness; I yet; so far, get no reply. So am wondering if things have happened.

Tis so very very long since we have had any sight of each other, that you may be curious as to why I am writing you to get me out of my difficulty. But hope you wont mind that. But kindly let me know when you can how things are.

We are down here at our little cottage & fairly out of the Bombing. But London got it badly, as you know. The Arlington Gallery was smashed long ago; &, since then, the windows of the flat in Earls Court blown in!

The poor old Temple was a sad sight when I saw it lately: & Fig Tree Court in a bad mess! Well, this is War – so things will happen and one wonders how much longer it is going to last: so that we all can return to normal conditions.

Came back from the South seas, for the second time, at Easter 1939: thinking the War would be on at once. And am glad I came, so much had to be seen to.

Wifie is fairly well, only nervy. The loss of the Gallery was a sad blow to her.

Well, I hope you are pretty well & well away from Bombs. (Can't have too many 'wells' these day – when so much is very decidedly otherwise!)

And with our love & hoping you wont mind letting me know what you can.

Affectionately yours
W. Alister Macdonald

In my rush north in 1935 had no time to stop anywhere: that was the last time I saw Sinclair at Inverness Station – he on

his way south – I north to Melvich. Little did I know then
I would never see him again. WAM

Miss Macdonald
Sea View
Invergordon
Ross. G.B.

From W. Alister Macdonald
Box Cottage, Tinhead Westbury Wilts[135]

A few years later he managed to make the journey north to reunite with his elder brother's family. There are family-owned photographs of Macdonald taken in Inverness in 1946 where he met up with his nieces and nephews of his older brother John. In a letter to his nephew Jack Mactavish he wanted to find a quiet cottage 'to write my memoirs'. A grand-nephew John Macdonald recalls him 'straight as a ramrod, of quiet demeanour and carrying what were probably his worldly possessions in a large leather bag over his shoulder'.[136] In the photo he wears a hat, looking thin in his dark suit with a worn expression on his face, a striking contrast to a more vivacious portrait taken eight years later on his last return to Tahiti. (7.6)

Outliving friends and last run

It is to his credit, and measure of their bond of marriage from 1898 surpassing a Golden Anniversary, that Macdonald remained with Lucy until she died in January 1951, following a long period of dementia and physical fragility. Their last years together were spent in rural Wiltshire, in Lucy's Box Tree Cottage, which she had bought in 1927 while he was away in Tahiti, and where they had moved to in 1941 to escape the bombing in London (7.7). With no evidence of correspondence available to understand more fully their relationship, this detail offers some proof that Lucy was clearly managing financially on her own while bringing up their son, Ian,

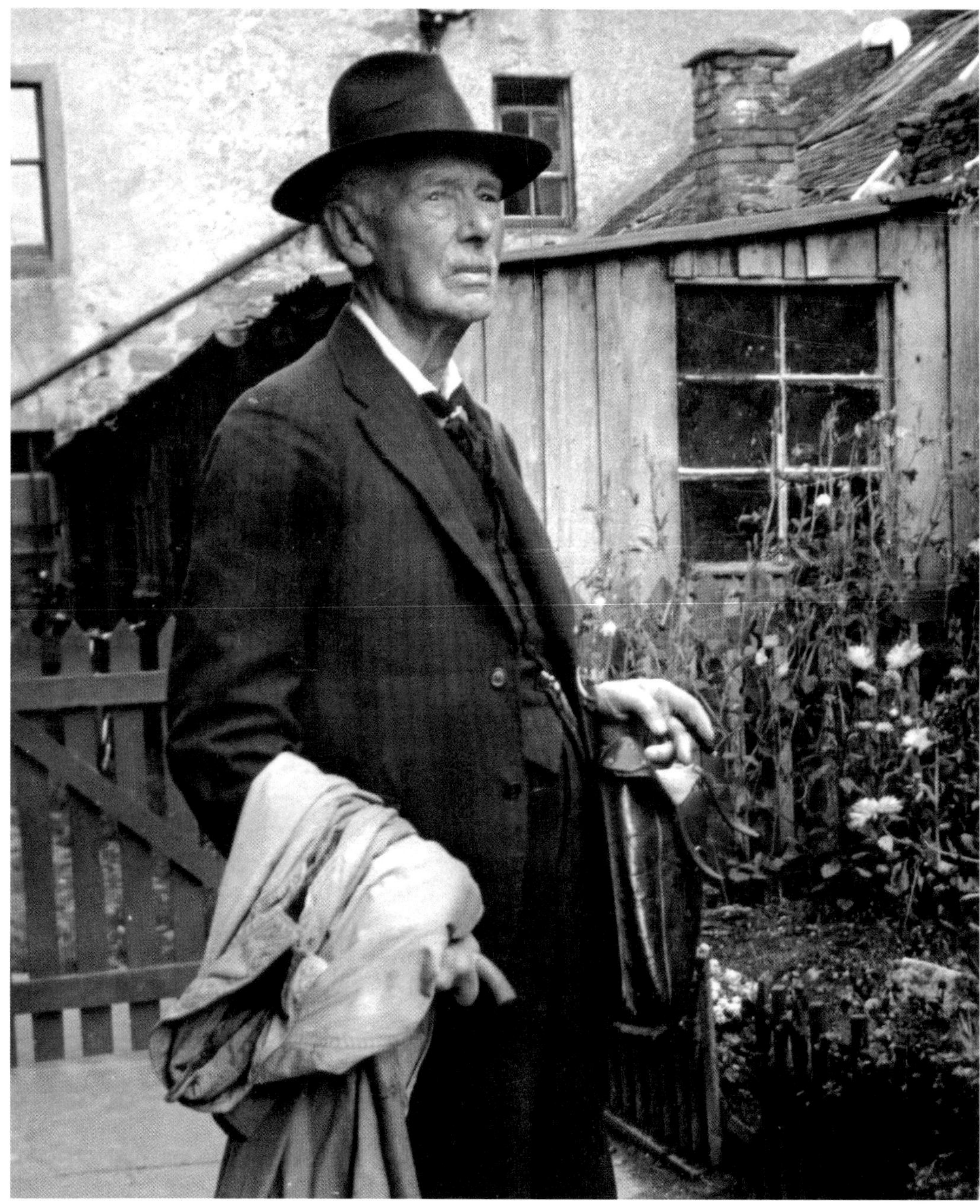

7.6 W. Alister Macdonald in Inverness 1946

7.7 Lucy Macdonald in Cotswold garden c. 1940s

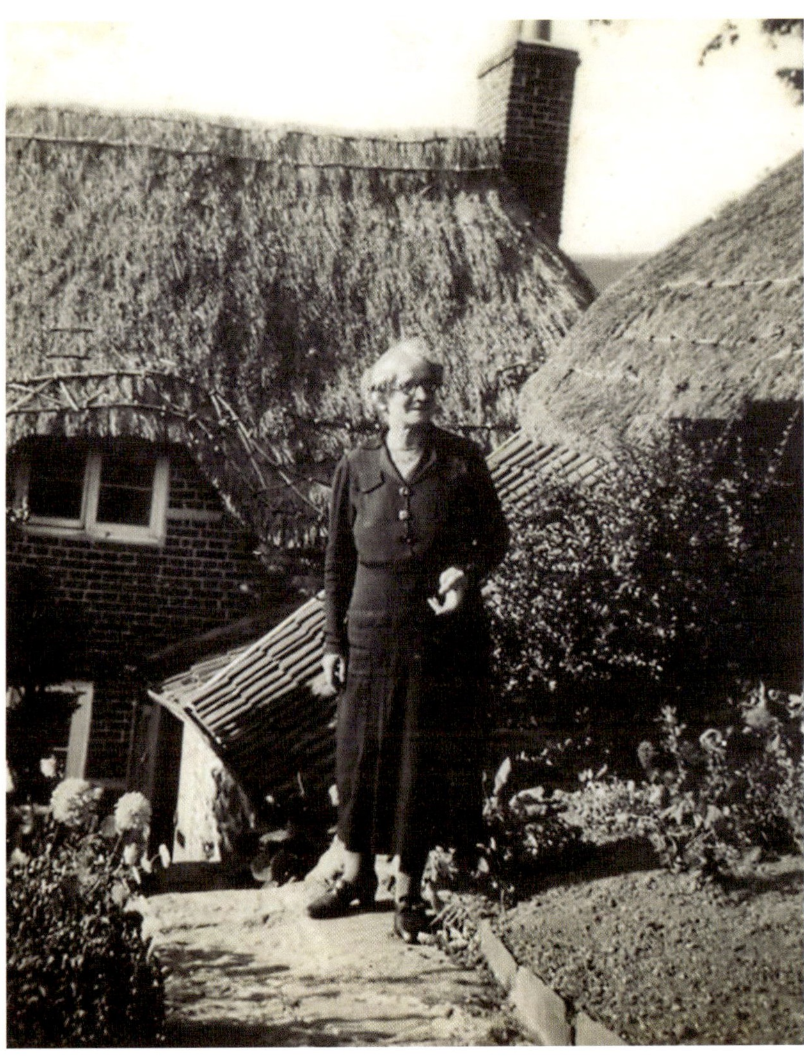

as a single parent in a time when many other women were surviving as war widows from the Great War. Compare this with the account of another constant traveller, the arctic explorer Ernest Shackleton, whose long-suffering wife, Emily, did not regard marriage as a 'life happily ever after'. 'When a man's heart is set in that direction,' she said, 'and especially when he is so suited for the work, one has to put one's own feelings aside – though you know how terribly hard it is sometimes.'[137] The modern-day explorer Sir Ranulph Fiennes's own wife, Ginny, empathised with a 'Strict stiff-upper-lip kind of way where you don't show emotions. You don't just sit down and weep. You have to get on with things.'[138]

In an interview taken by John Macdonald (a grand-nephew) in 2005, Melinda Watts, their neighbour in Westbury, described Lucy as a 'lovely lady' but he was a 'dour sort of chap who walked around with his nose in the air and was most unapproachable'.[139] Perhaps after enjoying the high society of Tahiti and Bond Street, the elderly artist had cultivated an aloofness, or even an air of snobbery over neighbourly countryfolk.

After taking a month following Lucy's death to tidy his affairs in England, on 19 February 1951 Macdonald departed Southampton one last time, on the SS *Madura* travelling east through the Suez Canal for Columbo and the South Seas. By the time he returned to Tahiti many of his old friends had already died. Nordhoff had divorced and returned to California where he died in 1947, Robert Frisbie had died in the Cook Islands. 'A man who destroyed himself through the search for beauty',[140] is how Michener described him. In some ways Frisbie's extraordinary journey also seems the 'standard' American literary life: so much purity of expression ending in frustration and drink. James Norman Hall had remained in Tahiti but had died in 1951, as had Tipari, Macdonald's *vahine*.

Macdonald had already lived a full life when he arrived in Tahiti aged sixty in 1921, now he was returning at ninety, cognisant that this must be his last resting place. Far away from his birthplace and childhood in Sutherland, Scotland, and yet it was a place living in its own time bubble, like many islands across the globe. When his nephew, Canadian artist Jock Macdonald (1897–1960), made a return to Thurso to visit the family having spent over twenty years living and establishing his painting career in Vancouver and Toronto, a man he barely recognised from his school days remarked in the street, 'Hullo James, nothing new, eh!' 'Time certainly doesn't exist for him…I cannot understand the people who have remained here all their lives + still feel that life has been a tremendous experience'.[141] Geographically Thurso and Caithness were like islands then, accessible by sea, although linked by a remote railway and a cliff-hugging single track road to Inverness over a hundred miles to the south.

'He was never seduced by fame and praise. Fleeing worldly vanity like a new Gauguin, he found his refuge in the quiet of the Islands, from then on living a primitive and happy life in Pao-Pao'.[142]

Having outlived his contemporaries and with his daughter and his grandchildren around him, Macdonald embraced the Tahitian philosophy of living each day as it came and enjoyed living in the moment. As long as his eyesight remained and he was able to hold a paintbrush in a steady hand every day would be a fresh canvas to see and capture the natural beauty that unfolded in front of him in ever-changing light and colour. As other artists have found, Moorea is an enchanted island, a place that would befit J.M. Barrie's *Peter Pan* (1904).

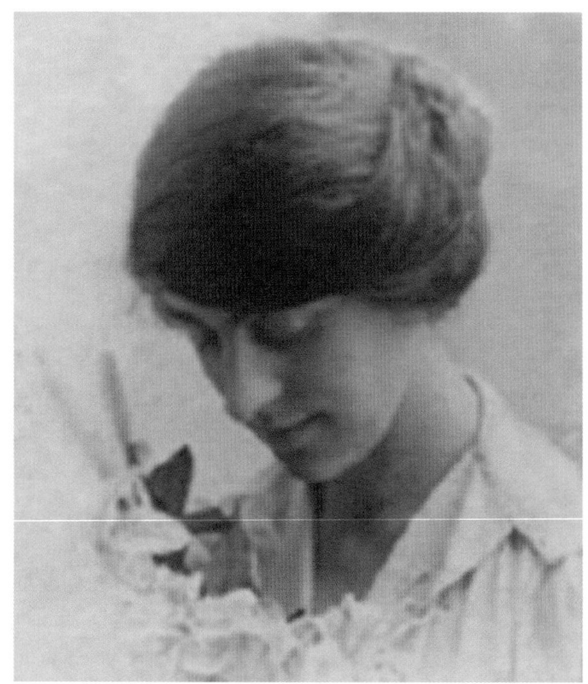

8.8 Dolly Myhill passport (detail) 1923

8

The Wife, Lovers and Daughter

Introduction

Macdonald's early childhood bonding with his mother, Barbara, was tragically cut short at the age of four when she died of puerperal fever ten days after the birth of his younger brother. Thereafter the most influential women in his life were his eldest sibling Jane, eleven years older, who helped to bring up her brothers, and their maternal Grandmother Jane Sinclair, under whose stern care they grew up with. It feels a long way from a Dickensian happy ending, but at least he grew up in a relatively financially and morally secure family environment surrounded by many siblings, typical of Victorian times.

Sent to boarding school in Aberdeen, over two hundred miles away to the south, at the age of eleven, he learned the hard way to develop his independence and competency for travel that would serve him for the rest of his life. Enclosed in a male environment at school and then at work in the bank he would have been limited to polite interactions with women. In later life he is recorded as having social friendships with society women, such as Lady Freake in Twickenham, and finds a long-standing and long-suffering wife in Lucy Winifred Carey.

The story might end there, but nearing the age of sixty, his relationships with women enjoy a romantic and new burst of life that take him to the other side of the world, in a mode similar to Paul Gauguin. There are perhaps four key women that contribute to a late flourish of youthful vigour that help extend his life into the

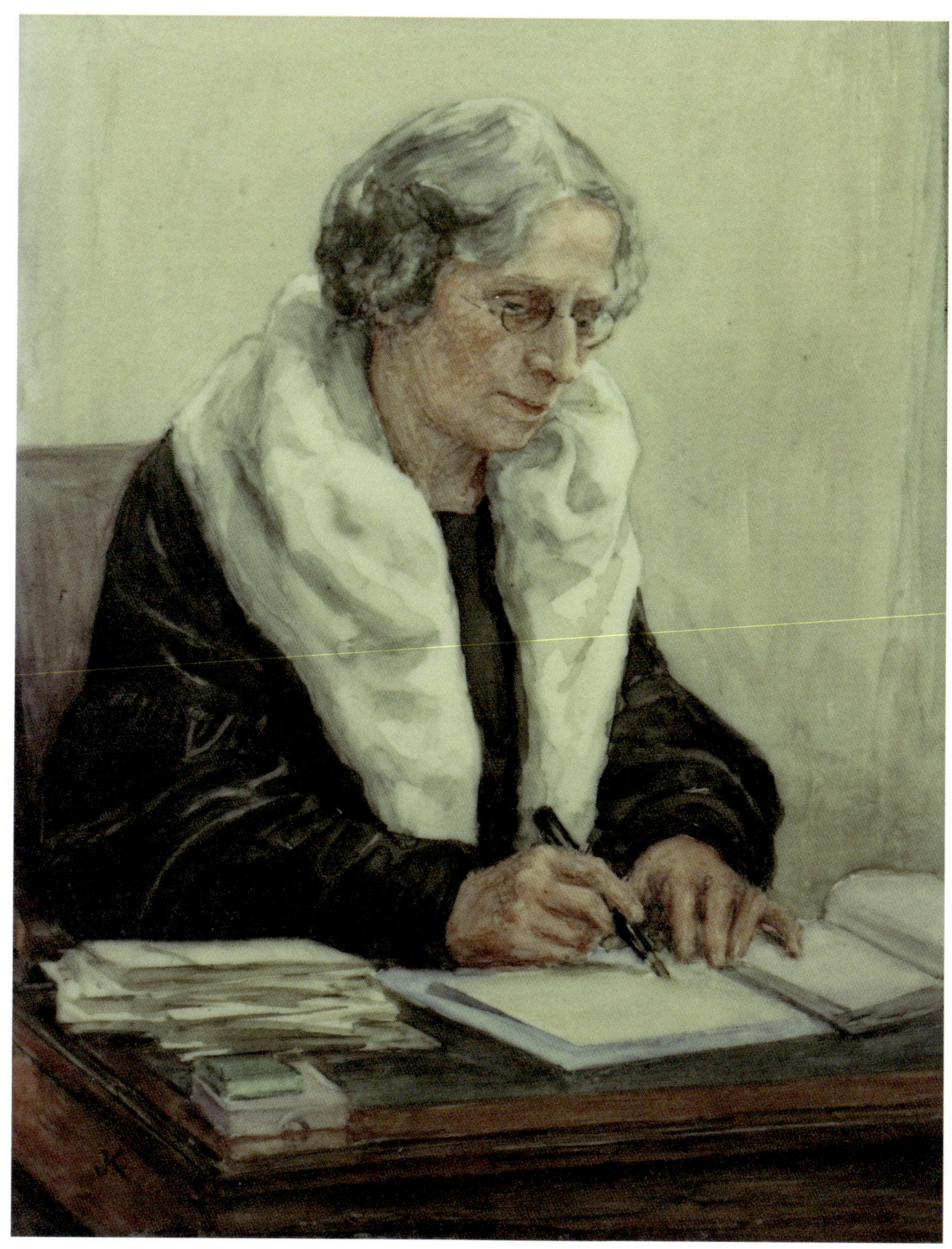

nineties: his wife Lucy, Dorothy Myhill, Tipari Tuera, and his daughter Avril. By all accounts they all share a common quality of independent and acute thinking, as well as strength of character and affection for him.

8.1 *Mrs Lucy Macdonald* by Mrs Joyce Kilburn

Lucy Winifred Macdonald (1872–1951)

Lucy Winifred Carey (8.1), born 12 April 1872, was the daughter of artist William Henry Carey. She grew up in London and with the encouragement of her father she developed her own artistic skills as a miniaturist painter. This very specialist field had great commercial value as treasured portable and wearable tokens and gifts amongst wealthy families in Victorian society. Her reputation was recognised as she exhibited at The Society of Miniature Painters' inaugural show in 1896, when her address was given as 17 Percy Road, Shepherd's Bush. She was elected a member in 1897 and then later became Honorary Secretary in 1917.

How she met W. Alister Macdonald is not known, but they could have met through society circles in the London art scene. Ten years older and likely well-spoken after a period working in the bank, his Scottish upbringing may have struck her as very romantic and something out of a Sir Walter Scott novel. They were married on 21 October 1898, she twenty-six and he a mature thirty-seven years old (8.2). Her father had died by then and so the witnesses were her sister Florence Elizabeth Carey, and her mother, Jane Matilda Hamnett now remarried.

They moved frequently in the first years of their marriage, up and down the Thames. Their first home together was at Danes Inn in the Strand, but by 1901 they were living at 15 St Helier Street, Richmond, Surrey. In 1906 they moved to a very superior address, 8 Fig Tree Court, in the Temple. They were enabled to secure this accommodation through a friend, Mr Etherington Smith, a Bencher of the Inner Temple. From here they could see the Thames and the

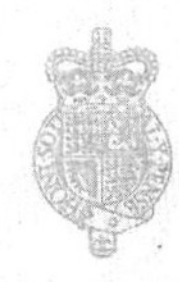

CERTIFIED COPY OF AN ENTRY OF MARRIAGE

GIVEN AT THE GENERAL REGISTER OFFICE

Application Number W136468

1898. Marriage solemnized at St Paul's Church in the Parish of Hammersmith in the County of London

Columns: 1	2	3	4	5	6	7	8	
No.	When Married.	Name and Surname.	Age.	Condition.	Rank or Profession.	Residence at the time of Marriage.	Father's Name and Surname.	Rank or Profession of Father.
118	27th Octr 1898.	William Alister Macdonald.	37	Bachelor	Artist	8 Danes Inn Strand.	John Macdonald	Minister
		Lucy Winifred Cary	27	Spinster	—	42 Mall Road	William Henry Cary (deceased)	Artist.

Married in the Parish Church according to the Rites and Ceremonies of the Established Church by ——— or after Banns by me,

This Marriage was solemnized between us, William Alister Macdonald, Lucy Winifred Cary; in the Presence of us, Jane Matilda Hamnett, Florence Elizabeth Cary; E. W. Langford

CERTIFIED to be a true copy of an entry in the certified copy of a register of Marriages in the Registration District of Fulham

Given at the GENERAL REGISTER OFFICE, under the Seal of the said Office, the 20th day of June 2003

This certificate is issued in pursuance of section 65 of the Marriage Act 1949. Sub-section 3 of that section provides that any certified copy of an entry purporting to be sealed or stamped with the seal of the General Register Office shall be received as evidence of the marriage to which it relates without any further or other proof of the entry, and no certified copy purporting to have been given in the said Office shall be of any force or effect unless it is sealed or stamped as aforesaid.

MXB 318099

CAUTION: THERE ARE OFFENCES RELATING TO FALSIFYING OR ALTERING A CERTIFICATE AND USING OR POSSESSING A FALSE CERTIFICATE. ©CROWN COPYRIGHT

WARNING: A CERTIFICATE IS NOT EVIDENCE OF IDENTITY.

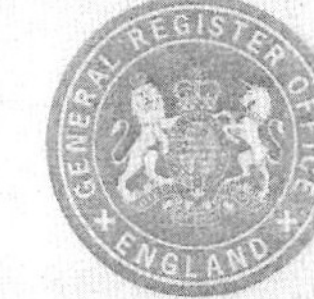

8.2 W. Alister Macdonald and Lucy marriage certificate 1898

Southbank, and it was a convenient base from which Macdonald could walk to paint the streets and river-shores of the city. Lucy spent a lot of time on her own while he went on painting excursions across Britain during the winter months and then further afield to Europe in the summer. In 1910 they had a son, Ian (8.3), and in that year alone Macdonald painted in Lincolnshire, Kent,

Ludlow, Fife, the Outer Hebrides, then a tour of Italy, Switzerland and Greece. Rather than sit at home helping his wife to nurse an infant, he maintained his busy schedule of painting trips until the outbreak of war in 1914. Sometime during the war they must have vacated their apartment in the Temple as they sub-let it to a Russian émigré who had escaped the Revolution. The 1921 census records Lucy Winifred Macdonald as the owner and occupier with her eleven-year-old Ian at 6a Penywern Road Earl's Court, with her place of work at Studio, 283 Fulham Road, SW10. This remained their home until around 1940 when their windows blew in during a bombing raid in the Blitz, forcing their escape to Box Tree Cottage in Westbury, rural Wiltshire that Lucy acquired in 1927.

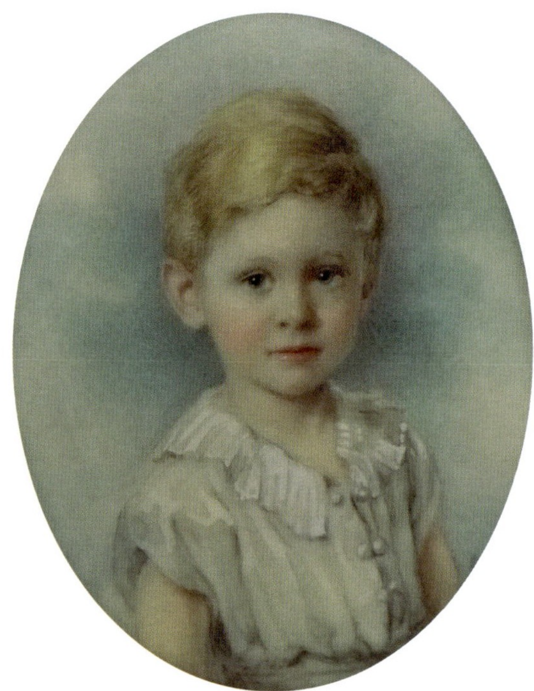

8.3 *My Little Son* by Lucy Macdonald 1912

Galleries

Lucy had a shrewd understanding of the London art market, cultivated as an artist and through her involvement with the Royal Society of Miniaturists. In 1910, motivated by Macdonald's frustration with his work being dictated by other gallery owners, they decided to open their own. The Little Gallery in Broad Street, off Victoria was their first. There they could exhibit and sell the work that Macdonald wanted the freedom to paint, while supporting other artists in their circle. Lucy ran the business while he was away for long periods to travel and paint across Europe and Britain.

In 1923 Lucy, by now effectively a single parent after her husband had departed for the South Seas in 1921, opened the Arlington Gallery at 22 Old Bond Street. The building was built by Sir Joseph Joel Duveen (1843–1908), the Dutch art dealer and benefactor of many art galleries and then owned by his son, Baron Joseph Duveen (1869–1939), who is considered one of the most influential art dealers of the twentieth century. The design of the building was based on a favourite palazzo in Venice. The integrity of the building's façade remains today despite having being bombed in 1941, an event that forced the Macdonalds to close the Arlington Gallery.

The Arlington Gallery attracted lesser-known artists of the period who probably found it harder to be exhibited in bigger galleries because they had yet to achieve a marketable reputation, or that those galleries took too great a commission. The gallery also exhibited artists associated with textiles, glass, jewellery, tapestry and metalwork. It regularly exhibited The Royal Society of Miniaturist Painters, Sculptors and Gravers who showed almost every year until its closure in 1941, and likely her own fine miniaturist work too. It was patronised by high society and reviews of openings regularly appeared in the *Bystander* and national and regional newspapers. Notable dignitaries, socialites and celebrities included the likes of George Bernard Shaw at the opening of the late John Collier (November 1934), Princess Alphonse de Chimay at American cartoonist Percy Crosby's show (June 1936), and the Duke of Connaught at Donald Wood's show (1934). Would the news of Macdonald's return from Tahiti in 1935 expose the existence of his Tahitian daughter, and so scandalise and jeopardise the valuable patronage and prestige of such society?

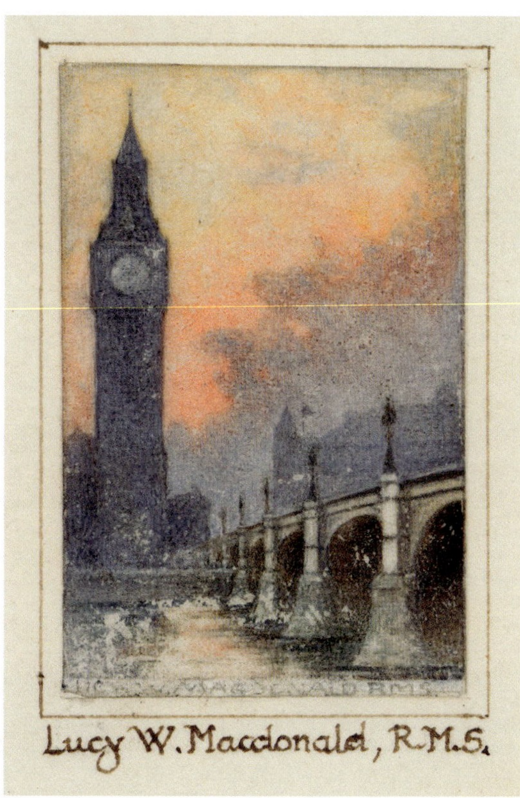

8.4 *Big Ben and Westminster*, by Lucy Macdonald RMS 1923

Works

Early in her career as a miniaturist painter, Lucy exhibited at the New Gallery, 121 Regent Street, which had held a major Burne-Jones retrospective in 1892 and 1893 and a memorial exhibition of his works in 1898. The last exhibition held there was the *Arts and Crafts Exhibition of 1910*. She also exhibited at the Walker Art Gallery, Liverpool, one that Macdonald returned to in 1941.

Lucy exhibited regularly in Royal Academy Summer Exhibitions, with a notable absence in 1938 and 1939 when her husband was back in Tahiti, and a long gap between 1920 and 1933 as she established her Arlington Gallery in Old Bond Street. Early works were of London theatres' leading Shakespearean actresses, and then latterly society portraits, *Miss Estelle Stead as 'Portia'* (1913) and *Miss Evelyn Grey as 'Hero' in Much Ado About Nothing* (1914).

The miniature portrait of *Mrs Jean McGuire* (1918) is typical of the society clientele she would have painted (8.5).

In 1923 she painted a miniature (4.3 × 2.8 cm) of *Big Ben and Westminster* for Queen Mary's Dolls' House, painted on lamb's skin, now in the Royal Collection (8.4).

In 1928 she wrote: 'Women's faces have changed because they have become more or less standardised. This is due to fashionable make-up. Women I consider, are more attractive in appearance and more seductive than they have ever been.'[143]

In other Royal Academy Summer Exhibitions in 1933 she exhibited *The Coral Reef Painter* (1149), in 1934 one of her three exhibits was *The Little Son* (1057) (8.3). There is speculation that the portrait of their son exhibited in 1912 as a boy of two years of age may also be the subject exhibited as *The Little Boy* in 1934, though he was twenty-four at that time. Could *The Coral Reef Painter* be a portrait based on her husband, then in Tahiti? By then Macdonald was an established artist there and had illustrated books for his American literary friends.

In 1937, the year Macdonald returned to Tahiti via America, Lucy exhibited *J.C. Anderson esq* (1080), and three miniatures in 1940, her last RA Summer Exhibition: *Dr George Wilkinson JP* (1115), *Mrs Violet Brunton-Angless RMS* (1095) and *Major Sir Neville R. Wilkinson* (1081).

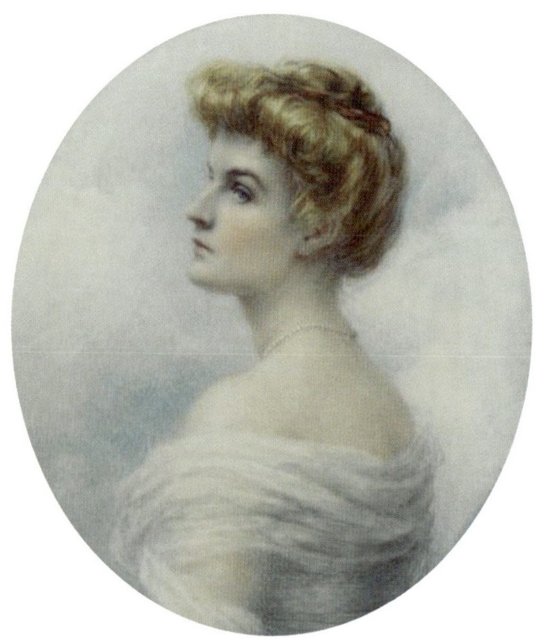

8.5 *Portrait of Mrs Jean Elizabeth McGuire née Adair*, by Lucy Macdonald RMS 1918

Tragedy and reconciliation

Unfortunately, there are no letters or correspondence between Lucy and Macdonald to reveal the nature of their relationship during any of his periods away in Tahiti. However, there are newspaper articles regarding Lucy in several American newspapers in 1924, such as the *Austin American Statesman*, in the 'Of Interest to Women' column:

> Mrs Lucy W. MacDonald of London, is a miniature painter of eminence, honorable secretary of the Royal Society of Miniature Painters and a director of two picture galleries. Mrs MacDonald's husband, W. Alister MacDonald, is also a well known painter.[144]

The same text is published in the *Tennessee Knoxville Journal and Tribune*, two days earlier. Perhaps this is Lucy putting it on record that she is the legal wife of Alister, and still very much alive? Later that month Dorothy Myhill departed Brisbane for England registered as Mrs Dorothy Macdonald, and she used this name again in her passport issued in 1929.

In July 1935, after a fourteen year sojourn, Macdonald boarded the SS *Barrabool* and returned from Tahiti to England, following the tragic death of their son.

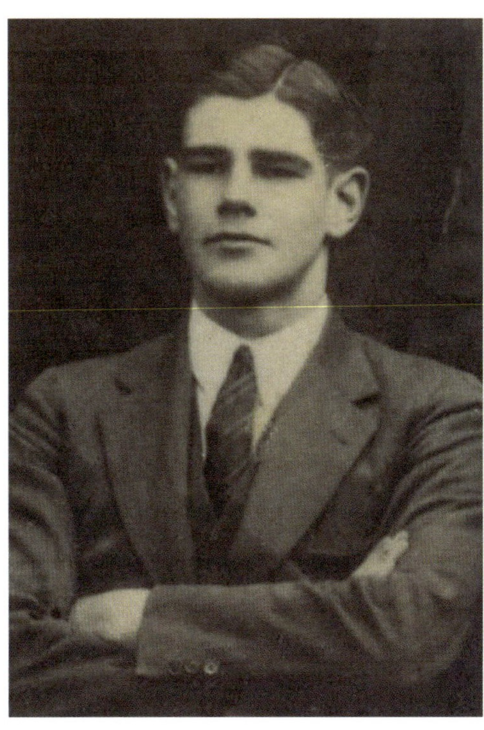

8.6 Ian Macdonald (1910–1934)

The *Kentish Times* reported that on 10 July 1934, during an evening sailing on the Thames, on a short yachting holiday from Twickenham, Macdonald's twenty-four-year-old son, Ian Alister Macdonald (8.6), a student of archaeology at London University, was attending to the jib when a gust of wind took them by surprise. He and his friend Richard Spires collided with a barge at Greenhithe and capsized (his mother 'did not think he had ever been on a yacht before').[145] Washed out of the boat, Spires was saved but despite the efforts of many bargemen, Ian was lost, tragically drowned, and recovered four days later on the Saturday, near the scene.

Soon after Macdonald's return to London, Lucy mounted an exhibition in October 1935, *Among the Islands of the South Seas*, of 119 pictures in the Arlington Gallery, followed by one in December of 101 forgotten watercolours of Old London painted in the early 1900s, an entire collection bought by Lord Wakefield for the Guildhall in London.

In February 1936, a third exhibition of a further 125 watercolours opened of *Pre-war Wanderings Watercolours Home and Abroad*. *The Times* reported 'Mr Macdonald, who seems to have been everywhere, has an admirable style for this kind of record on a small scale, crisp and articulate, and generally pleasing in colour.'[146]

Later that summer, Lucy herself exhibits a portrait miniature of her husband titled *W. Alister Macdonald* (1051) (8.7) at the Royal Academy. This is the portrait later used on his memorial stone.

In December 1936, Lucy found herself alone once more to run the gallery after Macdonald left Liverpool on the SS *Scythia* for Boston, America to exhibit the remaining unsold watercolours in the Robert C. Vose Gallery. There has been speculation that Lucy travelled to Tahiti with her husband, or later to join him on his second visit. However, as previously mentioned, there are no records of any Lucy Macdonald making a voyage to Tahiti, while records show her Arlington Gallery remained open and exhibited as many as ten exhibitions a year in the period 1937–9 while her husband was away.

His second sojourn in Tahiti came to an end in 1939, 'thinking the war will be on us at once',[147] no doubt concerned for her, the gallery and their home in London's Earls Court. He also had a sense of obligation to do his bit for his country as he had done in the Great War, in the Army Service Supply Department. Now in his eighties, he might very well have considered that his days of travels, if not war service, were over, and the remaining years would be spent together in quiet retirement.

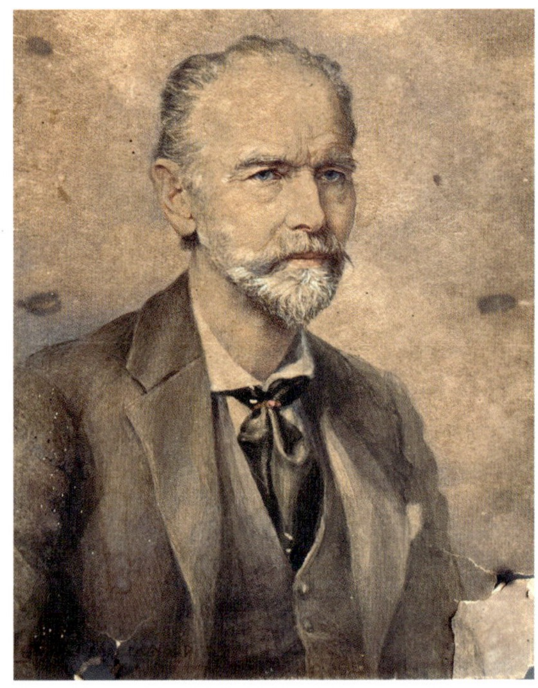

8.7 *W. Alister Macdonald* by Lucy Macdonald 1936

Lucy died on 4 January 1951, at Roundway Hospital, in Devizes following a long period of dementia and physical fragility from when the war ended. They spent their last years together in Box Tree Cottage, Westbury in rural Wiltshire, which she had bought in 1927 and they had moved to in 1941 after bomb damage to their apartment in Earls Court.

Dorothy Myhill (1890–1981)

Somerset Maugham's popular novel *The Moon and Sixpence* (1919) was perhaps an inspiration for the romantic Dorothy (Dolly) Myhill (1890–1981), who travelled to Tahiti with the much older Macdonald.

> But I was also a little shocked. Strickland was certainly forty, and I thought it disgusting that a man of his age should concern himself with the affairs of the heart. With the superciliousness

> of extreme youth, I put thirty-five as the utmost limit at which a man might fall in love without making a fool of himself.[148]
>
> 'There's only one explanation, and that is that he's not himself. I don't know who this woman is who's got hold of him, but she's made him into another man. It's evidently been going on a long time.'[149]

John Myhill (1948–), whose grandfather was Dolly's cousin, believes this was the case, prompting her to embark for Tahiti from the port of Hull. However, the fact that she is not on the passenger list that includes Macdonald on the SS *Arawa* of the Shaw, Savill & Albion shipping line bound for New Zealand, via the Panama Canal and Tahiti, would not surprise anyone in her family. Her life was unconventional, at times vague or foggy on detail, but never dull as she told it, and invariably never the same version was repeated.

Family legend

How the affair started is mired in the mists of memory and the fog that protects respectability in rural England. 'They are as fond of gossip in Tahiti as in an English village...'[150] On close inspection of the painting of *Monk's Wood* that Macdonald gave her, their initials: 'D. A M. W A. M 1919' can be seen carved into a beech tree, the punctuation identifying the first names they were known by: Dorothy and Alister (3.2). There is a Monk's Wood near the Norfolk coast by Cromer, about thirty-five miles from Dolly's home Grange Farm in the village of Fundenhall. He would have some familiarity of Norfolk having lived there briefly in his early days as an artist after leaving his office job in a London bank in 1884.

John Myhill remembers his great-aunts:

> Dolly and her sisters were all keen to prove they were as good as any man, so they dressed in tweeds, jackets cut in a masculine style, adopted boy's names, kept their hair short: there was nothing 'girlie' about any of them: reading, outdoor

> pursuits and smoking. They were all around five foot tall, but spoke with authority and took pride in their appearance and their clan.[151]

Indeed, Dolly, a diminutive of Dorothy, was also known as Bobby because at one time her hair was 'bobbed'. She was known to have two abiding passions, horses and art. She was educated at Lonsdale House, a boarding school in Norwich, it being presumed that her parents did not want her to be educated at the local village school, and the journey to Norwich in the 1890s would be more challenging than today. William Myhill (1839–1925) wanted all of his children to have a 'good' education, and boarding school for a girl was exceptional at the time. She was a good amateur painter and was believed to have had some art education. The family have one of her sketchbooks from 1903 and greetings cards that she painted throughout her life. Did she meet 'Mac' (as she called him) through this activity, or perhaps through a family acquaintance? Grange Farm was no stranger to artist or literary guests, the author Rider Haggard (1856–1925) of *King Solomon's Mines* (1885) and other popular adventure fiction romances, his wife, Marianna, and daughter, Lilias, would visit from their nearby home at Ditchingham House.

Another theory is that she met him through Alfred Munnings (1878–1959), regarded as one of England's finest painters of horses and an outspoken critic of Modernism, to whom her sister Evelyn (1894–1967) (known as Judy or Ju) had briefly been engaged to some time prior to 1914. Evelyn, during her engagement, was boarding a train returning to Fundenhall via Wymondham, which was very crowded with territorial soldiers on manoeuvres. Munnings approached a territorial in the Royal Army Medical Corps, Captain Thomas George Buchanan (1883–1976), and asked him to keep an eye on her welfare. The young captain, who was in his last year as a medical student, promptly did that with such enthusiasm that soon after she broke off her engagement to Alfred Munnings and on 7 September 1915 and married him instead.

A recently discovered address book from the loft of Hethel Farm reveals Dolly's work as a clerk in the civil service. Most of the addresses are military, regiments that reflect the span of the British Empire at the end of the First World War: Burma, East Africa, South Africa, West Africa, Army of the Rhine, and some in the Belgian Army. There are no family addresses, and the top half of the page for 'M' is ripped out. Did she meet Macdonald while he was working in the Army Office of Supply?

Both Dolly and Macdonald had lost their mothers early in life during childbirth, and this had had a profound effect on their fathers. It was a Myhill family legend, according to Evelyn's grandson, John-Henry Collinson (1952–2016), that their father William Myhill insisted that Dolly break off the relationship with Macdonald and forbade him to enter their house. Rather than take issue with him being married with a son, he was more concerned that 'Mac' was old enough to be her father. A widower since 1908 when their mother Agnes died in childbirth aged forty-six, he had given his seven daughters a strict upbringing in which he had developed an overpowering sense of guardianship, possibly out of fear of being left on his own. This was demonstrated on Evelyn's wedding day: her father was all dressed up to go to church to give her away when he baulked, unable to bring himself to do so, and instead went off to plough a field still dressed in his best suit.

Collinson's mother, Suzanne (1916–1993), (nicknamed Billie), remembered as a young girl, travelling with her mother Evelyn to London to meet 'Mac' and Dolly in either the Savoy Hotel or the Ritz where it seemed, they were staying. If Macdonald's marital status was general knowledge, it would explain why this visit had to be kept secret from her grandfather. Conceivably, this could have been 1921 when Billie was herself five years old, and a last goodbye between sisters before her aunt departed for New Zealand.

Another version of the relationship, according to Collinson, was that she met Macdonald returning from one of his painting journeys while travelling in the Mediterranean onboard a ship unknown in

Alexandria or Port Said, on her way back to England. The story, according to Dolly, was that both decided to go to Tahiti while on board. Dolly, talking to her family in later years maintains that he went to Tahiti to carry out a commission to paint, but there is no corroboration of this story available. Collinson's daughter Poppy asserts that Myhill women 'burn everything after someone dies' and 'as a family of storytellers they wouldn't let the truth get in the way of a good story'.[152] As one of the few women in the later family, Bobby, as she was known to Poppy, gave her special attention instilling in her a life of curiosity and unconventionality. She believes her great-great-aunt went for adventure, not for love.

There is evidence that both Dolly and Macdonald were avid readers, and so Maugham's bestseller could not have passed them unnoticed at such a point in their relationship. Perhaps they saw romantic parallels in the novel and sought a similar escape from the increasingly mechanised, socially chaotic upheavals of Europe to the exotic South Seas, following in the footsteps, as they would later discover, of the writers Charles Nordhoff and James Norman Hall? On Macdonald's return to England in 1935, following news of the death of his son, Chancellor (1937) gives an account that spares everyone's blushes and keeps a more respectable front:

> The War being over, and his beloved London becoming in all sorts of ways so drastically changed, Mr Macdonald determined to see what the new world was like. He forthwith sailed for New Zealand. The vessel, stopping at Tahiti, gave him the opportunity of making acquaintance with that spot, which he found – I use his own words – 'a Paradise for water-colour painters.' So Eden-like did it become to him that he made a long sojourn there, the years, he says, passing like weeks that at their end he never realized how long he had been away from his native land.[153]

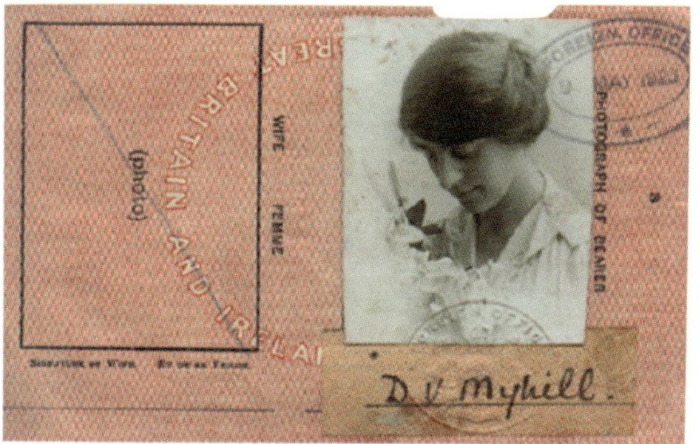
(photo)
WIFE FEMME
PHOTOGRAPH OF BEARER
D.V. Myhill.

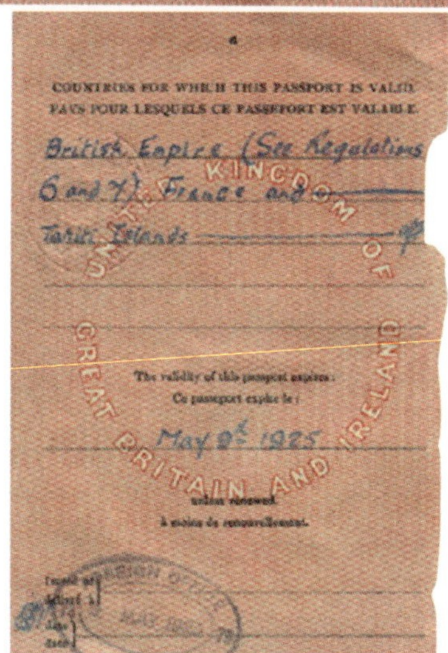
COUNTRIES FOR WHICH THIS PASSPORT IS VALID
PAYS POUR LESQUELS CE PASSEPORT EST VALABLE
British Empire (See Regulations 6 and 7) France and Tahiti Islands
The validity of this passport expires:
Ce passeport expire le:
May 9th 1925
unless renewed
à moins de renouvellement.

8.8 Dolly Myhill passport 1923

Hard evidence

The locations and dates of Macdonald's paintings and drawings provide a record of his movements, but there are no such traces to shed light on Dolly Myhill's travels. It was her great-nephew John Collinson who took on the family detective work to try and unravel her remarkable life. The passenger list that confirms Macdonald's departure from Southampton on 5 May 1921 does not include any mention of a Myhill. Dolly had a passport stamped 9 May 1923 by the Foreign Office for British Empire, France and Tahiti Islands, arguably a renewal as the earlier one would only have been valid for two years according to UK Foreign Office rules at the time (8.8). A painting of the ship *El Katara* in Papeete dated July 1923 that Macdonald gave to Dolly does establish some point in time that they were there together (3.10). Throughout his remaining life he kept a drawing of a young woman titled *Young England* from his voyage on the *Arawa* in 1921, one that poses a remarkable likeness to Dolly's early passport and surely someone of sentimental value (8.9).

There is a record that she returned to England alone under the name of Dorothy Macdonald from Brisbane, Australia on the ship SS *Moreton Bay* to Hull on 26 August 1924. A journey that would take around forty-three days and cost £38 (£1600 today) for a Third-Class ticket. A page in her address book reveals her thoughts on her fellow Australian passengers, which she loosely disguises as 'orstrylains'.

> So-called moralists of the Tell-it-to-God-&-the-curate type tea time the most comfortable of English hours. Orstrylians sunsets like impressionist sketches of the last judgement
>
> Sacre nom de Dieu
>
> deckchair on a verandah, where the refreshing trade wind gives one sufficient thought to stretch out an occasional hand for a banana or an orange – makes one want to scream for the sake of company.

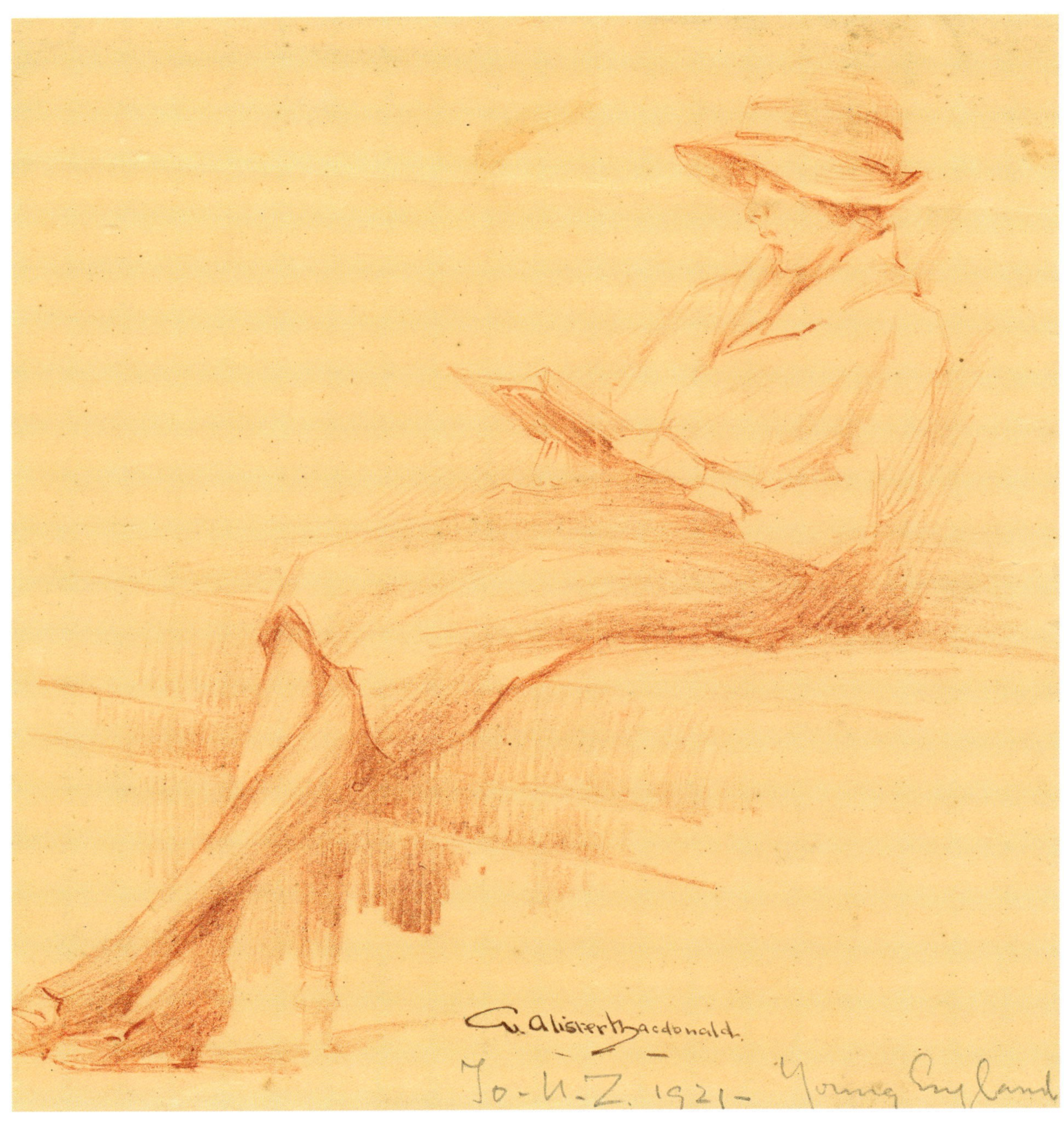

8.9 Young England (Dolly Myhill) 1921

8.10 Dolly Macdonald passport 1929

> The orstraylians are as omniscient query-what-they-do they know of England who only Sydney know – Answer Everything – sweltering heat, mosquitoes, flies, fleas & other pests are against quiet enjoyment.[154]

Her journal records that she was having a hard time dealing with loneliness on top of the climate and insects. A note written on the front page suggests she also suffered from malaria: 'In order to get malaria out of my blood & diminish risk of haemoglobinuria malarial cachexia'.[155] Her disaffection with the life of an artist is revealed with a note of Arthur Machen's *Hill of Dreams* (1907), and in the last page of her address book as she muses with reference to the German poet Heinrich Heine:

> Some say the goal & his life was spent in passionate endeavour to reach it. Heine also saw the goal, but in his heart of hearts was not quite sure if the gates were of gold or tinsel & in any case he was so much amused by the tragi- comedy of the race that he often preferred to sit by the wayside & laugh till bitter tears came into his eyes – & then began to laugh again – though disenchantment was the order of the day was he altogether without those passionate illusions which come only to enthusiasts of life.[156]

In 1924, even without applying the perspective of twenty-first century social values, there would have been different needs and expectations with an age gap of nearly thirty years between Dolly and Macdonald. At the age of sixty-three, he had found a spiritual home in Tahiti where he could live simply and paint. But for Dolly perhaps the romance of eloping, and allegedly 'marrying', waned as she missed her home and intellectual stimulus of Norfolk and England? Perhaps she had received news from England of her father's ailing health? William Myhill died nine months after Dolly returned, no doubt at peace with all his daughters around him once again.

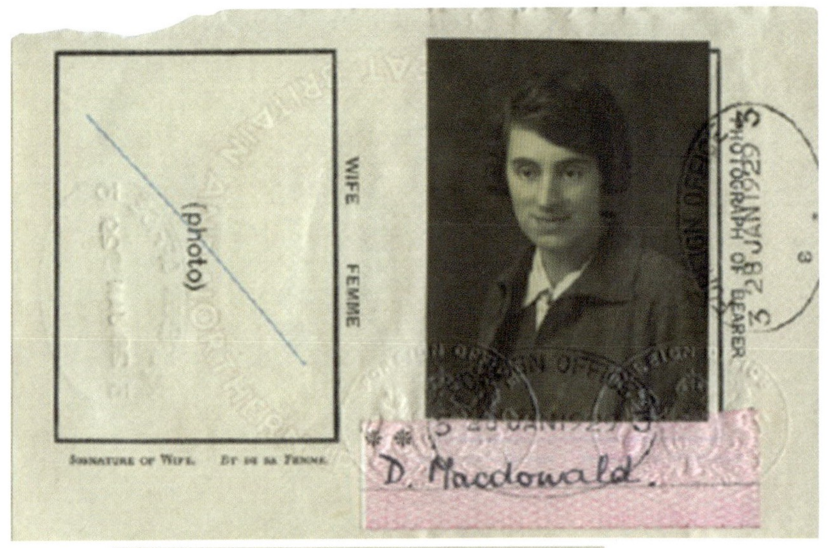
WIFE FEMME

(photo)

SIGNATURE OF WIFE. SIGNATURE DE SA FEMME.

D. Macdonald.

PHOTOGRAPH OF BEARER

FOREIGN OFFICE 3 28 JAN 1929 3

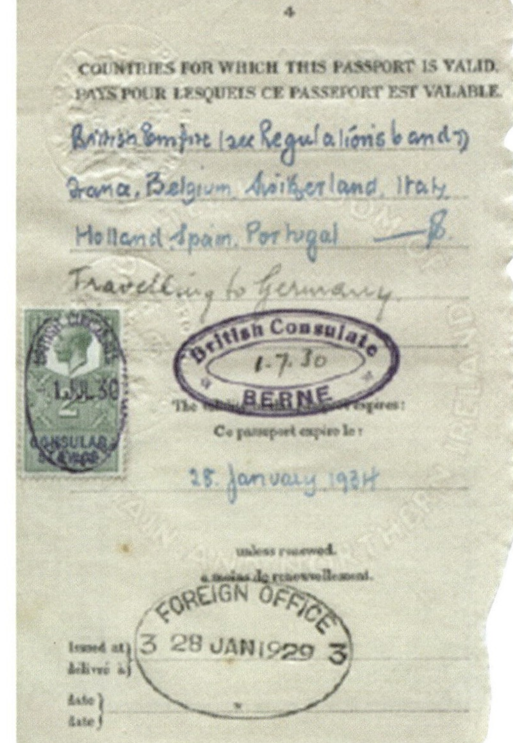
4

COUNTRIES FOR WHICH THIS PASSPORT IS VALID.
PAYS POUR LESQUELS CE PASSEPORT EST VALABLE.

British Empire (see Regulations 6 and 7)
France, Belgium, Switzerland, Italy,
Holland, Spain, Portugal

Travelling to Germany.

British Consulate
1.7.30
BERNE

CONSULAR STAMP 1 JUL 30

The [illegible] expires:
Ce passeport expire le:

28. January 1934

unless renewed.
à moins de renouvellement.

Issued at } FOREIGN OFFICE 3 28 JAN 1929 3
délivré à }
date }
date }

Who knows if Macdonald was expecting her to return to Tahiti. She left with a portfolio of paintings and a sketchbook, whether a parting gift or a means of financing a return ticket, can only be speculated. A later passport from 1929 was stamped Berne, Switzerland, so it appears that Dolly's overseas travels were restrained to Europe thereafter (8.10). Some years later she moved to Frederick Myhill's Church Farm in Hethel, and lived there rent-free for life as a widow from 1936, not spending more than one night away until she died in 1981.

Marriage

Maugham describes a Tahitian wedding celebration and feast; it is a party that involves huge amounts of food and dancing. Maybe under the Southern Cross they pledged their love and for months they may have lived happily in an extended honeymoon, as many tourists do to this day? The passenger list on her return from Australia to England in 1924 records her as Dorothy Macdonald, and her 1929 passport is in the name of 'D. Macdonald', with the correct spelling. Also, on the front cover of her address book she has written 'Macdonald'. According to Poppy Collinson, the sisters would sometimes use each other's documents to expedite matters, so using Macdonald's name would not have been viewed as a major transgression. Perhaps Dolly remained by that name until she married George Wrafter (1873–1936), a retired army officer from Burma listed among her contacts in her address book, on 2 January 1934 in St Pancras, London? The 1931 census could have revealed the answer had the entire Records Office not been destroyed by fire in 1942. Without a legal marriage certificate to Alister Macdonald, as he was still legally married to Lucy alive and well in Earl's Court, she would not be breaking any laws by marrying Wrafter. How did she explain her name? John Myhill recalls her referring to herself as 'the widow Macdonald'. Away in Tahiti he was as good as dead. Had she bumped into Macdonald on his return to London in 1935 it could have proved to have been an awkward moment for all, though at that time she was living with her husband Wrafter in Jersey.

> The artist, painter, poet, or musician, by his decoration, sublime or beautiful, satisfies the aesthetic sense; but that is akin to the sexual instinct, and shares its barbarity: he lays before you also the greater gift of himself. To pursue his secret has something of the fascination of a detective story. It is a riddle which shares with the universe the merit of having no answer.[157]

Church Farm, Hethel

Dorothy Myhill's marriage to George Wrafter barely lasted two years before he died in 1936, after which she returned from Jersey to Norfolk. John Myhill recalls many visits and long stays with his 'Aunt' Dolly in her home at Church Farm, where he now lives. During that time, from the 1950s to her death in 1981, she maintained a love for art and several friendships with artists and others in their association, such as Jo Sisley, whose husband's great-uncle was the artist Alfred Sisley (1839–99), and others in the artistic Norfolk set, such as the celebrated children's author Eleanor Fargeon. More interested in intellectual conversation than housekeeping, Dolly lived amongst a 'chaos of cats, cobwebs and mud'.[158] Being labelled 'artistic' was an excuse for unconventional behaviour. To the six-year-old John Myhill, Dolly then aged sixty-four, seemed 'as old as the house. I could not separate them in my mind. Her mind was full of low ceilinged, dark rooms, each with ancient furniture, books and cobwebs. A strange world, wholly beyond my experience, captured by Dickens' description of Miss Havisham's house'.[159] Dolly called it 'liberty hall' and told the children they could do as they pleased.

> The attics were our favourite place, looking at 50-year-old copies of London Illustrated News, or more recent art magazines from the era of Emma (1868–1944) and Millie (1868-1951), my

> grandfather's sisters. These poet spinsters had lived sparingly. They filled books with quotations from authors they admired and corresponded with aspiring authors.[160]

Dolly was a woman ahead of her time, a vegetarian, but one who lived on a dairy farm. Young John was astounded.

> Beef was my favourite meat and cows' milk my only drink... The thought that calves must die to produce these delights had not occurred to me, nor did Aunt Dolly enlighten me. My innocence was more important to her than a convert to the cause.[161]

A few years later in 1960, after the death of his grandfather William Myhill, John stayed for three weeks with Dolly, where he met her niece, Philippa.

> I decided we were in love and would marry when we were older and she went along with this game as she did with other pretend games. We told Aunt Dolly with great excitement and I think she was a little worried at first, till she realised this was Romantic imagination, not sexuality. Absence allowed us to discover new dreams.[162]

In 1976 John moved in to Church Farm to live with his Aunt Dolly while he worked as a trainee nurse at the Norfolk and Norwich Hospital.

> I would care for her in her dying years and be on site to take over the farm, when the tenant farmer retired. Dolly lived independently for ten more years without my support and Mr Rackham did not retire as tenant farmer until 1986, so my 'Great Expectations' were premature.[163]

Dolly died on 3 February 1981, and four days later John attended her funeral with family and friends. 'As a solid atheist, she would have hated the religiosity of the service. My first funeral put me off for another ten years: there was no God in it.' Some years earlier she had told the vicar of Hethel (1957–74), Rev. David Main, on their first meeting, 'You are not praying over me, I won't have it.' They became good friends competing in deafness and art appreciation.[164]

Avril Tuera-Macdonald (1926–2013)

> *These island girls make the best of wives down here, but take it from an old fellow who's seen it tried more than once – they never fit in at home.*[165]

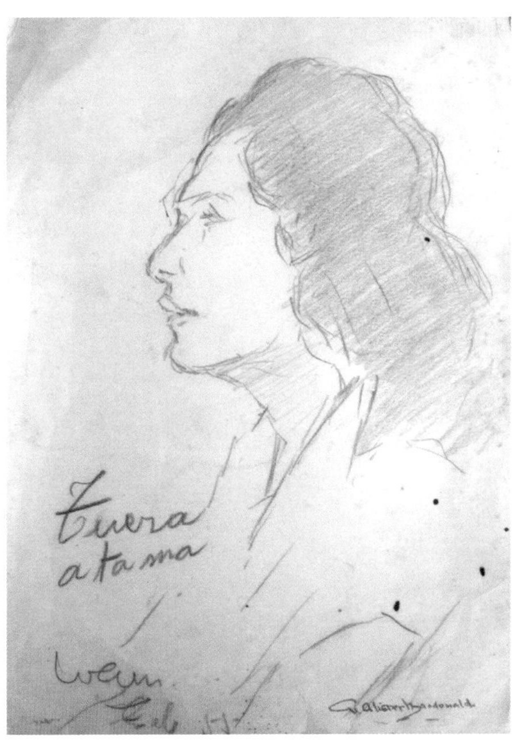

8.11 Drawing of Tipari

European men have never had to remain single or alone for long in Tahiti, unless by choice. After Dolly returned to England Macdonald spent time exploring the islands, painting and socialising with other expats in Papeete's Cercle Bougainville. Sometime between 1923 and 1925 he met Tipari Tuera (1885–1951), who had come from Rapa in the Austral Islands, the southernmost group of French Polynesia.

In her late thirties she had already been married once to another European, William Neagle with whom she had five children from 1906 to 1916: Rautiare (female), William (male), Catherine (f.), Teura (f.) and Tommy (m.). When she settled with Macdonald it is unlikely that she brought her family of children with her; teenage daughters marry young, and the youngest Tommy may well have been cared for by his sisters. In 1926, Tipari gave birth to their daughter Avril, named after the month she was born. Macdonald also gave her the name Marie Macdonald. As a family they lived simply but comfortably around other expats not far from the town of Papeete. The account given in Australian author Farwell's autobiography (1976) shows how acceptable and commonplace it was for families of mixed-ethnicity to live in Tahiti.

There are no surviving photographs of Tipari, but one drawing does exist that is attributed to being a portrait of her (8.11). She died in

1951, just a few weeks before Macdonald returned to the islands and was buried in the Uranie cemetery in Papeete.

Later in life Avril wrote down her own account of her life which gives some detail on her father's movements and the nature of their relationship.

> I was born on April 10, 1926 in Tahiti. It is my father who gives me the first name of Avril. We live in Patutoa at first. Later, my father bought a piece of land in Pirae where he built our house. I then attend the school of Pirae. My father's friends were the Norman Hall family in Arue. From time to time, in the afternoon, when my father went to see them, I went with him. We were walking along the beach. The girl was my girlfriend. I often accompanied my father on nato fishing in the river. My father had a rule to know if the caught fish was big enough otherwise he put it back in the water. My father was a very disciplined person. At 4 p.m., he had his tea with a small cake and I was entitled to a candy.
>
> In 1934 my father learned of the death of his son, my half-brother. Before leaving for England, he places me in boarding school in Papeete at the school of the sisters of St Joseph-de-Cluny, under the name of Marie MacDonald, and promises the sisters to have me baptized... I stay in boarding for 7 years. He will entrust the money to pay the pension and other expenses concerning me to Jean Vilmet, his trusted man.
>
> On weekends I go home to my mother Tipari in Pirae. I am not baptized while I am in a Catholic school. The sisters insist. So my mother is going to have me baptized but among Protestants like her.
>
> My father returns 5 years later with a lady who claimed to be the mother of his deceased son. They live in Paea where I go to see him from time to time. He wants me back and offers me to go back to England with him to continue my studies.

I don't want to because I prefer to stay with my mother. He continues to paint, travels a lot in the islands of Polynesia, then ends up leaving.

He returned to Scotland or England and stayed for many years. He writes to me from time to time to give and hear from me.

I then announce to him that I married Max Fogel on June 19, 1943, and that we have a daughter named Danielle. Danielle was 19 days old when we learned that my husband Max was assigned to Makatea to work for the Compagnie des Phosphates. He is a lieutenant of the port of Makatea. He knows several languages, which facilitates exchanges with foreign phosphate vessels. My mother Tipari comes with us to Makatea.

We will have 3 other children: Monique, Greta and Max. Four months after Max was born, my husband fell suddenly ill

8.12 W. Alister Macdonald's five grandchildren from Avril

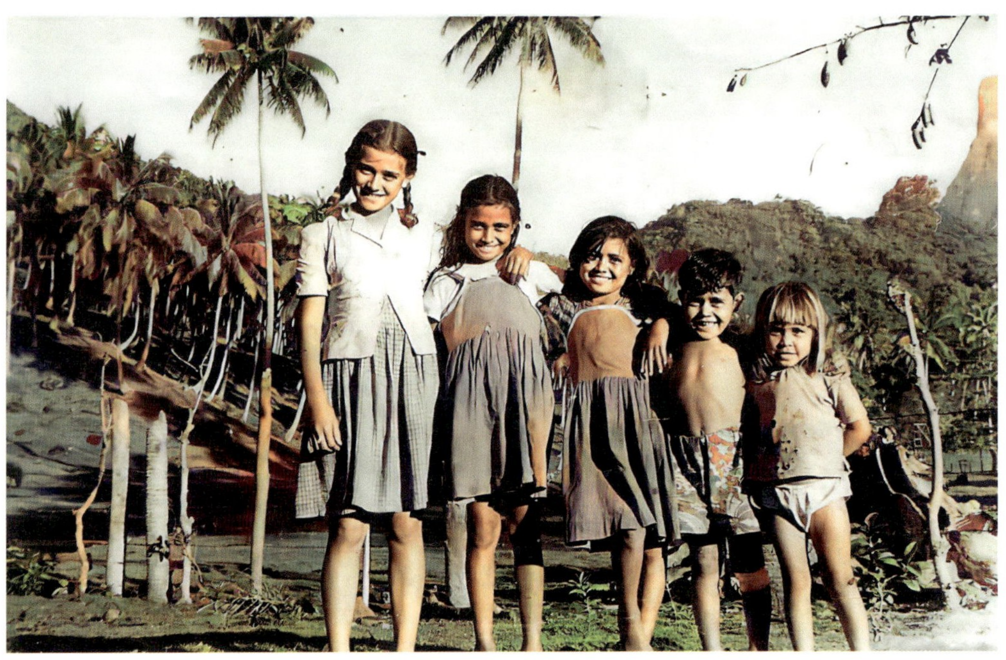

with peritonitis (appendicitis). He was urgently repatriated to Papeete. It takes a night crossing to get there. He spent the night at sea, but died two days later on July 15, 1950. He was only 29 years old.

I find myself a widow at 23 with my 4 children. The eldest is 7 years old and the last 4 months. With my mother Tipari we are going to live in Moorea, in the bay of Paopao, on the land of my husband Max. Benjamin Teraiharoa will be by my side because he knew the family very well and worked for us. He wanted to help me with my 4 children. We have two daughters: Andrine and Jacqueline and we got married in 1964 (8.12, 8.13).

A year after the death of my husband, I also lose my beloved mother Tipari Tuera (March 24, 1951 at the age of 66). It was then that I received a telegram from the English consul and then his visit to consider the request for the return of my father who wanted to come and live with me. To authorize his coming, I have to recognize that he is my father and that he paid for my studies, I owed him that. I do what is necessary with the English consulate with the letter certifying that he has always taken good care of me. He can return to Tahiti.

To accommodate my father, we built with Benjamin, a bungalow in 'niau' (coconut palm) and bamboo near our home. Alister likes to live alone and especially likes calm (he is 90 years old). He is happy in his bungalow, me and my little family we lived not far from his home. I prepared meals for him. His 4 p.m. tea was always very important.

He never leaves Moorea and likes to paint at dusk, sitting in his chair on the beach. He enjoyed the sunsets. As soon as the evening star (Venus) appeared, he said it was his star.

At that time, there was no public electricity in Moorea, so he wrote his letters at night by the light of an oil lamp. The courier as well as his painting orders are dispatched in the

8.13 W. Alister Macdonald, Avril, Monique and Max 1953

8.14 Avril and daughter and grandchildren

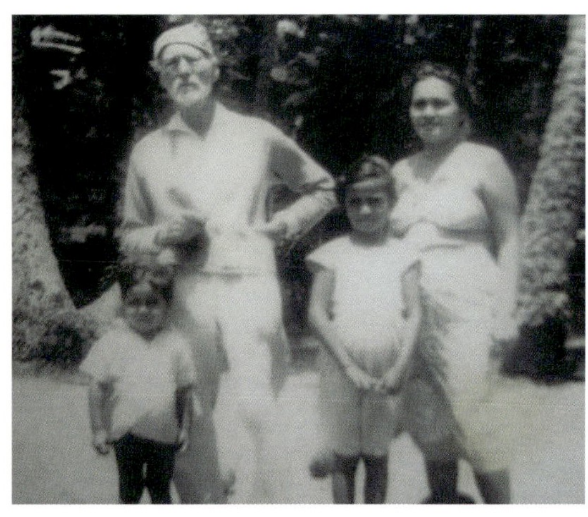

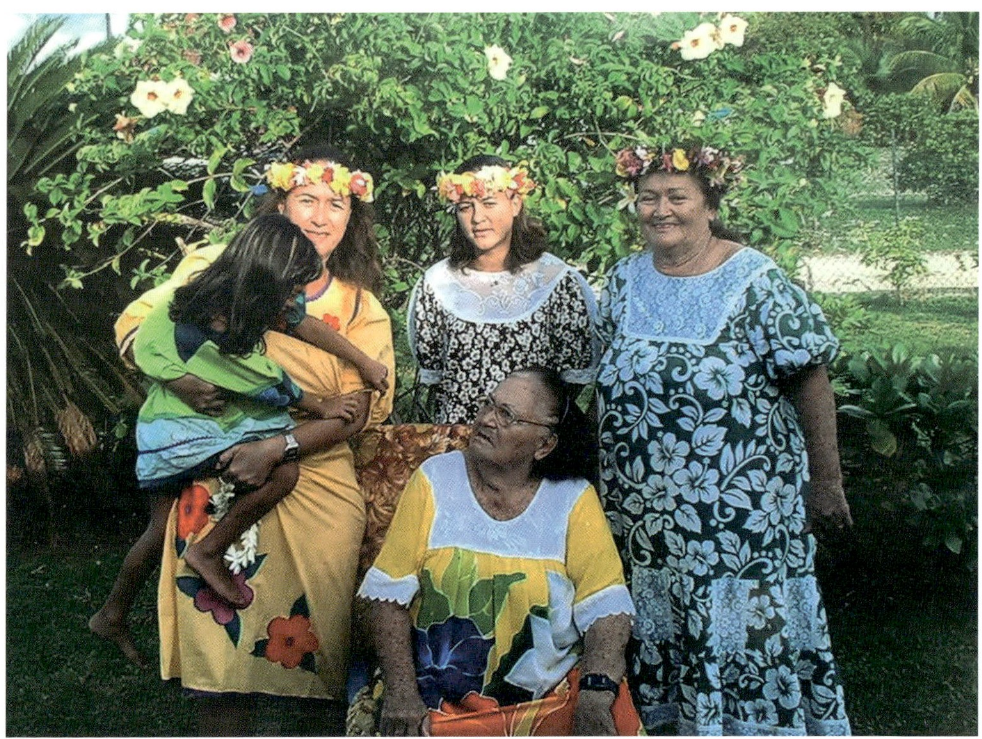

> morning. My father only had to walk along the beach to get to the wharf from where the boat left for Tahiti, not far from the house.
>
> It is Mr. Tiro, the captain of the Mitiaro, a boat linking Tahiti and Moorea, who takes care of the orders in Papeete, at the Donalds store on the seafront. The provisions are not delivered until the next day. At that time, the boat took two or even three hours to make the Tahiti–Moorea crossing.
>
> We live together like this for a few years. And one day, he catches a good bronchitis. He treats his illness with his own remedies and above all did not want to hear about a doctor. He did not hold out this time and died on August 11, 1956 at the age of 95.
>
> Walking together one day on the property he told me that if anything happened to him, he wanted to be buried there. And I did. His grave is where he wanted.[166]

She would often talk about her memories of Macdonald, less so or never about her mother. She was close to him and missed him when she was sent away to school. How she must have missed him when he left for England in 1939, imagining she would never see the old man again? There is a sense of family pride towards her father, one that has been handed down to her children, grandchildren, and their children. Her compassion and determination are defining qualities in her character, underpinned by a resolute Christian faith which remains within the family today. As a grandmother she was the first to accept and support Moana's gender transition from male to female. Steadfast and resolute, principled and just are some of the words used to describe Avril by her family.

Other stories of Avril's childhood have come to light. She was a childhood neighbour and friend of Gaston Flosse (1931–), President of French Polynesia on five separate occasions from 1984 to 2014. His little pet monkey reached through the fence to scratch her face leaving her with a permanent scar by her nose.

In adult life she was a leading business woman and tourism entrepreneur, the first manager of Air Moorea and the aerodrome, and with her husband Ben, ran a fleet of tour buses and taxis. She had several properties in Tahiti and Moorea and a house in Auckland, New Zealand. She was adored by her grandchildren, very much the boss of the family and though generous, would only provide financial support if the reason was well founded or properly thought through with a business plan. (8.14)

Her half-brother, Tommy Neagle, also lived in Moorea at the bottom of the Paopao Valley, not far away from their home. She would visit regularly with one of her daughters until he died in 1989.

In her obituary she is described as:

> A determined woman, she decided to get to work, first as a hostess for Air Tahiti, which would become Air Moorea. She would end her career as station manager. She will remain alongside Ben, one of the personalities of the island, close to the Evangelical Church, and who developed tourism as an entrepreneur in transport.[167]

I was very touched that on 22 September 2022, her youngest daughter, Andrine came to see me to share her memories of her mother with me on the anniversary of her death.

Aué! as Tahitians say, 'in the depths of grief'.[168]

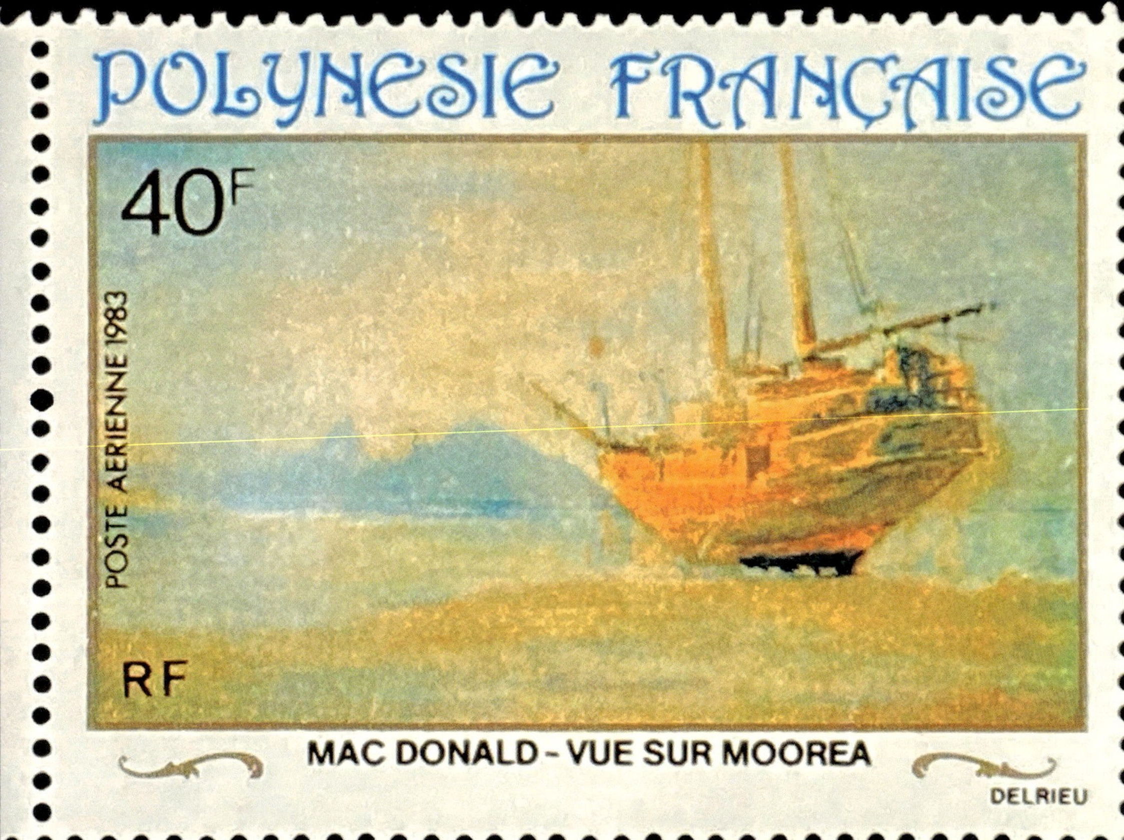

POLYNESIE FRANÇAISE

40F

POSTE AERIENNE 1983

RF

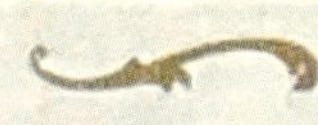
MAC DONALD - VUE SUR MOOREA
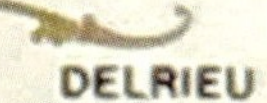

DELRIEU

9

Retrospective

What was it that drove Macdonald to travel? While D.H. Lawrence (1885–1930) barely stepped off the boat in Papeete on his passage from New Zealand to San Francisco in 1922, the writer does offer insight into the forces compelling an artist to seek freedom. 'Freedom is a gift inside one's soul,' Lawrence declared. 'You can't have it if it isn't in you.'[169] A gift it may be but it is not there for the taking. To actualise this capacity for freedom in yourself is a struggle. In attempting to follow in D.H. Lawrence's footsteps Dyer (2015) asks:

> Of what, then, did Lawrence's hard-won freedom consist?
>
> Catherine Carswell applauded Lawrence for the way 'he did nothing that he did not really want to do, and all that he most wanted to do he did'... The perpetual questions of where to go next, whether to stay or to move on, become crucial stations in the itinerary of one's destiny. In this light Lawrence's wandering becomes purposeful, and the gap between resignation and active creation almost insignificant.
>
> ...A destiny is not something that awaits us, it is something we have to achieve in the midst of innumerable circumstantial impediments and detours. A character in *A Question of Geography* (1987) by John Berger and Nella Bielski expresses this concisely:
>
> Each one of us comes into the world with her or his unique possibility – which is like an aim, if you wish, almost like a

9.4 French Polynesia postage stamps 1983

9.1 Alister at home in Moorea with an American tourist 1954

> law. The job of our lives is to become – day by day, year by year, more conscious of that aim so that it can at last be realised.[170]

The life of W. Alister Macdonald reveals an artist who enjoyed a privileged freedom that many of his generation and place of birth could scarcely dream of. He was single-minded, selfish even, and tenacious, but lived frugally enough to sustain his travels. He overcame the tragedy of losing a son, the impediments of wars and his own detours. Similar to Dyer's analysis of Lawrence, Macdonald's travels were purposeful and he followed an inquisitive nature that was stimulated by the intellectual company he kept.

The Scottish poet George Mackay Brown (1921–1996), himself brought up overlooking the Pentland Firth in the far north of Scotland, albeit from the Orkney side, argued that to be an artist you had to be regarded as on the fringe of society.[171] Macdonald preferred to work and travel alone, but enjoyed stimulating company and found friends with similar attitudes and values. These were not necessarily typical of Edwardian society in England or Presbyterian Scotland. In 1937 he made a brief return to Tahiti accompanied by the Hall family (7.4) and asked his daughter to come with him to England for an education in London. Her refusal provided an opportunity for him to return again in his nineties, while ensuring she avoided any racism and bigotry to be found in England and Scotland, and was later able to bring up her own children in Moorea.

A double-page profile article in *Pacific Islands Monthly* by Walter Smith in April 1954 describes Macdonald as 'a remarkable example of a man who has retained his mental and physical faculties far beyond the average span of life. He travels widely, always alone. Two years ago he circled the world'.[172] The article provides a fine portrait of him dressed elegantly with silk polka dot scarf, wearing a signet ring on his left little finger. With the camera looking up he strikes a commanding pose. Who would guess unless told that his eyesight was failing.

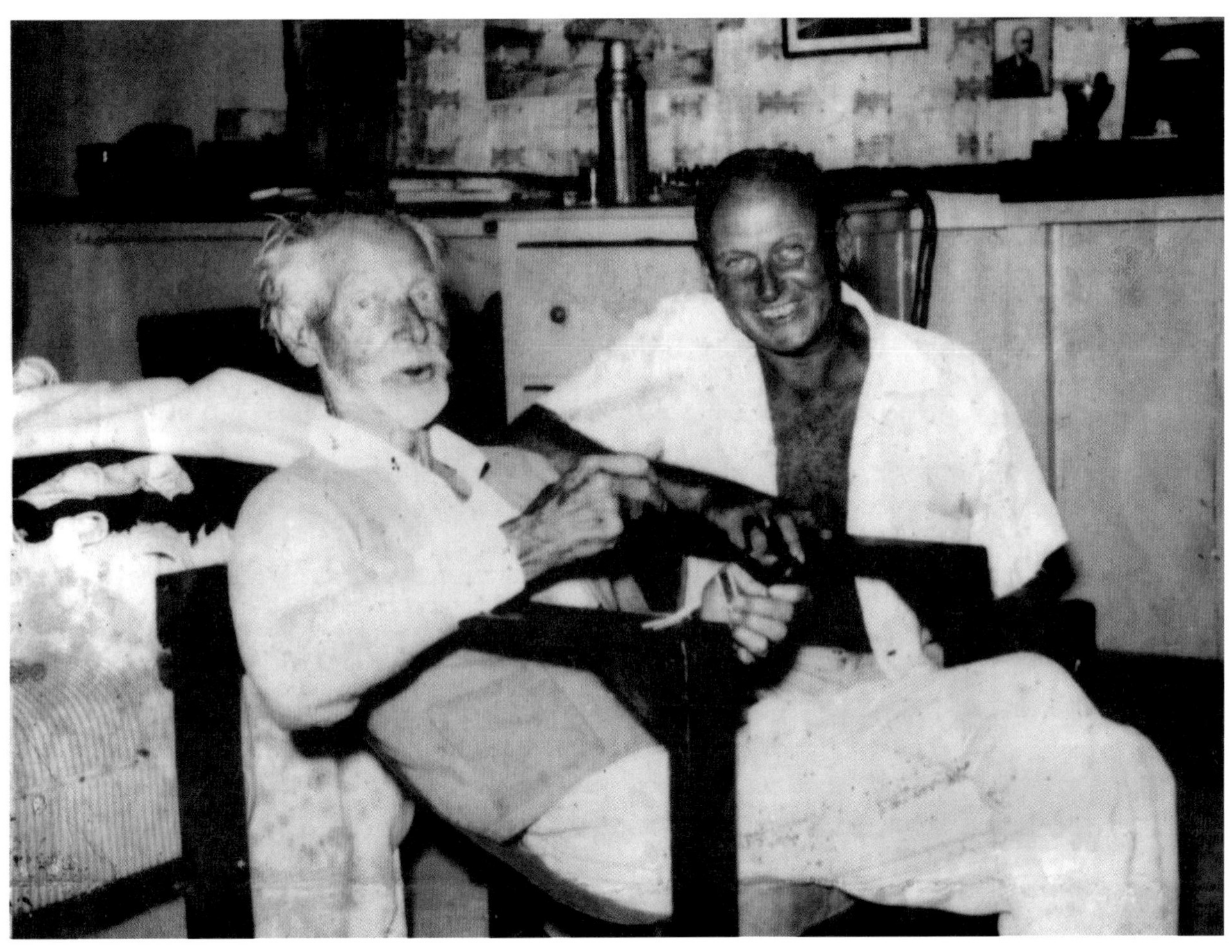

9.2 Vue de Moorea depuis Tahiti

> Frederick Simpson, the well-known photographer of Papeete, reproduces the physical appearance of Mr. Macdonald to-day ... He attributes his longevity to that wise maxim: moderation in all things.[173]

The occasional traveller from Europe and America who knew his work would seek him out (9.1), but life in Paopao was quiet and tranquil, away from the centre of Tahitian business and tourism in the now bustling Papeete (9.2). Macdonald lived in harmony with nature, totally detached from worldly goods, albeit a little whisky for a dram in the evening and tobacco for his pipe, lest not forget some change for a bag of sweeties for the grandchildren (9.3). After such an austere and challenging start to life, born in the rugged north of Scotland, in a manse overlooking a distillery, and orphaned aged four with his siblings, it could have easily been a short life of excessive drinking or abstinence of any pleasure at all.

In July 1955 the *Premier Salon de Tahiti* exhibition was held in a temporary gallery at the l'école Paofai, organised by Van der Broek d'Obrenan, Grandidier and Lyon. Judging by his correspondence, Macdonald was possibly too frail to attend in person to be photographed with his contemporaries, but three of his water-colours: *Baie de Cook, Tuamotu* and *Vue sur Moorea*, are included in the 329 paintings exhibited celebrating European painting in Polynesia dating from contemporary to the fifteenth century. Of his contemporaries he rated Adriaan Gouwe (1875–1965), who had arrived in Tahiti in 1927. 'Why make so much fuss over Gauguin?...We have a much finer artist now in Raiatea, Gouwe – a Dutchman. Only he will not finish things & does not paint studio pictures'.[174]

A few months later he wrote in a letter that he'd been unwell, and had suffered a bad tumble. One granddaughter admitted years later that she and her young sisters had removed the supports from his chair to tease him after being refused a bonbon, that had led to him tumbling off his chair! He died on 11 August 1956.

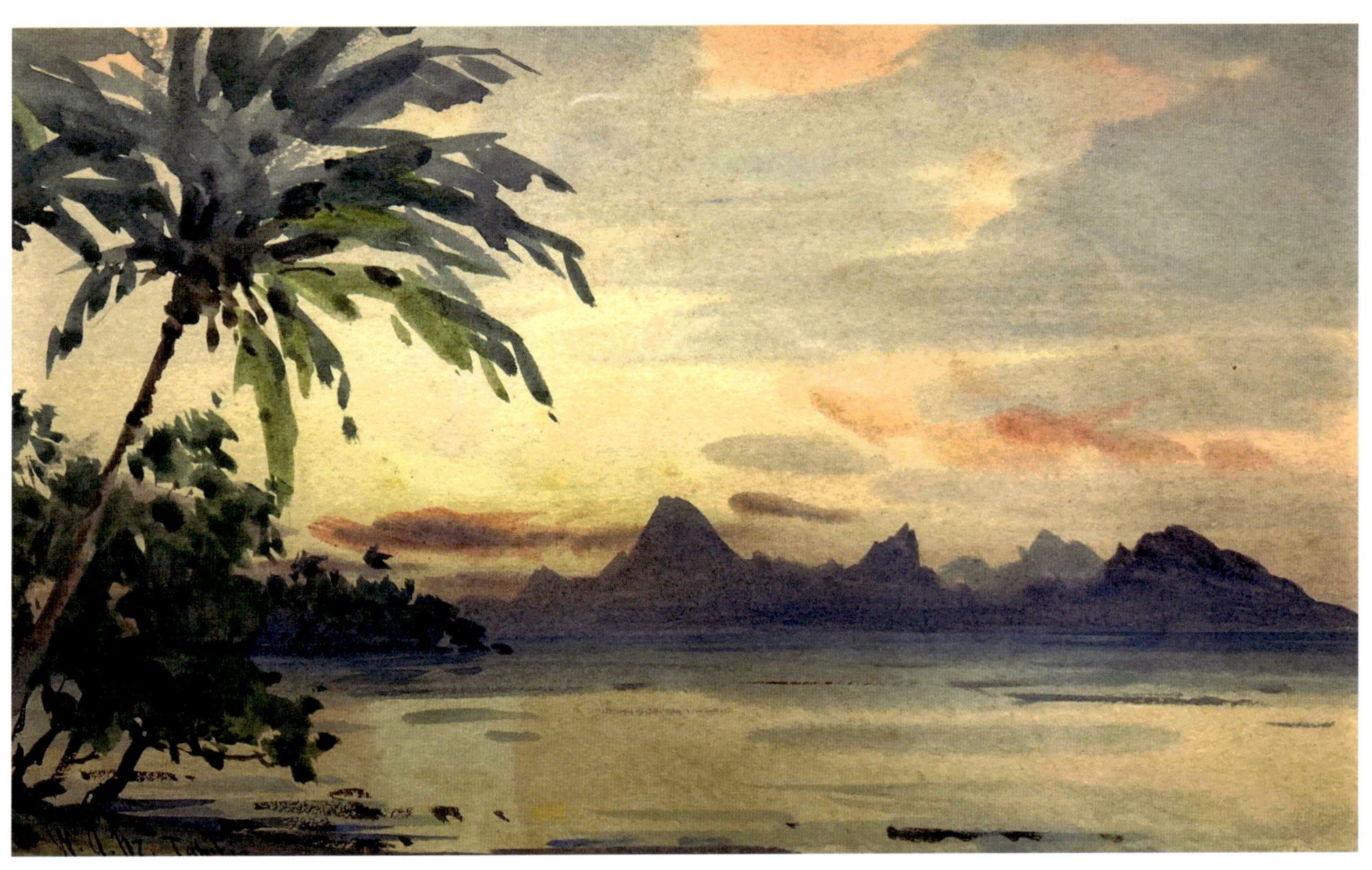

From April to May 1957, a year after his death, a large retrospective of sixty-six watercolours and drawings was mounted in the Tillet Library, Papeete, with a private view opened by Governor Toby.

> Citizens of Papeete showed a lively interest in the quality of work presented...of the more traditional school of English painters, exiled himself early in the 1920s to the South Seas, where he painted more freely.
>
> He was widely travelled and some paintings shown were executed in China, Japan, England etc. MacDonald [*sic*] painted until the end though these latter works were [less] assured in their treatment, and [colour] tended to muddiness, their [quality] was quite remarkable considering his age.[175]

Macdonald was a prolific artist, a work ethic only dimmed by the frailties of old age towards the end of his life. His paintings remain highly valued and popular amongst private collectors in Polynesia, America and the UK. One Tahitian collector remarked that his landscapes are timeless, the sunsets framed by palm trees and translucent lagoons remain to be discovered and enjoyed. None of his generation, or perhaps since, have quite caught the islands with as much 'candour, lightness and luminosity'.[176] In 1983 French Polynesia issued a commemorative set of postage stamps that included Macdonald along with his later contemporaries Gouwe, Mordvinoff and Lemoine who had all exhibited at the *Premier Salon de Tahiti* (9.4).

In Britain, he found acclaim late in life and through Lord Wakefield's generous gift to the Guildhall Art Gallery in London he secured a foothold in the history of British watercolour painting. That was nearly a century ago, and rarely have these works been seen in public. That he is not listed in Halsby and Harris's *Dictionary of Scottish Painters 1600–1960*[177] but appears in Wood's *Hidden Talents: a dictionary of neglected artists working 1880–1950*[178] says much for his lost status. Now, a fresh light illuminates his life and work that spans London and Europe before the mechanised age in the late Victorian and Edwardian eras, as well as his later landscapes of French Polynesia. The adventurous white European and American frontier men that came to the Tahitian shores have often been mythologised, but the influence of Tahitian culture and art on them and how they shaped Western impressions of the exoticism of colonial Tahiti deserves greater critical exploration. That Macdonald made Moorea his last destination, surrounded by his daughter and grandchildren, suggests that this was where he felt most at home and at peace with the natural world and the people that enveloped him.

Perhaps another lesson from this study and account of W. Alister Macdonald is that no one knows what our lives will hold, how many chapters will unfold. The artist's life does not need to be a flash of intense productivity cut short by excess and tragedy to be romantic. Maugham likens the search to understand the artist as a detective story, and this account is no exception. 'It is a riddle which shares with the universe the merit of having no answer.'[179]

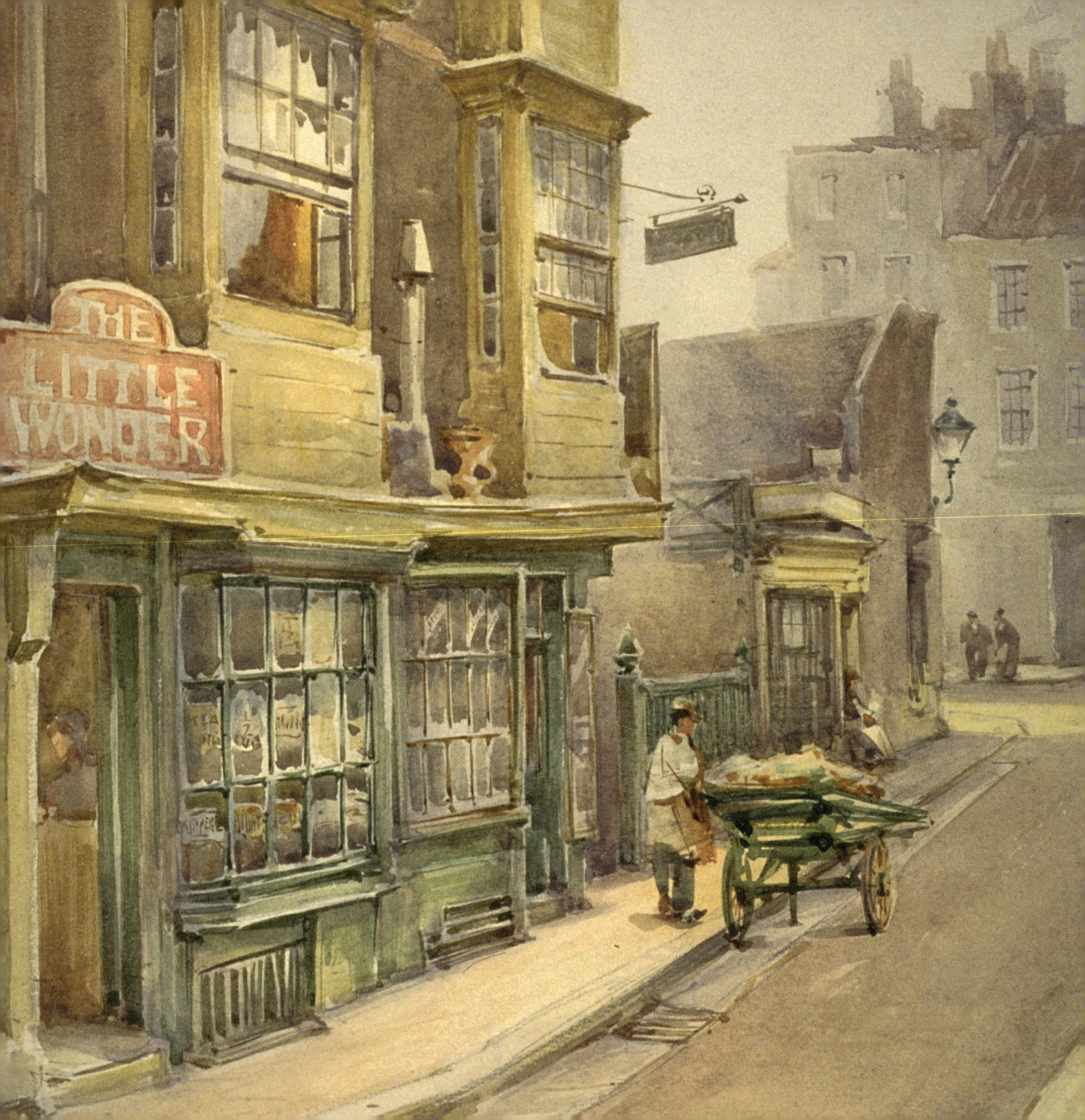
THE
LITTLE
WONDER

NOTES

1 W. Alister Macdonald, personal correspondence to Daryl Broderick, 21 July 1955
2 *Polynesian Web Directory* 2003
3 E. Beresford Chancellor, *London Recalled. Being a Topographical Description of the Collection of Water-Colour Drawings by W. Alister Macdonald in the Guildhall Art Gallery*, London 1937, p. 15
4 James Norman Hall and Charles Nordhoff, *Faery Lands of the South Seas*, Indiana 1921, p. 158
5 Walter Smith, 'He Paints in Tahiti', *Pacific Islands Monthly* (April) 1954, p. 79
6 James Norman Hall, *My Island Home*, Boston MA 1952, p, 302
7 W. Alister Macdonald, personal correspondence to Daryl Broderick, 27 February 1955
8 Daryl Broderick correspondence with author 2023
9 Enrique Bunster, *ia Orana Tahiti,* Santiago, Chile 1956, p. 120–1
10 Georges Di Giorgio logbook, Translated from Spanish, 14 September 1954
11 Théano Jaillet and Riccardo Pinari, *Après Gauguin,* Tahiti 2013, p. 60
12 W. Alister Macdonald, personal correspondence to Daryl Broderick, 21 July 1955
13 *Pacific Islands Monthly*, January 1935, p. 22
14 W. Alister Macdonald, personal correspondence to Daryl Broderick, 21 July 1955
15 W. Alister Macdonald, personal correspondence to Daryl Broderick , 4 December 1955
16 *Pacific Islands Monthly*, September 1956, p. 153
17 *Pacific Islands Monthly*, April 1954, p. 80
18 *Pacific Islands Monthly*, August 1951, p. 20
19 Tom M. Devine, *The Scottish Clearances*, London 2019, p. 305
20 E. Beresford Chancellor, *London Recalled. Being a Topographical Description of the Collection of Water-Colour Drawings by W. Alister Macdonald in the Guildhall Art Gallery*, London 1937, p. 9
21 *Ibid.*, p. 10
22 *Ibid.*, p. 10
23 *Ibid.*, p. 10
24 The *Illustrated London News*, 7 November 1885
24 E. Beresford Chancellor, *London Recalled. Being a Topographical Description of the Collection of Water-Colour Drawings by W. Alister Macdonald in the Guildhall Art Gallery*, London 1937, p. 11
26 *Ibid.*, p. 12
27 *Ibid.*, p. 12
28 *Ibid.*, p. 12
29 *Ibid.*, p. 12
30 Smith 2021: p. 9
31 E. Beresford Chancellor, *London Recalled. Being a Topographical Description of the Collection of Water-Colour Drawings by W. Alister Macdonald in the Guildhall Art Gallery*, London 1937, p. 13
32 Kenneth McConkey, and Charlotte Topsfield, *Arthur Melville: Adventures in Colour*, Edinburgh 2015, p. 111
33 E. Beresford Chancellor, *London Recalled. Being a Topographical Description of the Collection of Water-Colour Drawings by W. Alister Macdonald in the Guildhall Art Gallery*, London 1937, p. 14
34 Ranulph Fiennes, *Shackleton*, London 2022, p. 160
35 Zane Grey, *The Reef Girl*, New York 1977, p. 3
36 James Norman Hall and Charles Nordhoff, *Faery Lands of the South Seas*, Indiana 1921, p. 3
37 Patrick Barkham, P. *Islander – A journey around our archipelago*, London 2017, p. 284
38 *Ibid.*, p. 10
39 James Norman Hall and Charles Nordhoff, *Faery Lands of the South Seas*, Indiana 1921, p. 9
40 William Somerset Maugham, *The Moon and Sixpence*, London 1919, p. 69
41 Ranulph Fiennes, *Shackleton*, London 2022, p. 140
42 William Somerset Maugham, *The Moon and Sixpence*, London 1919, p. 23
43 *Ibid.*, p. 35
44 W. Alister Macdonald, personal correspondence to Daryl Broderick, 21 July 1955
45 Elizabeth C. Childs, *Vanishing Paradise*, Berkeley 2013, p. 1
46 Patrick Barkham, P. *Islander – A journey around our archipelago*, London 2017, p. 56
47 Elinor Mordaunt *The Venture Book,* London 1926, p. 60–1
48 *Ibid.*, p. 72

49 *Ibid.*, p. 95
50 *Ibid.*, p. 95
51 *Ibid.*, pp. 100–101
52 *Ibid.*, p. 107
53 *Ibid.*, p. 108
54 *Ibid.*, pp. 98–99
55 *Ibid.*, p. 82
56 *Ibid.*, p. 82
57 George Farwell, *Rejoice in Freedom*, Melbourne 1976, p. 102
58 *Ibid.*, p. 102
59 *Ibid.*, p. 102
60 James Norman Hall, *The Tale of a Shipwreck*, Boston MA 1934, p. 10
61 *Ibid.*, p. 10
62 George Farwell, *Rejoice in Freedom*, Melbourne 1976, p. 76
63 Charles Nordhoff, personal correspondence to his parents, 12 December 1924
64 Charles Nordhoff, personal correspondence to his parents, 24 November 1924
65 George Farwell, *Rejoice in Freedom*, Melbourne 1976, pp. 99–100
66 *Ibid.*, p. 102
67 Avril Macdonald-Teraiharoa, written testimony, translated from French, ND
68 George Farwell, *Rejoice in Freedom*, Melbourne 1976, p. 67
69 *Ibid.*, p. 74
70 *Pacific Islands Monthly*, March 1956, p. 78
71 *Ibid.*, p. 78
72 *Ibid.*, p. 75
73 Charles Nordhoff, personal correspondence to his parents, 1930
74 George Farwell, *Rejoice in Freedom*, Melbourne 1976, p. 102
75 *Ibid.*, p. 90
76 Walter Smith, 'He Paints in Tahiti', *Pacific Islands Monthly* (April), 1954, p. 79
77 Thomas H. Pauly, *Zane Grey: His life, his adventures, his women*, Illinois 2010, p. 271
78 Loren Grey, *Zane Grey, A Photographic Odyssey*, New York 1985, p. 93
79 Zane Grey, *Tales of Tahitian Waters*, New York 1931, p. 11
80 *Ibid.*, p. 48
81 *Ibid.*, p. 260
82 Loren Grey, *Zane Grey, A Photographic Odyssey*, New York 1985, p. 93
83 *Pacific Islands Monthly*, December 1932
84 W. Alister Macdonald, personal correspondence to Daryl Broderick, 27 February 1955
85 Robert D. Frisbie, *My Tahiti*, Boston MA 1937, dust jacket
86 Anthony Weller, 'Afterword' in R.D. Frisbie *The Book of Puka-Puka*, London 2019, p. 251
87 George Farwell, *Rejoice in Freedom*, Melbourne 1976, p. 91
88 W. Alister Macdonald, personal correspondence to Daryl Broderick, 21 July 1955
89 James Norman Hall, *My Island Home*, Boston MA 1952, p. 162
90 *Ibid.*, p. 163
91 *Ibid.*, p. 160
92 *Ibid.*, p. 211
93 Anthony Weller, 'Afterword' in R.D. Frisbie *The Book of Puka-Puka*, London 2019, p. 253
94 *Pacific Island Monthly*, 28 January 1935
95 Théano Jaillet and Riccardo Pinari, *Après Gauguin*, Tahiti 2013, p. 53
96 *Pacific Islands Monthly*, (January) 1935
97 The *Scotsman*, 24 June1935, p. 13
98 *The Times*, 2 November 1935, p. 10
99 Enrique Bunster, *ia Orana Tahiti*, Santiago, Chile 1956
100 *The Times*, 18 December 1935
101 *The Times*, 17 January 1936
102 *The Times*, 7 February 1936
103 The *Northern Whig and Belfast Post*, 18 January 1936, p. 6
104 Roger Quarm and John Wyllie, *W.L. Wyllie Marine Artist*, London, 1981
105 E. Beresford Chancellor, *London Recalled. Being a Topographical Description of the Collection of Water-Colour Drawings by W. Alister Macdonald in the Guildhall Art Gallery*, London 1937, pp. 8–9
106 *Ibid.*, pp. 17–18
107 *Ibid.*, p. 18
108 *Ibid.*, p. 23 with a quote from Henry Wadsworth Longfellow's *The Village Blacksmith* 1839
109 Jenny Uglow, *William Hogarth: A Life and a World, London 2011*
110 E. Beresford Chancellor, *London Recalled. Being a Topographical Description of the Collection of Water-Colour Drawings by W. Alister Macdonald in the Guildhall Art Gallery*, London 1937, p. 27
111 *Ibid.*, pp. 33–34
112 *Ibid.*, p. 41
113 *Ibid.*, p. 69
114 *Ibid.*, p. 99
115 *Ibid.*, p. 114
116 *Ibid.*, p. 108
117 *Ibid.*, p. 107
118 *Ibid.*, p. 105
119 *Ibid.*, p. 110

120 *Ibid.*, p. 125
121 E. Beresford Chancellor, *London Recalled. Being a Topographical Description of the Collection of Water-Colour Drawings by W. Alister Macdonald in the Guildhall Art Gallery*, London 1937, p. 16
122 A.J. Philpott, the *Boston Globe*, 22 December 1936, p. 17
123 *Ibid.*, p. 17
124 *Ibid.*, p. 17
125 *Ibid.*, p. 17
126 *Ibid.*, p. 17
127 Elizabeth C. Childs, *Vanishing Paradise*, Berkeley 2013, pxvi
128 W.C. Thompson, personal correspondence to Macdonald, February 1938
129 W. Alister Macdonald, personal correspondence to W.C. Thompson, 25 January 1938
130 W. Alister Macdonald, personal correspondence to W.C. Thompson, 8 September 1939
131 The *Daily Province*, 4 February 1937, p. 1
132 David L. Jones, *Famous Name Trains*. Calgary, Alberta 2006
133 Avril Macdonald-Teraiharoa, written testimony, translated from French, ND
134 James Norman Hall and Charles Nordhoff, *Faery Lands of the South Seas*, Indiana 1921, p. 179
135 Charles Nordhoff and James Norman Hall, *The Dark River*, Boston MA 1938, p. 135
136 W. Alister Macdonald, personal correspondence to Jeannie Macdonald, 15 May 1941
137 John Macdonald (great-nephew), personal memoir, 2001
138 Ranulph Fiennes, *Shackleton*, London 2022, p. 273
139 *Ibid.*, p. 273
140 John Macdonald (great-nephew), personal memoir, 2001
141 James A. Michiner, *The World is My Home*, London 1992
142 Jock Macdonald, diary 22 August 1949 in Hudson A., Thom I., et al. *Jock Macdonald Evolving Form*, London 2014, p. 185
143 Enrique Bunster, *ia Orana Tahiti*, Santiago, Chile 1956, p. 121
144 Royal Society of Miniaturists, biography of Lucy Macdonald
145 *Austin American Statesman,* 14 August 1924, p. 4
146 The *Kentish Times*, 20 July 1934
147 *The Times*, 19 February 1936
148 W. Alister Macdonald, personal correspondence to Jeannie Macdonald, 15 May 1941
149 William Somerset Maugham, *The Moon and Sixpence*, London 1919, p. 24
150 *Ibid.*, p. 33
151 *Ibid.*, p. 158
152 John Myhill, personal correspondence with the author, 2022
153 Poppy Collinson, interview with the author, 2022
154 E. Beresford Chancellor, *London Recalled. Being a Topographical Description of the Collection of Water-Colour Drawings by W. Alister Macdonald in the Guildhall Art Gallery*, London 1937, p. 15
155 Dorothy Myhill, personal address book, *c.* 1920–30
156 *Ibid.*
157 *Ibid.*
158 William Somerset Maugham, *The Moon and Sixpence*, London 1919, pp. 1–2
159 John Myhill, *Trials and Inspirations*, online, 2013
160 *Ibid.*
161 *Ibid.*
162 *Ibid.*
163 *Ibid.*
164 *Ibid.*
165 *Ibid.*
166 Charles Nordhoff and James Norman Hall, *The Dark River*, Boston MA 1938, p. 139
167 Avril Macdonald-Teraiharoa, written testimony, translated from French, ND
168 *La Dépêche de Tahiti*, translated from French, September 2013
169 Charles Nordhoff and James Norman Hall, *The Dark River*, Boston MA 1938, p. 336
170 D.H. Lawrence, *The Letters of D.H. Lawrence,* Cambridge 2002
171 Geoff Dyer, *Out of Sheer Rage*, Edinburgh 2015 pp. 141–3
172 George Mackay Brown, *For the Islands I Sing: An Autobiography*, Edinburgh 1997
173 Walter Smith, 'He Paints in Tahiti', *Pacific Islands Monthly,* (April) 1954, p. 79
174 *Ibid.*
175 W. Alister Macdonald, personal correspondence to Daryl Broderick, 4 Dec 1955
176 *Pacific Islands Monthly,* (June) 1957, p. 143
177 Jean Marie Dallet, Christian Gleizal, et al, *Le Memorial Polynesien,* Tome VI. Papeete 1977, p. 358
178 Julian Halsby and Paul Harris, *A Dictionary of Scottish Painters 1600–1960*, Edinburgh 2010
179 Jeremy Wood, *Hidden Talents: a dictionary of neglected artists working 1880–1950,* West Sussex 1994
180 William Somerset Maugham, *The Moon and Sixpence*, London 1919, p. 2

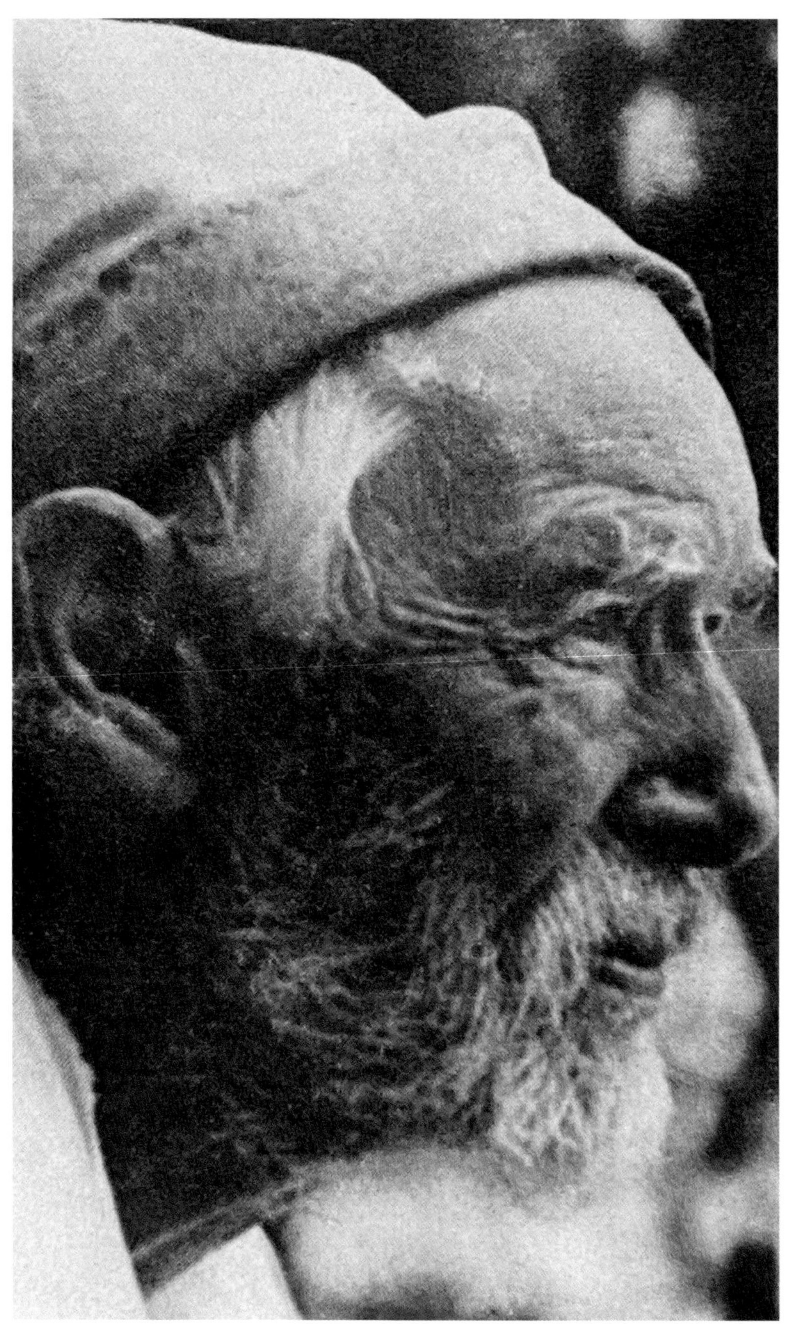

9.3 W. Alister Macdonald c. 1954

WILLIAM ALISTER MACDONALD

	LIFE EVENTS	CONTEMPORARY EVENTS
1861	12 July, William Alister born in Clyne, Sutherland, son of Rev. John Macdonald, Minister of the Free Church of Scotland and wife Barbara, née Sinclair. He was the fifth child, with four surviving siblings: Jane (1852–1907), Donald (1853–1909) and John (1858–1928), and deceased William (1856–1859).	American artist James Abbott McNeill Whistler (1834–1903) settles in London and spends next decade painting scenes of the River Thames.
1864	31 August, mother dies of puerperal fever following birth of Barbaratus Sinclair (1866–1936).	
1866	Father dies, children move north to Melvich on Sutherland coast to be brought up by maternal grandmother, Jane Sinclair, and their guardian uncle David Sinclair, along with three orphaned cousins. Strict upbringing and likely Gaelic spoken within Free Church.	
1871	Sent to Rattrays School in Aberdeen, 'highly commended' in painting and drawing by Mr Kennedy.	
1876	Begins work at fifteen as a clerk in Thurso bank on a salary of £10 a year through assistance of his uncle David Sinclair, a 'rather unscrupulous guardian'.	
1880	Through the offices of an aunt married to the head of the Consul Office in the Bank of England, he transfers to London & Westminster Bank in Lothbury, City of London. Attends evening classes at St Martin's School of Art under John Parker RWS and with the Gilbert Garret Sketch Club, spends spare time drawing along the Thames.	In 1882 English artist Walter Sickert (1860–1942) begins his artistic career in Whistler's London studio, adopting his tonal approach in oils, painting London street scenes and shop fronts.
		In 1883 Scottish artist Arthur Melville's (1855–1904) watercolours from his journey from Cairo to Constantinople are exhibited in London.
1884	Leaves employment at the bank to paint full-time. Now living in Greenwich, he goes on a sketching tour to the Norfolk Broads, with a group of fellow artists.	William Gladstone's government publishes Royal Commission on Highland Clearances in their *Inquiry Into the Condition of the Crofters and Cottars in the Highlands and Islands of Scotland*, by Lord Napier. English maritime artist W.L. Wyllie (1851–1931) exhibits *'Heave Away' Barges upward bound, shooting Rochester bridge* at Royal Academy. Patronage by Fine Art. Society increases the popularity of his paintings of the Thames.
1885	Watercolour of Yarmouth harbour. Wins second prize for landscape in a competition between 'metropolitan sketching clubs and Royal Academy students' at the Society of British Artists, as reported in the *Illustrated London News*, 7 November.	French artist Edgar Degas becomes Sickert's mentor, inspiring him to plan his compositions with preliminary drawings and to use bolder colours.
1886	The captain of a fishing boat moored under his window in Greenwich agrees to take him on a trip to the North Sea fishing grounds on Dogger Bank. He sells a watercolour and an account	W.L. Wyllie exhibits *Gabriel's Wharf* at Royal Institute of Painters in Water Colours.

	of Line Fishing to the *Illustrated London News*. He continues to paint around London and attends Westminster School of Art under Fred Brown. Further travels around Britain, often using the mailboats to explore the remoter coastal areas. During this time he spends periods back in Scotland in Inverness with his nephews, Alister and Jack Mactavish, and in Invergordon with his brother John, who owned London House, a general store, where he displayed and sold a number of watercolours.	
1892	Moves to Camden with a group of 'impecunious artists'. Submits first painting to Royal Academy, *Doubtful Weather, Loch Hourn*.	In 1891 French artist Paul Gauguin (1848–1903) sets sail for Tahiti, returning to France in 1893, exhibiting paintings at Durand-Ruel Gallery, Paris in 1894.
1893	Royal Academy exhibits *Her Palaces and Towers*, a view of the Thames from Blackfriars Bridge, first mention in *The Times*, commended by art critic George Moore.	
1895	Moves to Chelsea and focuses on painting River Thames. Begins to sell through the Kensington Fine Arts Society, as well as teaching part-time. Introduced to arts patron Lady Freake in Twickenham. First recorded visit to Europe: Portugal supported by Stephen Leitch of the British Embassy Lisbon.	Paul Gauguin returns to Tahiti where he remains in Papeete until 1901.
1897	Paints in the Norfolk Broads.	French photographer Eugene Atget (1857–1927) starts recording Paris street scenes of its foggy nights, architecture, River Seine and 'humble' urban life. He continues to document Paris until his death in 1927.
1898	Marries Lucy Winifred Carey (1872–1951), a well-known miniature painter and daughter of artist William Carey. They move to 8 Danes Inn, Strand.	Whistler and Sickert paintings of shop fronts in Dieppe show similar palette and loose handling of oil paint.
1901	Census records the couple now living in 15 St Helier Street, Richmond, Surrey. Paints in Wiltshire and Windsor.	Until 1905 Sickert travels frequently to Venice to paint repeatedly from favourite spots, exploring shifting light effects at different times of day, taking inspiration from Claude Monet's Rouen Cathedral series. W.L. Wyllie publishes first of two manuals on the painting of watercolours, *Maritime Painting in Watercolour*.
1902	Travels to Europe to paint in Spain and French Alps.	
1903	Painting trip to Skye, then Corsica and Italy, where Florence, the Lakes and Venice become frequent visits.	French artist Paul Gauguin dies in the Marquesas Islands in French Polynesia. American artist James Abbott McNeill Whistler dies in London. Royal Scottish Academy, Edinburgh exhibits retrospective in 1904. Joseph Conrad's *Typhoon & Other Stories* is published.
1904	Paints University colleges in Cambridge and Oxford, as well as Eton School. Painting trips to Florence and Dordrecht.	Scottish artist and watercolourist Arthur Melville RWS dies.

Year	Life	Context
1905	Painting trips to Scottish Hebrides, Venice, Locarno and Dordrecht.	
1906	Couple move to 8 Fig Tree Court (now Elm Court), Temple. Painting trips to Oxford, Cambridge, Salisbury, Eton, St Andrews, Italy and Norway.	
1910	Son, Ian Alister, born in New Kings Road, London, 14 June. With wife Lucy they open The Little Gallery in 40A, Victoria Street, Westminster. Painting trips to Geneva, Corfu, Naples, Assisi, Fife, Barra, Lincolnshire and Kent.	
1911	Painting trips to Cotswolds, Verona, Rome, Sicily and Tunisia.	
1912	Painting trips to Isle of Wight, Loch Maree, Skye, French Riviera, and Tunisia. Lucy exhibits *Little Son* at Royal Academy.	In 1911 Sickert is part of the formation of the Camden Town Group of English Post-Impressionists, based in his Camden studio, painting realist scenes of city life and landscapes in a range of post-impressionist styles. Scottish artist S.J. Peploe (1871–1935) exhibits in London to critical acclaim. His tonal effects are inspired by Whistler.
1913	Painting trips to Snowdonia, Skye, Perthshire and Inverness, and last European trip to Florence, Venice and Lake Geneva.	
1914	Aged fifty-three, he enters British Army to work with Army Supply Dept of the War Office under Colonel Morgan in Whitehall, then Major Poulton at Reading.	In February, English poet Rupert Brooke arrives in Tahiti having explored the South Seas. He forms a relationship with

Year	Life	Context
	Painting trips limited to Essex, Yorkshire and Snowdonia.	Taatamata who inspires the poem *Tiare Tahiti*. In August, outbreak of war in Europe.
1917	Lucy becomes Hon. Secretary of the Royal Society of Miniature Painters, 29 November.	
1918	He writes to younger brother Sinclair from Snowdonia, Wales, eager to see the sea again and travel abroad. A Russian is lodging in their apartment in Fig Tree Court.	11 November Armistice Day, end of war in Europe. With the return of soldiers from the Front, an outbreak of Spanish Flu killed over 228,000 in Britain alone.
1919	Gives a painting of Monks Wood, Norfolk to Dorothy (Dolly) Myhill (1890–1981) with their initials carved in a beech tree.	Publication of Somerset Maugham's *The Moon and Sixpence*, loosely based on story of Gauguin.
c.1920	Family move to 6a Penywern Road, Earls Court.	American writers Charles Nordhoff (1887–1947) and James Norman Hall (1887–1951) arrive in Tahiti to start a new life.
1921	He sets sail for New Zealand with Dolly Myhill on the SS *Arawa* of the Shaw Savill & Albion shipping line from Southampton on 5 May. They never reach New Zealand, having disembarked in Tahiti, French Polynesia. 1921 census taken in June records only Lucy and eleven-year-old son at Earls Court address, with her place of work at Studio, 283 Fulham Road, SW10.	
1922	He is introduced to European and American expatriate community centred around the Cercle Bougainville club in Papeete, including writers Robert Frisbie, Charles Nordhoff and James Norman Hall (all at least twenty-five years his junior).	D.H. Lawrence (1885–1930) visits Tahiti for three days on his way to San Francisco from Wellington, New Zealand. His postcards tell of his disappointment.

BBC starts daily radio broadcasts from London, 14 November.

1923 His wife, Lucy Macdonald, opens Arlington Gallery, 22 Old Bond Street in a building owned by arts philanthropist Baron Joseph Duveen.

He paints French ship *El Kantara* in Papeete harbour and is gifted to Dolly (remaining in Myhill family).

Australian travel writer Elinor Mordaunt disembarks from El Kantara and writes of meeting a British watercolourist.

1924 On and around the 12 August his wife, Lucy Macdonald publishes in several American papers a statement of her status as the Honourable Secretary of the Royal Society of Miniaturist Painters and wife of W. Alister Macdonald, 'a well known painter'.

Dolly, registered as 'Dorothy Macdonald' departs from Brisbane, Australia on *SS Moreton Bay* to Hull on 26 August, never to see him again.

In November he is commissioned to paint a watercolour of Charles Nordhoff's house that is sent to Nordhoff's parents in Santa Barbara, California as a Christmas present.

First group show of 'Scottish Colourists' in Paris (though the name is not coined until 1948 in Glasgow): S.J. Peploe, J.D. Fergusson, Leslie Hunter and F.C.B. Cadell.

French Cubist and Dadaist artist Fernand Léger (1881–1955) releases film *Ballet Méchanique*.

1925 Dolly Myhill's father William dies in Norfolk with all his daughters around his bedside.

Scottish Colourists group exhibition in London.

1926 He builds a plantation house in Patutoa, 1km north of Papeete for his partner, Tipari Tuera (1885–1950) originally from Rapa. Their daughter, Avril (Marie), is born on 10 April.

Moana, a silent 'documentary' film set in Samoa, made by R.J. Flaherty, is released in USA.

His nephew James (Jock) Macdonald (1897–1960) emigrates to Vancouver from Scotland as Head of Design at the School of Decorative & Applied Arts.

1927 Zane Grey (1872–1939) arrives in Tahiti in his three-mast schooner *The Fisherman*, meets Alister painting a watercolour of his yacht and a friendship begins.

In 1928 D.H. Lawrence publishes the short story *The Man Who Loved Islands*, based on his friend and best-selling author Compton Mackenzie (1883–1972).

1929 On 9 December he boards the Union Line *SS Makura* in Papeete for San Francisco, arriving 29 December.

1930 He returns to Tahiti in May on the *SS Marama* from his visit to San Francisco and broadens his money making activities to include Christmas cards and letterheads.

French artist Henri Matisse (1869–1954) visits Tahiti, Moorea and Tuamotu.

On 29 August 1930 St Kilda, the remotest isle of Scotland's Outer Hebrides, is evacuated after a millennia of inhabitation.

1931 He begins illustrations for Robert Frisbie's *My Tahiti* (1937). He is mentioned in the text and provides illustrations and the cover of Zane Grey's *Tales of Tahiti* (1931).

He paints decorative panels for the Compagnie des Phosphates of Makatea that are presented at the Colonial Exhibition of Paris.

W.L. Wyllie dies in London while putting finishing touches on three pictures for the Royal Academy.

Tabu, A Story of the South Seas, a 'docufiction' film by F.W. Murnau is released, promising 'a hundred pulsating thrills'.

1932 He accompanies the writer James Norman Hall to the Marquesas for *L'Illustration*. Often stays at the homes of friends Hall, and shipowner and businessman Oscar Nordman.

Nordhoff and Hall's *Mutiny on the Bounty* published.

1933 Now living in Pirae on land he has bought, an Australian author George Farwell (1911–1976) moves in next door.

1934 He illustrates Hall's *The Tale of a Shipwreck*.

On 10 July, Ian, his twenty-four-year-old son, drowns in an accident during an evening sailing on the Thames, at Greenhithe.

He places daughter Avril in boarding school in Papeete at the Sisters of St Joseph de Cluny.

In November, at Lucy's Arlington Gallery in London, George Bernard Shaw attends the exhibition opening of the late John Collier's work.

On 11 April Radio Club Oceanien, set up by amateur enthusiasts including Mayor of Papeete Georges Bambridge, begins broadcasting with a programme of music, notices and news on Wednesdays and Fridays. None can foresee how important a service it will become to Tahiti and the islands during WW2.

1935 The popular drinking spot, Cercle Bougainville holds its first exhibition with paintings by Macdonald, Gouwe, Engdhal, Machecourt and Gres.

In July returns to Briatain, via Sydney, Colombo, Aden, Port Said and Malta on *SS Barrabool*.

Makes a return to Melvich to see family and sees Sinclair (younger brother and architect) at Inverness Station.

He reconciles with his wife, Lucy. They mount an exhibition *Among the Islands of the South Seas* in October of 119 pictures in her Arlington Gallery, followed by one in December of 101 forgotten watercolours of Old London previous to 1914, an entire collection bought by Lord Wakefield for the Guildhall in London, for a record price of £750. Both receive good report in *The Times*.

MGM Studios began production for the movie of Mutiny on the Bounty in June 1935.

In Canada, his nephew Jock Macdonald takes his wife Barbara and young daughter Fiona to live in Nootka, BC to get closer to nature and find a spiritual connection with his art. In his diary he includes: W.A. Macdonald, Box 45, Tahiti, via San Francisco, indicating possible previous correspondence between the two artists.

1936 *The Times* (17 January) publishes an illustrated feature of the newly acquired Wakefield Collection at the Guildhall, City of London. That same week his younger brother, Sinclair dies (15 January) at home in Thurso, Caithness.

A third exhibition of a further 125 watercolours opens in February, *Pre-war Wanderings Watercolours Home and Abroad*.

Lucy exhibits a portrait miniature of *W. Alister Macdonald* (1051) at Royal Academy.

On 27 November he departs from Liverpool on Cunard *SS Scythia* for Boston, USA. In December the Robert C. Vose Gallery exhibits his paintings from Europe, North Africa and Tahiti, receiving a glowing review in the *Boston Globe*.

1937 In February he arrives in Vancouver, Canada where he accompanies James Norman Hall with Mrs Hall and daughter Nancy back to Tahiti.

While in Vancouver he spends time with his nephew, painter Jock Macdonald who had returned to the city from two years in remote Nootka. Through introductions to Hall, Jock finds set-painting work on film sets in Hollywood.

His first published biography is in E. Beresford Chancellor's *London Recalled* with colour plates from the Wakefield Collection at the Guildhall Gallery.

Lucy exhibits a portrait miniature of *J.C. Anderson esq* at Royal Academy.

The Hurricane, a film based on the book by Nordhoff and Hall, directed by John Ford, is released.

1938 Now in Tahiti he makes an attempt to adopt Avril. Avril refuses to leave her home and mother, and instead he pays for her education in Tahiti.

Year	Life	World events
1939	He returns to Britain in anticipation of another European war.	Friend and best-selling author Zane Grey (1872–1939) dies at home in Altadena, California. Outbreak of war in Europe.
c. 1941	Family home in Earls Court damaged by bombing, and Arlington Gallery destroyed. He and Lucy move to Box Tree Cottage, Tinhead Road, Westbury in rural Wiltshire, which she had bought in 1927.	
1942	Exhibition of *Watercolours and drawings of Old London* previous to 1914, at the Walker Gallery, London.	
1943	In Tahiti, daughter Avril marries Max Fogel (1921–1950) on 19 June, and soon have first daughter, Danielle (1943–2018). They move to Makatea and have two more daughters Monique (1944–2004) and Greta (1945–2019).	
1946	He travels to Inverness alone, photographed, and meets nieces and nephews of his older brother John. In a letter to his nephew Jack Mactavish he wanted to find a quiet cottage 'to write my memoirs'.	
1947		On 10 April, his friend Charles Nordhoff dies at home in Santa Barbara, California. On 28 April, Norwegian Thor Heyerdahl with five crew sets sail from Peru on *Kon Tiki*, a 13m-long balsa wood boat, to attempt a crossing of the Pacific to prove his thesis that Polynesians originated from America, now since disproved by DNA tracing that relates Polynesians to Asia.
1948		On 19 November, his friend Robert Frisbie dies in the Cook Islands.
1950	In Tahiti, Avril has fourth child, Max (1950–2007), but within four months her husband Max Fogel dies from appendicitis on 15 July, leaving her a widow with four children at age of twenty-four.	Outbreak of Korean War.
1951	4 January wife Lucy dies in their Wiltshire cottage, having been admitted to hospital suffering from dementia in summer 1950. Aged eighty-nine, on 19 February he leaves England for the last time on *SS Madura* for Columbo, Ceylon (now Sri Lanka) and the Seychelles. The P&O timetable extends to Singapore, Penang, Hong Kong, Freemantle, Adelaide, Melbourne and Sydney. In Tahiti his partner and mother of daughter Avril, Tipari Tuera, dies 24 March, aged sixty-six. He telegrams his daughter Avril to seek proof of his paternity in order to gain permission from the French Consulate to return to Tahiti.	His friend James Norman Hall dies in Tahiti. Monthly flying boat services operated by TEAL connect Tahiti with Cook Islands and New Zealand by air.
1952	He returns to live in Moorea, with few or 'no possessions', and is looked after by his daughter Avril and her second husband Benjamin Teraiharoa (1934–2017) who build a bungalow for him near the shore in Paopao (Cook's Bay). Ben's father is a close friend of Macdonald. Avril has a fifth child, Jacqueline.	In Toronto, Canada his nephew Jock Macdonald exhibits at the first *Canadian Abstract Exhibition* that establishes the Painters Eleven.

1954	15 September a Chilean schooner captained by Georges di Giorgio anchors off Paopao and the owner, his father Giorgio, and writer Enrique Bunster meet him painting their schooner from the beach. Giorgio Snr spends two hours negotiating the purchase of a large portfolio of watercolours including Polynesia, China and Japan. He keeps some back for personal reasons, including a drawing of a Young Englishwoman on deck from 1921 (Dolly).	Between 1953 and 1955 his youngest nephew, architect Hugh Macdonald (1903–1979) designs the renovation and restoration of the Castle of Mey in Caithness for HRH Queen Elizabeth the Queen Mother. Henri Matisse dies.
1955	In July and August he exhibits three watercolours in the *Premier Salon de Tahiti* exhibition celebrating European painting in Polynesia from the fifteenth century to then. He is possibly too frail to attend in person to be photographed with his contemporaries.	In London, Pop Art is born.
1956	He dies on 11 August following a fall and fractured hip injury, at home in Moorea. Survived by his daughter Avril, and six grandchildren including new baby Andrine, in Moorea.	
1957	Between April and May, the painter Tillet holds a retrospective of Macdonald's work including sixty-six watercolours in his bookshop.	
1960		Papeete airport opens and first commercial jet flights arrive in Tahiti a year later. A second movie version of *Mutiny on the Bounty* is made in Tahiti starring Marlon Brando and Trevor Howard. Members of the Hall family attend the shoot, and young Georges di Giorgio is an extra. In France, a cinematic revolution starts with the Nouvelle Vague and the release of Jean-Luc Godard's *A Bout de Souffle*.

REFERENCES

Austin American Statesman (14.8.1924: 4)
Barkham, P. (2017) *Islander – A journey around our archipelago.* London: Granta
Brown, G.M. (1997) *For the Islands I Sing: An Autobiography.* Edinburgh: Polygon
Bunster, E. (1956) *ia Orana Tahiti.* Santiago, Chile: Zig-Zag
Chancellor, E.B. (1937) *London Recalled. Being a Topographical Description of the Collection of Water-Colour Drawings by W. Alister Macdonald in the Guildhall Art Gallery.* London: Basil Blackwell
Childs, E.C. (2013). *Vanishing Paradise: Art and Exoticism in Colonial Tahiti.* Berkeley CA: University of California Press
Dallet, J.M., Gleizal, C. et al. (1977), *Le Memorial Polynesien,* Tome VI. Papeete: Hibiscus Editions
Defoe, D. (1719) (2008) *Robinson Crusoe.* Oxford: Oxford University Press
Devine, T.M. (2019) *The Scottish Clearances.* London: Penguin
Dyer, G. (2015) *Out of Sheer Rage.* Edinburgh: Canongate
Farwell, G. (1976) *Rejoice in Freedom.* Melbourne, AUS: Nelson
Fiennes, R. (2022) *Shackleton.* London: Penguin
Frisbie, R.D. (1929) (2019) *The Book of Puka-Puka.* London: Eland
Frisbie, R.D. (1937) *My Tahiti.* Boston, MA: Little, Brown & Co.
Grey, L. (1985) *Zane Grey, A Photographic Odyssey.* New York: Taylor
Grey, Z. (1934) *Tales of Tahitian Waters.* New York: Harper Brothers
Grey, Z. (1977) *The Reef Girl.* New York: Harper & Row
Hall, J.N. (1934) *The Tale of a Shipwreck.* Boston, MA: Houghton Mifflin
Hall, J.N. (1952) *My Island Home.* Boston MA: Little, Brown & Co.
Hall, J.N. (1952) *The Forgotten One.* Boston MA: Little, Brown & Co.
Hall, J.N. and Nordhoff, C. (1921) (2021) *Faery Lands of the South Seas.* Indiana: Alpha Editions
Halsby, J. and Harris, P. (2010) *A Dictionary of Scottish Painters 1600–1960.* Edinburgh: Birlinn Ltd
Hudson A., Thom I., et al. (2014) *Jock Macdonald Evolving Form.* London: Black Dog
Jaillet T., Pinari R., et al. (2013) *Après Gauguin.* Tahiti: Musée de Tahiti et des Iles
Jones, D.L. (2006) *Famous Name Trains.* Calgary Alberta: Fifth House
Lawrence, D.H. (2002) *The Letters of D.H. Lawrence.* Cambridge: Cambridge University Press
Macdonald, J. (2001) personal notes
Macdonald, W.A. (1918) personal correspondence
Macdonald, W.A. (1941) personal correspondence
Macdonald, W.A. (1955) personal correspondence, February
Macdonald, W.A. (1955) personal correspondence, July
Macdonald, W.A. (1955) personal correspondence, December
Macdonald-Teraiharoa, A. (no date)
Machen, A. (1907) *The Hill of Dreams.* London: Grant Richards
Maugham, W.S. (1919) (1999) *The Moon and Sixpence.* London: Vintage Random House
McConkey, K. and Topsfield, C. (2015) *Arthur Melville: Adventures in Colour.* Edinburgh: National Galleries of Scotland
Michiner, J. (1992) *The World is My Home.* London: Secker & Warburg Ltd
Mordaunt, E. (1926) *The Venture Book.* London: The Century Co.
Myhill, D. (No Date) Personal Address Book
Myhill, J. (2013) at https://johnmyhill.files.wordpress.com/2013/12/trials-and-inspirations.pdf
Myhill, J. (2022) personal correspondence with the author
Nordhoff, C. (1924) personal correspondence
Nordhoff, C. (1930) personal correspondence
Nordoff, C. and Hall, J. (1938) *The Dark River.* Boston MA: Little, Brown & Co.
Pacific Islands Monthly (1932) (1935) (1951) (1956) (1957)
Pauly, T.H. (2010). *Zane grey: His life, his adventures, his women.* Illinois: University of Illinois Press
Polynesian Web Directory (2003)
Quarm, R. and Wyllie, J. (1981) *W.L. Wyllie Marine Artist.* London: Barrie & Jenkins
Smith, J. (2021) 'William Alister Macdonald and his Drawings of the Thames'. In *London Topographical Society Newsletter.* 92 9–10
Smith, W. (1954) 'He Paints in Tahiti', *Pacific Islands Monthly* (April)
The *Boston Globe* (22.12.1936)
The *Daily Province* (4.2.1937)
The *Illustrated London News* (7.11.1885)
The *Kentish Times* (20.7.1934)
The Making of *Mutiny on the Bounty* available at https://youtu.be/8XchSYxkP1o
The *Scotsman* (24.6.1935)
The Times (2.11.1935) (18.12.1935) (17.1.1936) (7.2.1936)
Uglow, J. (2011) *William Hogarth: A Life and a World.* Faber & Faber
Weller, A. (2019) 'Afterword' in R.D. Frisbie *The Book of Puka-Puka.* London: Eland
Wood, J. (1994) *Hidden Talents: a dictionary of neglected artists working 1880–1950.* West Sussex

EXHIBITIONS

1892 *Doubtful Weather, Loch Hourn*, Summer Exhibition, Royal Academy, London
1893 *Her Palaces and Towers*, Summer Exhibition, Royal Academy, London
1906 *Venice, Strasbourg, Swiss and Italian Lakes*, Westminster, London
1918 *Watercolour Drawings of Exceptional Interest,* Finnigan's Showrooms, Manchester
1931 *Océanie Française*, L'Exposition Coloniale, Paris
1935 *Final Exhibition*, Cercle Bougainville, Papeete, Tahiti (Jan.)
1935 *Among the Islands of the South Seas*, Arlington Gallery, London (Oct.)
1935 *London Recalled,* Arlington Gallery, London (Dec.)
1936 *Pre-war Wanderings Watercolours Home and Abroad*, Arlington Gallery, London
1936 *London Recalled*, Guildhall Art Gallery, London
1936 *Europe, North Africa and Tahiti,* Robert C. Vose Gallery, Boston MA USA
1942 *Watercolours and drawings of Old London previous to 1914*, Walker Gallery, London
1955 *Premier Salon de Tahiti*, L'école Paofai, Tahiti
1957 *Retrospective*, Tillet Bookshop, Papeete, Tahiti
1989 Guildhall Library, London
1993 *City Antiques and Fine Art Fair,* Business Design Centre, London
2001 Guildhall Art Gallery, London
2008 Galerie Winkler, Papeete, Tahiti
2013 *Après Gauguin*, Musée de Tahiti et des Iles, Tahiti

PUBLICATIONS

1937 Chancellor, E.B. *London Recalled.* Guildhall London
1954 Smith, W. *He Paints in Tahiti.* Pacific Islands Monthly, April
1975 O'Reilly, P. *Tahitiens.* Musée de Homme, Paris
1976 O'Reilly, P. *Peintres de Tahiti.* Nouvelle Editions Latines, Tahitiens
1977 Mazellier, P. *Le Memorial Polynesien* Tome 6. Hibiscus Editions, Tahiti
1994 Wood, J. *Hidden Talents: a dictionary of neglected artists working 1880–1950.* West Sussex
1996 Pugin, G. and Laudon P. *Les Peintres Inspirés par Tahiti.* Vahine Editions, Tahiti
2013 Jaillet T., Pinari R. et al. *Après Gauguin.* Musée de Tahiti et des Iles, Tahiti
2021 *Newsletter 92* London Topographical Society, London
2023 Macdonald, I. 'William Alister Macdonald of Scotland and Tahiti: a portrait of the artist in the third age.' *The British Art Journal*, XXIV: 2 pp. 3–13

ILLUSTRATED BOOKS AND REFERENCES

Bunster, E. (1956) *ia Orana Tahiti.* Santiago, Chile: Zig-Zag

Farwell, G. (1976) *Rejoice in Freedom.* Melbourne, AUS: Nelson

Frank T. Verity, Edwin T. Hall, Gerald C. Horsley and W. Shaw Sparrow. (1906) *Flats, Urban Houses and Cottage Homes: A Companion Volume to The British Home of Today.* London: Hodder & Stoughton

Frisbie, R.D. (1937) *My Tahiti.* Boston, MA: Little, Brown & Co.

Gamble, W. (ed.) (1909) Penrose's Pictorial Annual, The Process Year Book 1908–9 (Vol. 14)

Grey, Z. (1934) *Tales of Tahitian Waters.* New York: Harper Brothers

Hall, J.N. (1934) *The Tale of a Shipwreck.* Boston, MA: Houghton Mifflin

Hutchinson, W. (ed.) (1920) *Hutchinson's Picturesque Europe.* London: Hutchinson & Co.

LIST OF PLATES

ARLINGTON GALLERY 1923–1941

In 1923 Lucy Winifred Macdonald (Royal Miniaturist Society) (1872–1951) opened the Arlington Gallery at 22 Old Bond Street. The building was built by Sir Joseph Joel Duveen (1843–1908), the Dutch art dealer and benefactor of many art galleries and then owned by his son, Baron Joseph Duveen (1869–1939), who is considered one of the most influential art dealers of the twentieth century. The design of the building was based on a favourite palazzo in Venice. The integrity of the building's façade remains today despite having being bombed in 1941, an event that forced the Macdonalds to close the Arlington Gallery. The building continues to be used as a commercial art gallery for an international art dealer.

The Arlington Gallery attracted lesser-known artists of the period who probably found it harder to be exhibited in bigger galleries because they had yet to achieve a marketable reputation, or that those galleries took too great a commission. The gallery also exhibited artists associated with textiles, glass, jewellery, tapestry and metalwork. It regularly exhibited The Royal Society of Miniaturist Painters, Sculptors and Gravers who showed almost every year until its closure in 1941. In 1935 her husband returned from fourteen years in Tahiti and there followed two shows of his work including *Old London pre-1914* which was bought in its entirety by Lord Wakefield and donated to the Guildhall City of London Gallery.

The Arlington Gallery was patronised by high society and reviews of openings regularly appeared in the *Bystander* and national and regional newspapers. Notable dignitaries, socialites and celebrities included the likes of George Bernard Shaw at the opening of the late John Collier (November 1934), Princess Alphonse de Chimay at American cartoonist Percy Crosby's show (June 1936), and the Duke of Connaught at Donald Wood's show (1934).

A catalogue of the Arlington Gallery exhibitions is available at the National Arts Library.

1924

Exhibition of the late Percy Dixon, RI, Dixon, Percy.
An exhibition of the works of E.J. Detmold.
Exhibition by the late Miss Henrietta Irvine.

1925

Catalogue of flowers and gardens by Juliet Williams.
Catalogue of landscapes by Lewis G. Fry.
Donald Wood : Wood, Donald.

1926

Catalogue of watercolours.
Exhibition of sculpture and landscapes by Eveleen Buckton.
M.E. Dignam : Dignam, M.E.

1927

Etchings by the late Sir Charles Holroyd.
Egypt, Algiers and portraiture by Giuseppe Amisani.
Landscapes, flower studies etc. by Wm. Cartledge.
Portraits, landscapes and drawings by Kenneth Green.

1928

An exhibition of paintings of things, people, places by Doris Pusinelli and William Milner.
Oil paintings of Oxfordshire, Wales and France by Henry Hiles.
Oil paintings of the landscape of Greece by Nicolas Himona.
Paintings and drawings by Lady Chalmers, Miss Madge Graham, Fergus Graham.

1929

Beautiful flower pictures by Mrs Amy C. Reeve Fowkes.
Modern Dutch etchings by Jan Poortenaar.
Oil paintings and drawings by Alfred Ward.

1930

Mesopotamia, Kashmir and the Lower Thames by John Peake Wildeblood.
Submarine paintings by Zarh Pritchard.
Watercolours of France and Italy by Alexander Waite, ARCA.

1931

More idiosyncratic drawings in coloured ink by V.C. Vickers.

1932

Memorial exhibition of works by Samuel H. Hancock, the postman artist.
Royal Scottish Society of Painters in Watercolours.

1933

Exhibition of pictures by Isabel Tweddle.
Exhibition of pictures by Mrs Violet Brunton-Angless, RMS, miniatures and watercolours, and Miss Eva Savory, flower paintings in watercolour.
Exhibition of pictures of South Africa and Rhodesia by Tinus de Jongh.
Marjory Watherston (Mrs H.L. Geare), Evelyn Watherston.

1934

Imaginative illustrations in black and white by Heather G. Hamer.
Mr H. Septimus Power.
Paintings in little by the late Hon. John Collier.
Works by Reginald Hallward.
Pictures of men, women, horses and dogs by Donald Wood.
Exhibition by Miss L. Kemp-Welch, RI, Mrs E.B.N. Kerr, Albert Collings, RI, J.W. Schofield, RI, RBC.

1935

Landscapes at home and abroad by
Owen B. Reynolds.
Percy Crosby.
Pictures by Miss Mary G. Cowland, Lt. Col. F.A. Goddard, OBE, Miss E.D. Tinne.
The spirit of China and Japan.
Among the islands of the South Seas,
by W. Alister Macdonald.
Old London previous to 1914,
by W. Alister Macdonald.

1936

Exhibition of paintings by Emma M. Saville.
Pre-war wanderings, water colours of home and abroad, by W. Alister Macdonald.
The sea in sun and storm.
Impressions from Exotic Malaya by Elna Bendixsen.
Exhibition of portrait, landscape and still life paintings by Archibald D. Colquhoun and Amalie Colquhoun.
Colquhoun, Archibald Douglas.
"Never more-!", a modern triptych, and other paintings by R.H. Sauter. Sauter, R.H.

1937

Fidler memorial exhibition.
Exhibition of classic and modern Japanese colour prints, under the patronage of the Japan Society.
Landscapes in Cornwall and the South of France.
Studies of the jewels, deserts, temples, streets and gardens of Egypt by Mrs W.M.N. Brunton, RMS.
Charles S. Brownlow.
N. Winder Reid.
Paintings by Colin Colahan.
Paintings by the late Benjamin Haughton, RBA.
Watercolours by Miss B.M. Seccombe Leech.
Works in oil and watercolours of South Africa, Egypt, India, France, etc.

1938

An exhibition of paintings by Albert Perry.
Perry, Albert.
An exhibition of paintings by Philip Maurice Hill.
An exhibition of pictures and sketches by Miss Lucy Kemp-Welch.
Exhibition of oil paintings of portraits, figures, landscapes, still life, birds and flowers by E. Mary Wilkinson.
Exhibition of paintings in oil and watercolours of Norfolk, Sussex, Devon and the south of France, by P.E.T. Fisher.
Exhibition of portraits of dolls, and a few from life, by Mrs N. van Bakel.
Exhibition of water colours of Switzerland, Malta, Surrey and other places by Dorothy Davies.
Landscapes in watercolour by Michael Teale, MA Oxon, MRCS, LRCP.
Memorial exhibition of the works of the late Miss Mabel F. Layng.
Paintings of Japan by Mordaunt Parker.
Watercolours of Cairo and Nile boats by J.W.A. Young.

1939

Surrey Water Colour Society : London : Fine Arts Publishing Co.
Exhibition of miniatures and illuminated manuscripts by Arthur Szyk.
Exhibition of oil paintings, sculpture and books by Jack Bilbo.
Exhibition of oils and watercolours of Palestine and Egypt by J.P. Wildeblood.
Exhibition of original pencil drawings by Henry Charles Low.
Exhibition of portraits etc. by Countess I. Karolyi-Szechenyi.
Little paintings in Sussex, watercolours by M.O. Goulden; London and other pictures by B.S. Pedder and illustrations by Margaret Tempest.
Portraits and studies in pastels and oils by Luigi Amato.
The land and water of the Nile by Mrs W.M.N. Brunton, RMS.

PHOTOGRAPHIC CREDITS

All artist's works and photographs reproduced courtesy of artist's family.

AUTHOR

Figs; 0.1, 0.2, 1.1, 1.4, 1.7, 1.8, 1.9, 2.2, 2.33, 3.4, 3.5, 3.6, 3.7, 4.2

POPPY COLLINSON

Figs; 3.1, 3.2, 3.9

GUILDHALL ART GALLERY, CITY OF LONDON

Figs; 2.8, 2.13, 2.14, 2.15, 2.16, 2.33, 6.1, 6.2, 6.3, 6.4, 6.5, 6.6, 6.7, 6.8, 6.9, 6.10, 6.11, 6.12, 6.13, 6.14, 6.15, 6.16, 6.17, 6.18, 6.19, 6.20, 6.21, 6.22, 6.23, 6.24, 6.25, 6.26, 6.28, 6.29, 6.30, 6.31, 6.32

TIPARI LE GALL

Figs; 2.17, 4.3, 4.8, 7.6, 7.7, 8.6, 8.9, 8.11, 8.12, 8.13, 8.14, 9.1

TIPARI GOODING

Fig.: 9.2

NAIA HALL

Figs; 3.8, 4.4

HARPER BROS

Fig.: 4.5

HODDER & STOUGHTON

Fig.: 2.20

HOUGHTON MIFFLIN

Fig.: 4.6

HUTCHINSON'S PUBLISHING

Fig.: 2.22

JAMES NORMAN HALL MUSEUM

Figs; 2.24, 4.1, 7.4

LITTLE BROWN & CO

Fig.: 4.7

LONDON METROPOLITAN ARCHIVE

Figs; 2.4, 2.5, 2.6, 2.7, 2.9, 2.10, 2.11, 2.12, 2.19, 2.21, 5.3, 5.4, 5.5, 5.6

ALAN MACDONALD

Fig.: 2.25

ALASDAIR MACDONALD

Fig.: 2.1

THE NATIONAL ARCHIVE

Fig.: 3.3

NEWSPAPERS.COM

Figs; 7.1, 7.3

PENROSE PICTORIAL ANNUAL

Fig.: 2.22

JM PETIT

Figs; 1.2, 1.3, 1.5, 1.6, 5.1, 7.5

ROYAL COLLECTION

Fig.: 8.4

ROYAL MINIATURISTS SOCIETY

Figs; 2.18, 8.1, 8.3

ANDRINE TERAIHAROA

Fig.: 8.7

THE TRUSTEES OF THE BRITISH MUSEUM

Figs; 2.26, 2.27, 2.28, 2.29, 2.30, 2.31

VICTORIA & ALBERT MUSEUM

Fig.; 8.5

VOSE GALLERY, BOSTON MA

Fig.; 7.2

DR REX WALTERS

Fig.; 3.10

INDEX

Locators in *italics* refer to illustrations.

Published in 2024 by Unicorn
an imprint of Unicorn Publishing Group
Charleston Studio, Meadow Business Centre,
Lewes BN8 5RW
www.unicornpublishing.org

Images – see photographic credits page 221

ISBN 978-1-916846-24-1

10 9 8 7 6 5 4 3 2 1

Book design by Philip Lewis

Printed at Malta by Gutenberg Press Ltd